THE
UNCROWNED
KINGS OF ENGLAND

THE UNCROWNED KINGS OF ENGLAND

The Black History of the Dudleys and the Tudor Throne

Derek Wilson

CARROLL & GRAF PUBLISHERS
New York

Carroll & Graf Publishers
An imprint of Avalon Publishing Group, Inc.
245 W. 17th Street
New York
NY 10011-5300
www.carrollandgraf.com

First published in the UK by Constable,
an imprint of Constable & Robinson Ltd 2005

First Carroll & Graf edition 2005

ISBN 0-7867-1469-7

Printed and bound in the EU

Contents

—◦◦◦—

List of Illustrations

John Dudley, Duke of Northumberland and Earl of Warwick, *Warwick Castle and its Earls*, The Countess of Warwick, vol. I, 1903

Dudley Castle, photograph by the author

The offer of the crown to Lady Jane Grey (1537–54), engraved by Charles George Lewis (1808–80) (engraving), Leslie, Charles Robert (1794–1859) (after)/Private Collection/www.bridgeman.co.uk

Inscription by John Dudley in the Beauchamp Tower at the Tower of London

Execution of John Dudley, from a 19th century engraving

Robert Dudley, Earl of Leicester (1532?–1588) from a painting in the National Portrait Gallery, London, *London in the Time of the Tudors*, Sir Walter Besant, 1904

Kenilworth Castle, an engraving of 1817 from a drawing made in 1716 by Henry Beighton, *Elizabethan England*, being the history of this country 'In Relation to all Foreign Princes' A Survey of Life and Literature, vol. 3, 1575–1580, E. M. Tenison, 1933

Introduction

⸺⊱◦◦◦⊰⸺

This is the story of the royal dynasty that England almost had. The Tudors were powerful and impressive monarchs who gave the crown a permanence and inviolability that had eluded their predecessors but, ironically, their hold on power was weakened by their inability to sire a line of healthy male heirs and within little more than a century, after only three generations, they had disappeared. If Edward VI or Elizabeth I had had their way the house of Tudor would have been succeeded by the house of Dudley, the first and only wholly English dynasty in the nation's history. The Plantaganets sprang from French stock. The Tudors were Welsh. The Stuarts were Scottish, and when England had had its fill of them, search had to be made in far distant German palaces for a suitable prince to fill the constitutional gap. Had sovereignty passed to the Dudleys the history of Britain would have been vastly different.

There was much to be said for the Dudleys as prospective rulers of England. They were fecund. Their sixteenth-century family tree bristled with sons. They came from solid baronial stock, could boast ancestors who had fought with Henry V at Agincourt and served successive monarchs in court and council. They were well connected and proud of their links with the great medieval families of Beauchamp and Neville. Just how much store they set by their noble origins can be seen in St Mary's Church, Warwick. Here Richard Beauchamp, Earl of Warwick caused a sumptuous chantry chapel to be raised for the repose of his earthly remains in the mid 1400s. A century later, it was appropriated by the Dudleys and, to this day, houses a group of spectacular Dudley tombs. Every Tudor sovereign, with the exception of Mary, reposed high trust in members of this family, and not without good reason. They proved themselves accomplished courtiers, politicians, administrators and generals.

Yet, not only did they fail to achieve all that their talents promised, they have also gone down in popular legend as perhaps the most execrated noble family in English history. Ironically, it was their very closeness to the throne which destroyed the male line of the Dudleys and earned them their evil reputation, which, utterly undeserved, has led to their neglect by historians for four centuries. It is extraordinary that scholars have until very recent years been content to accept the moral judgements of Tudor contemporaries who were either sworn enemies of the Dudleys or jealous of their influence. The assumption has largely gone unchallenged that the Dudleys were an avaricious, power-hungry brood interested in nothing but feathering their own nest. They have appeared in chronicles of the sixteenth century as unmitigated villains whose designs were, fortunately, thwarted by the magnificent Tudor monarchs. Edmund Dudley was presented as the evil councillor who urged on Henry VII's draconian financial policies and took his cut from increased royal revenues. Henry VIII unmasked him and sent him to the block. Edmund's son, John, heartlessly pursued to death the 'good duke' of Somerset, Edward Seymour, during the reign of the boy king Edward VI and crowned his villainy by trying to place his own daughter-in-law, Lady Jane Grey, on the throne. Mary Tudor made short work of him and the would-be king, Guildford Dudley. Yet, within a few years, Robert Dudley, Guildford's brother, had wormed his way into the affections of Elizabeth I and was moving heaven and earth to marry her, not forbearing to dispose of his own wife in the process.

The 'black legend' of the Dudleys is a monstrous injustice. It is based on the testimony of preachers, pamphleteers and rabble-rousers who rejected the policies Edmund and his descendants stood for but who, for the most part, did not dare to direct their criticisms at the sovereign. Edmund Dudley made powerful enemies among the aristocratic and mercantile communities for carrying out policies devised by the king. John Dudley, Duke of Northumberland, had multiple enemies. The old noble families regarded him as an upstart while activists among the common people hated him for executing Edward Seymour, whom they looked upon as their champion. Robert Dudley, Earl of Leicester, felt the brunt of virulent Catholic propaganda because he was the premier patron of the Puritans. What may well be the world's worst example of pernicious libel, *Leicester's Commonwealth*, accused him of every crime its author could think up, including a 'kind hearts and coronets' conspiracy in which the queen and all claimants to the crown were to be murdered so that Dudley could take their place. With all this mud being thrown it was inevitable that much of it would stick.

However, this book is not simply an attempt to rebut such calumnies; to right ancient wrongs. I have tried to avoid the hagiographical trap. It is the rescuing of the Dudleys from scholarly neglect that provides the justification for the following pages. Even if all the libels were true the story of this family would be well worth the telling. It is remarkable that, not once but twice, the Dudleys bounced back from total disgrace and ruin to occupy a major place in national life. Their destiny was closely interwoven with that of England's greatest royal dynasty and without them the history of sixteenth-century England would have been very different. Would Henry VII have found a lawyer/administrator as inventive and energetic as Edmund Dudley to lay down the financial foundations of centralized monarchy? Without John Dudley, would Edward Seymour's incompetence and ill-advised policies have led to the collapse of government? If Robert Dudley had not been at her side as unofficial consort, would Elizabeth have been able to bear the burden of solitary rule throughout three tense and troubled decades?

The adult Tudors were all strong characters and it might be thought fanciful to conceive of the Dudleys as being powers behind the throne. Yet it was precisely that reality which so scandalized observers of Elizabeth's court. The Spanish ambassador reported that Lord Robert 'does whatever he likes with affairs' and the queen herself envisaged that, in the event of her sudden death, her favourite would become Protector of the Realm as his father had been before him. When her own marriage to Robert became impossible Elizabeth seriously proposed him as a husband for Mary, Queen of Scots – which would have meant that his progeny would have been the inheritors of two crowns. When the Dudleys did not actually have their hands on the levers of power they were seldom more than a shadow away. Nor must we forget that, on two occasions, the House of Tudor really did come very close to being by the House of Dudley.

The unpredictable twists and turns of fate denied that experience to both the family and the nation. We can only speculate what kind of rulers Edmund Dudley's descendants might have made had they legitimately come by the Crown. They were crucial and, until now, overlooked players in England's story. Like them or loathe them, the Dudleys were remarkable people who lived, loved and died at the very centre of political life, and left an indelible mark upon it.

DUDLEY ALLIANCES 1553
AND THE CHILDREN OF HENRY VII

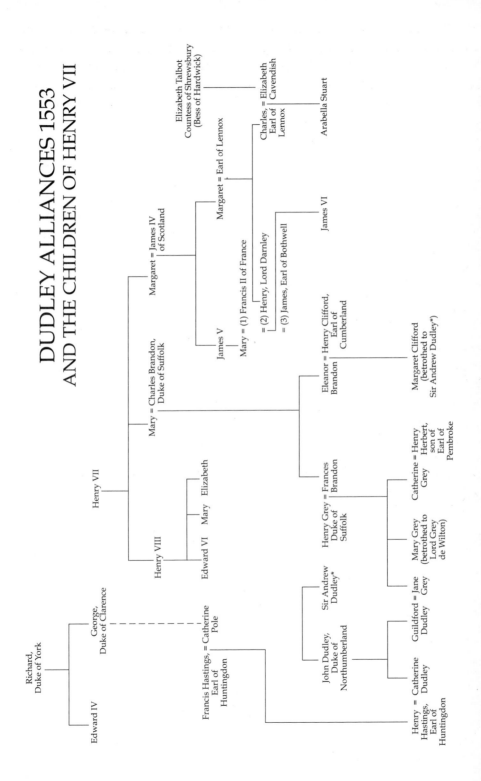

THE DUDLEY PEDIGREE

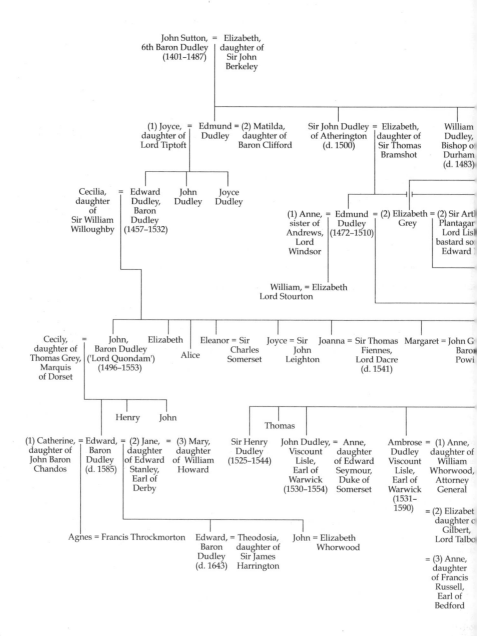

John Sutton, = Elizabeth,
6th Baron Dudley | daughter of
(1401–1487) | Sir John
Berkeley

(1) Joyce, = Edmund = (2) Matilda,
daughter of | Dudley | daughter of
Lord Tiptoft | | Baron Clifford

Sir John Dudley = Elizabeth,   William
of Atherington | daughter of   Dudley,
(d. 1500) | Sir Thomas   Bishop o
| Bramshot   Durham
(d. 1483)

Cecilia, = Edward   John   Joyce
daughter   Dudley,   Dudley   Dudley
of   Baron
Sir William   Dudley
Willoughby   (1457–1532)

(1) Anne, = Edmund = (2) Elizabeth = (2) Sir Art
sister of | Dudley | Grey   Plantagar
Andrews, | (1472–1510) | Lord Lis
Lord   bastard so
Windsor   Edward

William, = Elizabeth
Lord Stourton

Cecily, = John,   Elizabeth   Eleanor = Sir   Joyce = Sir   Joanna = Sir Thomas   Margaret = John G
daughter of   Baron Dudley   Alice   Charles   John   Fiennes,   Baro
Thomas Grey,   ('Lord Quondam')   Somerset   Leighton   Lord Dacre   Powi
Marquis   (1496–1553)   (d. 1541)
of Dorset

Henry   John

Thomas

(1) Catherine, = Edward, = (2) Jane, = (3) Mary,   Sir Henry   John Dudley, = Anne,   Ambrose = (1) Anne,
daughter of   Baron   daughter   daughter   Dudley   Viscount   daughter   Dudley   daughter of
John Baron   Dudley   of Edward   of William   (1525–1544)   Lisle,   of Edward   Viscount   William
Chandos   (d. 1585)   Stanley,   Howard   Earl of   Seymour,   Lisle,   Whorwood,
    Earl of   Warwick   Duke of   Earl of   Attorney
    Derby   (1530–1554)   Somerset   Warwick   General
          (1531–
          1590)   = (2) Elizabet
            daughter o
            Gilbert,
Agnes = Francis Throckmorton   Edward, = Theodosia,   John = Elizabeth   Lord Talbo
    Baron   daughter of   Whorwood
    Dudley   Sir James   = (3) Anne,
    (d. 1643)   Harrington   daughter
        of Francis
        Russell,
        Earl of
        Bedford

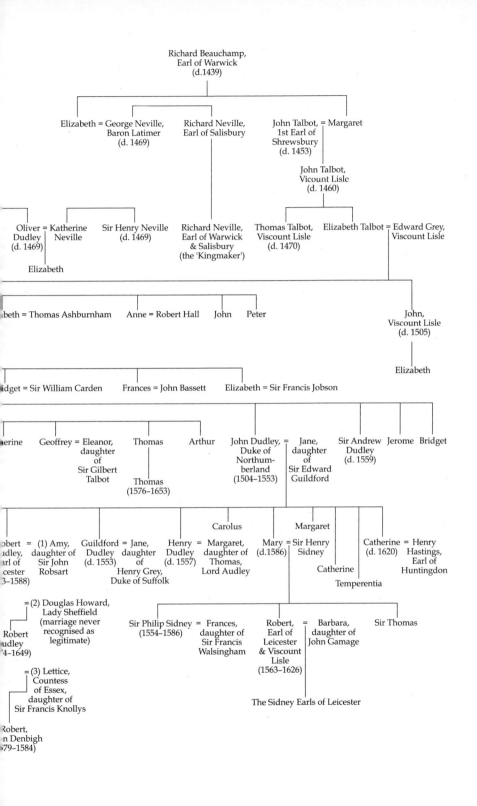

Richard Beauchamp,
Earl of Warwick
(d.1439)

Elizabeth = George Neville,
Baron Latimer
(d. 1469)

Richard Neville,
Earl of Salisbury

John Talbot, = Margaret
1st Earl of
Shrewsbury
(d. 1453)

John Talbot,
Vicount Lisle
(d. 1460)

Oliver = Katherine
Dudley | Neville
(d. 1469)

Sir Henry Neville
(d. 1469)

Richard Neville,
Earl of Warwick
& Salisbury
(the 'Kingmaker')

Thomas Talbot,
Viscount Lisle
(d. 1470)

Elizabeth Talbot = Edward Grey,
Viscount Lisle

Elizabeth

...beth = Thomas Ashburnham   Anne = Robert Hall   John   Peter

John,
Viscount Lisle
(d. 1505)

Elizabeth

...dget = Sir William Carden   Frances = John Bassett   Elizabeth = Sir Francis Jobson

...erine   Geoffrey = Eleanor,
daughter
of
Sir Gilbert
Talbot

Thomas

Thomas
(1576–1653)

Arthur

John Dudley, = Jane,
Duke of
Northum-
berland
(1504–1553)

daughter
of
Sir Edward
Guildford

Sir Andrew   Jerome   Bridget
Dudley
(d. 1559)

Carolus

Margaret

...obert = (1) Amy,
...dley,   daughter of
...rl of   Sir John
...cester   Robsart
3–1588)

Guildford = Jane,
Dudley   daughter
(d. 1553)   of
Henry Grey,
Duke of Suffolk

Henry = Margaret,
Dudley   daughter of
(d. 1557)   Thomas,
Lord Audley

Mary = Sir Henry
(d.1586)| Sidney

Catherine

Temperentia

Catherine = Henry
(d. 1620)   Hastings,
Earl of
Huntingdon

= (2) Douglas Howard,
Lady Sheffield
(marriage never
recognised as
legitimate)

Robert
...udley
'4–1649)

Sir Philip Sidney = Frances,
(1554–1586)   daughter of
Sir Francis
Walsingham

Robert,   =   Barbara,
Earl of   daughter of
Leicester | John Gamage
& Viscount
Lisle
(1563–1626)

Sir Thomas

= (3) Lettice,
Countess
of Essex,
daughter of
Sir Francis Knollys

The Sidney Earls of Leicester

Robert,
n Denbigh
79–1584)

I

THE LAWYER

1

Broad is the Path and Wide the Gate

A large crowd had gathered on the no-man's-land of trampled grass and bare earth which separated the eastern edge of the City from the intimidating bulk of the Tower of London. Executions of 'top people' were always major attractions but when the victims were the most hated men in England everyone who could do so wanted to get to Tower Hill to see them receive their just desserts. What they believed they were witnessing, on 17 August 1510, was the final act in the deliverance of England from a dark regime of tyranny and financial oppression into the sunlit rule of a young Adonis who would bring freedom and glory to his realm. It probably occurred to no spectator of that gruesome scene that a king who could bow to public opinion by sacrificing ministers whose only crime had been loyalty to their royal master might in the years ahead send many of his subjects to death for no better reason than that it would serve his interests.

The Dudley hate club sprang into existence very early and by 1510 it was already being noised abroad that Edmund Dudley was a jumped-up nobody, the son of a Midlands carpenter who had wormed his way into Henry VII's favour, then used his position to enrich himself and urge the king to pursue rapacious and unjust policies. In the highly stratified society of sixteenth-century England people were highly suspicious of men who rose from humble origins. It was assumed, and not only by the nobility, that kings should select their principal officials and advisers from among the nation's leading families. Renaissance princes, of whom Henry VII was one, swam vigorously against the powerful current, refusing to place their government in pawn to baronial clan leaders. In doing so they created a class of royal servants who formed a barrier between themselves and the petty princelings of the shires. Members of this class were rarely popular and always vulnerable. It was Edmund Dudley's fate to be considered of their number. In fact, he was very far from being a man of obscure origins. The thirty-eight-year-old lawyer who perished as a traitor beneath the headsman's axe was descended from a long line of Midlands landowners and royal servants. Their family name was Sutton but from the mid-fifteenth century they began to call themselves the lords of Dudley, Worcestershire after the manor which formed the basis of their power and wealth. Dudley Castle in Worcestershire, the impressive remains of which can still be seen, was begun soon after the Conquest, and testifies that these landowners had been men of substance for centuries. It is not surprising, then, that they played a significant part in what we have come to call the Wars of the Roses. Their motto, 'droit et loyal', indicated allegiance to the reigning monarch as liege lord but during the tumultuous decades of the conflict between the houses of York and Lancaster these petty barons had frequently had to question where their real allegiance lay. Their own survival was tied up with staying on the winning side and this they achieved with remarkable success.

The man who may be regarded as the founder of Dudley greatness was Edmund's grandfather, John, sixth Baron Dudley. Lord John was a burly man of war who fought beside Henry V at Agincourt and accompanied the king throughout his French campaigns. He bore the royal standard at Henry's funeral in 1422 and became a pillar of the government during the reign of the infant Henry VI. He served as Lord Lieutenant of Ireland from 1428 to 1430, a position of great power and prestige, and became a highly trusted diplomat and man-at-arms. In 1451 he was admitted to the exclusive brotherhood of Garter knights. In the previous year, when much of Kent rose in rebellion under Jack Cade, one of the king's men singled out for special complaint for brutishness and rapacity was John Dudley, a sure indication that the baron was a no-nonsense man of action, not squeamish in carrying out what he conceived to be his duty.

But we do not need such generalized complaints to obtain an understanding of Lord Dudley's turbulent character and the turbulent age which produced men like him. Thanks to fifteenth-century law court records we can see him in action in his locality. After his return from Ireland John received a stream of complaints about John Bredhill, rector of Kingswinford, some five miles from Dudley and a part of his estate. By all accounts Bredhill was the worst kind of arrogant, rapacious and immoral incumbent, more assiduous in collecting his tithes than in ministering to the needs of his flock. The crimes charged against him included arson, theft, poaching the lord of the manor's game, affray and rape. It was useless for the villagers to seek legal redress, for, when they did, Bredhill 'claimed his clergy', that is he demanded the right to be tried in an ecclesiastical court, knowing that he could rely on his peers to do no more than order him to perform an easy penance. Thus he avoided imprisonment, branding or death, the sentences that might have been imposed by a secular court, and remained in office to punish those who had presumed to raise their voices against him.

Whether John Dudley tried sweet reason with this unholy incumbent we cannot know. What we do know is that his temper soon snapped. The soldier who had laid about him with his broadsword against the king's enemies and ridden down rebels in Ireland was not about to tolerate clerical misdemeanours on his own patrimony. He gathered a small body of armed retainers and rode over to Kingswinsford where he, with,

> John Sheldon, John Clerk, Thomas Young and Thomas Bradley, the Tuesday in the feast of Whitsuntide last past, [1432] wrongfully entered into the parsonage . . . and there they broke up 4 coffers and bore away the goods that were in the same coffers and all other goods that your said suppliant had. Also they put his servants out of their place.[1]

This was no mindless orgy of spontaneous revenge; the spoliation was thorough and cold-blooded. The raiders waited until the incumbent was away and then removed everything that belonged to him: clothes, books, furniture, kitchen utensils, grain and hay from the barns and stock from the fields. Then they broke down his fences, filled his ditches, lopped his trees and trampled his standing crops. Bredhill reckoned the cost of the burglary and damage at £133.10s., some £150,000 in modern-day values. The parson sought legal redress but there is no record of Lord Dudley ever being brought to book. Bredhill, therefore, stoked up the feud by carrying out his own raids on the property of those he believed to be implicated in the outrage.

In his service to the Crown Lord Dudley was no less violent. When Henry VI's regime collapsed he transferred his allegiance to the Yorkist

Edward IV. However, 1470–71 saw a brief restoration of Lancastrian fortunes. Henry VI (now no more than a prematurely aged, feeble puppet in the hands of his own faction) was placed back on the throne. The triumph was short-lived. Edward rallied his forces and in the spring of 1471 crushed his enemies, first at Barnet and then at Tewkesbury (where the heir to Henry's throne perished). Edward purged the realm of his foes and had the rival king lodged in the Tower of London for safekeeping. The man to whom he entrusted the keys of the fortress as Constable was Lord Dudley. There could now only be one way to render the white rose victory permanent. On the very night following Edward's return to his capital someone entered the apartments of the fifty-year-old ex-king and battered him to death. The perpetrator was never identified but the deed could not have been carried out without the knowledge and, perhaps, the organization of the Constable of the Tower.

Such vicious exercise of realpolitik was not uncommon in a land torn by baronial faction fighting. For members of the political class advancement and survival constantly involved conflict between Christian morality, the law of the land and loyalty to the anointed king. Everyone acknowledged that without the framework of law society would collapse but just as important was the buttress of strong government.

Old Lord John saw each of his four sons well settled in life. One became Prince-Bishop of Durham, but three predeceased him and it was his grandson, Edward, who inherited his title and Midlands estates. Only the second son, John, survived his father. Like all younger sons, he was expected to make his own way in the world. Marriage was a standard route to wealth and respectability and, around 1470, he secured a moderately wealthy wife in Elizabeth, the co-heiress of Thomas Bramshot, a man of substance with lands in the Isle of Wight and Hampshire. John settled at Atherington on the coast between Littlehampton and Bognor, raised three sons and two daughters and became a member of the respected Sussex squirearchy. The year of Bosworth found him serving as sheriff of the county. It must have seemed that the Sussex Dudleys were on the way to descending into the relative obscurity reserved for the cadet branches of most noble dynasties. However, John had useful family contacts and made the most of them when it came to planning the career of Edmund, his eldest son.

By this time the power see-saw had tilted once more in the favour of the House of Lancaster. In 1483 Richard III usurped the crown which rightfully belonged to the son of Edward IV, his brother, and split the

Yorkist camp. Margaret Beaufort, mother of Henry Tudor, Earl of Richmond, intrigued with some of the leading political figures at home and with her son in exile. The plan was that Henry should pledge himself to marry Edward IV's eldest daughter, thus uniting the red and white rose factions, then lead a rebellion of all who were disenchanted with Richard III's regime. It was this plan which reached its bloody fulfilment at the Battle of Bosworth in 1485, where one usurper was killed and another usurper emerged from the fray as King Henry VII.

Margaret's go-between in all the negotiations leading to the coup was Reginald Bray, the steward of her household and a man with a fine head for administration and intrigue. The new king was devoted to his mother and it is not surprising that when he chose the men who were to form the inner circle of his government a prime position was found for Lady Margaret's agent. The chronicler Edmund Hall eulogized Bray as a man of principle and a fearless royal adviser. He was

a very father of his country, a sage and a grave person and a fervent lover of justice. Insomuch that if anything had been done against good law or equity, he would, after an humble fashion, plainly reprehend the king and give him good advertisement how to reform that offence and to be more circumspect in another like case.[2]

Bray was created a Knight of the Bath at Henry's coronation and soon afterwards Knight of the Garter. He was appointed to the privy council, awarded the chancellorship of the Duchy of Lancaster, and enriched with a steady stream of grants and offices, which not only made him very wealthy, but also demonstrated to all members of the political class the sort of royal servant who was most highly valued by the Tudor king.

Unlike most of those to whom Henry was beholden for the Crown of England, Bray was not a military man. He was an organizer, a fixer, a shrewd judge of character and a balancer of books. He had a vision for the creation of a new England, a land at peace in which piety and the arts could flourish. It is to his patronage and organizational skills, as much as to the talents of stonemasons, that we own such Gothic master-pieces as St George's Chapel, Windsor, Henry VII's Chapel at Westminster and Bath Abbey. Fittingly, his portrait appears in a fine transept window at Malvern Priory alongside those of Henry VII, his queen and his elder son. As a member of Lady Margaret Beaufort's cultured and pious circle, he took a close interest in her numerous benefactions to religious foundations and, particularly, to the universities. But it was as a financial administrator that Sir Reginald was of greatest value to his sovereign. Henry VII understood that a full treasury was the basis of strong government and Bray had long experience of extracting maximum profit from Lady Margaret's estates. As the reign progressed he exercised increasing control of the traditional sources of royal income and helped Henry to develop those policies that would earn him his reputation as a grasping, miser king. It was the administrative machine Bray created for the Duchy of Lancaster which became the model for royal government.

For any who hoped to advance themselves and their families in the service of the new dynasty Reginald Bray was a man whose patronage was to be coveted. This was obvious to Lord Dudley. Already in his eighties by the year of Bosworth, the Midlands magnate had lost none of his political acumen. He had always managed to stay on the winning side and knew how to cultivate the men in power. It is not surprising, therefore, to find him striking up a close relationship with Sir Reginald Bray. John named him as executor of his will, along with Sir William Hussey, Chief Justice of the King's Bench (who was related by marriage to Bray). John Dudley of Atherington shared his father's intimacy with several of the new men, including Bray, with whom he often had to work closely because of the latter's extensive lands in the southern counties and the Isle of Wight.

Young Edmund Dudley, therefore, grew up with access to the Tudor establishment and had an easy start as he set out on his own career path. Born in 1471 or 1472, he showed early promise as an intelligent boy. When he was barely into his teens he was probably sent to Oxford, perhaps at the instigation of his Uncle William, Bishop of Durham, who later became chancellor of the university.[3] Bray, steadily building up an efficient royal secretariat, was on the lookout for bright young men and recognized in Sir John's son someone with real potential.

If the England that Bray and his royal master wanted to build was to become a reality the first necessity was to centralize power in the person of the king. The Tudor dynasty must be assured and potential threats to it removed. Henry VII's overwhelming preoccupation for most of his reign was survival. He had spent all the years of his early manhood in precarious, uncomfortable exile and was resolved not to repeat it. *We* know that the Battle of Bosworth marked the end of the Wars of the Roses but that was far from clear to Henry's contemporaries. All over the land were powerful men who sneered at the Frenchified young man with the tenuous claim who had made a successful grab for the crown. For them the struggle was not over. They intrigued together, formed makeshift alliances and, from time to time, raised the standard of revolt. Rarely was Henry free from the anxiety that his throne might be shaken. In the spring of 1486, less than six months after the new king's coronation, three of Richard III's supporters broke out of the sanctuary where they had taken refuge and tried to raise forces in Yorkshire and Worcestershire. The insurrection collapsed, and Henry demonstrated his ruthlessness by dragging two of the ringleaders out of sanctuary.

However, within months a more dangerous plot was afoot. Yorkist leaders were claiming that ten-year-old Lambert Simnel, a tradesman's son, was the Earl of Warwick, son of the executed Duke of Clarence. The boy was taken to Dublin, a Yorkist stronghold, and proclaimed king. The conspirators, backed by their own levies as well as troops from Ireland and 1,500 German mercenaries, faced the royal army at Stoke in June 1487. The outcome was by no means a foregone conclusion and only after three hours of bloody fighting did victory go to Henry.

Still the enemies of the regime were not cowed. In Flanders they found another imposter in the person of Perkin Warbeck or Osbeck and groomed him for the role of Richard of York, one of Edward IV's sons who had disappeared in the Tower. Henry employed spies to penetrate the councils of the conspirators and this led to a spate of arrests and executions which effectively deterred more malcontents from joining the rebellion. At last, in the summer of 1497, the Yorkists' campaign fizzled out ignominiously in the west country. Even now the new regime was not secure. Genuine potential Yorkist claimants were skulking abroad under the protection of foreign princes, just as Henry had between 1471 and 1485. Efforts to winkle these would-be challengers out of their continental refuges kept Henry's diplomatic corps well occupied. To make matters worse, of the eight children born to Henry and his queen only two boys survived infancy and the elder died at the age of fifteen.

After the death of Prince Arthur in 1502 the survival of the Tudor dynasty rested entirely on the shoulders of Henry's remaining son, Henry, Duke of York, who did not in his early years show much sign of growing into a vigorous man with voracious appetites. If Prince Henry, like his brother, failed to attain manhood, then all that Henry VII had worked for would come to nothing and England would be plunged back into anarchy. Several dismal and menacing ghosts thus clustered round the Tudor throne – rebellion, diplomatic isolation, illness, impecuniousness, regional unrest, sudden death. They could not all be exorcized but

Henry VII increasingly wielded the law as a means of bolstering royal power and so needed the best legal and administrative brains available. He surrounded himself with experts in the common law and even the senior churchmen admitted to his court and Council tended to be versed in canon or civil law rather than theology. In his early years Sir Reginald Bray, described as 'secret, sober and well-witted', was joined as trusted adviser by Cardinal John Morton, Archbishop of Canterbury, whom Thomas More characterized as having 'a deep insight in politic worldly drifts'. The archbishop was Henry's Lord Chancellor for most of the reign, an expert in common and canon law and an advocate of the uncompromising use of royal prerogative. He has gone down in history as the inventor of 'Morton's fork', which suggested that any man who lived lavishly was obviously wealthy and could, therefore, afford to contribute to the royal coffers, while his more frugal neighbour had, equally clearly, laid aside sufficient cash to be able, similarly, to come to the king's aid. In fact, this tax collector's catch-all was around before Morton's time but its early attribution to the archbishop indicates the policy he advocated and suggests why he was widely unpopular.

It was the tidy-minded and industrious Bray who created the mechanism of 'chamber government'. He made the king and his personal, confidential staff the hub of the administrative and judicial systems, bypassing the offices of state and even the law courts and operating a network of agents and officials which ensured that the royal will was felt throughout the land. The most effective, and the most controversial, of all Bray's administrative innovations was the Council Learned in the Law, to which we shall return shortly.

The underlying motivation for these changes was financial. Henry was very far from being the miserable miser of legend. He spent lavishly on redesigning and decorating the royal quarters at Windsor. He completely rebuilt the palaces of Greenwich and Richmond in the latest style and he brought in craftsmen from France, Flanders and Italy. Henry's household was resplendent by the standards of the day and he understood the importance of making an impression. But his security depended on constant vigilance and preparedness. He needed armies to deter revolt. He needed spies to keep watch on those who might plan revolt. He needed diplomatic agents to persuade other princes not to support those who might become figureheads for revolt. For all this he needed money. Therefore, with the aid of Bray and other administrative experts, he set about reorganizing the royal finances – personally.

The Spanish ambassador reported that the king 'spends all the time he is not in public or in his council in writing the accounts of his expenses with his own hand',[4] and Henry's initials on page after page of royal accounts prove this to be true. In order to exercise this personal control he had to change the ways revenue and expenditure were recorded and channelled. During the years of exile he had observed the power and freedom enjoyed by the French monarch. After the end of the debilitating Hundred Years' War with England, Charles VII and Louis XI had painstakingly made themselves masters in their own domains. They reduced the power of the nobility, ruled with the aid of their own chosen favourites and, over much of the country, levied taxes without consultation. The antiquated and region-alized system of revenue collection was streamlined and all payments were made into the Treasury. The shrewd Spanish ambassador observed of Henry that, 'He would like to govern England in the French fashion but . . . he is subject to his council [though] he has already shaken off some and got rid of some part of this subjection.'[5] This certainly applied to financial administration. Hitherto the Exchequer, a separate office of state, had handled most government revenue. By 1485 outmoded practices and the disruptions of the wars had undermined its competence, but that was not Henry's principal motive for sidelining it; he wanted as much of the government's cash as possible to pass through his own hands. Therefore he ordered that all monies except the customs revenue should go to the Treasurer of the Chamber. The king changed the actual layout of royal apartments by adding to the Hall and the Chamber, staffed by men of high rank, the Privy Chamber, an inner sanctum where he was served by person-ally chosen men of low degree loyal to him alone. It was in this semi-reclusive lodging that he pored over his accounts.

Edmund Dudley, a gifted young lawyer of loyal family and a protégé of Reginald Bray, was being groomed to take his place in the intimate and secretive microcosm of Tudor chamber government. Edmund had not failed his mentor. After the university he entered Staple Inn or Barnard's Inn, lesser Inns of Chancery, before graduating to Gray's Inn, then the most prestigious of the four Inns of Court situated in the suburbs between London and Westminster, where barristers and judges learned their craft. This involved a rigorous mental discipline under the watchful eyes of harsh taskmasters. Edmund had to attend lectures by the seniors of his Inn. He had to take notes at the trials held in the courts which met in Westminster Hall. He had to argue cases with fellow students and with his tutors. Most arduous of all, he had to commit to memory hundreds of statutes and key precedents.

Like students of all times, Edmund and his contemporaries frequently let off steam in the alehouse and the brothel, the brawl and the demonstration. Rioting had become almost an official fixture on May Day, when respectable citizens shut up their shops and locked up their daughters. In 1515 Thomas More was among the City leaders who had to call in the soldiery to arrest over 300 unruly cudgel-wielding students and apprentices after a night of terrorizing inhabitants and looting their homes. Yet, whatever extra-curricular activities Edmund may have indulged in, he did not neglect his studies. He passed rapidly through the stages of his training and emerged as a more-than-competent advocate with a firm grasp of the intricacies of the law and an effective courtroom manner. By the time he was in his mid-twenties he had achieved quite a reputation for rhetoric and we can catch a glimpse of his style from his only extant written work, *The Tree of Commonwealth*:

> If there be no truth what availeth interchange of merchandise? What availeth cities or towns built? If there be no truth what availeth fraternities and fellowships to be made? And, for the more part, if there be no truth, what availeth laws and ordinances to be made or to ordain parliaments or courts to be kept? If there be no truth what availeth men to have servants? If there be no truth what availeth a king to have subjects? And so, finally, where is no truth can be neither honour nor goodness.[6]

In 1493 Edmund received his first official appointment, with his father on the commission of the peace for Sussex. By now he had established his own practice and had sufficient income to contemplate marriage. The young woman he chose was Anne, the sister of Andrew Windsor, later Lord Windsor of Stanwell, Berkshire. She was already widowed, having previously been married to Roger Corbet, member of an ancient Shropshire family. The Windsors and Corbets came from the same stratum of society as the Sussex Dudleys, moderately well-to-do landowners having strong connections with the legal profession. The couple had one daughter but within ten years Anne died, perhaps in childbirth.

1496 was a particularly good year for the twenty-four-year-old Edmund. He was nominated a lecturer at Gray's Inn and also elected by the City corporation as an undersheriff for London. His training equipped him to specialize in court work and also in the administration of estates and he seems to have divided his time between the two. He acted as a judge in minor cases and as an adviser to senior justices. Anyone who knew him at this time would have recognized a confident, well-connected, upwardly mobile young lawyer, destined for greater things. He was certainly very popular with the City fathers, for when he retired as undersheriff in 1500 they provided him with a generous pension and livery allowance.

At the turn of the century Edmund came into his own inheritance on the death of his father. John Dudley ended his life as a gentleman of considerable means, able to proclaim his status to later generations in the impressive marble memorial he had built in the magnificent collegiate church of the Holy Trinity at Arundel. There his remains rest still, in company with those of the Fitzalan Earls of Arundel.

By contrast, his son was soon mingling his genes with those of the ancient families of Beauchamp, Talbot and Grey. The death of Anne freed Edmund to aim very much higher, and he bought his way into one of the great noble dynasties. The wars of the fifteenth century had played havoc with the uninterrupted workings of the laws of inheritance. Husbands had been killed before they could sire sons. Sons had fallen in battle before they could be married. The hopes of leading dynasties had come to rest upon widows and children. Such was the fate of the Talbot Viscounts Lisle.

John Talbot, first Earl of Shrewsbury, was one of the most dashing military commanders of his age, another Hotspur, and was almost continuously on campaign in France from 1419 until his death in 1453. Very much a general of the old school, he finally perished because he failed to embrace revolutionary changes in the art of warfare, cut down before the walls of Castillon trying to storm the town in the face of murderous artillery fire. The earldom went to a son by his first wife but his younger son, John, had already been ennobled as Viscount Lisle in right of his mother, Margaret Beauchamp, Shrewsbury's second wife. Unfortunately, Lisle fell by his father's side at Castillon. It was thus his son Thomas who inherited the title and lands of the viscountcy. But then Thomas was killed in a skirmish during the Wars of the Roses in 1470 and, since he had no issue, everything reverted to his sister, Elizabeth and, on her marriage, to her husband, Edward Grey. This couple were delivered of two children who were still minors at the time of Edward's death in 1492. That meant that they became wards of the Crown.

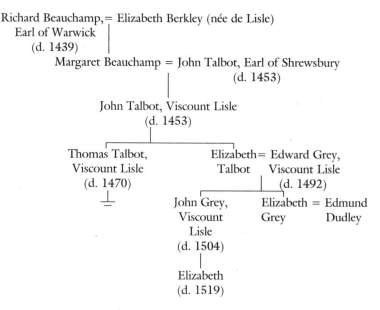

Wardship was a very valuable royal perk, a means of controlling the accumulation of lands and fortunes by acquisitive and power-hungry subjects and a source of revenue. The king did a brisk trade in wardships and there was never a lack of eager bidders. The man who obtained the wardship of little Elizabeth Grey was Edmund Dudley. This was a sign of his social standing and of his influence at court. It indicated that the king trusted the up-and-coming lawyer as a safe recipient of this valuable inheritance. As Elizabeth's guardian Edmund enjoyed the administration of her dower lands until she came of age but he could also lay permanent claim to her fortune by marrying her himself. This he did around 1503.

The importance of Edmund's forging this connection with the great medieval families of Beauchamp and Talbot cannot be exaggerated. It was something of which his children were extremely proud. It was particularly important to Edmund because the senior Dudley line had fallen on hard times. His cousin, Baron Edward, totally lacked the drive and charisma of his grandfather. He tried to make up for his lack of talent by living in spectacular style in London where he squandered his patrimony in a vain attempt to cut a dash in society and draw attention to himself at court.

Edmund, by contrast, had begun to receive marks of favour from a cautious King Henry. In 1501 he was nominated as justice of the peace for Hampshire and commissioner for concealed lands in Sussex. Both appointments were significant in terms of the direction of royal policy. Henry made increasing use of the county gentry in his campaign against those whose authority in their regions rivalled his own. One way to counter the local power of the great landowners was to widen the juridical competence of magistrates. By giving Crown appointees extended authority to examine breaches of the law and impose heavier fines Henry not only restricted the autonomy of the barons, he enhanced the prestige of the gentry and bound them as a class more firmly to the Crown.

Seeking out 'concealed lands' was another way of curbing the magnates and bringing money into the royal coffers. It involved the commissioners in investigation of a labyrinth of property deals, feudal dues, inheritance rights, customary law and local traditions. Theoretically all land belonged to the king and was held from him in return for feudal obligations in fee simple (outright possession) or fee tail (with restricted inheritance rights). Over the four centuries that had passed since the Conquest some feudal dues had been commuted, some had lapsed; property had passed from family to family by marriage or sale; boundaries had been surreptitiously extended; estates had been granted away, not always in accordance with proper legal procedures; tenants had been given grazing or other rights which had been legitimized by custom; royal demesne lands had been encroached upon. According to ancient statutes which had never been repealed, payments were due to the Crown when certain properties were passed from father to son or alienated. Very little had been done to untangle what had, by 1500, become an impossibly complex multitude of rights and relationships, and Henry VII was convinced, not without reason, that he was being cheated of an enormous amount of revenue. Hence the sending of commissioners to enquire into concealed lands which might be proved to belong to the king as a result of non-existent or faulty transfers of ownership.

Of course, the landowners in question regarded Dudley and his colleagues as royal 'snoopers' and resented the way they toured the country, attended by armed escorts, demanding access to family muniments and questioning tenants and servants. Edward IV had tried, in a very limited way, to rationalize the confused state of affairs but Richard III had abandoned the experiment because he was dependent on the support of the very men who were angered by enquiries into their affairs. Henry bowed to no such restraint. As he strengthened his position he could afford the calculated risk of displeasing his leading subjects. It was left to his agents in the field to suffer the abuse of the powerful men they were sent to investigate. There were, to be sure, some landowners who did not browbeat the commissioners, preferring, instead, to offer bribes. Years later, Dudley would be accused of using his position for personal profit, and we cannot know how much justification there was in such suspicions. He was meticulous in his habits and kept his account books in excellent order but, of course, they do not prove that unrecorded sums never passed through his hands. For royal servants to profit unofficially was the rule rather than the exception. They might pocket money in return for turning a blind eye to irregularities. They might earn the gratitude of some great lord in a position to do them return favours. They might help out their own friends by making a good report on them to the king. The role of middle man was beset by many temptations.

Edmund and his colleagues were thick-skinned when it came to enduring the complaints and abuse of the magnates because the one person they could not afford to alienate was their royal master. He had the power to raise them to still greater heights or to destroy them utterly and he was very sensitive to disloyalty. Henry, like many men in positions of power, felt betrayal very personally and was ruthless in avenging himself against those who abused his friendship. Dudley, could not be ignorant of the fact that he was in the service of a demanding monarch suspicious almost to the point of paranoia. Having deliberately set his sights on becoming part of the royal entourage, it is unlikely that the lawyer would risk stepping out of line, whatever temptations came his way. Edmund Dudley dedicated himself to his king's interests with unalloyed zeal.

This impression is confirmed by the crucial decision Edmund made in 1503. While advancing in royal service he was also being courted by the corporation of London. Impressed by his performance as undersheriff, they offered him appointment as common sergeant or sergeant at law. The sergeant ranked directly below the recorder, the senior judicial officer of the City, and for a lawyer in his early thirties to be advanced to this position was proof that he was on the fast track to the top of his profession. Yet Dudley did not hesitate to decline the honour, even though it cost him £46.13s.4d. to buy himself out. The reason is not difficult to see. At the beginning of the following year Henry VII instructed the newly elected House of Commons to appoint Edmund Dudley as Speaker. As such Dudley was the king's man in the lower chamber. There was no constitutional conflict between Crown and Commons at this time, but there were occasional differences between the king and the City and by making his choice Edmund Dudley had irrevocably taken sides. He would be Henry's agent to oversee the workings of the lower house and ensure that his legislative programme passed through smoothly.

But more important elevation to royal service was in the offing. Sir Reginald Bray died in August 1503 and was laid to rest in the chapel which he had helped to build at Windsor. One of his last services to the monarch to whom he was devoted was seeing Edmund Dudley summoned to the Council. Dudley now entered a new, privileged world, the world of the Privy Chamber. He became one of the elite confidential attendants permitted to pass the guards who strictly controlled the approaches to the inner sanctum from the presence chamber and other public rooms of the old royal residences and the new ones which Henry built close to the capital.

Edmund had every reason to congratulate himself on his good fortune. He was still in his early thirties and the king to whose confidential service he was now admitted seemed to have established his throne quite firmly. What matter that influential men grumbled about the harsh and intrusive policies of the government or that, as Dudley well knew from his contacts with nobles and gentlemen throughout the southern shires, the regime was becoming more unpopular by the month? For the time being Edmund could stifle the voice of inner protest, the voice that reminded him that he was sworn to uphold the glories of English law which enshrined the freedoms of English people. What the realm needed was firm rule and Henry Tudor was providing it.

2

Notoriety

———◦◦◦◦———

. . . the most Christian king and most natural lord, what praise, laud
or renown shall he have, as well of all Christian princes as of the
subjects, for having this tree of commonwealth within his realm . .
. rooted in himself and his subjects and plenteously garnished with
their . . . fruits.[1]

In the last months of his life, which he spent in the Tower of London,
Edmund Dudley had plenty of time to reflect on what makes for a fair,
just and secure society. *The Tree of Commonwealth*, in which Dudley set
down his ideas, is a work of conventional piety and idealism which
exhorts the king and all subjects in their due degrees to fulfil their
divinely ordained functions, which alone will produce the 'fruits' of
dignity, prosperity, tranquillity and good example.

In it Dudley insisted that the sovereign, had to act within the bounds
set by law and custom: 'though the cause touch himself, yet he must put
[his agents] in comfort not to spare to minister justice without fear.'[2]

Trusted royal councillors were especially vulnerable to the temptation
to abuse their power. It was one thing for a royal adviser to enunciate
such unexceptional Christian principles for the good ordering of
states. It was quite another to stand up for those principles on a daily
basis as a member of a regime determined to impose its own brand of
peace and security, come what may. It was also difficult to resist the
temptation to make full use of his position for his own ends.

When, in the autumn of 1504, Edmund Dudley was called to the Council, he found himself to be a very junior member of a large body numbering up to fifty men, including leading nobles, bishops, senior members of the judiciary, and some of the more substantial country gentlemen, as well as lawyers and clerks whose task it was to keep a record of business. The whole body only met when the court was at Westminster and seems to have been used by Henry, not for making policy, but as a sounding board and as a vehicle for making his own decisions more widely known. When the king was on progress or wished to discuss confidential matters he was attended by a much smaller group of councillors. When there were administrative details to be sorted out such work was assigned to committees of the Council. In the non-official hierarchy of royal attendants Edmund Dudley was not, and never became, a favoured companion or a trusted confidant of the king. In that he was on a par with most of those who were part of the household or government of this most secretive of monarchs.

Henry was at the centre of three interlocking circles, chamber, court and Council. Several men had their places in one or more of these influential fellowships but few enjoyed real intimacy with the sovereign. Henry was too cautious or canny to open himself up readily to anyone. He had few friends or favourites – perhaps none. A man might tend the king's needs at his bedside, or hold one of the great household offices, or accompany him for a day's hunting, or play cards with him until late into the night, or advise him on tricky diplomatic negotiations – and never gain access to the locked closet of his mind. By holding something in reserve and being as ready with a sharp rebuke as a warm greeting Henry ensured that no one came so close to the throne that he had any chance of manipulating its occupant. There were, to be sure, those whose company Henry enjoyed, who earned a greater measure of his trust and who were advanced to major honours. Such were selected by Henry's idiosyncratic will alone.

Dudley was never admitted to the elite corps of royal companions. He was a functionary, valuable to the regime for his legal expertise. It may be that he was not particularly popular with his royal master, for, although he profited handsomely in terms of cash and land, he never received any of those special honours that were marks of personal royal favour. For example, during the reign seven prominent men of law served as Speakers of the Commons. For all the others the office was a step to higher things. Some already were or became habitués of the court or close attendants on the king. Most were appointed to important positions in government or the household. All were knighted for their endeavours. Not so Edmund Dudley. Perhaps he lacked the fawning accomplishments of a courtier. Perhaps after the death of Sir Reginald Bray he had few friends in the inner circle prepared to advance his career. Whatever the reason, it seems that Dudley was someone useful to the king rather than admired by him.

He was brought into the administration for his detailed knowledge of the law and his success in applying it on various royal commissions. Dudley could devise hitherto unforeseen ways in which Henry might add to his revenues and Reginald Bray saw him as an ideal addition to the company of legal specialists whose expertise could buttress royal power. Dudley was one of the conciliar lawyers who heard cases on behalf of the Crown and of private plaintiffs. For almost two decades Bray had been developing the administration of the king's chamber, extending its authority and streamlining its procedures. It was an ever-growing task because as the army of royal agents and informers detected more alleged infractions of the law so the officers at the centre became busier and the need to improve the organization grew. For example, in 1503 the lucrative trade in wardships had developed so rapidly that a separate department had to be set up under the control of a Master of the Wards.

But more significant was the development of the Council Learned in the Law. It had been in existence for almost a decade when Dudley joined it. It was a conciliar court whose declared function was the closing of legal loopholes and the detecting of fraudulent evasion of feudal obligations. There is no doubt that the government did have a real problem in this area. We have already seen that Henry had despatched commissions into the shires to enquire into concealed lands but the issue of the treasury being cheated of its dues was very much wider. As well as property transactions the Council Learned's jurisdiction embraced wardship, marriage of heirs, retaining, maintenance and, in effect, anything that the king's lawyers chose to bring under their microscope.

Such was the official justification for the setting up of the Council Learned. Others put a somewhat different gloss on the royal initiative. The sixteenth-century chronicler, Edmund Hall, pictured the king reflecting that 'men through abundance of riches wax more insolent, headstrong and rumbustious' but yet being unwilling 'to repress and wrongfully poll and exact money of his subjects.' According to this interpretation Henry came up with a scheme for hitting potentially troublesome subjects in their pockets and reducing all wealthy men to dependence on the government for the peaceful enjoyment of their goods.

. . . it came into his head that Englishmen did little pass upon the observation and keeping of penal laws or [financial] statutes, made and enacted for the preservation of the common utility and wealth and, therefore, if inquisition were had of such penal statutes, there should be few noblemen, merchants, farmers, husbandmen, graziers, nor occupiers but they should be found transgressors and violators of the same statutes . . .[3]

Sixteenth-century commentators had a problem depicting the character of the first Tudor. His government was unpopular with the large number of his subjects who suffered from his legal/financial policies. However, Henry VII *was* a Tudor, the founder of the dynasty, and it was risky to impugn his memory. The convention such writers usually fell back on was to praise the dead king's virtues and to blame his vices on corrupt advisers. One of the first to grapple with the problem was Thomas More, a fellow law student (at Lincoln's Inn) with Edmund, though a few years younger. As soon as Henry VII was dead he expressed his feelings about the recent government in a Latin coronation ode addressed to Henry VIII. Although he did not accuse the late king directly, he was certainly far from circumspect in his comments. His praise for the new sovereign contained criticism of the previous regime which was far from veiled.

. . . the nobility, whose title has too long been without meaning, now lifts its head, now rejoices in such a king and has proper reason for rejoicing. The merchant, heretofore deterred by numerous taxes, now once again ploughs seas grown unfamiliar. Laws, heretofore powerless – yes, even laws put to unjust ends – now happily have regained their proper authority . . . Now each man happily does not hesitate to show the possessions which in the past his fear kept hidden in dark seclusion. Now there is enjoyment in any profit which managed to escape the many, sly clutching hands of the many thieves. No longer is it a criminal offence to own property which was honestly acquired . . . No longer does fear hiss whispered secrets in one's ear . . . Only ex-informers fear informers now.[4]

More's indignation at the injustices perpetrated by arbitrary rule and his fear that it could easily reappear never left him. He brooded on tyranny and treated the subject more fully in his most famous work, *Utopia*, published in 1516. He may still have been thinking about Henry VII and his councillors when he portrayed a 'hypothetical' king devising means of enriching himself at the expense of his subjects:

> One [councillor] advises crying up the value of money when he has to pay any and crying down its value below the just rate when he has to receive any . . . Another councillor reminds him of certain old and moth-eaten laws, annulled by long non-enforcement, which no one remembers being made and therefore everyone has transgressed. The king should exact fines for their transgression, there being no richer source of profit nor any more honourable than such as has an outward mark of justice![5]

Even Polydore Vergil, commissioned by Henry to write a history of the reign, could not avoid criticism. He praised the king's piety, his generosity, his political shrewdness, the splendour of his court and his love of peace. But there was a quality the Italian singled out for special note. Henry, he said, 'cherished justice above all things.' However, as the writer enlarged on this statement he made it clear that this did not imply the impartial application of the law. The king, Vergil explained, 'vigorously punished violence, manslaughter and every other kind of wickedness'. Having listed all his patron's good points, he concluded,

> But all these virtues were obscured latterly by avarice, from which he suffered. This avarice is surely a bad enough vice in a private individual, whom it forever torments. In a monarch, indeed, it may be considered the worst vice since it is harmful to everyone and distorts those qualities of trustfulness, justice and integrity by which the state must be governed.[6]

The word which served as something of an escape hatch for Vergil was 'latterly'. It suggested that Henry's less admirable characteristics could be put down to advancing years and the strains of kingship. Edmund Hall claimed that towards the end of his life Henry realized that he had been seduced into harsh policies by his henchmen and resolved to make restitution to all those who had suffered injustice at the hands of his over-zealous agents, a resolution sadly frustrated by his death. This attempt to whitewash the king's memory carries no credence.

More was absolutely right in identifying Henry Tudor as a dictator obsessed with drawing all power into his own hands and keeping it there. Nor can we believe that his harsh policies were the result of failing powers and unscrupulous underlings. Throughout his entire reign Henry had turned the screws ever tighter upon his subjects. Any suggestion that he only became autocratic in his last, fear-haunted years does not bear scrutiny.

Henry had no choice but to be ruthless. The mainstay of government revenue was not direct taxation. This was regarded as 'extraordinary' income and, to the chagrin of successive monarchs, could only be obtained by parliamentary consent, theoretically for such emergencies as war. The king was expected to meet all normal personal and national expenses from the profits derived from Crown lands, customs duties, feudal revenue and the law. Henry applied himself to maximizing all these sources and it was with the last two that the Council Learned was specifically concerned. Its activities were based to a very great extent on information gathered by anonymous accusers, known as 'promoters', whose victims were then proceeded against by the authority of the Council, without reference to any other court.

At Westminster a bevy of clerks was set to scan law books for precedents that might be turned to advantage. Other agents were despatched into the shires to study locally held muniments, to interrogate suspects, to encourage malcontents to air their suspicions and to turn a ready ear to gossip. The end result was that hundreds of wealthy and not-so-wealthy subjects found themselves designated tenants-in-chief of the king and therefore liable for arrears on a whole range of feudal dues. A man had to pay for the privilege of entering an inheritance. If he was unfortunate enough to die before his son was of age the boy became a royal ward and thus a commodity to be sold to a favoured courtier or magnate. When a landowner was succeeded only by a daughter, she was at the disposal of the king and her marriage rights also were sold. When there were no heirs all property reverted to the Crown. Moreover, when the royal snoopers could discern irregularities in property transactions they levied fines in addition to the relevant feudal payments. But beyond these imposts arising from the transfer of land there were other occasions when the king could demand contributions from all his tenants-in-chief. Such were the knighting of his eldest son and the marriage of his eldest daughter.

The regime soon discovered that putting financial pressure on rich and powerful Englishmen had other advantages beyond filling the royal coffers. It could be used as a means of political coercion. Henry applied himself vigorously to the problem of 'maintenance', the mainstay of nobles and others whose power in the provinces depended on retaining large bodies of servants whose first loyalty was to them rather than to the king. We have seen an example in old John Dudley's bullying of the vicar of Kingswinford, but that was a storm in a teacup compared with the way others employed mini-armies to enforce their will in their localities. Apart from the disruption this caused in the shires there was always the threat that such bands could be diverted from mere banditry to rebellion against the Crown. Armed retainers were not the only menace. Major landowners took onto their payrolls lawyers to pervert the cause of justice, clergymen to support them by means of the spiritual authority they wielded and farmers and merchants through whom they could exert economic pressure on any who dared oppose them. This was a serious evil and Henry was not the first king to address it but he did tighten the laws against maintenance, encouraged informers to report offenders and proceeded against suspects by direct action as well as through the common law courts. Edmund Dudley helped to steer through parliament the Act Against Illegal Retaining (commonly known as the Statute of Liveries 1504) which tidied up and stiffened previous legislation. With certain domestic exceptions it decreed that 'no person, of what estate or degree or condition he be . . . privily or openly give any livery or sign . . . or . . . by any writing, oath, promise, livery, sign, badge, token, or in any other manner wise unlawfully retain'. Not only was any convicted retainer liable for a 100 shilling fine every month for every servant thus hired, but every retainee would suffer a similar penalty.[7]

By this time the king's more substantial subjects had become painfully familiar with the threat of severe financial consequences which might follow any action which incurred Henry's displeasure – even if they were completely unaware that they had given offence. As royal agents unearthed ancient statutes and informers produced evidence that those statutes had been transgressed hundreds of people found themselves hauled into court. What frequently happened after the guilty verdict had been delivered was that the offender was offered a pardon that would clear his name – in return for payment. This procedure was even stretched to cover serious crimes. Thus a murderer might go free – if his purse was deep enough.

An extension of this was the exacting of bonds of recognizance. Actual or potential offenders were bound in a specified sum of money for their future good behaviour. Lord Bergavenny was fined a swingeing £70,000 for retaining. This figure, doubtless intended to *encourager les autres*, was well beyond the baron's means and was commuted to a bond of £5,000 attached to the condition that he never again went anywhere near his power base in south-east England, where his considerable family estates lay. A variant of the recognizance was the bond of obligation. The victim was obliged to enter an agreement to lend the king money or perform some other service, failure to comply with which would make him liable for payment of his bond. In such varied ways did Henry VII keep numerous people 'in his danger, at his pleasure', as Dudley later explained. It has been calculated that of the sixty-two leading families in the realm the king had forty-seven at his mercy by means of fine or bond at one time or another. From the beginning of the reign to 1504 royal income from all prerogative sources rose from around £3,000 to approximately £40,000 per annum. This was at a time when a skilled craftsman would consider himself fortunate to earn £2.10s. a year.

Edmund Dudley was in no way responsible for such policies. The programme was well established by the time he was brought onto the Council Learned in the Law. He joined a body whose remit and procedures were already clearly established. Its activities did not change after 1504 at the behest of a king grown more grasping with age. Any intensification of its activities was simply the result of its becoming more efficient. Morton and Bray were no longer alive to oversee it but the policies they had helped Henry to devise continued in the hands of a dedicated band of royal servants. The more senior members of the council were established lawyers and courtiers, high in the confidence of the king. The Council Learned was thus a formidable body of about a dozen men who served the king with an eager and ruthless efficiency and who marshalled a small army of industrious agents travelling to all corners of the realm. In 1622 Francis Bacon wrote of Henry that he did not 'care how cunning they were that he did employ, for he thought himself to have master-reach'[8] and the king and his specialist council were certainly well matched.

Dudley was, and always remained, one of the junior members of this body. A couple of charters refer to him as the 'president' but this can only mean that he conventionally acted as chairman/secretary of the council. The more exalted members were busy enough with their other duties and their attendance was sporadic. Routine business was, doubtless, attended to by the council's clerkly 'rump' and Dudley's gifts ideally suited him to organize their agenda. He was an assiduous keeper of books and taker of notes and his colleagues came to rely on his orderly, methodical approach to their varied tasks. He and his colleagues were zealous in the pursuit of their master's interests. They had very good reason to be so; their feet were well set on the ladder of advancement in royal service and they naturally wanted to show themselves to be efficient.

Being of comparatively humble origins they did not suffer the disincentive of other members of the establishment. The lords spiritual and temporal who clustered round the throne had relatives and friends who suffered as a result of Henry's rapacity and their loyalties were not always wholly undivided. The king knew that Dudley and his assistants were much more his own men, dependent on his favour alone and not on the aristocratic network of the shires. They were men who would not be intimidated. The other side of the coin was that the likes of Dudley were wholly dependent on royal protection. The great families of the realm, who regarded themselves as partners in government as of right, bitterly resented the Tudor monarch's reliance on commoners in central and local government. Such dissatisfaction remained bottled up while Henry lived but would be released as soon as a new reign dawned. Nor was it only felt by members of the elite. Thomas More was among several commentators who genuinely believed that the well-being of the realm was best safeguarded by king and peers acting in concert. Part of the fury directed against Dudley was on account of what he was rather than what he did. He was not a member of the aristocratic club. He was an upstart. Dudley's name came to be indissolubly associated with one other member of the Council Learned, Sir Richard Empson.

'Empson and Dudley' – two names forever linked in infamy, like Burke and Hare or Bonnie and Clyde. Francis Bacon did more than any other historian to blacken their names in an extended passage of unrestrained vitriol:

> . . . as Kings do more easily find instruments for their will and humour than for their service and honour, he had gotten for his purpose, or beyond his purpose, two instruments, Empson and Dudley; whom the people esteemed as his horse-leeches and shearers: bold men and careless of fame, and that took toll of their master's grist. Dudley was of a good family, eloquent, and one that could put hateful business into good language. But Empson, that was the son of a sievemaker, triumphed always upon the deed done; putting off all other respects whatsoever. These two persons being lawyers in science and privy counsellors

in authority, (as the corruption of the best things is the worst) turned law and justice into wormwood and rapine. [Here followed a list of Henry VII's financial-legal stratagems.] These and many other courses, fitter to be buried than repeated, they had of preying upon the people; both like tame hawks for their master, and like wild hawks for themselves; inasmuch as they grew to great riches and substance.[9]

Richard Empson was, another Bray protégé who had risen to the office of Chancellor of the Duchy of Lancaster and administered these lands on behalf of the Crown. The Council Learned was very closely allied with the administration of the Duchy. There was considerable overlap between the two bodies in both staff and methods. Empson, therefore, was an important directing influence in the activities of the Council Learned but he was not the only industrious member of that body. Nor was Dudley. So how was it that these two men were so completely identified with the harsh policies of the regime and came to bear the entire burden of its sins?

One reason we have already mentioned; they were arrivistes. As such they were resented both by those into whose ranks they were clambering and those from whose ranks they had ascended. Another reason, which appears on the face of it to be trivial in the extreme, was that they were neighbours. Each occupied a fine house close to the junction of Walbrook and Candlewick Street (modern Cannon Street) in the fashionable heart of the City, which backed onto the extensive garden of the town mansion belonging to the prior of Tortington. Reporting this a century later in his *Survey of London*, John Stow managed to impart some sinister significance to this topographical fact. There are, he recorded,

> two fair houses in Walbrook. In the reign of Henry VII, Sir Richard Empson, Knight, Chancellor of the Duchy of Lancaster, dwelled in the one of them and Edmund Dudley, Esquire in the other. Either of them had a door of intercourse into this garden, wherein they met and consulted of matters at their pleasures.[10]

By the time Stow wrote, the legend of the evil, scheming councillors was well established and readers would easily have envisaged clandestine meetings at which the harassing and ruin of the king's loyal subjects were planned. In reality, the arrangement whereby Empson, Dudley and their families enjoyed use of the adjacent grounds was much more innocent. Dudley's Sussex lands adjoined those of the priory of Tortington and Edmund had close relations with the community. His first wife was buried in their church and in his will he made provision for two altar cloths to be given to the brothers. What more natural than that the prior should have allowed his friend the use of his town garden? But the very presence of these two royal officials at the centre of the commercial community must have been a constant irritant.

It must have seemed that the two ministers were flaunting their affluence in the faces of their neighbours. They had numerous servants and fine horses. Their wives wore the latest court fashions. Their houses, built by an earlier generation of London merchants, were palatial and richly furnished. We have a description of Dudley's dwelling and we know that it comprised, as well as domestic offices and outbuildings, a great hall, a great parlour, a little parlour, a counting house, a long gallery, three principal bedchambers, an armoury, a 'little house for the bows', various galleries for indoor exercise, some open to the courtyard or the garden, two closets (small, private chambers) and a wardrobe (probably another privy chamber, rather than a room for the storage of clothes).[11] Such ostentation was quite sufficient to provoke the jealousy and resentment of their neighbours.

Henry's agents were rewarded with a percentage of the proceeds when prosecutions brought money into the chamber treasury. Thus, for example, Empson 'discovered' that pardons for outlaws could be granted on receipt by the Crown of the equivalent of one year's income from all the offender's landed property. For this he received one ninth of the income from the granting of such pardons. Edmund Dudley profited handsomely from the perquisites of office. He extended his Sussex and Hampshire estates and by fresh purchases spread his influence into Wiltshire, Dorset and Surrey. He also acquired extensive estates in Lincolnshire, Cambridgeshire and Oxfordshire. His personal fortune at the time of his death was valued at £5,000, a figure which put him on a par with some of the greatest in the land. Empson and Dudley were not unique among the servants of Henry VII who profited dramatically from their closeness to the throne. Dr Steven Gunn has pointed out that the king gave increasing amounts of money and land to courtiers as the reign wore on. From 1495 to 1501 the amount of royal income thus alienated was only £700, but in the last eight years of Henry's life this figure rose to £3,700.[12] Dudley's name rankled particularly with the City fathers. The king had for some time been at odds with the City elders over the status and privileges of the Merchant Taylors. The guild had gained (probably bought) Henry's favour and this had aroused the jealousy of the other guilds. In October 1506 they expressed their displeasure by rejecting the royal nominee for the post of sheriff because he was a Merchant Taylor. Henry was certainly not going to be balked. He sent one of his own advisers to the Guildhall to declare the corporation's election void and to demand the installation of his own man. The royal agent chosen for this task was Edmund Dudley. This action was a gross violation of the City's freedoms; an exercise of naked power. The guildsmen were incensed but because it was dangerous to murmur against the king, it was his messenger who took the brunt of their indignation. They complained, 'whoever had the sword borne before him, Dudley was de facto mayor and what his pleasure was was done.'[13] Henry's policies gave them many other opportunities to feed their resentment of Dudley. The long royal fingers reached over and again into the purses of the merchant community. Informers trawled the Thameside wharfs seeking evidence of customs dues avoided. Whether the victims were guilty or not they were angry at being summoned to answer before Dudley and his colleagues.

But they also levelled specific charges of arrogance and hostility against him. He supposedly bullied merchants into accepting royal decrees as faits accomplis. When the Mercers' Company declined to respond appropriately to a demand for an increase in the poundage rates he reputedly dismissed their prevarication with the comment that their answer would not satisfy the king. One of his servants was said to have boasted that his master would take the aldermen down a peg or two, making them 'wear cloaks of cotton russet instead of cloaks of scarlet'.[14] Such behaviour seemed nothing short of gross ingratitude in one who was himself a freeman of the City and was much indebted to it for his early advancement.

It was not only the propertied and mercantile classes who associated the royal lawyers with repressive and intrusive behaviour. Just as Henry interfered with the shrieval election in London, so he imposed his will in ecclesiastical appointments. In 1504 he obliged the Austin canons of St Mary's Priory, Walsingham to accept his nominee, William Lowth, as their new prior. His representatives informed the inmates that, according to ancient documents they had consulted, they required a royal congé d'élire (a licence telling them whom to elect), though they insisted that, as long as anyone could remember, the community had never had to seek the king's permission before choosing their leader. Who were the men sent from Westminster to overbear the canons of distant Norfolk? Empson and Dudley. The new regime at Walsingham seems to have been quite disastrous. A visitation ten years later found that the priory was run by the prior's mistress and her husband and that they and their cronies devoted their days to hunting and hawking and their nights to revelry.[15] It is, at first sight, surprising to find the pious King Henry determined to foist on this house of prayer so unworthy a shepherd but, as with most of his activities, financial motive was never far below the surface. Walsingham, one of England's primary centres of pilgrimage, had grown fat on the offerings of the devout and was made to pay for its alleged flouting of the royal prerogative.

Clearly, then, Edmund Dudley rapidly became a prominent feature of the unacceptable face of Tudor autocracy, an object of widespread loathing. But was he merely the all-too-prominent representative of a hated regime or had he done much to bring obloquy on himself? Was his a classic case of the ambitious man corrupted by power? Did he wield his authority with arrogance and a total disregard for the feelings of others? Somehow across the centuries we have to interpret his character and activities and set in perspective the complaints of those who held him responsible for their misfortunes.

For Edmund Dudley it was axiomatic that, 'every man is naturally bound, not only most heartily to pray for the prosperous continuance of his liege sovereign lord and the increase of the commonwealth of his native country, but also to the uttermost of his power to do all things that might further or sound to the increase and help of the same.'[16] Desire to be of service to the king was, naturally, bound up with ambition for prestige and wealth. Dudley profited handsomely from the position that talent and influence brought him but he was very far from being alone in that. Everyone who sought or gained employment in the Tudor court was doing so in order to feather his own nest and to establish the fortunes of his family. No less than his colleagues, Dudley could be charged with opportunism and profiting from the misfortunes of others but there is little concrete evidence of actual misdemeanour on his part. Rather was his wealth the result of careful husbandry and prudent speculation. He took his cut from government legal business and received grants from a grateful king. When the victims of Henry's stratagems were obliged to sell lands in order to pay fines or repay loans summarily called in, Dudley was at the front of the queue to snap them up. He often sold on such acquisitions at a profit and not infrequently employed his spare capital in trading ventures. Moreover, Dudley was far from being the best-rewarded of Henry's advisers. As we have seen, no titles or lucrative household appointments came his way. He entered and left the royal service as plain Mr Dudley, lawyer.

Because Edmund Dudley grew fat while other men grew lean it was inevitable that he would be suspected of sharp practice, maladministration and corruption. By the time Francis Bacon wrote his account of Henry's reign over a century later the legend was well established that Empson and Dudley had indicted innocent men and made them pay to have the charges dropped; that they had interrogated people in private at their own homes and that they had manipulated jury decisions. However, no evidence exists for such wholesale breaches of the law. The most telling reason to reject the legend is that no charges of extortion or false imprisonment were ever brought against the two ministers. If witnesses were clamouring to voice their complaints and ready to back them up with sworn testimony it is scarcely credible that a strong case would not have been made against them. Subjects certainly had to be careful when accusing ministers of the Crown: criticism of the servant might be taken to imply criticism of the master. Even so, the silence of the records is deafening. Some supplicants did appeal directly to Dudley, even when he was no longer in a position to help them:

> . . . an information was made against me, being justice of peace in my country, that I [had] let a man to bail and took sureties which were not sufficient, whereupon I was called before you and fined £20 to the king's use. I pray you cause the king's council to be moved that I may have my money again.

So ran one appeal in 1510. Dudley's reply is revealing:

> It is true I had this £20 and paid it to the king. I could make the fine no less. I think in my conscience you ought to have it again and I pray you to pray for me. If I were of power I would restore you myself.[17]

In other words, Dudley believed the levy, though lawful, was unjust and that the responsibility for it lay with the king. Had he ever been brought into court to face this and similar charges he could and undoubtedly would have made the same point – and that would have been embarrassing to Henry VII's son.

It is important to keep in mind that Dudley's activities were carried out under the close scrutiny of Henry VII. He would scarcely have dared to pervert royal justice for his own personal gain. Stretching the meaning of the law to the absolute limit in order to enrich the king was one thing; stepping beyond the law for his own gain was quite another. Moreover, Dudley, himself, was not exempt from the extension of the royal prerogative. In 1508, commissioners for concealed lands in Hampshire found that, seven years previously, the minister had entered on estates inherited from his mother without making due payment to the king. He was pardoned for the offence but the indictment brought home to him – if he needed any such enlightenment – that all his dealings had to be scrupulously open and above board. Caesar's wife must be beyond reproach, either by Caesar's critics or Caesar himself.

3

A Tree and its Fruit

—⧓—

. . . to enable a prince to form an opinion of his servant there is one test which never fails; when you see the servant thinking more of his own interests than of yours and seeking inwardly his own profit, such a man will never make a good servant, nor will you ever be able to trust him, because he who has the state of another in his hands ought never to think of himself, but always of his prince and never pay any attention to matters in which the prince is not concerned.[1]

Most politicians and senior administrators of all ages have not been self-avowedly amoral, and it is unthinking cynicism that insists 'They're only in it for what they can get out of it.' But it is equally true that most politicians and senior administrators of all ages have discovered that the job involves compromising principles. Idealism and realism are restless bedfellows. Faced with a determined king and a remit to make the Crown financially and politically secure, Dudley readily settled for the simple unwritten contract implicit in the inner circles of Tudor tyranny. The terms of that contract were clearly set out by Niccolo Machiavelli who had learned realpolitik in the seamy, ruthless world of the Italian Renaissance states. In return for unquestioning loyalty on the part of the servant,

. . . the prince ought to study him, honouring him, enriching him, doing him kindnesses, sharing with him the honours and cares; and at the same time let him see that he cannot stand alone, so that many honours may not make him desire more, many riches make him wish for more, and that many cares may make him dread changes.[2]

In other words, the successful autocrat will surround himself with talented yes-men whose loyalty he ensures by a judicious mixture of generosity and intimidation. Dudley knew nothing of power politics within the Italian states, but without being aware of it, he took Machiavelli's paragon as his model and devoted himself entirely to his master's interests. He unhesitatingly supported activities which, according to his own later testimony, troubled his conscience and in doing so he lost friends and became a public symbol of oppression.

It is, of course, possible that he had a genuine respect for Henry VII and was committed, in general terms at least, to the policies of the regime. The transformations the first Tudor had wrought in the internal life and external reputation of England were impressive in the extreme. Stability, freedom from civil war, and improved conditions for local and international trade were the more obvious benefits of the despotism. And the few who were in a position to view the wider picture saw a king who had enlarged the nation's prestige abroad without committing it to costly military adventures. Henry had taken an insignificant, strife-torn nation and allied it with the imperial Habsburgs and the rising power of Spain. The Intercursus Magnus with the Emperor Maximilian (1496) had forged strong commercial links between England and the rich, industrious Netherlands. The diplomatic advantages he had secured by the marriage of Arthur with the youngest daughter of Ferdinand and Isabella of Aragon and Castile had survived the prince's untimely death. Not only did Catherine become betrothed to Henry's younger son, but, after the death of Queen Elizabeth, the royal widower sent his agents to Spain to explore the possibilities of attracting a bride for himself and he did succeed in having his daughter, Mary, betrothed to the Emperor's grandson (the future Emperor Charles V). Though nothing permanent came of these latter negotiations, they indicate that England had become a significant player in European politics.

Dudley spent most of his time in a court whose ruler was determined to cede nothing to contemporary princes in terms of lifestyle and munificence. While watching the pennies, the king knew the propaganda value of sumptuous display and was fully prepared to lash out when occasion demanded. The new palace he created for himself at

Richmond was an impressive extravaganza of towers and cupolas in the French style (reminiscent of the slightly later Chambord) reflected in the river with a south-facing façade studded with windows which sparkled in the sunlight. It was no less splendid within. Visitors were impressed by the 'pleasant dancing chambers . . . houses of pleasure to disport in at chess, tables, dice, cards, bylys [skittles or, possibly, an early form of billiards], bowling alleys, butts for archers and goodly tennis plays'.[3] He considerably enlarged and beautified the palace at Greenwich and ensured that his earthly remains would be splendidly housed in the chapel he built at Westminster Abbey. Lavish celebrations with feasting, tourneys and pageants marked such important events as the betrothals of his children, but Henry was equally willing to spend money on spontaneous displays. On 7 January 1506, Maximilian's heir, Philip of Burgundy, together with his wife and several courtiers, were obliged to seek refuge on the Dorset coast when their ship ran into a winter gale. Henry pounced on this fortuitous visit by such eminent guests. He had the royal party conveyed to Windsor and there and in other residences organized so many splendid entertainments that Philip and his party were not able to escape till 23 April. The king of England brought craftsmen and scholars from the cultural centres of Italy and, three years after Columbus had reported his momentous discovery to Ferdinand and Isabella, Henry authorized John Cabot to enter the race for a western route to the Orient.

Henry VII's regime could not be described as 'dazzling' but it was certainly impressive and even some of the more substantial men who had suffered at his hands displayed a loyalty that was only partly based on self-preservation. However, inevitably, as the new century got into its stride, their thoughts turned to the future. The old king would not always be with them and what would happen then to the government of the realm and those most closely associated with the unpopular Tudor polity? In 1507 Henry entered his fifties and observers were already noting, 'the king's grace is but a weak and sickly man, not likely to be a long-lived man.'[4] In that very year he suffered a severe bout of tonsillitis that his physicians expected to be fatal and thereafter he frequently had to take to his bed. It is inconceivable that Edmund Dudley was not among those who watched the king's deterioration and took thought for the morrow.

Sixteenth-century English politics is dominated by two great figures, Henry VIII and Elizabeth I But their powerful personas conceal from us the essential fragility of the dynasty. Elizabeth came close to death at the

hands of her half-sister and their father's path to the throne was far from
being a straight, well-lit highway. For almost a century the great families
of the realm had been playing 'catch' with the crown of England and the
draconian measures to which Henry VII had resorted are proof positive
of his nervousness about the succession. He had many reasons to be
anxious. Enemies among the nobility might have been curbed by the
effective financial restraints he imposed upon them but they could be
expected to grasp the first opportunity to escape Tudor tyranny. Henry
had successfully seen off every challenge and the main surviving
contender for the throne was, after 1506, safely locked up in the Tower
(Henry had made a solemn pledge not to execute Edmund de la Pole but
had instructed his son to do so as soon as he came to the throne) but the
Yorkist family tree was flourishing with several healthy shoots. By
contrast, Henry only had one living son and he was still a minor. The
king's spies kept him well informed of plots, murmurings and clandestine expressions of discontent, so that he would have known, for
example, that malcontents gathered at Calais had seriously debated
whether to throw their support behind the Earl of Suffolk or the Duke
of Buckingham as soon as the present occupant of the throne was dead.

Henry's priorities, after 1502, were to keep his son safe and to live
long enough to hand over the crown to an heir who had attained his
majority. If the king was careful of his own security he was positively
paranoid about the prince's. Arthur, his eldest son, had been allowed to
set up his own court at Ludlow and to begin learning the business of
government but the adolescent Henry was kept almost as a prisoner in
his father's palace. He could go nowhere without a guard, access to his
person was strictly controlled and he was never allowed out in public.
The youngster was permitted his favourite tiltyard exercises but only
under the anxious eye of the king who watched from an upstairs
window.

Henry VII was a bundle of ailments although it was probably tuberculosis that was gnawing away at his constitution and making him a prey
to other afflictions. He recovered from his illness in the spring of 1507
but was laid low again within the year. Once more he rallied and it
seemed that his iron will might sustain his failing body until June 1509,
when the prince would attain his eighteenth birthday. Now the king
turned increasingly to thoughts of religion. In the autumn of 1508 he
made pilgrimages to both Canterbury and Walsingham. But his earnest
prayers seemed to go unanswered and by the end of 1508 he was
suffering increasingly from chest pains and shortage of breath. Now, the

monarch who had subordinated moral considerations to the establishment of his own power base made fervent efforts to buy divine grace and public approval. He directed precious reserves of energy into efforts to have his predecessor, Henry VI, canonized. He set aside money for the completion of the murdered Lancastrian's chapel at King's College, Cambridge and planned to remove the 'royal martyr's' remains from Windsor to Westminster. He made large donations to a variety of charities. Then, probably sometime in the early weeks of 1509, he ordered Edmund Dudley to go through his books and identify any men whom he might have treated unjustly so that he could make restitution. This flurry of activity was the action of a conventionally pious man who was about to meet his maker and render an account of his stewardship, but there was also in it an element of political calculation. By enshrining the legend of the saintly royal martyr he was creating a permanent reminder of his own Lancastrian credentials. By releasing from financial bondage some of those who were in his power he hoped to remove their cause for discontent. Henry knew how unpopular his policies were. That was a price he had been willing to pay for the establishment of strong central government but now he was about to hand the reins to an untried youth who would need the support of men of power and wealth. In his funeral oration Bishop Fisher revealed that, in his last days, Henry had discussed with his intimates the transformation that would come over his policies "if it pleased God to send him life', but it was political calculation as well as piety that demanded a significant reversal of policy.

Dudley obediently drew up a list of eighty-four persons, great and small, whom he adjudged to have genuine cause for grievance. It is an extraordinary document. An unwritten rule of all governments is that they should never admit to having been wrong but Dudley's catalogue of unjust exactions is a swingeing indictment of Henry's disregard for the rights of his subjects. Its items include massive bonds imposed on the nobility:

Item, the Earl of Northumberland was bound to the king in many great sums, howbeit the king's mind was to have payment of £2,000 and of no more, as his grace showed me. Yet that was too much for ought that was known.

Senior clergy fared no better:

Item, one obligation of my Lord of London for £500 to be had at the king's pleasure and recognizance of £300 to be paid at certain days. He was hardly dealt withall herein, for he said unto me, by his priesthood, the matter laid against him was not true.

The King's rapacity had reached into every corner of the realm:

> Item, Harper of Staffordshire was hardly dealt withall . . .
> Item, one Cooke of Coventry was sore dealt withall . . .
> Item, one Windial, a poor man in Devonshire, lay long in prison and paid £100 upon a very small cause . . .
> Item, the Baron of Elton and Sir Southward of Lancashire and Sir Andrew Fortescue had very sore ends upon office of intrusions.

Foreigners had not escaped the scrutiny of royal agents:

> Item, Peter Centurion, a Genoese, was evil entreated and paid much money and upon malicious ground, in my conscience.

The government had made use of biased and unreliable informants:

> Item, one Simms, a haberdasher without Ludgate, paid and must pay £500 for light matters only upon surmise of a lewd quean . . .
> Item, my Lady Perceval paid and must pay £1,000 for a light matter only upon the surmise of a lewd priest . . .
> William Curtis, customer of London, and his sureties upon the light information of one untrue man paid £500.

Dudley even hinted at duplicity on the king's part:

> Item, Sir John Pennington paid 200 marks upon an obligation of 500 marks wherein he was bound not to depart without the king's licence and yet for truth I was by when the king took him by the hand at his departure.[5]

Edmund was still compiling his damning catalogue when Henry VII died on 21 April 1509. His death was both expected and yet caught several people unprepared. The heir to the throne was still two months short of his majority – close enough to be of no real significance except to any bent on challenging the prince's right of inheritance. There might well be demonstrations in favour of rival claimants. There were certainly

Yorkist sympathizers waiting impatiently for the end of the regime and ready to set messengers galloping into the shires with the news. At the very least there would be crowds of angry petitioners thronging Westminster to obtain redress of their grievances. For the old king's leading councillors and courtiers there was one overriding priority, survival. They needed to ensure a trouble-free succession and the continuance of their own positions of power and influence at the side of the new king. For two days Henry's death was kept secret while members of the cabal made their plans. Some went to and from the royal bedchamber at Greenwich with smiles on their faces and nothing about their demeanour which might betray the doleful tidings. Others accompanied the new king to the Tower where they remained, 'closely and secret' according to Hall,[6] arranging the precise sequence of events which would ease the transition to the reign of the second Tudor. They readily decided that public anger would be best assuaged if they could convince people that the harsh regime of Henry VII was to be buried with him; that the son was an altogether different proposition from the father. The most dramatic way to signal England's emergence from a winter of discontent would be to throw some of the late king's ministers to the wolves.

The contemporary chronicler, despite his immense admiration for Henry VIII, was quite clear about the seamy scheming which underlay the persecution of the selected victims. Scapegoats were put forward, Hall said, either 'by malice of them that with their authority in the late King's days were offended, or else to shift [to others] the noise of [blame for] the straight execution of penal statutes in the late King's days'.[7] There must have been much argument and anxious pleading behind locked doors as to who was to be given the black spot. If everyone who had been a party to Henry VII's fiscal methods were to be brought to the bar of public opinion few would have escaped condemnation. It would be helpful to know about the rivalries and jealousies that pervaded the court and which came to a head in these frantic hours. Men scurried about the ancient, uncomfortable chambers and anterooms of the Tower's royal lodgings, sought audience with the new king, forged alliances and activated their clientage networks. Those who had shared with the Prince of Wales in the camaraderie of the tiltyard and the tennis court and those whose mature counsel had rendered them indispensable to the king were in the strongest positions. Among the more vulnerable members of the royal entourage were those who had concentrated all their efforts on serving their royal master without giving sufficient thought to building personal power bases.

Four names came top of the poll of those whom the evolving administration of the second Tudor could most readily jettison: Sir Edward Belknap, William Smith, Sir Richard Empson and Edmund Dudley. Belknap, has his brief place in the record as a courtier/lawyer appointed by Henry VII in the summer of 1508 as Surveyor of the King's Prerogative. This office came into being as part of the ongoing modernization of the bureaucracy connected with royal revenue. Henry had decided that the activities of the Council Learned needed the oversight of an individual and the fact that he was still casting an eagle eye over his prerogative rights must cast some doubt on his concern that he and his agents might have been over-zealous. As soon as Henry died Belknap realized that he had been left holding a hot potato. He hastily resigned and thereby ensured that his name was removed from the hit-list. Smith was not so lucky. At the beginning of Henry VII's reign he had been a page in the royal chamber, an attendant who looked after the king's clothes and helped him to dress. He was soon receiving little rewards and marks of approval, usually in the form of cash payments. These led to leases of Crown estates and numerous minor administrative offices, mostly in the north-west. By the turn of the century he was building up a tidy territorial empire. But he by no means abandoned his important position at the centre, becoming an indispensable agent of the Duchy of Lancaster and the Council Learned in the Law. Being away from court at the critical time, he was unable to marshal the support of influential friends. Orders went out from the Council for his arrest. He was brought back to London, stripped of all his offices and tried as an arch-informer. He spent several months in prison but once the new reign had got into its stride he was allowed to retire quietly to his Staffordshire estates.[8]

The death of Henry VII was made public on the evening of 23 April. The following morning members of the royal guard rode into Walbrook Ward to demand the surrender of Edmund Dudley and Richard Empson. They conducted the disgraced ministers, doubtless past jeering crowds, along Candlewick Street and Eastcheap to the Tower. The purge continued over the next few days as notorious promoters associated with Empson and Dudley were rounded up and exhibited in various pillories around the city. 'Howbeit, the most craftiest knave of all, called John Baptist Brimald, escaped and came to Westminster and there took sanctuary.'[9] Once the prisoners were safely lodged in the Tower, the new king and his Council had leisure to decide what to do with them. Their immediate inclination was to charge them, like Smith, with extortion. This was, after all, what most people wanted to see them punished for. But the men in power soon realized that such a course was fraught with problems, particularly since, to gain maximum propaganda effect there would have to be public show trials. Whatever the accused might say in their own defence would be sure to reflect on the late king and other members of his regime. Clever lawyers that they were, they would argue effectively that they had acted within the law, in obedience to their master's wishes and in collaboration with their conciliar colleagues. Both men could point to the fact that they were so completely in the confidence of Henry VII that he had nominated them as executors of his will. Under the circumstances, it took several weeks for the government to decide how to achieve the condemnation of Empson and Dudley while avoiding serious consequences.

The charge eventually brought against the two scapegoats, in July, was one of high treason. Empson and Dudley, it was alleged, had plotted to gain control of the country by massing armed troops in London, seizing the new king (presumably by a direct assault on the Tower!) and setting up a regency council. The two main advantages of this scheme were that witnesses could be bribed or threatened to provide the necessary evidence and that, since the supposed crime had taken place during the new reign, the accused would not have the opportunity to introduce material relating to the former regime. The principal disadvantage was the inherent improbability of the charge. The government proceeded cautiously, leaving nothing to chance. They decided to try the prisoners separately and to keep them apart to prevent them colluding in their defence. Empson was moved to Northampton for his trial, which did not take place until October. Dudley, by contrast, was arraigned on 16 July before a special commission of oyer and terminer (a judicial hearing to enquire into alleged crimes). The humiliating exhibition was staged in the cavernous Guildhall, where the largest number of gloating Londoners could be gathered to witness the degradation of the hated minister.

The accusation ran:

> . . . on the quinzaine of St John Baptist, 1 Henry VIII that Edmund Dudley conspired with armed forces to take the government of the King and realm, wrote several letters to Edward Sutton of Dudley,

knight, Thomas Turbeville, Thomas Ashburnham, William Scott, knight, Henry Long, Thomas Kynaston and John Mompeson to repair to him with all their power and caused these letters to be delivered to Richard Page and Angel Messenger, whereupon a multitude of armed persons came to London to the parish and ward aforesaid . . .[10]

The named correspondents seem to have been Edmund's neighbours and tenants in the south of England, with the exception of his cousin, Baron Dudley. They were all in a parlous situation: the only way they could avoid implication in the 'plot' was to say what the prosecutors wanted them to say. 'Co-operation', on the other hand, might well bring its rewards. Can it have been entirely coincidental that Baron Dudley was admitted to the Order of the Garter on 18 May? As for the jury, any body of London citizens could be relied upon to react with alarm and indignation to the suggestion that Edmund Dudley planned to bring a small army into the City.

The verdict was a foregone conclusion and Dudley was, accordingly, convicted on 18 July. Even though the motivation of his accusers was wholly political, their case cannot have been built entirely on sand. In all probability Edmund *did* send the letters he was accused of sending. If he was one of the few royal servants to know of Henry's death within hours of its occurrence, he would have shared the anxiety felt by all his colleagues in the inner circle and the realization that adequate safeguards needed to be put in place to ensure his own safety and a smooth transition to the new reign. In all likelihood every senior member of the regime did exactly what Dudley did: alerted his clients to be ready with arms and men to stave off any sudden crisis. It would always be possible to put a sinister gloss on such activity and that, it seems, is what brought down those few earmarked by the prominent court faction to bear the sins of the many.

How had Edmund Dudley spent the twelve weeks between his arrest and trial? It may have taken some days for him to get over the initial shock of disbelief, anger and fear but then he applied himself to attempts to escape his predicament. His first thought was to appeal to his former colleagues. He tried to make contact with the venerable Richard Fox, Bishop of Winchester and Lord Privy Seal, and doubtless messages were despatched to other members of the Council, some of whom were working only a matter of yards away within the confines of the Tower. They were as ready to offer succour as they would have been to visit someone suffering from plague. Realizing that he was totally on his own and hampered as he was by not knowing the details of the charge being preferred against him, Dudley settled to preparing his defence. His confinement was probably not very arduous. He could afford to pay for reasonable quarters and luxuries not enjoyed by the common run of prisoners. He had books, ink and paper and time in plenty to employ his agile legal mind marshalling cogent arguments. In the event they availed him nothing. No one who had been closely involved in the workings of what passed for royal justice could have imagined that a state prisoner in Dudley's position had the remotest chance of being acquitted. When he returned to his prison quarters after the trial he knew that a very unpleasant death awaited him, sooner rather than later.

It was now that he sat down with piles of his own records to write his 'petition', the document we have already referred to in which he listed eighty-four examples of royal extortion. The document was addressed to Fox and Sir Thomas Lovell, Chancellor of the Exchequer and Constable of the Tower by

> me, Edmund Dudley, the most wretched and sorrowful creature, being a dead man by the king's laws and prisoner in the Tower of London, there abiding life or death at the high pleasure of my sovereign lord (to whom I never offended in treason or thing like to it to my knowledge, as my sinful soul be saved) . . .[11]

Ostensibly Dudley wrote as one of the principal executors of the late king's will to remind his fellow executors of their master's wish that justice should be done to all who had suffered wrong. His motives, he declared, were the repose of Henry VII's soul and the discharging of those still subject to bonds. 'It were against reason and good conscience', he argued, that 'these manner of bonds should be reputed as perfect debts, for I think verily his inward mind was never to use them.'[12]

There is no reason to doubt Dudley's religious sensibilities. He believed, as most contemporaries did, that the dead suffered spiritual consequences if their sins were left unforgiven. Despite his confinement he knew that men were murmuring against the late king. Even Bishop Fisher, preaching the oration at Henry's funeral, had hinted at the unpopularity of the deceased now being openly voiced: 'Ah, King Henry, King Henry, if thou were alive again, many a one that is here present now would pretend a full great pity and tenderness upon thee.'[13] Dudley was loyal to his master to the end – and beyond. But there was more to his petition than that. He was drawing his plight to the attention of the new regime's leaders and, while offering no overt criticism of Henry VII, was distancing himself morally from the late king's decisions. He was also subtly reminding them that they had been just as involved as he in the policies of the old order. The recipients of this document took note of it – in secret. While using the information to alleviate the suffering of some of the individuals listed by Dudley, they continued to ignore the author.

At his trial in the autumn Empson rounded on his judges with an eloquent vigour which could only have confirmed for the survivors of the regime change just how potentially dangerous he and Dudley could be to them:

> . . . whoever yet saw any man condemned for doing justice, especially when by the king, the chief dispenser of the laws, the whole frame of the proceeding hath been warranted and confirmed? . . . And will you alone hope to escape this heavy judgement? If contrary to all equity and example, you not only make precedents for injustice and impunity, but, together with defaming, would inflict a cruel death on those who would maintain them, what can we then expect but a fatal period to us all? . . . Only, if I must die, let me desire that my indictment be entered on no record, nor divulged to foreign nations; lest, from my fate, it be concluded, that in England all law and government are dissolved.[14]

He was, of course, sentenced and sent back to the Tower to await the king's pleasure. After that – nothing. Weeks passed and neither the prisoners nor their families were given any news about the date of execution. They must all have begun to hope. Perhaps, like Smith, the condemned men would be quietly released after a suitable interval and allowed to retire into provincial obscurity. Some of Henry VIII's councillors may even have suggested a show of royal clemency and there is just a chance that a few consciences were itching. The ex-ministers were not entirely without friends at court; it was even rumoured that the new queen, Catherine of Aragon, might use her influence on their behalf. Hope and fear prowled warily around each other like the lions and the mastiffs sometimes sent to bait them in the royal menagerie not a stone's throw from the Tower's prison accommodation. Then, with the new year, came fresh confusion. Parliament was summoned and its members took the opportunity to add their voices to the chorus of condemnation against the prisoners. A bill confirming the attainders of Empson and Dudley passed both houses. Yet it never received the royal assent and this piece of business lapsed when the members were sent home.

However, the renewed threat had been enough to spur Edmund Dudley into making a desperate escape bid – or, at least, planning such a bid. When he heard that his attainder was being discussed in parliament he made preparations for a breakout with his brother, Peter, and a 'kinsman', James Beaumont. The escape was to have been effected with the aid of two of his servants. The scheme was abandoned for two reasons: his men refused to have anything to do with it and the parliamentary process was aborted. The failure of the attainder apparently persuaded the prisoner that royal mercy might yet rescue him and we would not know that Dudley had ever conceived of escaping from the Tower if news had not leaked out via one 'Brimley' in whom he had rashly confided. After this Dudley concentrated his efforts to secure his own future in completing his political treatise, *The Tree of Commonwealth*.

We must assume that he hoped, by this work, to impress the king with his political maturity; to show that he was the sort of seasoned and talented councillor that a young ruler needed at his side. Had he known the new monarch better he would have realized that Henry was far more interested in enjoying his sudden wealth, power and freedom than in poring over an elaborate and intricate piece of political allegory. *The Tree of Commonwealth* was nothing if not comprehensive as a manual for the edification of a Renaissance prince.

> The effect of this treatise consisteth in three special points, that is to say: first in the remembrance of God and of the faith of his holy Church, with which every Christian prince hath need to begin; secondly of some conditions and demeanours necessary in every prince both for his honour and for the surety of his continuance; thirdly of the tree of commonwealth, which toucheth people of every degree, of the conditions and demeanours which they should be of.[15]

Dudley began with a Polonius-like lecture. The king should be a loving father to the English church and appoint conscientious bishops. He should care for the universities and encourage learning. He must be faithful to all foreign alliances. He ought to avoid dangerous sports. And

Dudley (mercifully oblivious of the future) advised Henry VIII that if he remained true to his wife, God would bless him with healthy heirs.

Then follows the heavily laboured allegory. The ideal commonwealth is compared to a luxuriant tree beneath whose shade all subjects, from the highest to the lowest, are 'holpen and relieved'. To achieve this arboreal excellence the tree must have five secure roots: the love of God, justice, truth, concord and peace. Here Dudley comes very close to criticizing his former master, for he points out that in England the tree of commonwealth is 'wellnigh utterly failed and dead'. Fortunately, the new king is such a paragon that his people may confidently look forward to a vastly changed state of affairs. Led by the example of such a prince the various orders of society will be able to play their part in nurturing the roots with the most felicitous results. The author expands on this in a passage so reminiscent of Thomas More's coronation ode (see above p. 21) that it is difficult to imagine that he had not read it. Under the new dispensation,

> how glad shall every nobleman be of the company of another and one will trust and love another. What friendship and confidence shall then be between men and men from the highest degree to the lowest. How kindly and lovingly will merchants and craftsmen of the realm buy and sell together and exchange and bargain one thing for another. How diligently and busily will the artificers and husbandmen occupy their labour and business and how well content will men be, from the highest degree to the lowest to increase their household servants and labourers, whereby all idle people and vagabonds shall be set at work . . .[16]

Dudley explains that this marvellous tree will produce five fruits: the honour of God, honourable dignity, worldly prosperity, tranquillity and good example (to other nations). Again he exhorts the social orders to enjoy the fruits in manner appropriate to each. But let the harvesters beware; each fruit has a poisonous core which must be carefully removed and a poignant peel which may only be pared cautiously and distributed to those in need. From this point the allegory becomes tortuous.

What is interesting is the evaluation Edmund Dudley offers of contemporary English society after a lifetime spent in law and politics. His observations help us lay out a ground plan for the momentous events of the revolutionary decades which were soon to come.

The issue of overriding importance is the relationship between power and justice. Dudley recognizes that people will always use their wealth, position and influence to overawe those less well placed. At the beginning of Henry VII's reign the most pressing problem had been to curb the power of unruly nobles who held more sway than the king in their own territories. The dilemma of employing overmighty subjects as socially responsible servants of the Crown had not gone away by 1509. The king, Dudley advises, must continue to clamp down on maintainers, embracers and great men who ignore the statutes of liveries. This means putting the power of central government behind the judges and local commissioners. But that, in itself, is not sufficient to guarantee a fair deal for all. If greed, ambition and dynastic rivalry are the besetting sins of the realm's ancient families, those of the royal servants raised up to curb their power are arrogance and corruption. The king must appoint men as councillors, sheriffs and commissioners who are free from all taint of bribery and coercion. No one could have been more aware than Edmund Dudley of the resentment directed against 'new men' like himself. Despite the dislocation caused by decades of baronial conflict, there remained a deep-seated respect (expressed eloquently by writers like Thomas More) for the aristocracy of church and state, whose members were traditionally the 'proper' agents of the Crown, and an equally strong antipathy towards low-born royal officials who usurped the authority of their betters. Dudley had the activities of the Council Learned in the Law and his own fate very much in mind when he wrote,

> peradventure oftentimes the prince shall have councillors and servants that in his own cause will do further than himself would should be done, oftentimes to win a special thank of the king and sometimes for their proper advantage and sometimes for the avenging of their own quarrels, grudges or malice. Let these servants or councillors take heed that they do the party no wrong, for the rod of punishment dieth not.[17]

It was the closest he came to a confession.

Dudley is fully aware of the gulf between holy vocation and human failing in the church. He attacks simony, absentee clergy, the low level of clerical education, the use of political influence to gain preferment, the accumulation of landed wealth by bishops and abbots, the diversion of ecclesiastical income into personal fortunes, and the inadequate preaching of the word of God. He is revolutionary in his insistence that bishops should be obliged to reside in their dioceses and should not be appointed to major offices of state, though he does qualify this with the escape clause, 'unless their presence may not be foreborne about the king's person for his great honour or for the common wealth of the realm'.[18] Dudley was a friend of John Colet, to whom he entrusted the upbringing of his young son, Jerome, and Colet was a leader of that movement for scholarly and spiritual renewal known as the New Learning. He became Dean of St Paul's in 1504 and soon had people flocking to his sermons to hear the Bible expounded in a fresh, vibrant way and related to contemporary society. How closely Dudley was connected with the Colet circle we cannot know but certainly a breeze of New Learning indignation blows through parts of *The Tree of Commonwealth*:

> . . . ye send to the universities young scholars of 10 or 12 years, right near of your blood and they must be highly promoted with an archdeaconry or prebend before he can say his matins. He must go in his grained [finely dyed] clothes, lined with silk or furred with the best as though he of that university were the best, yet his cunning is but small.[19]

Here is a suggestion of that anticlericalism that would feed into the Reformation. Here, too, we may detect that concept of sovereignty which would enable Henry VIII to proclaim himself head of the church in England. Dudley's answer to all the possible ills of society is strong and virtuous kingship. Thus it is the king's task, 'not only [to] support and maintain *his* [my emphasis] church and the true faith thereof . . . but also to see that such as he shall promote and set in Christ's Church . . . be both cunning and virtuous'.[20] There is no mention here of the pope's proprietary claims and, though Dudley would not in his wildest dreams have envisaged England's new king breaking the ties with Rome, there is here a clear recognition that the temporal ruler has ultimate control over the spirituality.

Who has control over the king and where should he turn for guidance? Who can set the limits of his power? Dudley offers no answers to these questions. Other Renaissance theorists debated under what circumstances a prince might be held to account by his people or rebellion might be justified. Dudley does not paddle in these waters. Indeed, the whole object of his treatise is to urge the young Henry to follow the path of moral excellence and spiritual devotion which will ensure harmony in the state and thus render such considerations irrelevant. He observes, for example, that power without compassion is tyranny but he avoids any discussion of what might happen to a tyrant. Henry VII's rule, as he readily acknowledged, had become oppressive but for that the king was accountable to God alone, which is why Dudley was genuinely concerned that the minutiae of Henry's will should be meticulously observed. The king is responsible both to God and his people:

> God hath ordained him to be our king, and . . . every king is bounden [to maintain the tree of commonwealth] for it is his charge. For, as the subjects are bounden to their prince, so be all kings bounden to their subjects by the commandment of God them to maintain and support as far as in him is his power . . . though the people be subjects to the king yet are they the people of God and God hath ordained their prince to protect them and they to obey their prince.[21]

Thus Dudley lays out the main elements of the contract between ruler and ruled but does not venture into the small print of how the responsibilities of the contracting parties are to be worked out. The king must uphold and observe the laws handed down by generations of judges. He will be well advised to call into council wise and loyal servants. (By this Dudley means, specifically, servants well versed in the common law – like himself.) Beyond that there is no human agency able to limit the exercise of the royal will.

Dudley's life was now at the mercy of that will. He still had to wait to discover what the second Tudor would do with the man who had helped his father secure the dynasty and put it on a solid financial footing. Winter passed. And spring. The stones of the Tower grew warm in the summer sun and the fortress's more cramped quarters became stifling. In June, king, queen and court left the fever-prone city behind them and set out on progress through the southern counties. Were the prisoners forgotten? Henry was busy with other affairs which filled his thoughts far more agreeably than the dismal fate of two men who had been incarcerated for fourteen months.

> exercising himself daily in shooting, singing, dancing, wrestling, casting of the bar, playing at the recorders, flute, virginals and in setting songs, making of ballads and did set 2 goodly masses, every

of them five parts, which were sung oftentimes in his chapel and afterwards in divers other places. And when he came to Woking, there were kept both jousts and tourneys. The rest of this progress was spent in hunting, hawking and shooting.[22]

Perhaps Fox, Lovell and their colleagues were still debating what to do with the prisoners. Empson and Dudley were talented, experienced administrators who understood intimately important aspects of government business. The leading councillors had no intention of making sweeping changes in the way things were done. The new king was absorbed in his pleasures and seemed content to let his advisers attend to the day-to-day running of the country and they saw little reason to depart from the prudent and successful measures of the previous reign. If everyone waited until the clamour for the heads of Empson and Dudley died down it might be possible to reinstate them quietly. On the other hand there was the propaganda angle to be considered. The coronation had been splendidly staged and had got the reign off to a good start. Periodic court festivities had kept bright the image of a brave, youthful, popular monarch. A royal pardon had been issued to many imprisoned for minor offences and the government had cancelled some, but not all, of the bonds specified in Dudley's petition. It might be that enough had been done to win hearts and minds to the new regime. However, if public anger against Empson and Dudley showed little sign of ebbing, their execution would make a useful demonstration that the past truly had been buried.

According to Hall the summer progress of 1510 produced evidence of lingering animosity towards the two ex-ministers. Several complaints reached the king as he pursued his pleasurable way through the southern counties. It was for that reason that Henry sent word to the Sheriff of London to attend to the matter. This way of proceeding was to become habitual: a signature on a letter, a seal on a warrant – it was the matter of a moment. Then the king could return to his 'pastime with good company' and others would carry out the messy business for him. Hundreds of people – queens, ministers, courtiers and friends, as well as those who did actually pose some sort of threat – passed into oblivion by the same process and Henry never once had to watch his orders carried out.

The prisoners were given a few days warning. They were visited by their families and were able to say their farewells. Dudley wrote his will – more in hope than in any expectation that his wishes would be carried out. In it he protested his innocence before making a variety of bequests and asking for his body to be buried in Westminster Abbey. The usual sentence for convicted traitors had been commuted to simple beheading. It was carried out on Tower Hill on 17 August 1510. Afterwards Edmund Dudley's body was interred in the churchyard of Blackfriars, at the western end of the City. John Guy has succinctly pronounced the verdict of history on this cynical act:

> The executions were a calculated ploy to enable the new regime to profit from the stability won by Henry VII without incurring any of its attendant stigma.[23]

II

THE SOLDIER

4

Connections

———≈∘≈———

The next developments in the Dudley story were nothing short of astonishing. Within months the attainder on Edmund's name and estate, though never enacted was formally lifted. The rapid restoration of Edmund's widow and children is further evidence that his execution was nothing more than a shabby public relations exercise. But this pales into insignificance beside what happened next. Edmund's death became the major stepping stone in his family's climb to the heights of Tudor society. Without it his sons would have remained at the level of government officials and provincial landowners, instead of becoming prominent courtiers. A suitable match had to be found for the Dudley widow, a lady of good, aristocratic family. She was now brought by marriage into Henry VIII's extended family. The husband chosen for her was the king's uncle, his mother's half-brother, his closest unmarried male relative.

Arthur Plantagenet was Edward IV's son by a certain Elizabeth Lucy. His earlier life is very shadowy.

> Item, for my Lord the Bastard
> Item, for making of a coat of black velvet 5s.
> Item, for making of a gown of black 2s.
> Item, for making of a gown of russet 2s.[1]

This tailor's bill of 1472 is one of the very few and the earliest pieces of documentary evidence that survives about the early life of the man who married Edmund Dudley's widow within fifteen months of Dudley's death and became stepfather to her children. Arthur was in his mid-twenties when Bosworth was fought and lost. All members of the extended Yorkist clan who might have laid claim to the throne or supported the pretensions of a relative were closely watched by Henry VII, and, when necessary, disposed of but Arthur seems not to have aroused any suspicion in the mind of a king who was ready to suspect everybody.

Henry decided that the best way to ensure that the young man was not lured into plots and schemes was to keep him where he could see him. Arthur was, accordingly, taken into the household of the queen, his own half-sister, Elizabeth of York. He thus moved in the same court circles as the Dudleys and knew them well. Since he and Edmund were much of an age, they could have been quite close friends. Yet, despite the courtier's impressive connections, it was the lawyer who was by far the wealthier and more influential of the two. By the time of the queen's death in 1503, Arthur was described as a 'carver', which, however, implies a senior attendant and not just someone who waited on his mistress at table. He was a landless man, fully dependent on his quarterly salary of £6.13s.4d. After Elizabeth's death Arthur entered the king's household as a squire of the body, a close personal attendant whose duties were 'to array and unray him and to watch, day and night'.[2] Arthur had, by now, worked his way into the innermost ring of Henry VII's most trusted servants. The squires of the body were in the royal presence twenty-four hours a day and when Arthur was on the 'night shift' he had to sleep on a pallet in the king's bedchamber. No one was better placed to sue for favours. 'Study to serve me,' Henry told one of Arthur's colleagues, 'and I will study to enrich you.'[3] However, when it came to distributing lands and lucrative appointments, he was decidedly niggardly.

Things changed dramatically with the accession of the ebullient Henry VIII, who was determined to demonstrate a new, more open, style of kingship. Arthur was among those who received court offices and other perks in the early days of the reign. But keeping up appearances in the splendid new court was an expensive business. What Arthur needed above all was a rich wife. In this, too, the king obliged him. Thus, on 12 November 1511 Elizabeth Dudley was married to Arthur Plantagenet.

Arthur immediately stepped into Edmund's shoes as a major landowner and important royal officer in Hampshire and Sussex, frequently serving as a JP and on various commissions. As far as his wife and stepchildren were concerned it must have seemed that life had returned very much to normal.

Yet Arthur had no intention of burying himself in the country to live the life of a respected gentleman of the shires. Like Edmund, he intended to keep a high profile at court, for only through attendance on the king could further advancement be gained. Out of sight was out of mind and there were plenty of rivals jostling to fill every place left vacant in the royal entourage. That meant keeping his absences from the Tudor household as brief as possible and not allowing Henry to forget his face. But it also meant demonstrating his usefulness to the new young ruler. He could not follow in the footsteps of Edmund, the lawyer and assiduous administrator (although he was, in 1511, admitted as one of the members of Lincoln's Inn who was excused all professional obligations; the Inns of Court doubled as fashionable dining clubs for the elite of court and City). In any case, Henry VIII had no interest in the tedious business of contracts, charters, deeds and account books. His passions lay in showing off his own many skills, in the sumptuousness of his court and the military might of his nation. He was bent upon cutting a dash in Europe and making himself a vital force in shaping its destiny. The way to his heart, therefore, was to present oneself as a man of action. This was not the easiest of postures to adopt for a courtier who was nearer to fifty than forty at the outset of the reign.

Henry naturally chose his companions from younger men who were able to hold their own with him in the giddy round of knightly combat, feasting and dancing which he immediately embarked upon. His Spanish queen reported to her father that the court passed its days in 'continual festival'.[4] Every religious holiday and state event had to be celebrated with elan and almost exhausting vigour: Christmas, Shrove Tuesday, Easter, May Day, Midsummer, royal anniversaries, the reception of foreign dignitaries. No expense was spared to make each display more elaborate than the ones that had gone before and Henry's revel masters were kept occupied devising striking costumes and cunning *coups de théâtre*. The vivid word pictures left by contemporary chroniclers indicate the impact such festivities made on spectators.

First came in ladies all in white and red silk, set upon coursers trapped in the same suite, fretted over with gold, after whom followed a fountain curiously made of russet satin, with eight gargoyles spouting water, within the fountain sat a knight armed at all pieces. After this fountain followed a lady all in black silk draped with fine silver, on a courser trapped in the same. After followed a knight in a horse litter, the coursers and litter apparelled black with silver drapes. When the fountain came to the tilt, the ladies rode round about, and so did the fountain and the knight within the litter. And after them were brought two goodly coursers apparelled for the jousts: and when they came to the tilt end, the two knights mounted on the two coursers abiding all comers. The King was in the fountain and Sir Charles Brandon was in the litter. Then suddenly with great noise of trumpets, entered Sir Thomas Knyvet in a castle of coal black, and over the castle was written, *The dolorous Castle*, and so he and the Earl of Essex, the lord Howard and other ran their courses, with the king and Sir Charles Brandon, and ever the king broke most spears.[5]

Although Arthur was a member of the king's personal guard, it is not surprising that he left most of the tiltyard heroics to younger men. He is only mentioned in the records as taking part in one joust, at Greenwich on 1 June 1510. However, when it came to the real thing – war – he was determined not to be left out. Opportunities were not slow in coming. Henry VIII was set upon reliving the exploits of his legendary namesake, the hero of Agincourt.

His bellicosity, dressed in the iridescent garb of Christian chivalry, allowed him to be easily duped by Ferdinand of Aragon into joining a military alliance against France. Henry's wily father-in-law reckoned that England could be used as a useful irritant to his enemy while the main forces opposing French pretensions concentrated on the important task of ridding Italy of Louis' army. Henry's councillors, urged penny-pinching caution but the kings tiltyard companions encouraged Henry's quest for glory. Fortunately, Henry had at hand the man who could turn his dreams into reality. Thomas Wolsey, who at the start of the reign was merely the king's almoner, was an administrative genius. He assured Henry that he could have his splendid campaign and that he, Wolsey, would make all the arrangements about equipment, transport and victuals that would guarantee success. Henry eagerly put the thirty-seven-year-old priest in charge and fell to planning his grand strategy.

There were to be two English contributions to the war. A land force was to be put ashore near Biarritz in the far south-west of France and work its way northwards while a naval contingent harried the Channel and Atlantic coasts to prevent the French fleet supplying their own troops.

Arthur Plantaganet was not a member of the land army and he must later have been very thankful of the fact, for, once the English force were camped on the plain in the shadow of the Pyrenees, they were deserted by their Aragonese allies and wasted away with hunger and dysentery. Instead, he begged an honourable place in the naval force which was to scour the home waters under the command of the Lord Admiral, Sir Edward Howard, one of the king's boon companions. Henry did not immediately respond and it was not until the following year, 1513, that he gave his uncle charge of the *Nicholas of Hampton*. Sadly Arthur threw away his chance for glory. The Lord Admiral discovered the bulk of the French fleet securely anchored at Brest, one of the safest havens in the world. The foe declined to come out and fight and Howard was not the kind of commander to content himself with a dreary and inglorious blockade. He ordered his ships to attack the inner harbour and only discovered too late just how impregnable the French position was. Arthur was determined to be in the thick of the action, yielding nothing in valour to his younger companions. Under his command the *Nicholas* advanced boldly, her leadsman taking regular soundings on the depth of water beneath the hull. Arthur's impetuosity was his undoing. The ship struck a submerged rock with such force that, as Howard later reported, it was a wonder that she did not split in two. In fact, the warship stayed afloat long enough for most of her complement to escape and reach other vessels. Howard ordered the rescue of all survivors and then, learning the lesson of the *Nicholas'* fate, called off the attack. Later Arthur Plantaganet stood before the admiral to make his report and to beg him to intercede with his majesty on his behalf. Both men knew how angry the king would be at the loss of a ship through incompetent handling before a shot had been fired. Someone was going to have some hard explaining to do. Howard did his best for his captain. He wrote to tell the king that Arthur was 'the sorriest man I ever saw and no man here can comfort him.' He assured Henry in fulsome terms that there was no-one on the expedition more dedicated than Arthur to his royal master. Arthur had desperate need of this testimonial for he had to go back to court to face the royal wrath in person. Unpleasant though that prospect was, it was absolutely vital. Arthur had to present his version of the 'accident' before news of it reached the king from other sources and before the court gossip machine could get to work undermining his reputation. But hurrying home presented its own problem. Henry would want to know why his uncle had compounded his error by deserting his post instead of proving that devotion to duty of which Howard boasted. Captain and admiral came up with an explanation that may be genuine but which looks to the cynical reader like a clever and unchallengeable excuse. Howard went on to explain,

> I have given him licence to go home, for, Sir, when he was in the extreme danger [and hope gone] from him, he called upon Our Lady of Walsingham for help and com[fort and made] a vow that, and it pleased God and her to deliver him out of that pe[ril, he wou]ld never eat flesh or fish till he had seen her.[6]

Henry was very devout and Walsingham was a favourite shrine of both himself and the queen. Arthur must have been banking on the fact that the king was unlikely to challenge his commitment to undertake a holy pilgrimage.

The stratagem seems to have worked, for Arthur did not forfeit royal favour. Within days Arthur's misfortune was overshadowed by a greater. Edward Howard, leading another hotheaded attack on the French ships, was drowned. The English fleet, totally demoralized, immediately returned home, leaving the enemy at liberty to mount a reprisal raid on the Sussex coast. This threatened Henry's grand strategy for he had resolved to lead in person an assault on northern France and the plan depended on the Channel being kept free of enemy ships. However, by midsummer he judged it safe to attempt the crossing. What followed was part military campaign and part pageant. Attended by the menfolk of every noble and gentle house who could raise the money for fine accoutrements and impressive retinues, Henry made a stately progress inland. There was a minor skirmish with French forces which English propaganda soon turned into a great victory, dubbed the Battle of the Spurs, and then the invading force trundled on to invest the impressive fortress of Therouanne and the city of Tournai. These were not significant French strongholds, lying as they did in territory claimed by the Emperor Maximilian but under the 'protection' of King Louis. However, their capture was claimed by Henry as a great triumph of English arms and to celebrate he remained at Tournai for three weeks after its capitulation impressing his allies and the local citizenry with his prowess in the joust – the closest he ever came to actual military action. And Arthur Plantaganet was among those present on the campaign grabbing his small slice of glory. It was after the siege of Tournai that, along with several other commanders, he received a knighthood. The honour marked the end of his brief military career.

Another captain who was included in the mass dubbing of knights before the walls of Tournai was Edward Guildford, an old friend of the Dudleys and much more of a father figure to Edmund's heir than Arthur Plantaganet. All the lawyer's children with the exception of the eldest, Elizabeth (already married to William, Lord Stourton), were minors at the time of his death and, therefore, royal wards. In February 1512, Edward Guildford petitioned for and was awarded the wardship of the eldest boy, John Dudley, then seven years old. He removed the child from the care of his mother and stepfather and sent him to his own home at High Halden, near Tenterden in Kent, to be brought up with his own children.

As well as being one of the king's closest companions and a leading light at court, Guildford was one of the three leading landowners in south-east England. The family had been long established in Kent and Sussex but it was Edward's father, Sir Richard Guildford, who had firmly anchored their fortunes. A committed supporter of Henry Tudor, he had joined the exile in Brittany and fought by his side in 1485. The rewards bestowed by a grateful king had been lavish. As well as extensive lands and lucrative wardships, Sir Richard became a councillor, Master of the Ordnance and Keeper of the Tower Armoury, Comptroller of the Royal Household and Master of the Horse. But these perquisites were not merely the rewards for loyalty; he was a member of Reginald Bray's circle and a man of very similar stamp. Contemporary records reveal him to have been involved in organizing royal jousts, designing ships for the navy, going on diplomatic missions, draining marshland (the area around Rye is still known as the Guildford Level) and administering some of the estates held by Henry and his queen. The king showed the degree of trust he reposed in Sir Richard when he named him as a trustee in his will. He was unable to discharge that particular responsibility for he died while on pilgrimage to Jerusalem in 1506.

Richard Guildford's eldest son Edward, and his half-brother, Henry, followed careers at the centre of national life. Both men belonged to Henry VIII's inner circle and were his close companions in the tiltyard and in the campaigns against France. Edward followed his father as Master of the Armoury and was appointed Warden of the Cinque Ports. Henry became Master of the Horse in 1515 and was an efficient and enterprising organizer of jousts and court entertainments. He was not only fully conversant with all the details of chivalric ritual which strictly governed feats of arms in the tiltyard, he also delighted his royal master by devising impromptu diversions. In 1510, he decked out the king and a band of his friends 'in short coats of Kentish Kendal', borrowed for the occasion from his own servants, in order to disguise them as Robin Hood and his merry men, and they all surprised the queen in her chambers with music and dancing. Henry Guildford eventually became Comptroller of the Household. This was the family in whose midst John Dudley grew from childhood into adolescence.

Years later John observed, en passant, in a letter to his stepfather Arthur, 'You bare my father-in-law partly a grudge for doing as he did for to disherit me, being within age, and also should marry his own daughter,'[7] and indeed the events of 1512 contributed to a complex feud between Arthur Plantaganet and Edward Guildford. Arthur believed that Edward had used his influence with the king to deprive him of his rights. He doubtless assumed that when he married Elizabeth he would have all the Dudley properties at his disposal and that he would have the guardianship of the heir and, therefore, be in a position to make lucrative arrangements about his marriage. Now part of the estate had been alienated with John, whose upbringing had been taken out of his hands, and he was left with only the property that was Elizabeth's by dower or jointure for the term of his life. Being a courtier was an expensive business. Clothes, horses, tilt armour, and servants had to be found and maintained. It meant patronizing scholars and artists, offering lavish hospitality at impressive residences in town and country and displaying costly status symbols. The king's friends had to keep up with him in conspicuous consumption if they were to continue in his favour. This meant, for example, placing heavy wagers on the outcome of every sporting contest, for Henry was an inveterate gambler. All this could be crippling for the ambitious courtier. Hence the importance of land. Manors, farms and woodland brought in regular rents and they provided collateral when a nobleman or gentleman needed to go to the City goldsmiths for the ready cash necessary to support a lavish lifestyle. This is why wardships were so eagerly snapped up when they came on the market. It is easy to see why Arthur Plantaganet should have felt aggrieved when his expectations were not fully realized. However, in all likelihood, Arthur had himself largely to blame for losing out to Edward Guildford. He was not a very forceful character and he was certainly careless where money matters were concerned, so he was no match for a more skilful intriguer and one who had the ear of the king.

As for young John, we may reasonably speculate on the impact of his change of home and fortune at such a tender age. His earliest years had been passed in pampered luxury as the son of a prominent royal servant and he had spent most of his time in the large house in Candlewick Street with its extensive garden. Then, at the age of five, everything was snatched from him. His father was branded a traitor. Former friends and associates turned their backs on the family and his old playfellows were kept away from him. Two years later he was separated from his mother to be brought up in rural Kent. Still he may have had to endure the taunts of other children who had picked up from their elders stories about the loathsome Edmund Dudley. We do not have to rely solely on imagination and conjecture for this. John's reaction was to grow up intensely, defensively proud of his ancestry. In later years he resolutely defended his father's reputation and he was very strongly motivated to restore Dudley dynastic fortunes. As soon as he was in a position to do so he devoted considerable money and energy to rescuing his family estates, in danger of being totally ruined by the ineptitude of their baronial landlords.

The marriage of Edward Guildford's only daughter, Jane, to his ward was always part of the deal. In this way the girl was provided for and the Guildford–Dudley links would remain strong after John came of age and assumed control of his own affairs. The children were probably betrothed soon after John joined the household at High Halden, when Jane was only three or four. They were married as soon as propriety allowed, in 1523 or 1524, when she was fourteen and her groom nineteen. Theoretically, either of the young people could have declined to go through with the matrimonial arrangements made in their name but there is no indication that they registered any such objection. By the day of the ceremony John and Jane had been brought up together for a decade or more, and had got well used to the idea that they were destined to become husband and wife. Jane was an intelligent and well-educated young woman. She was tutored in Princess Mary's household by the radical educationalist Juan Luis Vives and in later years would be a patroness of scholars. All the evidence suggests that she and John were very fond of each other. John remained faithful to Jane through thirty years of married life. She supported him through good times and bad, bore him thirteen children and lived to revere his memory. The will which she wrote with her own hand contained several references to 'my dear husband' and, bequeathing a clock to her daughter, Mary, she pointed out that it had been 'the lord her father's, praying her to keep it as a jewel'. Back in the calm 1520s there may have been a more mercenary element to the bond between the young people. Edward Guildford had a son, Richard, who must have been about the same age as John and we must assume that, for some time, they were brought up together. However, Richard died young and Jane became sole heiress to her father's estate. John Dudley thus became a soldier–courtier with excellent 'expectations'.

In fact, from a financial point of view, John's early career was marked by several strokes of good fortune. Richard's death meant that he and his wife would, on the death of his mother and her father, unite all the substantial lands held by their two families in south-east England. Then, in 1519, his prospects became even brighter. His mother's niece, Elizabeth Grey, sole heiress of the Lisle estates and titles, died unwed at the age of fourteen. As the girl's closest living relative, Elizabeth Plantaganet was the sole beneficiary. The person who gained immediately was Arthur Plantaganet. In 1523, when the lawyers had made their ponderous way through the elaborate probate ritual, he became Viscount Lisle and the holder of lands in ten counties 'with remainder to his heirs male by the Lady Elizabeth, his wife'. But he had no heirs male by the Lady Elizabeth. She died a couple of years later, having presented him with three daughters. At that point John received the Dudley lands which had been his mother's, and the reversion of the Lisle estates, which would pass to him, along with the viscountcy, after Arthur's death. And his good fortune, as we shall see, did not end there.

All this was in the future when the seven-year-old boy was taken to Kent to begin his new life. There his education was vigorous and demanding. From the beginning he was trained in the skills of a soldier and courtier because those were the skills most valued by the king. For Edmund the law had been the obvious route to royal service. His son and those responsible for his upbringing understood that the new king prized men of action rather than subtle-minded scholars. Guildford knew exactly what was required of those who hoped for high office under the second Tudor and he took a close interest in his ward's progress. John was trained in horsemanship, weaponry and military strategy, with little emphasis on book learning, though he would have made a good scholar for he had his father's keen mind. The commonest criticism of him during his years in power was that he was a subtle, amoral schemer, a man who weighed up the pros and cons of every option before deciding on the one that would be most advantageous to himself. Such clearheadedness served him well as a field tactician and as a politician. What he lacked was the breadth of understanding that a grounding in philosophy and ethics would have given him. It was a deprivation of which he became acutely aware as the years passed.

Having found in John Dudley an apt pupil and one whom he came to look upon as a son, Guildford awaited opportunities to bring him to the attention of England's two rulers, the king and his chief minister. Wolsey, who had become a cardinal in 1515, was now widely acknowledged as having at least equal standing with his master. He held the offices of Lord Chancellor and Archbishop of York and in his residences at York House and Hampton Court he received ambassadors, dealt with a range of petitions, exercised tight control of government business and lived in princely splendour. The poet John Skelton pointed out in his verse satire, *Why Come Ye Not to Court*, what many observed with growing resentment:

> To which court?
> To the King's court?
> Or to Hampton court?
> Nay, to the King's court!
> The King's court
> Should have the pre-eminence!
> And York Place
> With 'my lord's grace',
> To whose magnificence
> Is all the confluence,
> Suits and supplications,
> Embassies of all nations . . .

Wolsey's position might appear to observers as unshakeable but it relied, as the corpulent cardinal knew, on three interlinked skills: efficient administration, careful management of the king and vigilant watchfulness of potential rivals. Wolsey was no less assiduous than Empson and Dudley had been in keeping a tight reign on overmighty subjects and he used the same methods as his hated predecessors. He hauled great men into court before him for supposed offences against the laws of livery and maintenance and other ancient statutes and imposed heavy fines on them. However, even Wolsey could not be in two places at once. While he was keeping court in one of his great palaces the king might be at Whitehall or Greenwich or on progress where other people could have access to him. The cardinal was particularly nervous about the gentlemen of the Privy Chamber, including the Guildfords, who were always close to Henry and who might, he feared, use their influence to undermine his policies or become a conduit for those hereditary magnates he had shouldered aside. Events in 1516 and 1517 indicated the currents that were running beneath the surface of court politics. In May 1516, Wolsey harangued the council about the presumption of certain well-placed men and assured them that no one was beyond the reach of the law. He followed this up by having the Earl of Northumberland thrown into the Fleet prison and subjecting others of the king's entourage to interrogation. The attempted showdown failed when the Earls of Shrewsbury and Surrey led a protest against such high-handedness and won Henry's grudging sympathy. The gentlemen of the Privy Chamber followed up this little victory the following year when Wolsey was laid up for several months with the sweating sickness. The king fell into the habit of dictating sensitive correspondence to some of his trusted gentlemen. As soon as Wolsey was back in circulation he had the 'offenders' banished from court. A year later the feud was still bubbling, for once again the cardinal had some of the king's household companions dismissed for allegedly unruly behaviour. The position for which John Dudley was being groomed was not just one of military and court service; it carried political potential and it could not avoid involvement in intrigue.

An active and athletic teenager could not fail to be impressed by the splendour of the royal court. John watched the popular heroes of the tiltyard, the headstrong but skilful Duke of Suffolk, the flamboyant Sir Nicholas Carew and, of course, the king, whose polychrome embroidered surcoats, gilded helms and gleaming Nuremberg armour outdazzled his opponents, and he longed for the day when he would enter the arena to draw admiring gasps from the ladies and be feted by his peers. But, like all the other young gentlemen jostling for notice, John also longed to disport himself on a wider military or diplomatic stage and his chance was not long in coming.

In 1519, Sir Edward Guildford was appointed Knight Marshal of Calais, which meant that he was charged with keeping law and order among the king's subjects in the town and its pale. It was a responsible position at any time but had a special importance at that moment. Calais was about to become the stage for the most sumptuous diplomatic display that Europe had ever seen, and vigilant security and policing were vital if everything was to run smoothly. Wolsey had discovered that indulging Henry's passion for military adventure was ruinously expensive. Money had been poured into the early campaigns of the reign and there was nothing to show for it.

Somehow the king had to be deflected into relying on diplomacy rather than warfare, but without appearing to be weak. The answer was a series of meetings between Henry and his royal rivals, Francis of France and the Emperor Charles V, at which Henry would play the pivotal role of broker of universal peace and Christian brotherhood. But there was to be much more to these royal get-togethers than discussions round the table. Wolsey designed them to be high theatre in which the king of England would outdo his fellow monarchs in the splendour of his personal presence and the magnificence of his retinue.

The high point of all these demonstrations of national hubris took place in June 1520 at the Field of Cloth of Gold, a temporary township built near Calais to receive English and French delegations. The diplomatic festival went on for three weeks.

> It was an Olympic Games: the jousts tournaments, archery and wrestling. It was a musical and dramatic festival: the solemn chart of royal choirs, the evenings' minstrelsy, the masques. It was an architectural competition: the English raised a large temporary palace, the French a myriad tents and pavilions. It was a wine and food festival: the banquets with every luxury in food and drink, and free wine for all. It was an international 'concours d'elegance' in dress and costume, in jewellery, and in caparisons for the choicest mounts.[8]

Everyone wanted to be there. From one end of England to the other gentlemen desperately urged their friends at court to pull strings to engineer an invitation to be a part of the Tudor retinue and pawned lands to acquire the necessary finery to join the cavalcade.

Sir Arthur Plantaganet was there, as were the Guildfords. It is more than likely that a place was found for John Dudley in his guardian's entourage. If so, the memory would have remained vividly with him to the end of his days. As a military leader in after years John often displayed a love of dramatic gesture and a regard for the niceties of honourable combat that were already becoming old fashioned. It seems likely that early exposure to the overwhelming productions of the cardinal-impresario made a lasting impression.

Sir Edward's protégé had certainly come to Wolsey's attention, for a year after the Field of Cloth of Gold the cardinal chose John Dudley to be one of his attendants when he travelled in state to Calais in a further attempt to make peace between the Habsburg and Valois rivals. Weeks of talking had no positive result, except to tie England firmly to the imperial cause. The big issues of statesmanship would have been of little interest to John. What mattered to him was the excitement of being at the centre of international affairs – and he was still only seventeen.

There was someone else within whose ambit the impressionable young man came at this time who must also have had a marked influence. That was John Bourchier, Baron Berners. This ebullient courtier–soldier was another of the king's bosom companions and frequently borrowed money from his majesty in order to maintain the state which his position necessitated. Unlike many of the macho action men of the royal household, Berners was no mean scholar. He had an excellent command of French, Spanish and Latin, he collected the works of contemporary artists and his greatest solace was his library. Henry valued Lord Berners as a cultured man of letters and employed him on various foreign embassies but he also recognized his friend as a valiant knight who shared his love of military glory and the paraphernalia of chivalric etiquette and knightly display. Berners had his place in most of the early campaigns of the reign but his impact on later ages was of a different order. He was the most accomplished author/translator of his day, and it is to him that we are indebted for the English version of Froissart's *Chronicles*, written by the Frenchman over a century earlier, which provided many sixteenth-century schoolboys with their basic knowledge of history and became the pattern for the even more influential works of Hall and Holinshed. Berners revelled in stories of the past or, rather, in the romanticized, chivalric image of the past. He translated the French Charlemagne adventure, *Huon of Bordeaux*, and, in so doing, introduced into English literature the figure of Oberon, later developed by Shakespeare. He made his contribution to native legend with *The History of the Most Noble and Valyaunt Knight, Artheur of Lytell Brytaine*. It was this multi-talented royal servant whom Henry made his Deputy Governor of Calais in 1520 and who thus became the superior of Sir Edward Guildford and John Dudley.

This was a crucial time and Berners carried a major responsibility in Calais. Henry and Charles entered into an offensive alliance against Francis I in 1521 (so much for the elaborate celebration of Anglo-French amity of the previous year) and the port was England's gateway to the realm of the enemy. Berners' duties were manifold. He set about strengthening the defences of the town. He sent skirmishing parties into the surrounding countryside to impress the inhabitants with the force of English arms. And his remuneration included the significantly large annual sum of £104 as 'spyall money'. In the spring of 1522 the French began harassing the garrison and Berners sent out several sorties to see them off. It was in these minor engagements that John Dudley had his first taste of real action. He quitted himself well enough to gain the attention of Lord Berners and, in August 1523, he received his first salaried military appointment. The Deputy Governor raised the nineteen-year-old soldier to the position of Lieutenant of the Calais Spears. This gave him command – under the direction of a more experienced officer – of a formidable body of pikemen.

The appointment was part of the arrangements that were being made for a major campaign. After months of diplomatic wrangling a joint Anglo-Imperial strike into the heart of France had been agreed. The troops from Calais joined the Duke of Suffolk's contingent in the Low Countries and from there the army moved south during the autumn. For a while all went well. On 14 November, Sir Edward Guildford distinguished himself by leading a successful assault on the supposedly impregnable Ardennes fortress of Bohan. John Dudley had already proved his mettle for, a week earlier, he had been knighted on the field of battle by the army commander, Charles Brandon, Duke of Suffolk, that same hero of the joust whom John had so long idolized. The duke did not distribute honours rashly and there can be no doubt that the young commander fully deserved the recognition he now received. John's shrewd judgement was still masked by the dash and bravado of youth but his natural battlefield talents were already evident.

Henry wanted his best fighting men in France but he also liked to have his household graced by lusty, virile courtiers who were proficient in the tiltyard and projected the image England's monarch wished to project. Thus, while what Wolsey called the 'dribbling war' went inconclusively on, hampered, as was becoming commonplace, by the competing ambitions of the allies, the young knight was summoned home to be made an esquire of the body to the king. At the end of 1524 we find him among those who competed in the Christmas tourney.

It was probably on his return from the continent that Sir John was married to Jane Guildford. The newlyweds set up home on one of the

Dudley estates and John divided his time between there and the royal court. His mother's death soon afterwards transformed this son of a condemned traitor into a man of property advancing steadily in royal favour. Thus, by the time his royal master set in train that sequence of events which were to bring about the greatest changes in the nation's history, John Dudley was well established at the centre of national life. As long as his own ambition kept him there he could not avoid being involved in political and religious conflicts such as England had never seen.

5

Crises and Calculations

———◇◇◇———

Three major elements rendered the decade of the 1530s explosive. First came the unstable European political situation, shaped by the bellicose Habsburg–Valois rivalry and the English king's determination to remain on equal terms with the neighbouring monarchs. To this was added religious revolution which began in an insignificant Saxon town and spread rapidly across all national boundaries. Finally, Henry flung into the pot his own insecurity about the survival of the Tudor dynasty.

The volatility of Europe was the product of the competing anxieties and ambitions of Charles V and Francis I. We cannot speak in any meaningful way of 'French policy' or 'Imperial policy'; wars, massacres and treaties were embarked upon by the will of two superpower leaders who hated each other with total conviction. Charles, a cold, duty-bound automaton, had by various means, inherited and acquired a miscellany of territories which built into the most formidable personal fiefdom Europe had seen in over seven hundred years and, theoretically at least, he had the fabulous wealth of his New World possessions to sustain it. Francis, a death-or-glory extrovert, was ruler of a state only recently united under his crown, and encircled by Habsburg territory which stretched from the Netherlands, via Franche Comté and Milan, to the whole of southern Italy and Spain. To the east, it also incorporated the kingdoms of Austria, Hungary and Bohemia. Each ruler regarded himself as the arbiter of Europe's destiny, the true heir of Charlemagne, and what finally made them irreconcilable was their competition, in

1519, for the crown of the Holy Roman Empire, vacant following the death of Maximilian I. Despite their solemn avowals to be the defenders of Catholic Christendom, Charles and Francis subordinated religious and moral considerations to the pursuance of their personal aims. The French king was not averse to making alliances with Lutheran heretics and even the infidel Turk, while the Emperor shocked Europe profoundly by sending his troops to sack the Eternal City and hold the pope a virtual prisoner. Henry VIII and Wolsey were outclassed by the energetic malevolence of these combatants and lacked the resources for effective competition. Thus, most of their policies were doomed to frustration.

When, in 1517, Martin Luther, a lecturer at the recently-founded university of Wittenberg, on the banks of the middle Elbe, proposed a debate on the controversial hawking of indulgences he unwittingly set a match to several powder trails. He was very far from being alone in condemning the 'pay now, live later' propaganda of papal agents who preyed upon the fears and hopes of the gullible and superstitious by offering remissions from purgatory in return for cash, and it was not just this narrow issue which an ever-widening circle of supporters took up. There were hundreds of thousands of ordinary people throughout Europe who felt angry yet powerless to stand up to a domineering priesthood whose motto was 'Do as I say not as I do'. There were scholars who studied the Bible in its original languages and believed that the authority and dogmas imposed by the Vatican and its lieutenants had no warranty in the word of God. There were peasants who lived in squalor and were no longer easily overawed by the glittering splendour of shrines and altars or the richly adorned senior clergy who lived among them in unashamed state. There were German nobles and princes whose national pride was offended by the taxes and obeisance claimed by a distant Italian pontiff on the far side of the Alps. There were scores of petty rulers within the confines of the Holy Roman Empire who resented the 'conspiracy' of pope and emperor to keep them in subjection. And there were the multitudes who found it difficult to rationalize the resentment they felt with the existing order but who were ready to listen to fiery preachers who proclaimed God's wrath against a corrupt church and invited the faithful to purge themselves of error and throw off the yoke of priestly subjection.

So rapidly had the contagion of Lutheranism spread in less than four years that Charles V denounced the Wittenberg monk at an imperial diet in 1521. The reformer's books were burned throughout Europe and he would have met the same fate had he not been protected by his own prince, the Elector Frederick, who was determined to advertise his own autonomy. Henry VIII was eager to demonstrate his immaculate orthodoxy and he published a book, the *Assertio Septem Sacramentorum,* in refutation of Luther's heresies. For this a grateful pope rewarded him with the title 'Defender of the Faith', which put him on a par with his 'Catholic' majesty, Charles V and his 'Most Christian' majesty, Francis I. But when his own interests came into conflict with his loyalty to Rome Henry proved himself just as ready as his brother monarchs to set aside his obedience to the holy father.

The issue that set the English king at variance with Rome was the same fundamental concern which had motivated his father, the security of the dynasty. He kept up Henry VII's policy of seeking out Yorkist cells and eradicating possible claimants to the throne. In sporadic purges between 1513 and 1538 a dozen or more descendants of Edward III (some very distant from the throne) and their suspected supporters were executed or vanished while in the Tower in circumstances every bit as suspicious as the death of the 'little princes'. The problem was that Henry was the last of the male Tudor line. He had no brothers, so securing the throne his father had grasped some forty years before depended entirely on the birth of a male heir. The tragedy was that the Spanish bride Henry had eagerly married in 1509 had suffered a series of miscarriages and infant deaths, leaving her husband with only a single child, a daughter, Mary. By 1525 Henry was in his thirties and Catherine, five and half years his senior, was approaching the end of her child-bearing days. The king desperately wanted a son and he was not accustomed to being denied anything he wanted. Those close to him were aware of his increasing perplexity.

And no one was closer to him than Anne Boleyn, younger daughter of one of Henry's close companions. Not especially beautiful, Anne returned, in 1522, from years of training at the refined French court, a vivacious, witty, strong-willed fifteen-year-old and took her place as one of the queen's maids-of-honour. She made no especial impact on the life of the royal household for several years. The king, who was now often looking outside his marriage for sexual gratification, was taken up with Anne's sister, Mary, who became his established mistress. But as Anne grew into womanhood she turned many heads about the court, and eventually aroused the king's interest. As they grew more intimate, Anne became fully aware of Henry's concern about the succession and, in his longing to get the younger Boleyn girl into bed, he told her that relations between him and his wife were becoming increasingly strained. For her part, Anne was determined not to go the way of her sister. She genuinely abhorred adultery and it is likely that her resolve was stiffened by members of her family who saw a possible road to advancement opening up before them. If Henry truly loved her and if he was a king in more than name then he would dispose of the only obstacle to their happy union. The king was in full agreement. He had by now convinced himself, through careful study of the Bible's teaching on marriage, that he had been wrong to take to himself his dead brother's widow. For this act a papal dispensation had been necessary and Henry reasoned that what one pope had done another could undo. As his own mind became more firmly made up he assumed that everyone else would fall into line, including Clement VII in distant Rome. There was nothing uniquely arrogant about this; Henry's fellow monarchs no less blithely assumed that popes could be bullied, bribed or cajoled into obliging them in such delicate matters.

It was in the spring and summer of 1527 that these three powerful forces combined to push England in a wholly new direction. The influence of Lutheranism was reaching into scholarly and fashionable circles. Students at university and the Inns of Court were discussing the new ideas, as were merchants, free-thinking clergy and even members of the royal household. In recent months copies of a revolutionary book had begun to circulate. William Tyndale, in voluntary exile in the Low Countries, translated the New Testament into English and despatched it across the North Sea. The bishops banned it and, when they could lay hands on copies, they burned them and threw their owners into jail. This only emboldened radical spirits and proved to them that the pope and his minions were afraid that the searchlight of holy scripture would illuminate their corrupt ways and their false doctrines. Wolsey received a growing volume of complaints about preachers who were proclaiming heresy. He refused to be pushed into overreaction by alarmed tradition-alists, reasoning that it was unwise to make martyrs. Occasional demon-strations of government determination would be sufficient to ensure that the latest intellectual fad went the way of all other challenges to religious convention. In this he grossly underestimated the power of reformist sentiment which was churning up a religious war in Germany which cost 100,000 lives, shattering monastic cloisters and tearing down the objects of 'superstition' that had adorned church walls for centuries.

Henry was, as ever, preoccupied with international diplomacy. Currently he was going through a pro-French phase. In February 1525 an imperial army had inflicted a humiliating defeat on their enemies at the Battle of Pavia. Francis I was taken prisoner and conveyed in triumph to Madrid, where Charles V demanded a massive ransom, including a third of French territory. Had Francis agreed to these humiliating, draconian terms there would have been an end to French pretensions in Europe, which would have become in large measure part of the Habsburg empire. In England this gave rise to serious alarm. The Emperor was now worryingly powerful and, if that was not cause enough for concern, he made it quite clear that he no longer had need for allies. Any hope that Henry might have entertained of sharing in Charles' good fortune and picking up for himself some tasty morsels of French land were soon dashed. He was furious at having once again been the victim of Habsburg perfidy. Domestically, his rage was vented against Queen Catherine, the Emperor's aunt, and this added to the tension between them. Diplomatically the king was ready to be drawn into an alliance with the French.

Not until May 1527 was all in readiness for a ceremonial demonstration of Anglo–French accord but then Francis' ambassadors were received in splendour at Greenwich. They were treated to four days of banquets, 'combats', masques and balls in beautiful pavilions specially constructed for the purpose. Henry signed the treaty. Wolsey preened himself as the architect of the new-found friendship between his master and the King of France while the pro-imperial party glowered in impotent silence.

But those in the know were aware of a significant sub-text to the celebrations. A powerful rival to the great cardinal had, at last, emerged. It was during the Anglo–French festivities that courtiers first observed and began to interpret the body language of the king and Mistress Boleyn. Henry now secretly confided to his minister that he was conscience-bound to seek the annulment of his marriage, so Wolsey used his legatine powers to summon an ecclesiastical court to deliberate on the validity of the royal marriage. The senior churchmen and canon lawyers were in the unenviable position of having to juggle nice theological and legal arguments with their desire to please their sovereign and they were also aware that if they delivered the verdict Henry wanted, his outraged wife would, as a matter of course, appeal over their heads to Rome. It must have been with a profound sense of relief that they received some shattering news that provided an excuse for adjourning their deliberations: Charles V, had despatched imperial troops to sack the papal city and drive the vicar of Christ into the Castel Sant' Angelo, where he was now a virtual prisoner.

All of Europe was shocked by this audacious sacrilege but to Wolsey it seemed that the Emperor had played into his hands. None of his political enemies could argue with his policy of alliance with the French to contain soaring imperial ambition. The papacy was, to all intents and purposes, out of commission and that left a vacuum at the heart of Christendom, a vacuum someone had to fill in order to challenge Charles V, achieve Clement VII's release, stop the spread of heresy, restore equilibrium to the affairs of the continent, reform the Church and settle a variety of specific inter-state issues, including the little matter of the king of England's marital problems. Cardinal Wolsey was in no doubt whatsoever who was the only man to shoulder this immense burden.

In July 1527, he set out with more than even his accustomed splendour to carry his master's fraternal greetings to Francis I at Amiens and then proceed to Avignon where he had summoned a solemn conclave of cardinals to meet with him. But Wolsey's power had been built upon the king's confidence in him and that confidence was now being undermined by Anne Boleyn and her faction, prominent among whom was her uncle, Thomas Howard, Duke of Norfolk. He had for years been a violent if covert enemy of the 'upstart' cardinal who had usurped that position at the king's right hand that he believed was his by hereditary right. Wolsey's opponents ensured that the imperial ambassador knew of Wolsey's plans, with the result that Charles V put pressure on the Pope to forbid his cardinals to travel to Avignon. The emperor was also informed of the slight being offered to his aunt, Queen Catherine, and he set himself staunchly to prevent Henry casting her aside. Anne, meanwhile, was only concerned about the divorce. Having no confidence in Wolsey to secure it, she urged the king to bypass him by a direct appeal to Clement. All this inept and malicious activity muddied the waters and ensured that the king's 'great matter' would drag on for years and have monumental, unforeseen consequences.

Feelings ran high in the towns and villages of the realm. They may have been focused on what many saw as the heroic queen Catherine and the despised cardinal but what lay behind them were the jumbled emotions of anti-French sentiment, religious discord and discontent over taxation.

John Dudley cannot have failed to be aware of the feelings running through London and his own estates, but his perspective on events was very different. He was at the centre of things. He attended the king at Westminster and on progress. He featured prominently as one of the new stars of the tiltyard in the martial contests laid on to entertain the king and foreign dignitaries. He was a member of Wolsey's impressive entourage in the summer of 1527. He witnessed himself or shared gossip about those incidents which were the very stuff of court tittle-tattle: incidents such as the cardinal's reception on his return from his failed diplomatic venture. Within hours everyone knew that Henry had kept his minister waiting for an audience and had then interviewed him in the presence of Mistress Boleyn. Yet, no more than any other habitué of the court, could he have fully understood the forces that were threatening to pull his world apart. He was aware of the clash of personalities, of the greater freedom with which men expressed their resentment of Wolsey's power and ostentation, of the growing estrangement between king and queen, of the widespread sympathy which Catherine enjoyed and of the slow emergence of factions, but he was not a political animal and he was preoccupied with pursuing his own advancement. That did not yet involve him in taking sides in any of the personal, political or religious rivalries that were emerging.

Pope Clement prevaricated over the annulment of the royal marriage, because he had no alternative. Wolsey's heart was not in the business though he prosecuted it with all the vigour and guile at his command, to no effect. Meanwhile, in 1529, Charles V and Francis I patched up their quarrels at the Peace of Cambrai and England was, once more, pushed out into the diplomatic cold. Henry readily believed what Anne lost no opportunity to suggest to him, that the cardinal was opposed to the king's wishes and was secretly trying to frustrate them. He also began to pay attention to all those criticisms of Wolsey that he had always dismissed before: the servant was become too powerful, rivalling his master; he outshone the king in splendour; while pretending to work on his sovereign's behalf he pursued his own policies and ambitions.

But it was not just the man against whom the king's suspicions were raised. He began to think that the writers of heretical pamphlets and banned books might have a case when they complained about the usurped temporal authority of the senior clergy.

> . . . the bishops, abbots, priors, deacons, archdeacons, suffragans, monks, canons, friars, pardoners and summoners . . . have gotten into their hands more than the third part of all your realm . . . What money pull they in by probates of testaments, privy tithes, and by men's offerings to their pilgrimages and at their first masses . . . by hallowing of churches, altars, superaltars, chapels and bells . . . Is it any marvel that the taxes . . . that your Grace most tenderly of great

compassion hath taken among your people to defend them from
the threatened ruin of their commonwealth hath been so slothfully,
yea, painfully levied, seeing that almost the utmost penny that
might have been levied hath been gathered before yearly by this
ravenous, cruel and insatiable generation?[1]

So wrote Simon Fish in *A Supplication for the Beggars*, from the safety
of the Low Countries. The Boleyns drew Henry's attention to the
diatribe and Henry not only read it but extended his protection to the
author. It was, doubtless, Anne who encouraged Henry to think daring
new thoughts and he, driven almost to distraction by what he saw as the
'obstruction' of the ecclesiastical establishment, was not the man to
shrink from draconian measures if they might serve his purpose. Wolsey
was dismissed from office and only his sudden death saved him from a
charge of treason.

The Boleyns and their friends were now unchallenged and
unchallengeable and courtiers scrambled to win the favour of the second
family in the kingdom. The twenty-six-year-old Sir John Dudley was
among those who emerged triumphantly from the scrum. He was no
original thinker but he was in tune with those who were championing
reform and urging the king on. Now he displayed a new confidence,
boldness and aggression in all his dealings. The 1530s would be the
decade that transformed his fortunes as well as those of the nation.

It was only three months after Wolsey's death that Dudley achieved
his first public office, as a member of the commission of the peace for
Surrey and Sussex. However, it was not the southern counties that
engaged John's attention. Throughout 1532 and 1533 he was engaged
in a monumental series of land transactions that removed his base from
south-east England to the Midlands. His eyes were fixed on the ancient
Dudley estates and he was determined on nothing less than the
restoration of his family's greatness. The spur to this sudden burst of
energy was the state of the barony. It had fallen on hard times since the
days of Lord John Sutton de Dudley, due largely to the ineptitude and
fecklessness of the great man's heirs. Perhaps we should not judge
Edward, the seventh baron too harshly. He did correctly assess the
changing nature of English politics. Realizing that attendance on the
king was the key to advancement rather than remaining in
Worcestershire and patiently building up his estates, Edward had rented
one of the new houses in Tothill Street, Westminster, specifically built
in response to the demand of gentlemen and noblemen who wanted to

be close to the court. From there he tried to cut a dash in Tudor society. In order to maintain an impressive style, over the years, he ran himself further and further into debt and mortgaged many of his lands. He had, in addition, a large family to keep. We know of eleven children who survived infancy. For some of them he managed to engineer alliances with other ancient families, but such connections were only through daughters or younger sons. The children of Lord Dudley were not regarded as good catches because, despite his efforts, he lacked the talent, character or sheer pushiness to gain the king's favour. Edward died in January 1532, at precisely the right moment to facilitate the upward mobility of his second cousin.

The man who succeeded to the barony was another John, Lord Edward's eldest son. He was a wastrel and a simpleton and in short measure completed the dismantling of his patrimony that his father had begun. Sir John, now the most prominent member of the family, was not prepared to stand by and see its property dispersed. He spent several months in feverish activity with influential friends and wealthy potential backers putting together a rescue package. On 3 July 1532, a consortium consisting of the Earl of Shrewsbury, Baron De la Warr, Thomas Fitzalan, Lord Maltravers, William Whorwood, Sir Thomas Arundell, Sir George Carew, Sir Thomas Wyatt and Sir Andrew Dudley (Sir John's brother) paid £4,200, on behalf of Sir John, for,

> Dudley Castle, the manor of Sedgeley, 50 messuages, 3,000 acres of [arable] land, 1,000 acres of meadow, 5,000 acres of pasture, 1,000 acres of furze and heath and £25 of rent in Dudley, Sedgeley, Ettinghall, Brierly, Coseley, Woodsetton, Upper Gornal, Nether Gornal, Darlaston, Cotwall End and Gospel End, the manors of Dudley and Himley and the manor of Deoder in Shropshire.[2]

Lord Dudley now mortgaged the remainder of his lands directly to Sir John for £6,000. This was a huge sum and the courtier had to use every means at his disposal to raise the necessary capital. He borrowed. He obtained mortgages. He sold some of his Sussex property and what he could not sell he found other ways to turn into cash. His stepfather had a life interest in some of the lands which John had inherited from his mother. John now sold the reversion of these lands to his friend at court, Sir Edward Seymour (so they would transfer to Seymour's ownership on the death of Sir Arthur Plantaganet). Seymour, in his turn, seems to have borrowed the money from the king. This meant that Dudley had to accept a much lower valuation of the property but he was happy to do so in return for ready cash. It was the same with the Lisle lands. Since they, along with the title, would now be his when the viscount died – because Arthur and Elizabeth had had no heirs male – John could sell their reversions too. He also looked to the king for help. He had, by now, achieved that prominence in the royal household that enabled him to sue for favours. Thus it was that, in March of this same year, 1532, he received the wardship of Anthony Norton, orphaned son of a Worcestershire landowner, whose property lay conveniently close to the old Dudley lands.

Sir John's virtual assumption of family leadership and his grasping of the Dudley lands could not fail to provoke the resentment of his relatives. Lord Dudley's affairs were in hopeless disarray and he defaulted on his mortgage repayments. His cousin, not unnaturally, foreclosed and the wretched baron was left with virtually nothing. He became a laughing stock throughout the capital and was commonly referred to as 'Lord Quondam' – 'Lord Once-upon-a-time'. It was left to his dependants to go cap in hand to the king on his behalf and to appeal desperately to their friends for help. Quondam's son, Edward, thanking one of Henry's ministers for aid in 1536, assured his benefactor, 'Had it not been for your compassion I must have sought my living from door to door.'[3] And Cecily, Lady Dudley, threw herself on the mercy of one of the religious houses that, in better times, her family had generously patronized: 'I have little above £20 a year, which I have by my lady mother, to find me and one of my daughters, with a woman and a man to wait upon me,' she explained when the nunnery was faced with closure, 'and unless the good prioress of Nuneaton gave us meat and drink of free cost I could not tell what shift to make.'[4]

Lord Edward and Lord John were responsible for their own downfall but it was inevitable that they should blame their dashing and successful kinsman for their plight. Quondam feebly excused himself from appearance at court by claiming that Sir John lay in wait for him to have him hustled off to prison. The baronial family looked upon their cousin with both envy and resentment as an ogre who had used sharp practice to bring them all to beggary. They themselves were not above acting outside the law in their efforts to thwart him. One of Quondam's brothers, Arthur, a priest, took matters into his own hands as we know from a plaint Sir John entered against him in the Court of Chancery:

. . . minding utterly to disherit and wrongfully to put your said orator from the premises for ever, [he] of late wrongfully entered into the castle of Dudley and thereupon brake up certain chests and coffers, then being in the said castle, wherein remained divers evidences, charters, writings, court rolls, rentals, terriers, etc., of the said Sir John Dudley and took them away with him and keepeth them in his possession and custody and that [he] at all times denied and utterly refused to return them . . .[5]

All who knew Sir John recognized that he was a shrewd and ambitious young man. It was said of him that he 'had such a head that he seldom went about anything, but he conceived first three or four purposes beforehand'.[6] He was certainly an energetic go-getter but he was far from being unique among the courtiers of his generation in using position and contacts to enlarge and rationalize his land holdings. Edward Seymour was embarked upon a consolidation programme which would make him the most powerful man in Somerset and Thomas Wriothesley, an up-and-coming member of Wolsey's secretariat, would shortly embark upon a similar programme to achieve prominence in Hampshire. What was different about John Dudley was his transferring his attention to the inheritance of his baronial cousins. If he was merely interested in building a power base he could have concentrated on those counties where he already had a considerable stake. That would have been less complicated and would not have involved raising a huge amount of loan capital all at once. But the land deals he opted for in 1532–3 involved him in an enormous risk.

Family pride must have played its part in his decision. For Sir John, who had won his spurs on the field of battle and become a trusted companion of the sovereign, it must have been intensely frustrating to see the Dudley barons become objects of fun or pity. Striving to establish his own good name had toughened him and he was now not the sort of man who could stand by and see his once-great family dwindle into obscurity. It would be naive to suppose that personal wealth and prestige did not enter into John's thinking. If his gamble paid off he stood to become one of the great landholders of the central shires. He already knew that the Lisle title would be his on his stepfather's death and he was establishing an impressive estate to support the dignity.

Vital as these negotiations were for Sir John, they took place against a background of events that were immensely more momentous. Henry

VIII had bludgeoned his way to the marriage annulment that he had so impatiently sought for six years and had found himself new men who were willing and able to do his bidding in the matter. The Norfolk clique had fondly imagined that once they had got rid of Wolsey there would be a return to the authority of the Council and that they would play a leading role in government. They were rudely disappointed. Rule by committee did not suit Henry's style. He was a consummate actor who lived the dream of glorious imperial power, relying on a trusted subordinate to take care of all administrative matters (and to accept the blame when anything went wrong) and he did not want to change the system. His great good fortune – a fortune he neither deserved nor appreciated – was in being presented with ministers who had the rare talents necessary to handle the multifarious tasks of government. The man who emerged from Wolsey's shadow was the lateral-thinking genius, Thomas Cromwell.

This self-made lawyer, entrepreneur and jack-of-all-trades was the same age as the Tudor dynasty. The son of a Putney brewer, he had had little in the way of a formal education but, as with many successful men down the centuries, this proved to be a positive advantage: it meant that the windows of his mind were not curtained by second-hand theories and also that he was spurred on to prove himself over against those born with greater advantages. By the 1530s he had travelled widely in Europe, seen military action, amassed a modest fortune through trade, practised successfully as a lawyer, become Wolsey's indispensable right-hand man and survived the fall of his master by showing Henry possible answers to his most pressing problems – the impasse over his divorce and his empty treasury. Cromwell was, in some ways, a model for John Dudley. He was a man who clearly saw and boldly grasped opportunities that presented themselves. He was never daunted by the big idea. He read voraciously and possessed a library that was large for a non-scholar. No one understood more clearly than he the deep anticlericalism that gripped a substantial section of the populace. In a series of measured steps throughout the 1530s Cromwell acted through parliament to sever the link with Rome, to make his master supreme head of the church in England, to bring to an end the centuries-old monastic tradition; to appropriate for the Crown all the wealth of the dissolved houses, to set up the administrative machinery necessary for selling on, granting or leasing the estates, farms, buildings and building materials that now glutted the property market; to remove objects of 'superstition' from all parish churches and to make available to all the people the Bible in English.

In all this he had the eager support of the other man who, with Cromwell, stepped into Wolsey's ample shoes. Thomas Cranmer was an obscure Cambridge don but more importantly a protégé of the Boleyns when Henry promoted him over the heads of all the English bishops to be Archbishop of Canterbury.

The king now very clearly saw the practical advantage of pursuing the policies advocated by the growing number of Protestant visionaries in his entourage. But he also had a genuine aversion to heresy, a trait which Catholic courtiers and councillors could make use of to frustrate the process of reform. Thomas More, the Lord Chancellor, was the passionate foe of those who were coming to be called Protestants. The Duke of Norfolk was a died-in-the-wool reactionary, who boasted that he never had and never would read the English Bible. Stephen Gardiner, Bishop of Salisbury was the leading conciliar Catholic opponent of Cranmer. Beyond these there were several who deeply resented the injustice suffered by Catherine of Aragon and who heartily loathed Anne Boleyn. The remainder of the reign was marked by deep divisions within the inner circle of the king's advisers and conflict between factions which had their supporters in the court, the City, the nation and the international diplomatic community. Everyone at court had to be careful about what he said and to whom he said it and anyone who was ambitious, as John Dudley certainly was, could not be neutral. The time had come to take sides on the great issues of the day.

There was no doubt that Thomas Cromwell was the man whose patronage could be the most valuable and Sir John was careful to cultivate him. However, we should not assume that he was motivated only by cynical self-interest. The two men had an affinity and Cromwell had good reason for extending his patronage to the soldier–courtier whose star was obviously in the ascendant. He needed supporters among those who were close to the king. The relationship between Cromwell and Dudley was definitely symbiotic. The first evidence we have of it is a note among the 'remembrances' Mr Secretary wrote for himself in order to keep tabs on the minutiae of the innumerable items of business that crossed his desk daily. In April 1534 he reminded himself to do something for Sir John Dudley regarding the prestigious household post of vice-chamberlain. Behind this simple aide-memoire lies a significant and convoluted story of family feuds, clashing religious convictions and competition for places at court.

The first strand concerns the vice-chamberlainship. The current holder was Sir John Gage, a well-respected courtier who had long enjoyed the king's friendship. But, as a staunch Catholic, Gage was rigorously opposed to the new direction of royal policy. His happy relationship with the king came to an end in 1533 when Gage told Henry that he was unable to accept the putting away of Catherine and the installation of Anne as queen. Henry angrily banished him from the court and subsequently ordered him to be examined 'about the Lady Catherine'. The king relented and no proceedings were taken against Gage but he, for his part, was in no hurry to seek a reconciliation. On the contrary, early the following year he renounced his court office and declared his intention to become a Carthusian monk. This news must have been something of a red rag to Henry, for the Carthusians were the most stubborn opponents of the divorce and, as an order, made no secret of their support of the pope. Under these circumstances the vice-chamberlainship became vacant and John Dudley applied for it.

This is where family conflict enters the story. The prospect of John Dudley benefiting from his action did not please Gage at all. The two men were cousins by marriage, Gage's wife being the daughter of Richard Guildford, one of Sir Edward's brothers. Whether there was longstanding personal animosity between the two Johns, as well as political and religious disagreement, we do not know. What is clear is that the events of the next few weeks permanently soured their relations. Dudley's father-in-law Edward Guildford was by now very infirm. For some months he had been unable to fulfil his duties as Master of the Tower Armouries and Dudley had been deputizing for him. It seemed likely that he was not very long for this world and that the Dudleys would shortly inherit all his property. At the beginning of June 1534 Gage rode down to Leeds Castle in Kent where Guildford was currently living and tried to persuade the old man to make a will in favour of John Guildford, Sir Edward's closest male relative. The fact that he volunteered the services of a lawyer who was one of his own kinsman and subsequently sought the intervention of Thomas, Lord De la Warr, John Guildford's brother-in-law, suggests convincingly that Gage was part of a conspiracy to deprive the Dudleys of Jane's inheritance. Sir Edward cheated them by dying before a testamentary document could be pushed under his pen. Notwithstanding this, John Guildford went immediately to Halden to try to take possession. He claimed that Gage had assured him that his uncle had fully intended to nominate him as his heir. Such a claim, of course, had no standing in law and the Dudleys were eventually confirmed in possession of Sir Edward's estate but not before John Guildford and his supporters had mounted a long campaign in which they tried to prove a Dudley–Plantaganet plot to alienate Sir Edward's property from his family. It was at about the same time that Gage made his peace with the king and resumed his office of vice-chamberlain. We may wonder whether this volte-face was, in part at least, to spite John Dudley. Any such malice, however, could not harm Sir John who, immediately on his father-in-law's death, had been given the Mastership of the Tower Armouries.

One problem with the fragmentary nature of surviving documentary evidence is the inevitable distortion that it involves. Court records tend to be preserved more carefully than many other kinds of written material and might suggest that our sixteenth-century ancestors spent most of their time invoking the law against each other and, by implication, harbouring grudges or mercilessly pursuing their legal rights. This was certainly not the case with John Dudley. In the 1530s he was engaged in an enormous empire-building exercise. This was largely fortuitous; the death of his mother and his father-in-law, the difficulties of the baronial family and, later, the sudden availability of vast tracts of former monastic land constituted a unique convergence of circumstances of which he energetically took advantage. Some of this activity certainly created ill-feeling and engendered long-running feuds. John had made a permanent enemy in Sir John Gage. But others with whom he was involved in litigation did not allow this to sour their relations. Self-interest often prevailed where a forgiving spirit did not. Sir John Dudley was becoming a man of consequence in good standing with the king and a friend of Thomas Cromwell. Most of his aggrieved relatives set aside prejudice and clamoured for his patronage. Even Arthur, the burglarious priest, made his peace with his upstart cousin and, as a result of John's influence, was appointed Prebendary of Worcester.

Sir John's relationship with his stepfather was respectful rather than affectionate. Arthur Plantaganet, Viscount Lisle, had received several marks of royal favour over the years and these culminated in his appointment as Lord Deputy of Calais, a post he took up in June 1533. This was no sinecure (in fact, involvement in the affairs of the tiny colony would bring about Lisle's downfall) and Arthur and his family had to take up residence on the other side of the Channel. A fortunate result for us is that he had to exchange occasional letters with his stepson. One matter which involved some unpleasant wrangling arose out of the reversions that John sold to Edward Seymour. He asked for and received Arthur's permission for the transaction and all proceeded very amicably until Seymour discovered and began exploiting a loophole in the legal arrangements. Having undertaken to pay rent on some of the property during Arthur's lifetime, Seymour discovered that, through a faulty drawing up of the indenture, some land was not covered by this agreement and he declined to make the annual payment to which Lisle had believed himself entitled. Lisle, as he admitted in correspondence with his lawyer, was largely to blame because he had signed certain crucial documents without reading them. Nevertheless, he believed that the two young courtiers had conspired to defraud him and resorted to the law. The dispute dragged on month after month until Lisle's advisers counselled that, though he had a good moral case, legally he had no leg to stand on. The aggrieved Viscount now appealed directly to Cromwell:

> . . . Sir, I sustain great wrong but I remit it wholly into your hand and will abide your award in it . . . But I fear not but the matter being opened unto you as the truth is, you will say that I have sustained great wrong, and also that it were against reason that I should depart from possession during my life. And as touching Sir John Dudley, I think he may say I have rather used me like a father therein than a father-in-law [a sixteenth-century alternative for stepfather], as the King's highness and the Council doth right well know. And I have little deserved towards them that he so should handle me.[7]

Another year passed before a conclusion acceptable to all parties was arrived at by order in Chancery.

From all this we might expect to discern a decided tension between Lisle and his stepson but while the lawyers were arguing the two men were exchanging friendly letters. Thus we find Sir John asking Plantaganet to buy a tilt horse for him in France, 'for I can get none here for no money' and passing on the latest news from court. He offers to act as host should the king while on progress call at Lisle's manors of Painswick or Kingston Lisle – no small undertaking when we consider the size of the royal entourage that would expect to be housed and fed in suitable style. He assures his stepfather that if he needs to rest at one of the Dudley estates in Kent on his journey from Calais to London, 'your lordship shall demand it as your own.'[8] But we come closest to gaining a flavour of the relationship in a letter of October 1535. John forwards to Calais an affidavit requiring Lisle's signature which was important to Dudley as he sought to counter the objections still being raised to his inheritance of the Guildford estate. Patiently he explains to the old man that one of the masters of Chancery has made a fair copy because 'the other that you have already put your hand to is so scribbled that with pain it can be read.' The writer, knowing what a poor head Lisle has for business, gives a careful précis of other support documents he is enclosing and cajoles his stepfather into a prompt reply: 'this week that cometh the matter shall be heard between my adversary and me, wherefore it will be too late to send unto you again.' He adds that in order to scotch any suggestion that his own marriage to Jane Guildford was part of a deep laid plot he has made it known that Plantaganet was actually against the union. 'And this I have heard your lordship often say, which I trust is no dishonour to you to have the same reported but rather to your honour.'[9] The whole tenor of John's letters to Lisle is respectful and not without affection.

Guildford's death brought John into public life in a new capacity; he was voted into parliament to fill the vacancy created by Sir Edward's demise. There can be no doubt that he served Cromwell's interest in the Commons nor that his presence at debates gave him a clearer understanding of the arguments being urged in favour of the wide-ranging revolution upon which the government was embarked. Cromwell needed his supporters in the lower house, for not all the measures placed before what has come to be called the 'Reformation Parliament' (1529–36) reached the statute book without significant opposition. By the time John took his seat the anti-papal campaign which had begun cautiously with attacks on clerical abuses was reaching a draconian crescendo. The Act of Supremacy formally endorsed Henry's headship of the English church and required subjects to swear an oath affirming his position as their spiritual leader. Any who refused to do so were, by simple logic, traitors. It was Thomas More's refusal of this oath that brought him to the block the following summer and which trapped many religious conservatives by making them liable to the appalling sentence of death by hanging, drawing and quartering.

The Supremacy Act was followed by a treason law which made it an offence to

maliciously wish, will or desire by words or writing or by craft imagine, invent, practise or attempt any bodily harm to be done or committed to the King's most royal person, the Queen's or their heir's apparent, or to deprive them or any of them of the dignity, title or name of their royal estates, or slanderously and maliciously publish and pronounce, by express writing or words, that the King our sovereign lord should be heretic, schismatic, tyrant, infidel or usurper of the crown . . .[10]

It was now obvious to many that the Tudor regime was assuming dictatorial powers. But there was no longer any part of the political realm that could withstand it. Henry VII had broken the nobility and his son had now brought the church to heel.

But the government did not rely on *force majeure* alone to obtain the support of Lords and Commons. Men who paraded their enthusiasm for royal policy did so to attract or hold the attention of those who were in a position to reward their loyalty. After March 1536 the Crown was able to be especially generous towards its supporters. That was the month in which the Act for the dissolution of smaller religious houses was passed. Parliamentarians, courtiers and others in the know had been waiting eagerly for this massive land grab, from which they had every hope of profiting. Early the previous year Cromwell had instigated an investigation of all church property and there were few who doubted that this was the precursor to confiscation. The only matter in doubt was the extent of the takeover. In the event, Cromwell decided as a first step to appropriate to the crown all religious houses with an annual value of less than £200 and having fewer than twelve inmates. To no one's very great surprise the royal investigators concluded that all the monks, nuns and friars of these lesser houses

spoil, destroy, consume and utterly waste as well their churches, monasteries, priories, principal houses, farms, granges, lands, tenements and hereditaments, as the ornaments of their churches and their goods and chattels to the high displeasure of Almighty God, slander of good religion, and to the great infamy of the King's Highness and the realm . . .[11]

We must place John Dudley among the enthusiastic supporters of government policy in parliament. He was by now joined hip and thigh to Cromwell. The minister was careful to take no one completely into his confidence but Dudley had definitely been admitted to his trusted inner circle and the two men were jointly involved in a variety of activities, both official and private. Sir John reports the suspicious activities of a Kentish priest. He describes the trial of a horse thief in

Lichfield. He shares in land deals with Cromwell. And, in September 1535, he borrows the considerable sum of £1,400 from the minister in order to invest in yet more land in the West Midlands. The build up of his territorial base was proceeding apace and the apparent fact that he did not profit from the first tranche of monastic land to be made available was probably due to his being already financially extended. As soon as he obtained probate of the Guildford estate he set about dismantling it. Although he kept some Kentish property, he disposed of most of it in order to acquire more land in the vicinity of Dudley.

By this time John had a sizeable family to look after. Throughout the early years of their marriage Jane gave birth almost annually. Of the children who survived infancy there were, by 1533, Henry, Mary, John, Margaret, Ambrose and Catherine. On St John the Baptist's day (24 June) in that year another son was born.[12] The Dudleys already had one John among their children and decided to christen the new arrival Robert. Thus the most famous member of the family made his entry into the world. (Eleven weeks later Anne Boleyn was brought to bed of a daughter. She was named Elizabeth.) The following year, about the time of Sir Edward's death, John and Jane had another son. He was called Guildford in memory of the grandfather he would never know. After him came another five siblings. The Dudley menage of the 1530s was a busy, noisy, bustling place.

By the standards of the time John was an affectionate, even an indulgent father.

> What should I wish any longer this life, that seeth such frailty in it? Surely, but for a few children which God has sent me, which also helps to pluck me on my knees, I have no great cause to desire to tarry much longer here.[13]

So he wrote in the dark days near the end of his life when the reversal of his fortunes persuaded him to reflect on the things that really matter, but even during the days when he was determinedly pursuing wealth and influence his family provided a comforting base. In later years he was accused of every kind of moral failing but no public lampoon or private letter exists which suggests that he was a womanizer. When he was abroad on diplomatic business he wrote home often and always returned with gifts for his wife and children. When he had to report to the Council unhappy tidings from the disturbed northern border he appended a personal note to his despatch: 'I pray you keep this from my wife.'[14] Dudley's concern extended beyond his immediate flesh and blood. When the Plantaganets took up residence in Calais John and Jane received one of their daughters, Elizabeth, into their own home. John took the responsibility seriously, even to the extent of remonstrating with the girl's father:

> . . . for my part I have and will do as becometh a brother to do to his sister; but if your lordship should not be as good lord and father unto her as to the rest of your daughters ye may be sure there is but few would harken unto her [regard her as a good marriage prospect]; for of late there was one brake off from communication of marriage only because it was bruited that you had given your land wholly to my sister Frances – as knoweth our Lord, who keep you in his blessed tuition.[15]

If the following letter is any indication of their father's general attitude it seems that the Dudley brood were pretty well spoiled. It was written when the eldest boy was on his first foreign mission and running into the usual temptations that beset young greenhorns away from the restraints of home.

> I had thought you had more discretion than to hurt yourself thorough fantasies or care, specially for such things as may be remedied or helpen. Well enough you must understand that I know you cannot live under great charges. And therefore you should not hide from me your debts whatsoever it be, for I would be loth but you should keep your credit with all men. And therefore send me word in any wise of the whole sum of your debts, for I and your mother will see them forthwith paid and whatsoever you do spend in honest service of our master, so [long as] you do not let wild and wanton men consume it, as I have been served in my days, you must think all is spent as it should be, and all that I have must be yours and that you spend before you may with God's grace help it hereafter by good and faithful service, wherein I trust you will never be found slack . . .[16]

Jane added a PS: 'Your loving mother that wishes you health daily.' There is every reason to envisage the growing family who lived in the Dudley town house much of the year and retired to one or other of their manors for the hot, unhealthy summer months as contented and well-to-do.

Their first serious shock came in May 1536. On the tenth of that month John wrote to Lady Lisle (Plantagenet's second wife):

> . . . As touching the news that are here, I am sure it needeth not to write to you nor to my lord of them, for all the world knoweth them by this time. This day was indicted Mr Norris, Mr Weston, William Brereton, Markes [Mark Smeaton] and my Lord of Rochford. And upon Friday next they shall be arraigned at Westminster. And the Queen herself shall be condemned by Parliament.[17]

6

The Pendulum and the Pit

———⧫———

No one has ever offered a fully satisfactory explanation for the downfall of Anne Boleyn. Sometime in the early months of 1536 Henry VIII, who had been utterly enraptured with the new woman in his life and for six long years had defied pope, emperor and English public opinion in order to make her his queen, instructed Cromwell to find a pretext for her death. There were several factors which might have affected the timing of this decision. In January the discarded Catherine of Aragon died. Henry could not have ended his second marriage while she was still alive because he would have been expected to take Catherine back. Now, however, he could re-establish relations with the Emperor and the sacrifice of Anne upon the altar of their friendship would dramatically demonstrate his sincerity. In January also the king had a bad fall in the tiltyard. For a couple of hours (according to some sources) he was unconscious and his physicians feared the worst. Some historians have identified this crisis as marking a drastic personality change in Henry. He had always been self-willed and capable of gratuitous cruelty but now his mood swings became quite unpredictable and his behaviour often irrational. Yet another event in the fraught early weeks of 1536 was Anne's miscarriage of a man child. It was the sad conclusion of her third pregnancy, and all she had to show for her ordeals was one child, a daughter. This, for Henry, was uncomfortably like a rerun of his first marriage – and time was not on his side. Henry's brush with death brought home to him the increased urgency of establishing the dynasty.

These three events indicate why Henry might have regarded this as a propitious time to take fresh thought about ways to secure a male heir but they do not explain why he resolved to murder not only his wife but other members of the court, some of whom had been close friends. There have been those who have seen the hand of the 'machiavellian' Cromwell in all this. In those winter months of 1536 he was putting the finishing touches to his plans to despoil the monasteries and there could be no doubt that the measure would provoke widespread alarm, discontent and, possibly, even rebellion. This was, above all, the time for the king to be seen to be strong, determined and ruthless. Getting rid of Anne and her 'accomplices' would serve a double purpose: it would gratify all those with whom the queen was enormously unpopular and it would send a signal to those opposed to the course of government policy that no one who offended the king could expect to escape retribution. Yet the suggestion that Cromwell could have conceived such a risky stratagem, persuaded the king to endorse it and calmly seen it through without, apparently, fearing that rivals would get to Henry and change his mind strains credulity. The minister had risen with the support of the Boleyns. They had shared not just a common concern to rid the king of his first wife but a commitment to a reformist programme. There could only have been one place where the fate of Anne Boleyn was decided and that was in the mind of England's tyrannical ruler. As ever, Henry proposed the policy and demanded its efficient execution by his loyal servants.

By mid-March rumour was spreading through the court like spilled oil. The queen herself set a match to it on 2 April when she had her almoner preach a sermon in which Cromwell was compared to Haman who, in the book of Esther, tried to encompass the downfall of the Persian queen and ended up on the gallows he had erected for his enemy. Thereafter the atmosphere in the royal household was crackling with nervous static. At the end of the month the arrests began and on 2 May Anne herself was conveyed by barge to the Tower.

Still no one outside the circle of Cromwell and his confidential agents knew precisely what was going on and it was a week before the minister called a meeting which was designed to put an end to speculation. Twenty-two gentlemen of the privy chamber were summoned to the great man's presence, among them John Dudley. They must have been in urgent need of reassurance. As well as Anne's brother, Lord Rochford, three of their privy chamber colleagues were marked to die for treasonable adultery. It was the following day that Sir John was able to assure Lady Lisle that it was resolved upon that 'the Queen herself shall be condemned by Parliament.' The chilling words indicate clearly that Anne's fate had been settled well before the travesty of a trial had been held. Writs for the new parliament had been hurried out on 27 April, its immediate object being to set the seal of a spurious legality on the execution of Anne, the bastardizing of her daughter and the legitimizing of Henry's offspring by his next wife. To those evaluating their alliances and friendships these were bewildering and hazardous days. The Boleyn network was torn to shreds. But the Catholic faction which hoped to benefit from the queen's fall and to be poised to strike at Cromwell failed to make the most of their moment. Their tactics depended largely in persuading Princess Mary to grovel her way back into her father's good books, but she refused to demean herself and sully her mother's memory by such a submission until it was too late to help her friends back into power. Even Cromwell's position was not secure. He was playing for high stakes and a moment's miscalculation could have brought upon him the fatal wrath of his unpredictable master. This was probably another reason for the meeting he called on 9 May; he was building his own faction based on old friends and new allies in the privy chamber.

Was it chance or shrewd judgement that once more placed John Dudley within the victors' camp? Not only did he remain loyal to Cromwell throughout these tense and troubled weeks; he had another alliance which would, in the long run, prove even more valuable. Edward Seymour, John's friend, colleague and partner in various land deals, was about to be rocketed to wealth and influence. Edward was almost John's exact contemporary but he had lagged behind in promotion within the household. He lacked John's impressive ancestry and his rise had been much slower and more problematic. He was a younger son of a Wiltshire gentleman who had served in the early campaigns of the reign and had managed to see Edward and his sister, Jane, placed at court. From there on Edward had to rely solely on his own talents if he was to take full advantage of his position. His chief attributes were a certain cultured charm and driving ambition. Whereas Dudley had become an esquire of the body in 1524, it was not until 1529 that Seymour joined that select band. However, Henry enjoyed his company, especially at the gaming tables, and various loans and grants came the young courtier's way. But in 1535–6 his career accelerated dramatically. The spur was Henry's attraction to Jane Seymour, who was one of the queen's ladies. Her portrait and contemporary accounts agree: Jane Seymour was no beauty. But she was bright and Henry liked intelligent women – as long as they were submissive. It may have been her ambitious brother or some other scheming courtier with a dislike of the Boleyns who saw the potential offered by the king's latest infatuation: what Anne had achieved Jane might also bring off. She was tutored to guard her virtue devoutly in the hope that her resistance would only fuel Henry's determination. It was the availability of another young, fecund potential wife that underscored Henry's determination to be rid of Anne. As Jane rose, so Edward rose with her. In March he was appointed a gentleman of the privy chamber. Both at Greenwich and at Hampton Court he and his sister were allotted quarters conveniently close to the king's so that his majesty could pass privily to and fro. On 17 May Cranmer obligingly pronounced Henry's second marriage null and void. On 30 May Anne was beheaded in the precincts of the Tower and within a fortnight the king and Jane Seymour were married.

Thus the pendulum of power swung away from the Boleyns and towards the Seymours. Over the next seventeen months Edward became Viscount Beauchamp, Governor of Jersey, Chancellor of North Wales and Earl of Hertford. He was admitted to the Council and received substantial grants of land to support his new dignities. The new balance of power at court was clearly indicated in August 1537 when Edward's sister, Elizabeth, was married to Cromwell's son, Gregory. How did John Dudley respond to his colleague's meteoric rise?

To all outward appearances – and those are all the historian has to go on – Dudley accepted the changed relationship with a good grace. It was, of course, in his interests to do so. Patronage and royal favour were now in the gift of the Cromwell–Seymour caucus. The minister had also reached new heights of personal aggrandizement. He was raised to the peerage as Baron Cromwell of Wimbledon and took over the office of Lord Privy Seal, which had been stripped from Thomas Boleyn. In the tiny world of the Tudor court every nuance of status and precedence was carefully noted and carried great significance. Thus, for example, Baron Cromwell, the most junior member of the aristocracy, declined to take a lowly place on entering the House of Lords. He had an Act passed which provided that the Vicegerent in Spirituals (himself), as the king's direct representative, should have the place of honour in the assembly even (and especially) above the premier peer, the Duke of Norfolk. If John was at all upset at being overtaken by someone less talented, he had little time to brood. Within the year he went to war again.

1536 was an *annus horribilis* for Henry VIII. Scarcely had he put the events of the spring behind him and settled into his new marriage than his only son, the illegitimate Duke of Richmond, died of tuberculosis. Seventeen-year-old Henry Fitzroy had filled an important place in his father's life. As his wives produced healthy daughters and a succession of sickly babies the existence of the young duke was living proof that Henry was capable of siring a man child. And there was always the possibility that Fitzroy could become the heir to the throne. His claim was just as good as that of Henry's daughters, both of whom had now been bastardized. The king was desperate for a legitimate male heir but should fate continue to deny that to him Richmond was a fallback and Henry contemplated the possibility of willing the crown to him. Now death had removed that option and the spectre of the dynasty's end reared up more frighteningly than ever. But that was nothing compared to the new threat to the regime which erupted in September – rebellion.

It had all started at Louth, a market town on the edge of the Lincolnshire fens. On Michaelmas Day (29 September) the citizenry gathered outside their church of St James, but recently refurbished and provided with an impressive 295 foot spire by the devoted parishioners, for the annual procession of crucifixes, statues and precious reliquaries. The building and its comforting rituals had always connected the people to a supposedly changeless past, but as they came together in 1536 they did so in a spirit of anxiety and foreboding. A shout from the crowd summed up the prevailing mood: 'Go ye and follow the crosses, for if they be taken from us we are like to follow them no more.'[1] Reality and rumour had profoundly disturbed this remote locality. Nearby religious houses were in the process of being torn down. Royal commissioners (inevitably regarded as snoopers) were travelling from village to village assessing the wealth of the churches. Cromwell had delivered injunctions instructing clergy to preach in support of the king's supremacy and to abolish superstitious practices. To many conservative countrymen it seemed that tyranny and heresy were in league to overthrow all that was valuable in traditional society. They believed that worse was to come: backbreaking taxes were about to be imposed; churches were to be stripped of anything valuable which could be appropriated for the king's pleasure; and what else might a monarch not do who had disposed of the pope, the monastic orders and both of his queens? The country folk decided they would not wait to find out. Next day self-appointed leaders took all the church ornaments into safe keeping and resolved to send the king's commissioners packing. What began in Louth spread rapidly throughout the fenland. Summoned by church bells and egged on by their clergy, an anxious crowd became an angry mob and, within days, the first blood of the rebellion had been shed.

If Cromwell was surprised by the turn of events he certainly had no excuse; for weeks his agents in several areas far from the capital had been warning him of the discontent caused by the changes he was forcing on the nation. But he had been dismissive of such alarmist reports and quite unrepentant. In fact, shows of resistance by unruly subjects helped his cause because they made the king angry. Henry contemptuously dismissed the Lincolnshire malcontents as 'the rude commons of one shire and that one of the most brute and beastly of the whole realm,'[2]and Cromwell took his cue from his master. As the expressions of discontent spread to neighbouring counties he instructed his agents,

> There can be no better way to beat the King's authority into the heads of the rude people of the North than to show them that the King intends reformation and correction of religion. They are more superstitious than virtuous, long accustomed to frantic fantasies and ceremonies, which they regard more than either God or their prince. They are completely alienated from true religion.[3]

But the messengers who galloped into Westminster were soon bringing more disturbing news: thousands of people were flocking to the rebels' pious banners representing the wounds of Christ and among them were some of the nobles and gentlemen to whom the government looked to maintain law and order. The dissidents were armed and determined, and defiant words were not going to stop them. Even the king was soon forced to acknowledge that the Lincolnshire Rising and the Pilgrimage of Grace which followed hard on its heels in Yorkshire constituted the biggest crisis of his reign. Not only were his policies being challenged, there was a real threat that England would return to the anarchy that had preceded his father's grabbing of the crown.

For days the government was at sixes and sevens. Forces were mustered to be sent north then ordered to stay where they were to defend the capital. Henry announced that he would march at the head of his army to face the rebels, then thought better of it and despatched the Duke of Suffolk to Lincolnshire and the Duke of Norfolk to Yorkshire. Ordnance was taken from the Tower to the rallying point of the royal forces at Ampthill but when fresh intelligence reported that the rebel host was on the road south it was trundled off to Windsor where the king had resolved to establish his headquarters.

John Dudley was at the centre of all this frenzied activity. As Master
of the Tower Armoury he was kept very busy supervizing the supply of
weapons and equipment. Then, on 9 October, he was ordered to muster
two hundred men in Sussex and join Norfolk's army. His contingent
was one of the largest contributions to Howard's force of about 8,000
men which made its way up the Great North Road. Meanwhile,
Richmond, York, Pontefract and the surrounding areas were in rebel
hands, recruiting bands were active throughout remoter regions and the
leader of the Pilgrimage of Grace, Robert Aske, was variously reported
to have between 20,000 and 40,000 armed men at his back.

Somewhere ahead of the Duke of Norfolk lay a fanatical horde
which far outnumbered his own. Behind him was a king who
expected him to crush that horde and who sent repeated messages to
that effect. Moreover, Henry, as the duke was well aware, did not
fully trust him. Howard's conservative sympathies were well known
and, in order to ensure that he did not make common cause with the
rebels, Henry had ordered him to leave his two sons behind. The
word 'hostages' was not used but Norfolk knew that that was what
they were. He was not being overly dramatic when he wrote to
commend his family to royal care in the event of his failure to return.
John Dudley must have shared his commander's anxiety. His life was
increasingly at risk with every northward mile of the royal troops'
advance. Even if he survived the fighting there might be question
marks over his future. He was known to be an ally of Cromwell and
committed to his programme of religious and social reform. If the
minister fell and was replaced by advisers who had the support of a
large traditionalist constituency he might, at best, be allowed to retire
to his estates and, at worst, lose his head.

It was Dudley's popularity with Cromwell and the king that kept him
out of harm's way. Norfolk had to keep his master fully informed and
that meant explaining why he had decided to disobey his instructions to
go for all-out military victory. As he sat up late at nights composing
draft after discarded draft of his reports he needed messengers who
would be well received at court and who would be able to handle cross-
examination by the king and the Lord Privy Seal. Thus Dudley became
one of the principal intermediaries between a woefully unhappy general
and an anxious, impatient monarch. Norfolk grovelled. He would, he
insisted, 'rather be torn in a million pieces than show one point of
cowardice or untruth to your majesty'.[4] And when he offered a truce to
the enemy and promised that the government would consider their

grievances (which was all that, given the circumstances, he could do), he dragged up every excuse he could think of to explain his decision:

> . . . it was not the fear of the enemy [that] hath caused us to [negotiate], but three other sore points. Foul weather and no housing for horse nor man, at the most not for the third part of the army, and no wood to make fires withall, hunger both for men and horses of such sort that of truth I think never English man saw the like. Pestilence in the town marvellous fervent . . .[5]

Doubtless the general was in some difficulty. Aske's army, encamped at Doncaster, was much better organized and they had commandeered most of the available victuals and fodder. Norfolk's rapidly assembled force lacked an adequate commissariat. But it was the military situation which really tied his hands. He was obliged to forsake any thoughts of honour and to make all manner of promises in order to persuade the enemy to disperse. These lessons were not lost on John Dudley when he led the king's men against the next major rebellion thirteen years later.

Norfolk's trickery worked. The leaders of the Pilgrimage of Grace abandoned their position of advantage and sent their followers home. Within weeks many of them were hanging from gibbets and church towers throughout the north. The Duke of Norfolk revenged himself enthusiastically for his humiliation and wrote his loyalty to the king in the blood of peasants. But Dudley had no part in the final sanguinary scenes of the failed rising. In January 1537 he was appointed one of the vice-admirals of the coast and went to sea immediately with a small squadron of ships. Naval command was thought to require no maritime expertise. Warfare at sea was traditionally only an extension of warfare on land; ships were floating platforms for conveying troops to where they were needed or for grappling enemy vessels whose crews could then be engaged in hand-to-hand fighting. Slowly, this situation was changing: the fighting ship was coming into its own as artillery experts and marine architects experimented with ways of increasing the firepower of naval cannon and providing vessels with the necessary stability to keep up a sustained bombardment. Europe's rulers were vigorously competing with each other to construct bigger and better ships and no one was more enthusiastic than Henry VIII. It was an enthusiasm Dudley came to share. Perhaps he volunteered for naval command in order to stay in the king's good books and to avoid touring the northern counties as an agent of royal vengeance. Whatever his motives, the sea definitely got into his blood.

Dudley's commission was to patrol the eastern end of the Channel and keep it safe for English and other merchant vessels. The country was not at war but piracy was ever present. The king's captains and sailors had every incentive to hunt down marine raiders because every legitimate capture meant prize money. After several months, during which his commission had been extended to cover the whole of the Channel, Dudley was frustrated at not having apprehended a single marauder. The situation was redeemed, however, on 22 August 1537 when he brought four Breton pirate ships to action in Mount's Bay and, after five hours' fighting, took two of them prisoner. Unfortunately, his triumph came to naught thanks to the interference of politicians. Following a protest by the French ambassador, who insisted that the impounded vessels were legitimate traders, they were released. Weeks later the captains of these 'merchantmen' were up to their old tricks and waylaid an English trading vessel out of Calais.

By this time the Seymour clan were cock-a-hoop. The long-awaited outcome of Queen Jane's first pregnancy was a boy, born at Hampton Court on 12 October. Henry was delirious with joy and relief. This was the vindication of all that he had done over the past decade. God had rewarded him for his patient suffering. The dynasty was secure. Everyone currently in favour shared in the rejoicing and the outpouring of royal bounty that accompanied it. John Dudley was among the courtiers, diplomats and church dignitaries who crowded into the chapel for Prince Edward's christening three days later. The good news from England had political significance internationally and messengers were rapidly despatched to courts throughout Europe, among them Dudley.

He was sent to the imperial court with letters for the English ambassador, Sir Thomas Wyatt, and had been selected for the mission because Cromwell trusted him and because he was an old friend and privy chamber colleague of the ambassador. Wyatt's career had closely mirrored Dudley's and though the courtier–poet had almost been ensnared in the plot against Anne Boleyn, the king's friendship had saved him and later exalted him to one of the top diplomatic jobs. There were important and delicate matters on which the minister needed well-informed, confidential information. The international situation was, once again, finely balanced and he wanted a shrewd, intelligent assessment of the attitudes of the principal players. John

Dudley was, therefore, more than a mere messenger. He found the peripatetic imperial court at Barbastro, in the Pyrenean foothills half way between the Biscayan port of San Sebastian and Barcelona on the Mediterranean.

What the Lord Privy Seal required of Wyatt was nothing less than that he would make diligent enquiries, 'in such discreet and temperate sort, as at the return of . . . Mr Dudley, your good friend, his highness may perceive that thing which his grace desireth to know, that is the Emperor's good inclination towards his majesty or the contrary, if it shall otherwise appear unto you.'[6] Dudley had brought back an offer from the emperor to mediate between Henry and the pope. However, reports from elsewhere suggested that Charles was guilty of 'fraud and deceit'.[7]

For the next couple of years John Dudley absented himself from court and capital for long periods of time and devoted his energies to consolidating his territorial empire. There may have been an element of pique in this. He had entertained hope of being advanced to a senior post in the royal household but nothing had come of this and he had watched while the likes of the Seymours passed him by in the race for wealth and rank. But he also had a genuine desire to rebuild his family's prestige in the Midland counties and the Welsh border lands. At the same time the dangerous rivalries of the court were making life at the centre increasingly perilous.

Sir John associated himself more and more with the social and political life of the Midlands and believed he could serve the Crown effectively on the border, certainly more effectively than his own relatives had in the past. In July 1539 he sent a poacher in chains up to London to be examined by the Council, explaining that the leniency he had displayed up to that point had not effected any change of behaviour by the offender and his kin. 'When let off,' he pointed out to Cromwell, 'these men get worse and worse, as they did in the old Lord Dudley's days.'[8]

Lawlessness in the principality and the adjacent shires was a constant irritant and establishing effective royal power there was one of Cromwell's major concerns, as Dudley knew. The Lord Privy Seal had given the old Council in the Marches of Wales sharper teeth and, in 1534, appointed Rowland Lee, Bishop of Coventry as its president. The bishop was at odds with many of the nobles and gentlemen who held sway in the area and resented being under the thumb of an ecclesiastic who was determined that his own authority should be totally superior to and independent of the common law courts.

Cromwell received a string of complaints from Lee and his opponents and there were definitely rumours in 1538–9 that Lee had fallen from favour and was about to be replaced.

In the summer of 1539 Sir John asked for Lee's job. Being President of the Council of the Marches would give him enormous power and prestige and he probably felt that, as an established leader of border society, he had a better chance of being accepted by his peers than had the abrasive bishop. He wrote to Cromwell, 'I have spent a great deal of my life and my youth in the court about my master [continuing that he was] now drawing homewards where I trust to make an end of my life in God's service.'[9] Strange words for a man of thirty-five! Whatever Cromwell thought of the letter, he did not agree to replace Lee with Dudley.

From this point we can observe competing, almost schizophrenic, aspects of Dudley's character. Alongside the old self-confidence and drive there appears a diffidence, a desire to distance himself from the pressures of court politics. He still lost no opportunity to add to his territorial empire. For example, in March 1540, two guests, Andrew Flammock and his son, arrived at Dudley Castle and, within days, showed signs of plague. Sir John reported this to Cromwell, lamenting that the king was on the point of losing a staunch servant but, at the same time, suing for 'the office at Kenilworth' that Flammock held. Yet he refused to make a great show of his own importance. Thus, for instance, he kept no impressive establishment in Westminster or London.

Dudley's letter to Cromwell reads like the world-weary plaint of a man who is disillusioned with the court and the constant struggle for worldly wealth and success. He writes about devoting the rest of his life to God. It has been customary to regard him, and other leaders of the reforming party, as opportunists, men who climbed on the religious bandwagon as soon as they saw that it was gathering momentum. This is to underestimate the impact of the fervour that was gripping large numbers of people in the 1530s. At the end of his life Dudley dated his conversion to the evangelical faith to around 1536–7 and he was far from being alone in being won over to evangelical religion at that time. The intoxicating new ideas were being taken up at all levels of society and church authorities were no longer able to dismiss heresy as the errors of simple-minded peasants and semi-literate tradesmen. 'What made the Reformation successful was not the support (if any) it received from deviants and the marginalised, but the support it received from the established elites in

Church and state.'[10] The educated and the powerful were being targeted by preachers and pamphleteers. Their campaign was, in part, political. Cromwell and his agents and protégés were engaged in an ideological struggle against Rome which both transcended national boundaries and aimed to influence national policies. But the outer cladding of bellicose realpolitik would not have survived and in several countries prevailed without a solid framework of personal devotion and conviction theology. The fundamental ingredient of Lutheranism and the other evangelical strains which diverged from it was salvation for the individual sinner by faith alone. The sacrifice of Christ called forth from men and women, not observance of ecclesiastical rites, but *metanoia*, a turning from the world, the flesh and the devil and a reliance on nothing but the mercy and love of God.

It was impossible for John Dudley, as he went about his daily life in the court and the capital, to avoid exposure to zealous exponents of evangelical religion. For one thing, Cromwell was energetically patronizing preachers, pamphleteers and others whose talents could be useful to him. John Dudley was no scholar and he was certainly not the stuff of which religious martyrs are made. No extant document contains a summary of his fundamental beliefs, but he aligned himself with the new movement in English Christianity and during his years in power promoted it vigorously. For those, like him, at the centre of national life it was impossible to avoid the ideological battle that was raging throughout the middle decades. When rival preachers were vilifying each other from their pulpits; when 'papists' were being hanged, drawn and quartered for treason and 'sacramentaries' burned for heresy; when Protestant zealots were smashing statues and Catholic zealots ransacking people's homes in search of banned books; when the king's pendulum conscience swung between new revelations and old orthodoxies; when, for the first time, the framing of foreign policy had to take into account the confessional allegiance of European rulers; when the biggest land speculation in English history was in full swing, in short, when men had to face the devastating fracture of western Christendom, taking sides became inevitable.

The new spirituality was in fashion at court. Several of John's colleagues were devotees who eagerly listened to Latimer and other avant-garde preachers, acquired pocket New Testaments and suspect books, and attended secret meetings in London back rooms. The king's brother-in-law, Edward Seymour, was an evangelical. So were his physicians, Doctors Butts and Huick. So were members of the Council and the privy chamber staff, Ralph Sadler, George Blagge, Philip Hoby, Anthony Denny and others. Younger courtiers climbed on the bandwagon because the religious novelties were new, exciting, dangerous and challenged old-fashioned assumptions but there were many others who were genuine converts with convictions that ran deep. All of them had to be circumspect about the public expression they gave to private faith. If pressed most of them would probably have given the answer that Thomas Cromwell gave to those who sought to probe his doctrinal allegiance. An envoy from one of the German princes reported that the minister inclined to Lutheranism but that, 'as the world stood, [he] would believe even as his master the King believed.'[11] It was the only safe answer that could be given by men who were close to the quicksilver Henry and well aware of the eager ears around the court waiting to detect any unguarded word. First and foremost in their thinking had to be their allegiance to the king.

This was no problem for John Dudley. His father and his guardian had schooled him in unswerving loyalty to the Tudors. What the Reformation did was provide a luxuriant theological apparel in which to dress up what had hitherto been an emotional rather than a closely reasoned commitment.

> . . . the office, authority and power given of God unto kings is in earth above all powers; let them call themselves popes, cardinals or whatsoever they will. The word of God declareth them (yea and commandeth them under pain of damnation) to be obedient unto the temporal sword, as in the Old Testament all the prophets, priests and Levites were.

So Miles Coverdale pronounced, in the preface to his Bible. William Tyndale, in *The Obedience of a Christian Man* (1528) had stated – or overstated – the case for royal authority: 'The king is in this world, without law and may at his lust do right or wrong and shall give accounts but to God only.'[12] Monstrous though such a justification of tyranny may seem to us, it had a distinct appeal to those whose fathers and grandfathers could tell them tales of fifteenth-century anarchy and to those patriots who supported England's casting off of the papal yoke. For John Dudley the arguments for unlimited royal power based on biblical exposition chimed perfectly with his own deepest feelings.

The raging politico-religious debate touched another spot deep in John's psyche, his admiration, bordering on veneration, for the intelligentsia. Walter Haddon, one of England's leading classicists, writing in later years to Robert Dudley, observed, 'your father, although he acknowledged himself uneducated, was yet most devoted to learning.'[13] Jane Guildford, his wife, though not a bluestocking, was one of a growing band of Renaissance ladies who benefited from the enlightened ideas of contemporary educational reformers. The Dudleys paid close attention to the schooling of their own children. At least one, John, the scholar of the family, was attached to Prince Edward's household and benefited from the instruction of Richard Cox, Anthony Cooke, John Cheke and Roger Ascham, top-drawer academics and formidable members of the New Learning brotherhood. As for Sir John, he enjoyed the company of thinking men, often corresponded with Cranmer, Cheke and Sir Thomas Wyatt and patronized promising authors. He was particularly interested in the developing sciences of mathematics, cosmography and astronomy. It is far from fanciful to imagine this intelligent man of mature years deciding that he wanted to escape the atmosphere of religious controversy and live quietly in the country, devoting himself to 'God's service'. There was much of the introvert in John Dudley. He was given to self-examination. But this could also metamorphose into self-dramatization and he frequently wore his heart on his sleeve.

By the middle of 1539, John Dudley had come to accept the tenets of the evangelical reformers and as a result, he was a man torn. The habit of seeking self-advancement through close attendance on the king had become ingrained. But at court religious controversy was distasteful and the risk of becoming caught up in the rivalry between Cromwell and his opponents seemed to be increasing. These were dangerous days for men of religious conviction, when courtiers were at a loss to know what to believe and how to behave. John Foxe, writing a generation later, described the confusion and anxiety of King Henry's latter years:

To many who be yet alive, and can testify these things, it is not unknown, how variable the state of religion stood in these days; how hardly and with what difficulty [the truth] came forth; what chances and changes it suffered. Even as the King was ruled and gave ear sometimes to one, sometimes to another, so one while it went forward, at another season as much backward again, and sometimes clean altered and changed for a season, according as they could prevail who were about the King.[14]

Thomas More had once compared Henry to a caged lion, as vicious as he was unpredictable. He warned courtiers who boasted of their intimacy with the king, 'Often he roars in rage for no known reason and suddenly the fun becomes fatal.' More himself had fallen foul of royal wrath in 1535, and in the years that followed more and more of Henry's erstwhile companions, advisers and close servants felt his claw marks. In the early weeks of 1539 Dudley was called to play his small part in executing his master's revenge against those who had fallen from favour. Furious at the machinations of Cardinal Reginald Pole and his clandestine communication with English dissidents, Henry had tried, without success, to have him assassinated. The 'meddlesome priest' might be beyond his reach but Pole's relatives and friends were not. The king ordered a ruthless purge and sixteen high-ranking people, including the Marquess of Exeter and Baron Montague, were caught in the net of royal vengeance. Exeter had Yorkist blood, being the son of Edward IV's daughter Katherine, and so too did Montague. He and his brother the Cardinal were grandsons of Edward IV's brother George, Duke of Clarence. A series of state trials were staged, and John Dudley was sworn a member of the jury that on St Valentine's Day dutifully proclaimed his old privy chamber colleague, Sir Nicholas Carew, guilty of high treason. Carew had been a great favourite with the king and a member of the highly select Order of the Garter. He had often taken part with Dudley in tiltyard contests and had served on important foreign embassies. But the one privilege neither Carew nor anyone else close to the king was permitted was independent judgement and Sir Nicholas had been too open in his disapproval of the drift of policy since the fall of Catherine of Aragon.

Throughout 1539 the court was alive with rumours and there was plenty of scope for personal vendettas. Someone, wanting to make trouble for John Dudley, tried to involve him in the downfall of the Exeters. The story went round that letters implicating the imperial ambassador, Eustace Chapuys, had been found among the Marchioness of Exeter's papers and that Dudley had taken it upon himself to warn the ambassador. Chapuys was at pains to deny that he had written anything incriminating or that he had been approached by Dudley. Nothing happened as a result of this slander and, for the moment, Sir John was safe. But greater danger reared up in the summer. The conservatives had just achieved their greatest triumph, the passage through parliament of 'An Act Abolishing Diversity in Religion', better known as the 'Act of Six Articles' or, in Protestant circles, as the 'Bloody Whip with Six

Strings'. The new legislation prescribed belief in traditional doctrines and increased the powers of ecclesiastical courts to seek out heretics. Norfolk, Gardiner and their allies hoped to use it to mount a major purge of evangelicals in high places and this alone could well have convinced John Dudley that it was time to retire from the political centre and 'make an end of my life in God's service.'

Not that he was idle. Accumulating, exchanging and speculating in property took up a great deal of his time and energy. His closeness to Cromwell paid off as more monastic lands passed through the Vicegerent's hands. After the confiscation of the lesser monasteries the government put pressure on the larger houses to close voluntarily. In the summer of 1538 the Premonstratensian priory of St James, Halesowen (some seven miles from Dudley) was surrendered to Cromwell's visitors and immediately granted, with its four manors and extensive acreage, to Sir John Dudley. The year 1539 saw the second Dissolution Act by which all remaining monastic property was appropriated to the Crown and more parcels of land came John's way. He did not keep them all and it would now be impossible to trace the deals struck in these years. In the booming market there was money to be made by careful speculation. Property passed rapidly from hand to hand as landowners great and small consolidated their holdings and tried to make quick profits. Dudley was just one of those who kept the lawyers busy drawing up deeds of sale and purchase and new leases.

The dissolution of the monasteries provided the greatest boost to domestic architecture before the industrial revolution. Noblemen, gentlemen and merchants were buying up abbey churches, conventual buildings, tithe barns and farms with the intention of converting them into fine houses or stripping them of all materials that could be sold or used for building elsewhere. Sir John was not one of those who indulged in an orgy of erecting status symbols. He did modernize Dudley Castle but he did so with an eye to comfort rather than spectacle. There were no professional architects in Tudor England but there were men who had a flair for house design and Sir John employed one of them to advise him. This was William Sharington, later famous for his work at Lacock Abbey, Wiltshire and infamous for abusing his position as vice-treasurer of the Bristol mint to defraud the Crown of thousands of pounds.

A modern visitor climbing the steep escarpment above the town to Dudley's ruined castle is confronted with a seemingly homogeneous jumble of broken, roofless walls ringing a wide area of greensward. Only careful study of guidebooks and plans unfolds the architectural history of the site and places Sir John's activities in perspective. He ensured that it remained a defensive fortification by retaining the twelfth-century curtain wall and fourteenth-century gatehouse and keep. Its formidable military structure was able to withstand a parliamentary siege during the Civil War. Sir John concentrated his efforts on the domestic range along the eastern side of the site. According to a twentieth-century expert, 'Nothing too high can be said of the beautiful simplicity of the design, or of the splendid manner of the execution . . . the convenience of the arrangements and the advanced nature of their comforts is little short of wonderful.'[15] Several features of this house anticipated the great age of Elizabethan domestic building. Having entered by the gatehouse and dismounted in the courtyard, Sir John and his guests were confronted by a flight of steps leading up to a loggia fronted by a row of ionic columns. This gave onto a porch from which a door led into the great hall, twenty-four metres in length, which was, very unusually, on the first floor. Morning and evening light streamed into this impressive space through large rectangular windows. As in all traditional major secular buildings, this was the centre of the household's life. However, Sir John's alterations added a private great chamber for himself and his family, partly created by reducing the size of the adjacent chapel. Over the extensive kitchen and buttery area there were four or five bed chambers. As noblemen's residences went Dudley Castle was certainly not large but the standard of its decoration, furniture, fixtures and fittings marked it out as something special.

On the evidence of his lifestyle John Dudley cannot be convicted of overweening pride, particularly when we compare his building programme with that of some of his contemporaries. Cromwell acquired the enormous site of the Austin Friars priory in London's Broad Street as well as several neighbouring properties in order to create for himself a town house of impressive splendour. At Ewhurst in Surrey he erected a new country mansion of no less striking proportions. Edward Seymour, also, built himself magnificent palaces in town and country, Somerset House and Syon House.

At the beginning of 1540 John returned to the centre of affairs, perhaps on the orders of Cromwell. The minister had, he thought, brought off a major political coup. He had arranged a marriage between King Henry and Anne, the sister of the Duke of Cleves-Mark-Julich-Berg, a strategically placed Rhineland territory. Although Duke William was not a Lutheran this alliance could tie England into a relationship with the reformist princes of the Schmalkaldic League, thus creating a third force in European politics and ensuring the establishment of the Reformation at home. The new queen had to be provided with an entourage and this gave Cromwell an opportunity to establish more of his supporters at court. John Dudley now received the office of Master of the Horse to Anne of Cleves and his wife became one of her ladies in waiting. These were senior positions in the royal household and necessitated close personal attendance on the sovereign and his consort. Dudley's role involved him in supervising all the queen's travel arrangements as well as attending her on ceremonial occasions. If he was looking for a breakthrough into the upper air of power and influence this should have been it. Unfortunately fortune's wheel had not stopped spinning. In the next few months its accelerated revolution threatened to fling him down once and for all.

7

King's Knight and God's Knight

───✦───

John had his first sight of his new mistress on 2 January 1540 as part of a delegation sent to meet her party near Deptford and escort her to London.

> the Earl of Rutland, who is to be her Lord Chamberlain, Sir Thomas Dennis, Chancellor, Sir Edward Baynton, Vice-chancellor, Sir John Dudley, Master of her Horse, and all others to be appointed to her council . . . 30 in all, shall meet her and be presented by the Archbishop of Canterbury and the Dukes of Norfolk and Suffolk, as her own train and household, and so to wait upon her till she approach the King's presence, when all the yeomen and meaner sort shall avoid.[1]

Soldiers were out early on 3 January putting up crush barriers to contain the thousands of people who congregated on Blackheath during the morning. Even more citizens watched from gaily decorated boats which crowded the river. All were eager to see the spectacle and to catch their first glimpse of the new queen. Anne and her retinue arrived about midday and if the focal point of all those eyes was nervous she must have been much heartened by the warm welcome of the people who would shortly be her subjects. With her close attendants she immediately retired to brightly coloured pavilions which had been erected for the occasion. Here she took refreshment and changed into a gown of cloth of gold overlaid with jewelled chains to await Henry's arrival. When news was brought to Henry that Anne was ready to proceed he left the palace mounted on a magnificent horse caparisoned in cloth of gold. To the sound of trumpets his elaborate procession of guards, courtiers, councillors and foreign dignitaries made its way across the park for the ceremonial act of public greeting. Anne rode out to meet her husband-to-be with all her ladies and her German and English attendants. The royal couple exchanged courtesies, then the entire procession made its way back to the palace, all in due order according to protocol. After the armed escort rode civic and court dignitaries, then the gentlemen of the privy chamber with Anne's ladies in waiting. They were followed by members of the diplomatic corps,

> then the Lord Privy Seal and the Lord Chancellor, then the Lord Marquess with the King's sword, next followed by the King himself, equally riding with his fair lady, and behind him rode Sir Anthony Brown with the King's horse of estate . . . and behind him rode Sir John Dudley, Master of her Horses, leading her spare palfrey . . .[2]

On 6 January the marriage took place but the new union was doomed before it started. Henry had been shocked when he met Anne and he went to the bridal bed feeling more like a condemned criminal marching to the scaffold than an eager husband. When it came to the point he was unable to consummate the union though, as he assured his doctors, it was not for lack of trying. Of course, there was no question in his mind but that the fault for his impotence lay with Anne; she failed to stimulate his desire. He felt trapped and humiliated. Diplomatic realities prevented him wriggling out of the marriage: as long as Charles and Francis were parading their new found amity he did not dare upset the Duke of Cleves. Yet his new wife was obviously not going to provide him with the two things he craved above all other – pleasure and children. In his unchecked egotism Henry indulged the fantasy that within his bloated and increasingly pain-racked body there lurked a lusty young buck ever ready for sexual adventure. Anyone who was the instrument of bringing him face to face with reality ran the risk of encountering his terrible wrath. It was his energetic denial of the truth which, within weeks, set him chasing after another young chit-about-court, Catherine Howard.

Well schooled by her uncle, the Duke of Norfolk, and other members of the mighty Howard clan, the teenage Catherine led the king on and a besotted Henry fancied himself in a rapture of love. Here, at last, was the woman who would give the Tudor line a bevy of princes and provide him with comfort for his remaining years. Henry was not going to let that chance slip through his fingers and he began casting round for ways to escape his fourth marriage without courting diplomatic disaster. He dispatched Norfolk to France to explore the possibility of prising Francis away from the Habsburg–Valois alliance.

It seems scarcely credible that for some weeks the knowledge that all was not well with the royal marriage was kept from the members of the queen's household, yet such seems to have been the case. It was important to prevent rumours from reaching foreign diplomats and so the councillors with whom the king shared his dilemma were sworn to secrecy. But did Anne not drop any hints to her attendants? The answer is no, because she was not aware that anything was wrong. There were two reasons for this. She was a stranger in England bending all her concentration on getting to grips with the native customs and language. She was also incredibly naive. She genuinely believed that when her husband came to her chamber several nights a week and kissed her and spoke kindly to her that that was all marital relations entailed. Eventually the queen's ladies, eagerly awaiting signs of a royal pregnancy, deduced the truth of Henry's nocturnal inactivity and, by the Spring, tongues started wagging about the king and Mistress Howard. The Dudleys were among the first to be aware of the gossip but if John was concerned about the impact of a royal estrangement on his own prospects such reflections were soon elbowed aside by other anxieties. A political storm was blowing up which threatened men to whom he was dangerously close.

Henry sometimes referred to Calais as the most troublesome of all his dominions. It was the resort of spies, fugitives and intriguers who dreamed of influencing affairs in England but feared getting any closer to the island. Inevitably, the ideological storms of the Reformation wrought disproportionate havoc in the small community. Every shift in the religious wind was nicely gauged by political meteorologists in the pay of Charles and Francis. The disruptive activities of rival preachers and gangs of image-breakers were a constant annoyance to the Deputy but Plantagenet discovered that the more he complained to his superiors, the less notice they took. There was good reason for this. Arthur put all the blame for religious strife on the evangelicals. Cromwell and Cranmer, on the other hand, were much more concerned about papal agents and sympathizers getting the upper hand. Thus, when Plantagenet arrested troublemakers and sent them across the Channel for investigation, he suffered the humiliation of seeing them return after a few weeks with the blessing of the Lord Privy Seal or the archbishop. He knew, moreover, that they and their friends had been carrying tales about him to the court and he was obliged to protest his utter loyalty to Cromwell, a man he increasingly loathed. As if that was not worrying enough, he had to suffer the Lord Privy Seal's written sermons about not authorizing witch hunts:

. . . he or they, whatsoever they be that would without great and substantial ground be authors or setters forth of . . . rumours may appear rather desirous of sedition than of quiet and unity . . . And therefore mine opinion is that you shall by all means devise how, with charity and mild handling of things, to quench this slanderous bent as much as you may . . .[3]

By 1539 Arthur's patience was at breaking point. He embarked on the dangerous game of court intrigue, using his own contacts among the king's more conservative advisers to draw his majesty's attention to the fact that Calais was becoming a breeding ground of vile heresy. He knew that he was playing with fire. 'I beseech you keep this matter close,' he urged one of his correspondents, 'for if it should come to my Lord Privy Seal's knowledge or ear, I were half undone.'[4] Norfolk and his friends noted well that they had a potential ally in Arthur Plantaganet and as soon as Cromwell was in difficulties over the Cleves alliance they used his complaints in the dossier of evidence they were compiling about the dangerous spread of religious radicalism throughout the king's realm. One result was that a commission was despatched to Calais in March 1540 to enquire into the religious situation there.

Going over Cromwell's head in this way is a further indication of Arthur's naivety. He was well out of his league in pitting himself against such a seasoned and ruthless politician. The minister could not stop the commission but he could make sure that his own clients appeared before it to give evidence of suspicious activities at Calais taking place under Plantagenet's nose and not reported by him. Certain 'sacramentaries' were arrested and referred back to London for trial but so, too, were a group of men involved in the 'Botolf conspiracy'. Gregory Botolf, an ardent papist, had been one of Plantagenet's domestic chaplains. He had obtained a pass allowing him to return to England but had instead made a clandestine journey to Rome and there met with representatives of

Cardinal Pole. The plot which resulted was a hare-brained scheme, almost entirely of Botolf's devising, to betray Calais into the hands of the king's enemies. In mid-April Cromwell engineered the Deputy's recall. The royal summons informed Plantagenet that Henry wished to have the benefit of his representative's personal advice on matters relating to the town. Arthur hastened to obey. At last he was going to have the opportunity of a personal interview with the king and would be able to make clear how the Vicegerent in Spirituals was encouraging heresy and frustrating the endeavours of royal servants to ensure the smooth running of Calais. He also believed that a grateful king had it in mind to bestow fresh honours on him, perhaps the earldom of Essex, recently become vacant by the death of Lord Bourchier. Arthur was, indeed, well received at court, where Henry greeted him affectionately. But Cromwell was carefully accumulating his evidence and on 19 May Arthur Plantagenet, Lord Lisle was suddenly arrested and conveyed to the Tower on suspicion of treason. A few weeks later a new Earl of Essex was named – Thomas Cromwell.

These were nerve-racking days but all John Dudley could do was fulfil his court duties and stay close to his all-powerful patron. Though past his athletic best, he was still a formidable contender in the tiltyard and in the May Day celebrations he took the star role. Challenges were sent to France, Spain, Scotland and the Low Countries inviting the courts to send their best champions against a home team led by Sir John Dudley. To open the festivities at Westminster he led his colleagues, Thomas Seymour, Thomas Poynings, George Carew, Anthony Kingston and Richard Cromwell (the minister's nephew) into the lists, 'richly apparelled and their horses trapped all in white velvet'. There followed six days of competition featuring every kind of mounted and foot combat and the highlight of the week was a banquet which Dudley gave for the king and queen and all the court at Durham House in Holborn. On another day 'they cheered all the knights and burgesses of the Common house in the parliament and entertained the Mayor of London with the aldermen and their wives at a dinner.' It was a costly exercise but Dudley and his comrades in arms were well rewarded, for the king presented each of them with, 'one hundred marks [about £66] and a house to dwell in of yearly revenue out of the lands pertaining to the Hospital of St John of Jerusalem.'[5] This complex of buildings between Smithfield and Clerkenwell had recently come into royal hands with the dissolution of the order (the last item of monastic real estate to be confiscated).

The May Day celebrations were the last public events at which Queen

Anne presided with her husband. Thereafter, Henry abandoned the pretence of his marriage. He was spurred on by his infatuation with Catherine Howard but also by the fact that the Cleves match had lost its diplomatic importance. The Franco-Imperial alliance had fallen apart and, as Norfolk and his cronies readily pointed out to Henry, he no longer needed close relations with the heretic Germans and the religious opprobrium which this carried.

Now Cromwell's enemies in the Council threw everything into a desperate attempt to destroy him and he responded in kind. Catholic and Protestant activists were arrested and examined in frenzied attempts to find damning evidence. Spies and informers did a brisk trade. The French ambassador accurately assessed the situation: 'things are at such a pass that either the party of . . . Cromwell must succumb or that of the Bishop of Winchester [Gardiner] with his adherents.'[6] In such an unstable situation momentous events could be decided by minor, even trivial, circumstances, such as the timing of a messenger's arrival with the latest news from abroad, or what rumour emerged about fresh heretical activity, or what mood the king was in, or who happened to have access to him at the psychological moment. Such eventualities could not be foreseen and none of the principals concerned could anticipate when he might be transformed from trusted adviser to doomed traitor in the twinkling of an eye. In the event it was Cromwell who was dealt the ace of spades. Arriving for a Council meeting on 10 June he was astounded to be arrested and rushed to the Tower. On 28 July a bungling headsman dispatched him on Tower Hill.

John Dudley must have reflected that his earlier decision to distance himself from the court had been the right one. Henry's divorce from Anne of Cleves deprived him and his wife of their positions. His patron had been executed for treason. His stepfather daily expected the same fate. With relief John made his way back to the relative calm of the English heartland.

The king was deliriously happy with his nubile young wife, the Howards and their conservative clique were firmly ensconced in royal favour and radical preachers were subdued by anti-heretical legislation. The evangelical caucus in the royal household had not dissipated but its members were now obliged to be very circumspect. Most would have echoed the advice of one of the junior members of their party: 'Let us not be too rash or quick in maintaining the Scriptures. If we wait quietly and do not oppose [the Duke of Norfolk and the Bishop of Winchester], but rather suffer a while in silence, they will overthrow *themselves*. For they stand so obviously against God and their prince that they cannot long survive.'[7] The speaker was John Lascelles, a Nottinghamshire gentleman who was one of the senior attendants at the king's table. He was soon to cast his caution to the winds and grasp eagerly an opportunity to attack the enemies of the Gospel.

London and its environs held little attraction for Dudley in the aftermath of Cromwell's death. Conservative vigilantes were trying to cash in on what they believed to be a return to pre-Cromwellian orthodoxy. Informers were denouncing men and women for alleged breaches of the Act of Six Articles and the Catholic backlash was vigorous and merciless. At one point Bishop Bonner of London had five hundred accused heretics penned up in foetid prisons in the heat of one of the most sweltering summers in living memory. Moreover, the reactionaries were determined to purge the establishment of all the fallen minister's allies. Early in 1541 Dudley's friend, Sir Thomas Wyatt, was among those who had to endure a spell in prison before the king intervened to set him free.

Cranmer and his colleagues were by no means quiescent under this new wave of persecution. The archbishop came to the rescue of clergy denounced by their enemies, carried the attack into his opponents' camp and made sure that the king was informed of all manoeuvres aimed at bringing down those who enjoyed royal favour. What was now beginning to appear at the centre of English political life was a bifurcation largely along religious lines. The Howard–Gardiner faction was counterpoised by Cranmer, Seymour and their friends in chamber and Council. Both groups of leaders had their sympathizers throughout all levels of the royal household. The resultant dialogue of the deaf was inevitable for two reasons. One was the inner momentum of the Reformation. The religious revival could not be stopped. Men and women in the grip of confessional fervour who felt themselves betrayed by the institutional church were only emboldened by persecution. However, those who saw the traditions of their fathers being uprooted were by no means convinced that the Reformation was irreversible and were bitter in their resentment. Clergy who witnessed the alarming disintegration of the structures which guaranteed their power and their accustomed place in society were determined to resist further change.

The other reason was a revolution in the workings of government. For over three decades the king had relied heavily on powerful, semi-independent chief ministers to undertake the tedious routine of running the nation's affairs. After June 1540 Henry was sometimes heard to complain angrily that he had been tricked into getting rid of Cromwell, but he never found (and probably never sought) another political major-domo. For their part, councillors who had resented being lorded over by one of their own number were determined to resist the emergence of another Wolsey or Cromwell. Council deliberations, therefore, had more importance and that meant that rivalries became more acute. Indeed they sometimes took on homicidal intensity, as we shall see. But Henry was still king and still determined that his will should prevail, whatever his advisers might propose. There were henceforth two vigorous currents engaging with each other in the dynamic of government. Councillors and members of the chamber staff constantly sought Henry's support for their schemes, while the king pursued his own agenda and expected his servants to carry it out. For a man like John Dudley, who had little stomach for party fervour and confrontation, property speculation and estate building in the Midlands had distinctly more appeal than attempting to resurrect a court career.

Meanwhile, court radicals were handed on a plate a spectacular opportunity for revenge. Gossip around the royal household suggested that Catherine was not the pure, utterly devoted wife she pretended to be. One courtier, moved by what he believed to be the highest of motives, resolved to discover the truth. His name was John Lascelles. This earnest evangelical had a sister, Mary Hall, who had been a servant in the household of the Dowager Duchess of Norfolk at a time when Catherine had been billeted there and she had been a party to secret assignations which the teenage girl and her friends had carried on under the nose of their chaperone with various lusty young bucks. Lascelles persuaded Mary to tell all she knew then, armed with names, dates and salacious details, he sought out Archbishop Cranmer at Whitehall and laid the information before him. Cranmer discussed these serious revelations with his colleagues and they all decided that Henry must be told (it would, indeed, have been treason to conceal the unpalatable truth from him). Cranmer wrote the details of Lascelles' story in a confidential note and waited an opportunity to pass it to the king. On 29 October, Henry came to Hampton Court and it was in the chapel there, four days later, that the archbishop handed over his bombshell.

Far from flying into a rage, the king simply declined to believe what he was told but he did order discreet enquiries to be made into this 'malicious gossip'. While the inquisition was taking place, Henry removed to Whitehall and never saw his fifth wife again. After some days Catherine also travelled downriver but only as far as Syon Abbey, the grand house Edward Seymour was creating from the surrendered monastic establishment near Brentford. It was here that Cranmer finally extracted a full confession from the distracted queen, not only of her pre-marital sexual adventures, but of various indiscretions she had committed since becoming queen. The damning document was carried and delivered to the king by John Dudley. Why was he at his old friend's house at this critical time? Why was he entrusted with this delicate mission? It would be helpful to know the exact circumstances of his involvement, but in the absence of such knowledge we are thrown back on intelligent guesswork. It may be that, realizing that a crucial turning point in the faction struggle at court had been reached, he judged the time right to reappear at court. If Lord Hertford [Edward Seymour], Cranmer and their supporters were about to assume the ascendancy, he wanted to be among their number. What is clear is that he was trusted by the evangelical leaders and was sufficiently intimate with the king to be able to bear the ill tidings of Catherine Howard's irresponsible behaviour.

That behaviour brought her to her sorry end beneath the headsman's axe on 13 February 1542. Seventeen days later another death occurred within the Tower which had an even greater impact on John Dudley's fortunes. Arthur Plantaganet had been languishing there ever since his arrest in May 1540. He and his family had expected him to be released in the aftermath of Cromwell's fall but month succeeded anxious month and the old man remained incarcerated. No indictment was brought and, if his case was thoroughly investigated, no record has survived. His miseries seem to have been occasioned by the continuing nervousness about Yorkist–papist rebellion and Henry's determination to make examples of any suspected of the slightest whiff of treason. In the spring of 1541, the king put down a minor rebellion in Yorkshire and also ordered the execution of Margaret Pole, Countess of Salisbury, the daughter of George, Duke of Clarence. The death of this cousin, also a long-term prisoner in the Tower, must have been very alarming for Arthur. But still he was kept in ignorance of his fate. In January 1542 he was restored to the Order of the Garter but he remained in prison – it was all very confusing. At last, on 3 March, Henry sent his secretary to the Tower with a token of his favour and a promise of imminent release. Alas, the rush of euphoria, following months of listlessness and depression proved to be too much for the octogenarian peer. As John Foxe succinctly and moralistically explained,

When the king's majesty minded to have been gracious unto him and to have let him come forth, God took him out of this world, whose body resteth in the Tower and his soul with God, I trust, in heaven, for he died very repentant.[8]

The viscountcy of Lisle was now vacant and, under the ordinary rules of inheritance John might have automatically succeeded to it in right of his mother. Ironically, his own eager property dealing had created a problem. One condition of holding the tenure of the title was ownership of the manor of Kingston Lisle, Berkshire, and John had sold it in 1538. A new patent was required if he was to attain the peerage he had always looked forward to gaining.[9] It is a mark of the favour he enjoyed that, within days, the heralds had drawn up the necessary document and the king approved it. On 12 March, Sir John Dudley stood before his sovereign in the privy chamber at Whitehall to be mantled in velvet and ermine and to hear his new honours proclaimed: 'Viscount Lisle, Baron Malpas and Lord Basset of Tyasse.' He was now the senior member of the ancient family of Sutton de Dudley. He was also thirty-eight years of age. Promotion had come none too soon.

From this moment John Dudley was thrust into the very forefront of national life. Honours and appointments that had hitherto eluded him now came his way. In part this was a belated recognition of his qualities. He was an established courtier and a tried and tested military leader. Throughout the difficult years he had kept himself out of trouble, sometimes by absenting himself from court. Though loyally committed to the Tudor regime, he always had his father's fate at the back of his mind as a warning not to associate himself too closely with unpopular policies. Up to this point he seems not to have been closely identified with radical religious activism. However, friends like Seymour, Cranmer, Anthony Denny, Chief Gentleman of the Privy Chamber, and Sir William Butts, the king's physician, who were the leading evangelicals at court, knew their man and may well have used their influence on his behalf. At a time of acute religious polarization they took every opportunity to strengthen their party.

The timing was certainly fortuitous for Dudley. Henry ran his own unique form of ecumenical movement by publicly punishing undue religious zeal, whether Catholic and Protestant. For example, immediately after Cromwell's death he had six men executed at Tyburn. Three 'sacramentaries' were burned for heresy while three 'papists' suffered the penalty for treason. In the same spirit of knowing what was best for his country he determined to put an end to seventeen years of peace. His belligerence, no longer tamed by cost-conscious ministers, reasserted itself in a decision to wage war against Scotland and France. This ruinous, wilful change of policy, which frittered away the massive financial gains which the great ecclesiastical land grab had brought into the treasury had a very dubious basis in logic.

He had invited the Scottish king, James V, to meet him at York, during his summer progress in 1541 to discuss relations between their two countries but James did not turn up. This was enough to form a calculated pretext for war. Henry was about to go campaigning again in France and he had to secure his own postern gate before he ventured across the Channel. With two military adventures in the planning the king needed generals. Since some of England's tried and tested leaders had died and others were too old for active service it was inevitable that a new generation of field officers would have to take their places. John Dudley rose rapidly to prominence among them. Within weeks of his ennoblement he was sent north as part of a commission to examine the strengthening of Berwick's defences, a necessary preparation for forth-coming hostilities with Scotland. The king's representatives discovered that all was far from satisfactory in the border garrison and they had to take a tough line with the local authorities and workmen in order to complete work by the end of the summer so that the town could be used as a secure base when the Duke of Norfolk arrived with an army of 20,000 to harry the Lowlands.

Having done his job, Dudley returned to court but he was soon back on the border with a much more exalted title. The position of Lord Warden of the Marches became vacant on the retirement of the Earl of Rutland and Henry appointed Edward Seymour, who was on the spot as part of the military contingent. However, the ambitious Seymour did not relish the prospect of a long absence from the centre of power and excused himself on the grounds that 'the country knew not him nor he them.' After considering various other candidates, Henry decided to confer this important political and military position on Dudley. As well as his more obvious qualifications, Dudley's commitment to religious reform may well have commended him to Henry. In his negotiations with the Scots it suited the king to show his radical face. He urged the ruler north of the border to follow his own example in throwing off papal allegiance, ridding his realm of monasticism and redistributing ecclesiastical property. In order to make this transformation as palatable as possible it would be necessary to instruct the people in the 'truth'. Henry knew that Dudley would enthusiastically support such a policy and, indeed, we find the new Lord Warden, a few months later, organizing the despatch of vernacular Bibles to evangelical colporteurs in Scotland.

Dudley arrived back at Berwick at a crucial moment. When he was still on the road news reached him of the Battle of Solway Moss. James V had been provoked into launching a large but inadequately prepared force across the border. On 25 November 1542 it was challenged by a smaller English army north of Carlisle and comprehensively routed. A large number of Scottish noblemen were captured and sent to London to become sources of information and valuable bargaining pieces in Henry's diplomacy. Even more significant was the death of James V. The disaster of Solway Moss helped to undermine a weak constitution and the thirty-year-old king died on 14 December. He left a bevy of illegitimate children and one heiress only a few days old, Mary, Queen of Scots.

In Edinburgh all was now confusion. The rival factions were far too busy jockeying for position among themselves to give a great deal of thought to relations with England. The situation was scarcely less difficult for Henry and his representatives on the border. They did not know whom to deal with and whether to proceed by diplomacy or force. For Dudley the immediate problem was what to do with the thousands of men he had under arms. If there was to be no immediate military campaign he would have to pay many of them off as quickly as possible. He was seriously short of money (a not-unusual situation for Tudor commanders) and had no desire to feed and quarter through the winter more men than was absolutely necessary. Logistical problems will have been uppermost in his mind when he offered the king seemingly charitable advice: 'seeing God hath thus disposed his will of the said King of Scots, I thought it should not be to your Majesty's honour that we your soldiers should make war or invade upon a dead body or upon a widow or upon a young suckling, his daughter.'[10] Henry seems to have agreed – for the time being. He needed to gather information about the state of the parties and to consider his options. Whereas he had been thinking about bullying his nephew into neutrality and quiescence, now a greater prize lay within his grasp; nothing less than the union of the crowns. He bent all his efforts towards securing an alliance cemented by the marriage of the infants Edward and Mary.

8

Tempestuous Seas

In January 1543 John Dudley received the appointment that of all the positions he ever held he found the most congenial. Hardly had he begun to stamp his personality on the administration of the north when he was instructed to take up the post of Lord Admiral. Again, there seems to have been some suggestion that Hertford should assume this role but, in the reshuffle, he managed to secure the more influential position of Lord Chamberlain, which, being the chief office of the royal household, ensured him regular access to the king. Dudley's promotion was an enormous step up the ladder, for the position was a political one and carried with it membership of the Council, and to enhance his new dignity he was admitted to the Order of the Garter. He had arrived at the 'high table'. His appointment was to prove of vital significance in the history of the royal navy.

The Lord Admiral was one of the great officers of state. Hitherto, the position had not necessarily demanded any great knowledge of naval matters. It was often bestowed as a reward for service and usually involved some mix of military, diplomatic and ceremonial activities. The previous holder, Lord John Russell, who had only occupied the post since 1540, was typical in that he was an intimate of the king with access to the chamber, had served on several foreign embassies, had attended the king on campaign and had been, since 1538, a member of the Council. Henry was fascinated by ships. The proud man-o'-war with gleaming paintwork, bulging sails and streaming pennants was a brave and powerful status symbol and a potent demonstration to brother monarchs. However the construction and maintenance of new vessels was an extremely costly undertaking and even the self-aggrandizing Henry could only justify it in time of war. The traditional custom followed by his government was to sponsor a modest shipbuilding programme and augment the fleet by hiring merchantmen when a national crisis demanded extra expenditure.

It was when England became caught up in (or plunged headlong into) an arms race that this cautious policy was threatened. A mix of strategic needs and royal pride led to the rapid build up of a permanent navy. It began early in the reign. James IV of Scotland astonished everyone by launching, in 1511, the *Great Michael*, the biggest and best equipped ship in northern waters. Henry took this as a challenge, almost a personal affront, and responded by ordering the massive, 1,000 ton *Henri Grace à Dieu*, which left the dockyard in 1514. At the same time the government became alarmed by the appearance of French galleys in the Channel. These oared vessels had been brought from the Mediterranean in the belief that their speed and manoeuvrability would give them an advantage in a stretch of water where wind force and direction were notoriously unreliable. The experiment, in the event, was unsuccessful but it did prompt shipbuilders to explore methods of dealing with this perceived threat. One way of preventing galleys from getting close enough to grapple was to provide naval vessels with effective firepower. The age of naval artillery had begun. Within three decades the emphasis changed from relatively small bow chasers to large cannon housed in the stern and amidships, firing through ports which could be closed when not in use. This involved using new construction techniques to create ships that were strong enough and stable enough to carry heavy armament.

Throughout the 1530s, when Henry was not involved in foreign adventures, construction was very limited. Many vessels were sold or laid up. It was the last years of the king's reign that witnessed a virtual frenzy of rearmament. Almost half of the new vessels added to the national fleet were acquired between 1540 and 1546 and fifteen of them were in excess of 300 tons. This involved building or extending the royal dockyards at Deptford and Woolwich and the creation of a massive naval base at Portsmouth. Nor was this the only kind of construction that the southern sea-facing counties witnessed. As part of an overall offensive–defensive strategy Henry studded the coast from Kent to Cornwall with castles to guard principal havens. All this was part of a well-conceived plan which was to enable Henry to launch his major attack on France. But, of course the king did not personally draw up all the blueprints, keep the books and scrutinize every major item of expenditure. There had to be an effective central administration. Clearly, the old, makeshift organization for the navy would no longer serve. Throughout 1545 a series of discussions took place which eventually led to the establishment of the Council for Marine Causes, the direct forerunner of the Navy Board and the Board of Admiralty. Its establishment marked – if the pun may be forgiven – a sea change in the nature of the royal navy. And the man who presided over this transformation was John Dudley.

It is no accident that the single most important institutional reform in the whole history of the navy occurred as soon as John Dudley had settled into his role as naval chief. He was a new kind of Lord Admiral, a hands-on leader with experience of command by land and sea, but also a permanent official, rather than a 'sea general' only active in wartime. He might not have notched up any dramatic victories in the field by 1543 but he had shown himself an effective general. Furthermore, his long service at the Tower armoury had provided him with a detailed working knowledge of artillery which was playing an increasingly diverse role in warfare by land and sea. But was he in any way gifted as an administrator? If we took his own protestations at face value we should have to assume that he was not. Dudley was always aware of his shortcomings. A couple of years earlier, when reporting as Warden in the North, he had claimed to be a simple soldier, out of his depth in matters of high politics and administration.

> Your Lordships doth know my bringing up. I have never been practised nor experimented in no matters of council before this time. At my first coming hither it was open war; it was then more easier to conduce those affairs than these which be presently in hand. Therefore, knowing mine own infirmity and the fear that it puts me in day and night, lest anything should pass through my negligence contrary to the King's majesty's pleasure, I can no less of my bounden duty and for mine own discharge but still to trouble your lordships herewith.[1]

Had he been as utterly lacking in self-belief as such letters suggest he would have been a poor commander, which clearly he was not, and he would not have enjoyed the king's confidence, which manifestly he did.

What we have to make allowance for is that both convention and prudence demanded humility in official correspondence. A certain obsequiousness was expected of all royal servants, from the lowest to the highest and all those who were about the king's business were ever at pains to be seen to be carrying out the *king's* will and not their own, to the best of their ability and to make sure that Henry appreciated this. Working for tyrants always has an inhibiting effect on the exercise of individual initiative and Dudley had the fate of his father and stepfather to remind him of what happened to men who could be represented as having gone beyond their instructions. It is scarcely surprising, therefore, to find him writing from his flagship to the Council for clarification of orders and insisting, 'it shall be most requisite that the King's majesty's instructions . . . be devised by your lordships and to be signed by the King's majesty and to be sent hither with speed.'[2]

The reality behind this almost painful prudence was that John Dudley had arrived in a job he loved and to which he now devoted enthusiasm, industry and creative thought. He played a central role in the shaping of the new Council for Marine Causes, which was modelled on the Ordnance Office. It comprised six officials directly answerable to the Lord Admiral, each with clearly defined responsibilities and a salary commensurate to the considerable volume of work he had to undertake. But, busy as he was in overseeing the administration of the navy, he remained first and foremost a man of action, never happier than when on campaign.

The new Lord Admiral's mettle was put to the test in 1544. Henry was determined to launch his invasion of France as soon as the campaigning season was open but first he decided to make sure of Scotland by means of a rapid strike against Edinburgh. Seymour was given overall command and Dudley was charged with conveying the bulk of the 16,000 strong army to Newcastle. Dudley embarked the troops on sixty-eight ships at Harwich and reached Tynemouth on 18 April. Joined by the commander-in-chief and the force that he had assembled in the north, Dudley now conveyed the entire army to the Firth of Forth. As soon as the complex task of landing men, horses and equipment had been completed Seymour set his battle plan in motion. He gave command of the vanguard to Dudley and followed with the main force. It was Dudley's men who had the only military encounter of the campaign, though it was one scarcely worthy of the name 'skirmish': 'at first the Scots made towards the Englishmen as though they would have set on the vanguard but when they perceived the Englishmen so willing to encounter with them . . . they made a sudden retreat and, leaving their artillery behind them, fled towards Edinburgh.'[3]

Dudley's men occupied Leith, where 'they found such riches as they thought not to have found in any town of Scotland.'[4] The most exciting loot took the form of two modern ships, the *Unicorn* and the *Salamander* (the latter a present from Francis I to the Scottish king). The army moved on to invest Edinburgh and, Seymour having refused terms, Dudley positioned his culverin and blasted open the Canongate. The invaders surged through determined 'utterly to ruinate and destroy the said town by fire.'[5] According to Hall, the conflagration raged for three days, although most citizens were safe within Edinburgh's virtually impregnable castle. Seymour then went on to harry his way through the Lowlands as a vivid expression of his master's indignation and to ensure that the border region would be safe as Henry turned his attention towards France. Meanwhile, Dudley was ordered to embark 5,000 men immediately for the forthcoming trans-Channel campaign. He hurried back to London preceded by Seymour's well-deserved commendation:

> Pleaseth your Highness to be advertised that, forasmuch as my Lord Admiral repaireth unto your Majesty, I can do no less to recommend him unto your Highness as one that hath served you hardly, wisely, diligently, painfully and as obediently as any that I have seen, most [humbly] beseeching your Majesty that he may perceive by your Highness that I have not forgotten him.[6]

By mid-June Dudley had seen the king and his army of 30,000 safely across to Calais and he then took his place as second in command to the Duke of Suffolk in the siege of Boulogne. As a member of the headquarters staff he was constantly in the royal presence, and Henry was in buoyant mood. He quickly abandoned the strategy agreed with the emperor and directed all his attention to besieging Boulogne and Montreuil. It was 1513 all over again and Henry was dazzled by the prospect of adding significant mainland towns to his empire. The Duke of Norfolk failed in his attempt to invest Montreuil but the main thrust of the English attack was reserved for Boulogne and, on 18 September, Henry VIII was able to make a triumphal entrance to his new Channel port. Dudley basked in the king's favour but for him the glory of conquest was soon to be overshadowed. He had been accompanied from England by his eighteen-year-old son and heir, Henry, who was having his first taste of military action. It was also to be his last. A proud father saw him knighted by the king but shortly afterwards the young man died, either from wounds sustained in battle or from camp fever.

There was little time for his father to grieve. His military duties kept him very busy. Then, when the fighting was over, he was ordered to stay behind as Captain of Boulogne. This was a dubious honour. For one thing, the town's defences had taken a heavy battering. If the French attempted to recapture it, as they most assuredly would, Dudley and his garrison would be hard put to hang onto Henry's proud possession. Furthermore, Dudley feared that he had been manoeuvred into this position by more powerful men who were determined to avoid the poisoned chalice themselves. They returned home with the king, leaving Dudley far from the centre of influence in what could rapidly become a backwater (his stepfather's fate cannot have been far from his mind). Specifically, he was worried that the Admiralty might be taken away from him and bestowed upon some importunate courtier with ready access to the king. He put his anxieties in writing, probably in a memo for the Council:

> My trust is that I shall have the King's majesty's favour to enjoy the office of High Admiralty of England, for it is an office of honour, of estimation and of profit and within the realm; and, having his gracious favour thereunto I may occupy it with a deputy and serve this [post] notwithstanding, which I beseech your lordships to consider.[7]

'Honour', 'estimation', 'profit' and 'within the realm' – Dudley was quite up front about why he wanted to retain the Lord Admiral's office. It was a position which he genuinely valued for itself and in which he believed he could serve effectively. It was certainly profitable; the head of the navy received a major share of all prizes taken in war and of all pirate vessels apprehended. He had the placing of contracts for supplies and equipment and also the granting of commissions, all of which had financial strings attached. And it involved frequent attendance at court, close to the centre of power. Dudley had, it seems, overcome his nervousness about the turbulent waters which eddied around the throne. Now he was concerned about being kept *away* from the place where reputations and fortunes were made: he had passed the point of no return. It was becoming increasingly likely that Henry would not achieve his aim of staying alive until his son had come of age, and that meant that there would be a regency. Therefore the rival groups in court and Council manoeuvred with a vigorous and ruthless sense of urgency. Colours had to be nailed to the mast. Anyone who wished to stay at the centre of power could not afford to wait and see which way the wind blew.

Dudley was fully committed to the radical, progressive platform of the evangelical 'party'. Those in diplomatic circles were quite clear about government realities. It was almost in despair that, in 1546, the imperial ambassador reported,

> If the king favours these stirrers of heresy, the Earl of Hertford and the Lord Admiral, which is to be feared, both for the reasons I have already given and because the queen [Catherine Parr], instigated by the Duchess of Suffolk, the Countess of Hertford and the Lord Admiral's wife, shows herself infected, words and exhortations, even in the name of your Majesty, would only make the King more obstinate.[8]

However, we are ahead of ourselves. Part of the reason for Dudley's position of influence as the reign drew to its close lay in his conduct during the crisis of 1545. He had remained at Boulogne, working under great difficulties (not least of which were the lack of money and victuals for his men) to repair the fortifications as rapidly as possible. He was obviously successful, for in February the garrison beat off a large amphibious attempt to recapture the town and inflicted heavy losses on the French. By then Dudley had already been recalled. The government was fully expecting Francis I to launch an invasion attempt now that he was at peace with the Emperor and could direct his undivided attention against England. Dudley was needed to take charge of his country's first line of defence. He assumed this enormous responsibility under the grand title of 'Lieutenant General of the Army and Armada upon the Sea in Outward Parts against the French'.

For the first time since 1485 the English government was, in a state of great agitation, facing the prospect of a seaborne invasion. Their agents reported impressive movements of French ships and men, and rumour added frightening details to what could be deduced from intelligence sources. Thanks to the building works that had been progressing since 1539 the coast was fairly well defended and local authorities raised levies for the manning of the garrisons. What was in short supply was money. Henry had run through his monastic windfall and was already heavily in debt. He now had to resort to the debasement of the coinage in order to put his realm into a state of readiness, leaving his heir an appalling legacy. Yet, somehow, Dudley and his Council for

Marine Causes managed to get together the largest royal fleet England had ever seen. By June they were able to muster 160 ships and sufficient crews to man them. This involved having the shipyards working at maximum capacity, hiring and commandeering merchant vessels, sending out agents on a frenzied recruiting drive and paying the highest seamen's wages ever offered. So many mariners were added to the government payroll that along the Devon coast only women were left to take the fishing boats out.

The campaign of 1545 was a baptism of fire for the new Tudor navy. From reports of the various actions that took place we can gauge some of the improvements and innovations Henry and his Lord Admiral had been putting in place. They had not been slow to learn from the French. They had experimented with galleys (sometimes called 'galleases' or 'galliots'), propelled by both sails and oars. They had begun the development of naval artillery by commissioning iron cannon which could be ranged along a warship's sides and not just located in the bow (the *Mary Rose*, for example, carried ninety-six guns). They had induced leading French cartographers and hydrographers to cross the Channel. And, in order to provide the navy with a kind of auxiliary wing, they had introduced the system of letters of marque. These authorized the masters of merchant vessels to attack and plunder the ships of enemy nations. This legalized piracy immediately proved popular with the bolder captains and it played a significant part in securing England's mastery of the Narrow Seas. English vessels, prowling singly or in packs, preyed not only on French merchantmen, but also on those of Spain and the Netherlands, on the dubious grounds that the emperor's neutrality was, in fact, helping England's enemy. When foreign ambassadors protested the Admiralty court usually turned deaf ears to their complaints or ensured that judicial proceedings dragged on for months or years. Audacious raids culminated in March 1545 in Robert Reneger's capture of the Spanish *San Salvador*, inward-bound from the Americas with £4,300 in gold bullion. The king's Council managed to reach the conclusion that no law had been broken and Henry pocketed a sizeable proportion of the loot, which his government desperately needed. The activities we usually associate with Elizabeth's 'sea dogs' became common practice during the years that John Dudley was in charge of maritime affairs.

Dudley's patrols reported that his French opposite number, Claude d'Annebaut, had gathered groups of ships totalling somewhere between 160 and 300 in the harbours of Le Havre, Harfleur and Honfleur in readiness to embark the army. The existence of this formidable force lent substance to the rumours of a major invasion attempt. There seemed no point in waiting until Francis was ready to make his move. Dudley decided on a pre-emptive strike. With his best warships he made a sally into the Seine estuary, his objective being to inflict as much damage as possible on the enemy fleet. With this in mind, he set aside the usual tactic of grappling and boarding. He determined instead to remain in the deep water channel and use his artillery to best effect on the stationary shipping. Whether this plan would have worked he never discovered. The wind changed before he could come in range and he was obliged to break off the attack for fear of being driven into shoal water. He had to content himself with a skirmish between Alderney and Guernsey in which he sank several French galleys.

The best result of this action was that it stung d'Annebaut into retaliation. The French strategy had been, not the invasion of England, but the retaking of Boulogne. A land army was already advancing on the port and was to be heavily reinforced by sea. Now, however, the French admiral decided to strike at Dudley's fleet, the greater part of which was anchored at Portsmouth. The approach of 200 enemy sail served to reinforce the worst English fears. Armies were drawn up in Essex, Kent and Devon while Seymour commanded another on the Scottish border. Prayers were said in all churches and the king personally toured the southern counties to inspect the defences. He was actually in Portsmouth on 19 July when news arrived that d'Annebaut was in the Solent. With many other concerns on his mind, Dudley cannot have been entirely enthusiastic about entertaining his sovereign aboard the flagship, *Henri Grace à Dieu*. In fact, the dinner he hosted in the great cabin had to be brought to a hasty conclusion in order to convey the king safely ashore and prepare the vessel for battle.

In the event there was no real battle at all. The French made sporadic landings on the Isle of Wight, which were easily repulsed. Then, while Dudley's ships were confined at anchor by an onshore breeze, d'Annebaut sent a squadron of galleys to attack them. Fortuitously, the wind changed and Dudley was able to order his fleet to sea to engage the enemy. It was while turning into the wind with her gunports open in readiness that the *Mary Rose* heeled over and sank with the loss of Sir George Carew and 500 of his men. Lessons still had to be learned about the balancing of fire power and manoeuvrability. The disaster was a severe blow to the morale of Dudley's crews and to Henry who was among the crowd watching from the shore, but its actual significance at the time was not as great as its place in naval legend might suggest. Accidents of this magnitude were not uncommon. D'Annebaut had experienced a similar setback only days before when his flagship, the 800-ton *Caraquon*, had been completely burned out at anchor as a result of negligence. Dudley only paused to order a salvage crew to set to work on the sunken vessel before wearing out of the harbour to confront the foe. But the Spithead 'action' turned out to be a mirror image of Dudley's attack on the French fleet three weeks earlier. D'Annebaut drew his force off and made a few desultory sorties on the Sussex coast before crossing to Boulogne to land the 7,000 men for whom Francis was impatiently waiting.

There was now a pause, while Dudley took counsel with the king and his advisers. He was in a defensive posture and the initiative lay with the enemy. Until he could be sure what the French admiral planned he could not devise his counter-tactics. Not until 15 August did he get to grips with the opposing fleet. The engagement which followed off the Kent coast may be regarded as the first modern sea battle in history, inconclusive though it was. Both admirals drew their fleets up in formation (a departure from the traditional proceeding by which, because of the difficulties of communication, ships' captains had acted largely autonomously) and manoeuvred for position. D'Annebaut, whose force outnumbered the English two to one, gained the early advantage and he despatched his galleys. Then Dudley's warships grabbed the opportunity of a shifting wind to bear down on the oared vessels, which were forced to withdraw. The conflict now became a gun battle but neither side had done much damage to the other before night fell and the French used the darkness to retire to the safety of their own coast. The campaign was, to all intents and purposes, over and its termination was due more to circumstances beyond human control than to any decisive military advantage. Fickle Channel winds had prevented the fleets from grappling and plague now forced both admirals to downsize their crews and decommission ships. Henry ordered a reprisal raid against the French coast and, on 2 September, Dudley crossed to Normandy and put the small harbour town of Treport to fire and sword. Thereafter, he was obliged to allow impressed fishermen to return home and resume their livelihood.

Dudley had quitted himself well. His involvement in military affairs in three eventful years had shown him to be an industrious, intelligent and resourceful commander. His name was not associated with spectacular victories by land or sea but he had done all that was required of him and more. He had earned the king's esteem and made his mark in the life of the nation. Above all others John Dudley was seen as the man who had saved England from invasion.

On 24 August Henry had suffered a serious blow in the death of Charles Brandon, Duke of Suffolk. Throughout the whole reign Brandon had been at the king's side. He had filled the role of friend, jousting companion, military commander, brother-in-law (1514–32) and leading household official. As a last personal gesture of friendship Henry ordered that Brandon's body be interred at Windsor. The duke's demise left a highly important vacancy at court. Since 1540 Brandon had held the most senior of the household offices, the Lord Great Mastership. There seems to have been a possibility of Dudley's promotion to this exalted position. The appointment went to the veteran career courtier and political tactician, William Paulet, Lord St John. Did Dudley not have sufficient 'clout' to achieve his ambition or was he thwarted by being away from court at the crucial time when rewards were being handed out? It may be that powerful jealousies were active among the senior members of the household. Edward Seymour, in particular, would have found his own position as Lord Great Chamberlain strongly challenged if Dudley had become Lord Great Master. Seymour must already have been recognizing in his old colleague, even if he did not acknowledge it to himself, a greater military talent than his own. May we see here the first tiny crack in the old Seymour–Dudley friendship which was to widen into such a tragic fissure? Dudley did not, however, go unrewarded. Fresh grants of land came his way and, by 1546, he was among the ten wealthiest men in England.

Whatever he may have felt about his position in the household, Dudley had plenty to keep him occupied in the Admiralty. Plans for the new council were nearing completion. In January we find Dudley recommending Sir Thomas Clerc for the post of Lieutenant of the Admiralty and Sir William Woodhouse for that of Master of Ordnance to the king's ships. Both appointments were duly made and the Council for Marine Causes was constituted by letters patent on 24 April following. From that date the Lord High Admiral, who had previously only functioned in time of war, was involved regularly, with his colleagues, in the administration of the navy. The importance of the new body can scarcely be overstressed. It was the most sophisticated and efficient government office for maritime affairs in the whole of Europe. It gave the royal navy both permanence and individuality. It involved the government directly in all aspects of shipbuilding and seamanship.

One area of seamanship to which Dudley gave close and immediate attention was the art of navigation. Control of home waters was one thing but if English captains were to venture across the oceans and challenge the commercial monopolies of Spain and Portugal they needed training in the latest techniques and skills. The greatest living expert in such matters was Sebastian Cabot, Pilot Major to the emperor. The Venetian mariner, who as a young man had ventured across the Atlantic with his father, had frequently appealed in vain to Henry VIII in the early days of the reign to patronize further voyages of exploration. Eventually, he had turned his back on England and put his talents at the service of Charles V. He became head of the Spanish naval academy, the Casa da Contratacion, and compiled numerous charts from the information brought back by pioneer captains. He would be a valuable asset to any government seeking to expand its maritime commitment. Dudley and his agents made vigorous attempts to lure the veteran mariner back. The emperor's advisers worked just as strenuously to prevent him leaving. It was only after a great deal of determined hard bargaining that Cabot arrived in London in the middle of 1548.

In 1546 Dudley also displayed his negotiating skills in the diplomatic sphere. Henry and Francis were both broke and tired of war, yet too proud to be seen to be suing for peace. They therefore continued to make bellicose noises and visible preparations for renewed hostilities while opening up secret channels for talks. By the spring, the main burden of negotiation had fallen upon Dudley and d'Annebaut. They met for frequent discussions at the English camp at Ambleteuse, near Boulogne. But between sessions the admirals hurried back to their flagships to harry each other's vessels and coastal installations in their efforts to improve their bargaining positions.

It was Dudley who came out on top in the contest of bluff and counter bluff. He who had spent over twenty years building up one of the biggest landed fortunes in England was a master of the hard bargain. Even so his achievement in what was called the Treaty of Camp was quite remarkable. The French had come to the negotiations determined above all else on the return of Boulogne as the price of peace. Henry's Council were ready to cede the point, knowing how ruinously expensive the port was to defend. The king, however, would not hear of it and Dudley's instructions were to yield not one inch of England's continental territory. The terms he finally agreed were that Boulogne was to remain in English hands until the French redeemed it for 2,000,000 crowns, a sum so vast that it was never likely to be forthcoming. The treaty was signed on 7 June and when news of it reached England there was universal rejoicing.

> The 12th day of June after was Whit Sunday, and then was a general procession from St Paul's unto St Peter's in Cornhill with all the children of St Paul's School and a cross of every parish church with a banner . . . all the clerks, all the priests, with parsons and vicars of every church in copes . . . and the bishop bearing the sacrament under a canopy with the mayor in a gown of crimson velvet, the aldermen in scarlet, with all the crafts in their best apparel. When the mayor came between the cross and the standard there was made a proclamation with all the heralds of arms and pursuivants in their coats of arms, with the trumpets, and there was proclaimed a universal peace for ever between the Emperor, the King of England, the French king and all Christian kings for ever.[9]

However, joy was not unconfined for everyone. Edward Seymour was in command of all his majesty's forces in France in 1545–6 and might reasonably have expected to play a major role in the treaty making. Once again he was outshone by his old friend. Henry had decided that Dudley was the better man for the job and the French had made it quite clear that they preferred to do business with him. But any resentment Seymour might have guarded was not allowed to be seen. The political situation made it vital that the leading evangelicals appear completely united. At no time was this more crucial than in the summer of 1546. When Dudley returned to England in mid-June he found himself in the midst of a religious storm that threatened him and his wife.

They belonged to a tight-knit group who were so close to the king as to appear unassailable. There was Catherine Parr, Henry's patient nurse and the only person he would allow to change the dressings on his suppurating legs. There was Thomas Cranmer, one of the few royal servants to whom the king showed loyal friendship. There was Sir Anthony Denny, Groom of the Stool, the man who controlled access to the sovereign. More importantly, Henry entrusted into Denny's keeping the royal dry stamp, a device which impressed the king's signature on paper so that a clerk could go over it in ink to authenticate it. This could be a formidable tool for those who wished to guide government policy.

Those committed to turning back the clock were almost in despair at the power of their enemies. The Duke of Norfolk, indeed, had bowed to what he considered to be the inevitable by arranging marriage alliances between his family and the Seymours. But, in March, Bishop Gardiner returned from a five-month diplomatic mission in the Netherlands and, with 'Wily Winchester's' appearance the activity of the reactionaries stepped up several gears. Their overall strategy soon became clear: they would strike at known or suspected heretics who had court connections in the hope that small fish would lead them to the bigger ones.

They set in motion a fresh round of Six Articles persecutions. Prisons rapidly filled once again with artisans, clergy and tradespeople suspected of reading forbidden books or attending heretical conventicles, and interrogators set about dragging from their victims names of co-religionists higher up the social ladder. One of those now brought to the capital for examination was a Lincolnshire gentlewoman, Anne Kyme (nee Ayscough), better known to history as Anne Askew. She was a gentlewoman born, had a brother in the king's guard of Gentlemen Pensioners, was well known in the London evangelical underworld as a bold 'gospeller' and had patrons among ladies of the queen's entourage. The conservative leadership decided that she might have valuable infor-mation to give them about suspected heretics in Catherine Parr's circle. On 19 and 20 June she was brought before the Council to answer questions about her religious beliefs.

It was around this time that John Dudley returned to court and he was, therefore, present for Anne's interrogation. Since the whole Council could not spend time examining one woman, they delegated the task to a committee of three: Bishop Gardiner, William Parr, Earl of Essex (the queen's brother) and John Dudley. It was an uncomfortable experience for the two noblemen, who sympathized with the prisoner and who under-stood the bishop's agenda only too well. Anne certainly did not make things any easier for them. According to her own account, when she was pressed to consent to the Catholic doctrine of transubstantiation (that the flesh and blood of Christ are really present in the Communion service after consecration, in the form of bread and wine) she turned the attack on her interrogators. 'Then said I to my Lord Parr and my Lord Lisle that it was great shame for them to counsel contrary to their knowledge.' They returned her a brief, non-committal reply, 'in few words they did say that they would gladly all things were well.'[10] The returning hero who had faced the fire of battle and brazened it out with the diplomatic opposition was circumspection itself when it came to unfurling his religious colours.

The next few weeks were uncomfortable ones for Dudley and his family and friends. The ceremonial ratification of the treaty had yet to take place and Dudley had been ordered to Paris to lead the English delegation.

There was some urgency about this because it was generally feared that when Francis I had had time to reflect on just how much his representative had yielded he might renege on the agreement. Furthermore ratification had to take place within forty days. Yet, despite the pressure Dudley was under, he remained in London. He received final instructions on 2 July but still he did not set out. Eventually the terms of the treaty had to be changed to allow for the delay.

Dudley's hesitation has to be seen against the background of political and religious tension at court. The conservatives were in a frenzy of accusations, arrests and interrogations in and around Westminster. Members of the chamber staff, including John Lascelles, marked out for revenge by the Howards, were being imprisoned or placed under house arrest. Then, in early July, Gardiner and his allies moved against the queen and her ladies. In the most extraordinary sequence of events they gambled for desperately high stakes. Anne Askew was subjected to several interrogations in various locations, some dire, others quite comfortable, in an attempt to disorientate her. Finally, on 29 June, she reached the Tower. There she was subjected to an act of sheer barbarism. Not only was she put to the rack, something quite unheard of in the treatment of female heretics in England, but the officers who personally operated the engine of torture were none other than Lord Chancellor Wriothesly and Sir Richard Rich. They questioned her closely and repeatedly about ladies of the court who, they said, had sent her money. The Duchess of Suffolk, the Countess of Hertford and Lady Denny were among those specifically named. But, they suggested, Anne had more exalted confederates. 'You had help from some of the king's Council, did you not?' they demanded. But Anne remained mute.

An oblique attack having failed, Gardiner now mounted a direct assault on the queen. On 8 July he and his friends achieved a major triumph in the issuing of a proclamation against pernicious books. 'From henceforth,' it ran,

> no man, woman or person of what estate, condition or degree soever he or they be . . . shall have, take or keep within his possession the text of the New Testament of Tyndale's or Coverdale's translation in English, nor any other that is permitted by the Act of Parliament made at Westminster in the four and thirtieth and five and thirtieth year of his majesty's most noble reign, nor any manner of books printed or written in the English tongue . . . in the names of Frith, Tyndale, Wycliffe, Joy . . .[11]

This catch-all measure was something they had twice tried unsuccessfully to get through parliament. Now Gardiner used it as a net to catch some exotic fish. Finding Henry in one of his tetchy moods, he observed that the queen seemed to have set herself up as some sort of authority on religious matters, even to the extent of presuming to instruct her husband. How topsy-turvy the world was becoming, he suggested, when women turned theologians. He managed to persuade the king to allow Catherine to be examined as to her faith and arranged that she would be apprehended while she and her husband walked one afternoon in the privy garden. Gardiner had played his ace but his opponents were able to trump it. The ploy was discovered. Catherine hurried to throw herself on the king's mercy. All was forgiven. And when Wriothesly turned up at the appointed time with some of the king's guards, Henry angrily dismissed him for his presumption.

The conservatives had overreached themselves. Henry extended his protection, not only over the queen, but also over some of the courtiers who had fallen under suspicion. They were allowed a few victims, including John Lascelles and Anne Askew who perished together in the flames on 16 July, but their deaths drew a line under the last persecution of the reign. Four days earlier John Dudley had decided that the crisis had passed and that he could set out for France. 'The Viscount Lisle, Admiral, with the Bishop of Durham and divers lords and above a hundred gentlemen, all in velvet coats and chains of gold, went to Paris and were there solemnly received and feasted.'[12] At the end of the month Seymour returned to court and by 12 August Dudley had resumed his seat at the Council table. Their position was henceforth unchallenged though on one occasion feelings ran so high that Dudley reached across the table and struck Bishop Gardiner a blow across the face. For this severe breach of etiquette he was banished to his estates for a month. On 29 January 1547, the imperial ambassador gloomily summed up the situation for his master:

If (which God forbid) the King should die . . . it is probable that these two men, Seymour and Dudley, will have the management of affairs, because, apart from the King's affection for them, and other reasons, there are no other nobles of a fit age and ability for the task.[13]

But the great tyrant was already dead.

III

KING JOHN

9

Feast in the Morning

———∘✧∘———

Woe to you, O land, when your king is a child and your princes feast in the morning

Ecclesiastes 10:16

The eleven years and ten months during which first Edward VI, then Mary Tudor, occupied the throne of England have often been regarded as a sort of hiatus between the longer and more spectacular reigns of Henry VIII and Elizabeth I. Little of significance occurred, has been supposed, during the rule of the Protestant boy and the Catholic woman, except a lot of disastrous wrangling over religion. Edward, particularly, remains for many people a shadowy figure whose short life was dominated by powerful and unscrupulous men who milked the country for their own advantage. That is not the way that modern historians see the reign of the boy king, and specifically the years 1549–53.

> . . . it is possible to imagine that, had the King lived, the Dudley years would have allowed Edward VI to operate at the heart of one of the most radical, dynamic, and personal adult male monarchies of the Tudor century.[1]

John Dudley, who had served Henry VIII loyally and effectively as courtier, soldier and diplomat, went on to serve his son in the office of government leader, and most commentators now believe that he made a pretty good job of it.

In the early months of 1547 there were, doubtless, many people up and down the country who pondered the warning of Ecclesiastes. Minority rule meant unstable government and the potential rivalry of noble factions vying for power. That had invariably been the pattern in the past. But what happened in 1547 was something truly remarkable: a nine-year-old boy came to the throne, supported by a Council and a chamber staff who worked together and were in agreement on political and religious fundamentals. Over the next few years there were certainly personality clashes and policy changes. There would be rivalries, some of which would prove fatal, but the whole reign was marked by an underlying unity and continuity of purpose. The debilitating divisions that had cleft the government for the past twenty years were things of the past. An unwavering, idealistic course was set towards a religious and social revolution and dissentient voices that might have effectively challenged it either fell silent of their own accord or were silenced.

Paradoxically, it was the old king, whose religious opinions could never have been clearly labelled as 'Catholic' or 'Protestant', who launched the unequivocally evangelical regime on its way. Determined at the last, when even he had to recognize the imminent reality of death, to ensure that the Tudor dynasty would not be torn apart by religious factions, Henry quite deliberately entrusted the governance of the realm to Seymour, Dudley, Cranmer and their supporters. His motivation was expressed most clearly in the reason he gave for excluding Gardiner from the council of regency. When it was suggested to him that the bishop's name might have been omitted by an oversight, Henry fiercely replied,

> Hold your peace! I remembered him well enough and of good purpose have left him out. For, surely, if he were in my testament and one of you [executors] he would cumber you all, and you should never rule him, he is of so troublesome a nature . . . I myself could use him and rule him to all manner of purposes, as seemed good unto me, but so shall you never do . . .[2]

Henry intended that his young son should have a tranquil start to his reign. He, himself, had been able to enforce a religious stalemate on the realm and subordinate religious principles to diplomatic necessity. (Even in his last year he flirted with both Imperial and German embassies by encouraging one to hope for a rapprochement with the pope and the other to look for an alliance of Protestant states) but he was not passing the crown on to a strong-willed and self-assured heir who would be able to continue his policies. That being the case it was necessary to hand real power to one of the prevailing factions.

And when it came to deciding whether traditionalists or progressives should be in the ascendant he really had no choice. If he settled Seymour and his colleagues in the dominant position it was not because of any shift in personal conviction towards the evangelical position. Henry's arrangements for the new reign were based upon purely pragmatic grounds. Seymour and Dudley were the young, up-and-coming men. They had shown themselves to possess military prowess and diplomatic acumen. Moreover, they were his own creation. He could rely on them in a way that he could never rely on the Howards, proud in their ancient lineage, or Gardiner, whose first loyalty would always be to the church. Henry also recognized that Seymour and Dudley did not stand alone. Not only did they have numerous friends and supporters at court, they were also backed by a coterie of churchmen, scholars and lawyers who had a coherent political programme: Cranmer; Nicholas Ridley, Bishop of Rochester; Thomas Goodrich, Bishop of Ely; young Edward's 'New Learning' tutors, Sir John Cheke and Richard Cox, among many others. But what must have weighed heaviest in Henry's thinking was that only in the hands of the evangelical group was the royal supremacy safe. The Crown's control of the church in England had been bought at enormous cost and the old king was not going to put that at risk by placing at his son's Council table those who hankered after the 'good old days'.

It has sometimes been thought that pure chance played a major part in the swings and roundabouts of the last months of Henry's reign. Gardiner foolishly fell out with the king by demurring when he demanded an exchange of diocesan and Crown lands. Norfolk was caught up in the *folie de grandeur* of his son, the Earl of Surrey, who was reported as boasting that when the king died his family would be in power and who compounded his stupidity by quartering Plantagenet arms with his own. For this offence father and son were both committed to the Tower, found guilty of treason and sentenced to death. Surrey suffered the supreme penalty on 19 January and Norfolk, who had been a close royal servant since the first days of the reign, would undoubtedly have followed him to the block if Henry's death had not brought him an eleventh-hour reprieve. But to believe that the balance of Edward's Council depended on his father's pique with the bishop and his indignation with the leading nobleman is to misjudge Henry's motivation.

He had frequently destroyed men and women on a whim – or, perhaps, it would be truer to say that he had more often allowed their rivals to destroy them while keeping his own hands relatively clean – but he was the driving force behind the downfall of Gardiner and the Howards. He devoted an enormous amount of his dwindling energies to ensuring the convictions of Norfolk and Surrey and he refused to allow the repentant bishop into his presence. Lord Paget, a few years later, remembered that 'his majesty abhorred [Gardiner] more than any man in his realm' and only referred to him 'with such terms as the said Lord Paget is sorry to name'.[3] These men had certainly played into Henry's hands, and without the machinations of their rivals, but the king had their measure and would, one way or another, have excluded them from the government of his son.

The new rulers lost no time in securing their position. Within hours of Henry's death Seymour sped out to Ashridge to collect Edward and bring him, first, to Enfield where Princess Elizabeth was living, then, to the Tower. Only when this had been done was the news of the late king's passing released. Immediately the executors named in Henry's will (authorized by that famous dry stamp) set about securing their positions. There were sixteen of them and the shape of the minority government had been left in their hands. As they deliberated and bargained within the Tower's old, draughty, outmoded chambers they agreed that they should have a leader and that the obvious man for the job was the king's uncle, Edward Seymour. He now took the titles of Lord Protector of the Realm and Governor of the King's Person. He was elevated to the dukedom of Somerset and granted lands to the annual value of £800 to support his new eminence. His colleagues also had to be rewarded if they were to carry the dignity of their position and to remain loyal to the duke. Sir William Paget, the Secretary, produced a 'book' which, he claimed, the old king had instructed him to draw up in order to fill gaps in the ranks of the nobility which had of late become 'greatly decayed'.

John Dudley came out with enormous gains and one significant loss. He was raised to the next order of nobility with £200 per annum in land. It was first proposed to revive for him the earldom of Coventry, extinct since soon after the Conquest, but Dudley had his eye on a much more prestigious title. Claiming descent from the younger daughter of Richard Beauchamp (d. 1439), premier earl of England, he asked for the earldom of Warwick. The title and lands had reverted to the Crown in 1471, since when the Tudors had leased or sold away substantial portions of the estates which had supported this ancient and illustrious peerage. Warwick, a flourishing market town, recently incorporated, overlooked by its 'most stately and magnificent castle,'[4] was at the centre of the region where Dudley had been building up an impressive patrimony over the years and this was his chance to become undisputed master of a wide swathe of central England. He had some hard bargaining to do because it seems that the Council or, perhaps, Seymour, showed initial reluctance in granting him all the traditional appurtenances of the earldom. On 24 March he had to appeal to Paget to use his influence with his colleagues to make good the deficiency. The letter is highly revealing, not only of Dudley's ambition, but also of his dynastic pride and his sense of tradition.

> Some may allege consideration concerning the non-assignment of the lordship of Warwick [to me], saying it is a stately castle, a goodly park and a great royalty. But the castle is itself unable to lodge a good baron with his train. All on one side, with the dungeon tower is in ruins. The late King sold all the principal manors belonging to the earldom and castle, so that now only the rents of some houses in the town and meadows in Wedgnock Park belong to it. I am Constable, High Steward and Master of the Game of the castle, park and town, with herbage for life. Because of the name and my descent from one of the daughters of the rightful line I am the more desirous to have the thing. [5]

Dudley obtained the lordship of Warwick and from this point he adopted as his family badge the bear and ragged (more accurately 'raguled') staff, the badge of the Beauchamp earls. The bear supposedly represented Arthal, a Saxon earl ('Arctos', Latin for the Great Bear), and the staff was an uprooted ash tree from which the branches had been lopped.

Within the court Dudley received the senior position he had apparently craved eighteen months before, when he was appointed Lord Great Chamberlain. However, at the same time he had the chagrin of seeing the Admiralty taken from him and granted to a less worthy suitor. Somerset had to find perquisites for his younger brother, Thomas Seymour. There was little love lost between the siblings but, as the king's other uncle, Thomas could not be ignored. And he had a not undistinguished military record. During the recent war with France he had served as one of Dudley's admirals and played his part in maintaining England's mastery of the Narrows, but he lacked Dudley's energy, enterprise and commitment to detail. However, his besetting sin in the eyes of his predecessor was putting his own interests before those of his country. Baron Seymour of Sudeley, as he now became, was a notorious patron of pirates. Now that England was not at war letters of marque were not being issued to privateers but this did not deter him from encouraging his captains to set upon merchant vessels of all nations and taking a share of the proceeds. It was the Council who had to cope with the diplomatic backlash from these activities. If Lord Seymour's mind was not wholly on his naval duties it was because he had other personal concerns. Basically, he was jealous of his brother and saw no reason why he should not share the honour and the profits of his nephew's guardianship. When Somerset would not give him what he wanted, he went other ways about getting it. He paid court to Princess Elizabeth and, according to gossip, also to Princess Mary and Anne of Cleves. Then, a mere few weeks after Henry VIII's death, he secretly married his widow, Catherine Parr, imagining that this gave him a double claim on overseeing the king's upbringing. Soon he was wheedling his way into young Edward's favour by giving the boy presents and encouraging him to act independently of his governor.

All this was a problem for the Lord Protector but Thomas Seymour's irresponsibility and hubris rankled with Dudley also. He deeply resented handing over the navy, for which he was still working with energy, industry and flair. In 1549 the Imperial ambassador reported an argument he had overheard in which Dudley told the younger Seymour, 'be content . . . with the honour done to you for your brother's sake and with your office of Lord High Admiral, which I gave up to you for the same motive; for neither the King nor I will be governed by you; nor would he be governed by your brother, were it not that his virtue and loyalty towards the King and the kingdom make him the man fittest to administer the affairs of the country during the King's minority.'[6]

Yet it was precisely that last assertion that John Dudley was beginning to doubt. It has been customary to emphasize the material benefits obtained by Dudley and his colleagues once they held undisputed sway. Dudley certainly made significant gains. He was assiduous in campaigning for the lands he wanted and in buying and selling properties which enabled him to continue enhancing his position as the leading Midlands magnate. But such acquisitiveness pales into insignificance beside the landed fortune (reckoned at £7,500 per annum) built up by Somerset to support his semi-regal estate. The showy centrepiece of his property holdings was the new

Somerset House in the Strand, a vast waterside palace. It stood in stark contrast to his own modest building projects and can only have reinforced his growing suspicion of his old friend's deteriorating character.

Dudley and Somerset were ideologically committed to the same broad programme and any rifts in the government could only give comfort to the likes of Gardiner, Howard and Wriothesley, who were watching closely from the sidelines of power. Dudley would not play into the hands of the reactionaries by letting them know his reservations. At the same time he suffered the frustration of the talented subordinate obliged to watch his superior making a mess of things. Somerset 'clearly lacked the character and personality necessary for the office he held'[7] and like, most men in such a position, he progressively distanced himself from his colleagues, became increasingly dictatorial and resented those who bade fair to outshine him.

Dudley's allegiance had been severely put to the test in the relinquishing of the Admiralty. It was a job in which he had invested an enormous amount of himself. It is possible that he had already begun grooming his close friend and protégé, Sir Edward Clinton, as his eventual successor. Clinton was a soldier–courtier in the same mould as Dudley and the two men had worked well together on campaign and committee ever since Dudley had been appointed Lord Admiral. Instead, he had been obliged to place the navy in the hands of a flashy, unstable, untrustworthy subordinate. Lord Seymour's performance (or non-performance) of his duties soon confirmed Dudley's worse suspicions. During the campaigns of the next couple of years he was very rarely to be found at sea and he was becoming daily more notorious for his support for pirates. Seymour also made no secret of his enmity towards Dudley. In January 1549 councillors and courtiers were remembering that the Lord Admiral delighted to point out how his own landholdings were located in relation to those of Dudley and Somerset and how many gentlemen and tenants he had pledged to his service. He boasted of having thwarted Dudley's plans by refusing to exchange his manor of Stratford upon Avon for land of greater value. And, when he was trying to win over the Marquess of Dorset, he urged him to keep his house in Warwickshire, 'chiefly to match Lord Warwick'.[8]

What made matters worse was that naval hostilities with France were resumed before the reign was many months old. The peace that Dudley had laboured so hard to secure scarcely survived the death of Henry VIII. Within weeks Francis I also died and the new king, Henri II, abandoned his father's 'weak' treaty. He was determined to wipe out the shame of the loss of Boulogne and to forge an alliance with Scotland involving the marriage of Mary Stuart to his own heir. The old threat to England's security had surfaced once more. From a military and diplomatic point of view it was a matter of 'business as usual'. Somerset decided that the best way to bring the Scots to the negotiating table was to give them another demonstration of the superiority of England's armed might. He personally assembled an army of 18,000 at Berwick, supported by a force of 24 ships under the command of Edward, Lord Clinton. What was planned was a repeat of the triumphs of 1542 and 1544. Once again Dudley was given the major responsibility of commanding the vanguard. He performed with his usual combination of calm efficiency and flair. He crossed the border at the head of 4,000 men and advanced towards the Firth of Forth. At one point he found himself ambushed with only a small escort. Undeterred, he charged the enemy and put them to rout. On another occasion the Earl of Huntly, the Scottish commander, proposed that the issue be settled in single combat between himself and Somerset. Immediately Dudley volunteered himself for the confrontation. Somerset, of course, refused to allow it. He had no use for chivalric gestures and, whatever the outcome of such a combat might have been, it would not at all have suited him. He could not risk sacrificing his best general but, equally, he had no intention of letting that general return home as the hero of the hour.

The two armies finally met at Pinkie, near Inveresk. The result was a technical victory for the English but it was a long and bloody fight and casualties were heavy on both sides. To the winners the situation they found themselves in was painfully familiar. The border had been temporarily secured but how were they to turn a brief tranquillity into a lasting peace? Somerset's solution was twofold: he would leave behind him in the Lowlands a number of garrisoned strongholds and he would impose a marriage treaty which would bind the two nations firmly together. Having organized the first part of the programme, he left Dudley at Berwick to head a team of commissioners to negotiate with the Scottish leaders and took the bulk of his men back to London. The policy failed. The English outposts that were supposed to overawe the surrounding country were too far away to be readily succoured when necessary and thus were themselves vulnerable, especially when French reinforcements were sent to aid the local levies. As for the treaty, it never materialized because the Scottish negotiators simply failed to turn up. Huntly famously observed that though he approved in principal of the proposed marriage between Edward and Mary, 'I like not this wooing'.

English bullying achieved the exact opposite of what it had intended because it drove Scotland into the arms of the French. The leaders in Edinburgh looked to Henri II for aid and he agreed to be the nation's guardian in return for a Franco–Scottish marriage treaty. In the summer of 1548 little Mary Stuart was shipped across the North Sea and Henri greeted her with the words 'France and Scotland are now one country.' The government at Westminster was alarmed. Was this 1545 over again? They ordered Lord Clinton to sea with all haste.

From March 1547 to November 1548 Dudley was absent from the capital for long periods of time, surprising self-denial for a man widely regarded as the most effective and popular member of the governing group. Just as in 1539 and 1541–2, he turned his back on the court. In seeking to understand this behaviour we do not need to assume, as some have done, that Dudley was giving way to a prolonged fit of pique or was actively plotting against Somerset. In fact he was being intensely loyal under increasingly difficult circumstances, and had decided that he could best show that loyalty by distancing himself from political events. It was not Dudley's hostility that kept him away, but Somerset's paranoia and jealousy.

All members of the political and diplomatic elite were watching with intense interest the experiment in regency government. They noted Somerset's behaviour, his relationship with the Council and the reactions of his colleagues. They observed the Protector getting into difficulties both at home and abroad (discussed further below). Under these circumstances nothing would have been easier for Dudley than to skulk around Westminster, feeding off the disaffection of others and holding clandestine meetings behind the Protector's back. Dudley, however, was not an intriguer, but he was careful to keep himself well informed about national and international events and took every opportunity to assure the Protector of his desire to be of service.

He chose to communicate, not with Somerset in person, but with the men who were closest to the nation's leader. His chief confidants were Sir William Paget and William Cecil. Paget was Secretary to the Council in the early weeks of the reign and was subsequently raised to the position of Comptroller of the Household. Cecil, a young man whose remarkable career in English politics was just beginning, was Somerset's private secretary. Through these intermediaries Dudley offered advice, sought favours, conveyed information and displayed his support. Thus we find him writing with news he has discovered about French naval manoeuvres. He entreats for a lady who 'having been destroyed by bad London surgeons, has been eased by the surgeon of Boulogne. Please have my lord let him remain or she may lose a leg'. When Stephen Gardiner, who steadfastly opposed the religious innovations of the new regime, was brought to Whitehall for interrogation by the Council, Dudley was eager for news:

> I write to ask if [the Lord Protector] has proceeded with the arrogant bishop according to his deservings. I heard he was to be before my lord's grace and the Council yesterday, but had it been so I suppose it would have been more spoken of. I fear his accustomed wiliness and the persuasions of his friends will again let the fox deceive the lion. Tell me something of the matter.[9]

And in the same letter he adds a note which tantalizingly refers to an earlier letter about a subject close to his heart: 'Remind my lord about the navies.'

In the summer of 1548 Dudley requested a government job that would give him every excuse to spend most of his time at Dudley. (This was still his principal residence. He never seems to have changed his opinion of Warwick Castle and did not bother to engage in a grandiose building programme there.) He asked to be given the oversight of Wales and the border. This was the same position of responsibility he had sought from Cromwell almost a decade before, when he had declared himself tired of the stressful life of court and capital, and it is tempting to think that he found himself once again under the same emotional pressures. This time his request was granted and he became President of the Principality of Wales and its Marches. Via Cecil he expressed his thanks: 'I have received my lord's letters, being glad he accepts my offer to serve, which is but my duty. For his friendship I would do more if I could.'[10]

Now Dudley's correspondence begins to reveal a man expressing his devotion to Somerset, as it were, through gritted teeth. The two were soon at loggerheads in relation to Dudley's new role. Dudley wanted to stamp his own authority on the principality but found there a group of officials who were well set in their ways and reluctant to bow to their new superior. The president had reason to suspect the chief judicial officer, one Townsend, of gross corruption and some of the councillors as his aiders and abettors. Dudley asked permission to replace Townsend with John Gosnold, a lawyer in the Court of Augmentations whom he knew well to be an extremely efficient officer and a devout evangelical. Somerset received the request and at first considered it sympathetically. Then he changed his mind; Townsend had been granted his office for life and he would not remove him. Reluctantly, though with an acute sense of political realities, Dudley accepted the decision: '[Townsend] cannot be removed without a great cause and I will not advise my lord to break any of the King's grants by letters patent, for the same may happen to me and others afterwards.'[11] He did, however, ask for some of his fellow council members to be removed so that his own judgement would carry more weight. Again, the Protector seemed to accept the recommendation, only to go back on his word afterwards. Dudley was furious. However, by the time he responded to Cecil he had calmed sufficiently to divert his criticism from Somerset.

> By whose persuasions this happens I know not but am sure I have base friends who smile to see me so used. But I trust, despite my charges and pains, I have made my provision there. Despite mockery I shall be as ready to serve as those who have now won their purpose, not the first or last to be worked with my lord. If they work no more displeasure I will be more willing to forgive.[12]

Those lines suggest the frustration of a man who has tried to escape the negative effects of factional jealousies, only to find that they have pursued him deep into the shires and who realizes that he has no support from the man to whom he has pledged his allegiance. Whatever friendly comradeship had once existed between Somerset and Dudley had by now been squandered.

Dudley was very far from being the only member of the political class to be alienated from the Lord Protector. In the spring of 1549 Paget wrote to Somerset in words that Dudley might have used had he been prepared to wear his heart on his sleeve.

> No man dares speak what he thinks, although necessary . . . you sometimes nip me so sharply that if I did not know you well and were not assured of your favour, I might often have blanched for speaking frankly. If other honest men, not so well acquainted with your nature, say their opinions honestly and are snapped, God knows what you shall lose . . . A King who discourages men from saying their opinions frankly imperils the realm. A subject in great authority as you are, doing so, is likely to endanger himself as well as the commonwealth . . . relent sometimes from your own opinions. Your surety will be greater, your burden less.[13]

It took Edward Seymour, Duke of Somerset, less than eighteen months to alienate himself from most of his conciliar colleagues. The disaffection cannot be ascribed to religious faction. By the summer of 1548 the conservative leaders, Norfolk and Gardiner, were both in the Tower. Thomas Wriothesley, Earl of Southampton, the only other effective reactionary, was deprived of the Lord Chancellorship and did not regain his seat on the Council until January 1549. The remaining members were reformists, temporizers or Catholic sympathizers keeping their heads well below the parapet. Somerset only had himself to blame for the development of a conciliar majority which would eventually force him from power.

Character defects aside, Somerset's problem was that he was a man with a mission. Edward VI and his uncle inherited a dislocated realm. Widespread changes in land ownership, coupled with rapidly rising inflation had created or exacerbated a variety of social problems. Landlords, in order to maximize profits or simply to make ends meet, turned arable land into pasture and raised rents. Itinerant workers and beggars (often lumped together as 'vagrants') swelled the population of towns, placing pressure on food prices, rents and local services. Taken individually most problems facing the economy were not new but they were widespread and they were worsening rapidly.

Contemporaries were hard pressed to understand what was happening to them (why should the price of flour go up in a year of good harvest?) and economic historians still disagree about some aspects of the sixteenth-century crisis. Those caught in the poverty trap and several social commentators tended to identify the causes of distress with the more obvious recent events. They looked at the roofless abbeys and lamented the disappearance of monastic hospitals, schools and alms distribution. They gawped at the fine houses being built by 'new' men in town and country and inveighed against the arrivistes who had no care for local people and ancient ways. Preachers condemned the culture of pitiless greed encouraged by massive land speculation and the pursuit of quick fortunes.

> . . . London was never so ill as it is now. In times past men were full of pity and compassion but now there is no pity; for in London their brother shall die in the streets for cold, he shall lie sick at the door between stock and stock . . . and perish there for hunger . . . When any man died they would bequeath great sums of money toward the relief of the poor . . . but now charity is waxen cold;

none helpeth the . . . poor . . . Repent therefore, repent, London and remember that the same God liveth now that punished Nebo and he will punish sin as well now as he did then . . .[14]

Such perceptions were as faulty as 'golden age' nostalgia usually is but they were ubiquitous and powerful.

They were fed by the feelings of insecurity and bewilderment engendered by religious change. Parishioners had seen their churches stripped of ancient shrines and images. Local pilgrimage centres that had brought business to many areas had ceased to function. The replacement of familiar objects of veneration by chained bibles forced men to alter their spiritual compass bearings. If the process of change had been all in one direction it might not have been so disruptive but Henry VIII's stop-go Reformation could only leave people confused and apprehensive.

Somerset determined to come to their aid. He would provide clear policies and firm leadership. He would protect the people from their voracious social superiors and lead them into the lush pastures of pure faith and religious truth. He pledged himself to what has been called a 'commonwealth' programme which coupled unequivocal evangelical revival with the redress of social ills. Edward Seymour emerges from the historical record as a man with two faces, one that of the 'good duke', which he showed to the general populace, and the other the ambitious and ill-tempered autocrat so familiar to those who tried to work with him. Of few men has the verdict of historians varied so much over the centuries. Susan Brigden neatly exposes the dilemma:

As the soldier who had left the poor in the Borders to live like animals in their ruined homes; as rack-renter, sheep-master and encloser; as the ruler who presided over the Vagrancy Act which imposed slavery upon those who, willingly or not, left their homes, he was ostensibly an unlikely social reformer. Yet to that role he aspired. Here was a man as ambitious of virtue, the badge of nobility, as of riches.[15]

Somerset was not the first politician and certainly not the last to suffer from messianic delusions; to believe, quite sincerely, that he was the people's friend while feathering his own nest and developing a monumental ego. Moreover, his position was not one of total isolation. He did have behind him a coterie of enthusiastic supporters who gave his regime philosophical respectability and spiritual sanction. This group embraced ecclesiastics like Thomas Cranmer, now eagerly pushing through parliament and convocation a programme of doctrinal and liturgical change, the king's reformist tutors, Roger Ascham, John Cheke and Richard Cox, the radical parliamentarian John Hales, leading academics and literary propagandists for social reform such as Sir Thomas Smith and a bevy of preachers who came to court to preach before the king, foremost among them was the veteran Hugh Latimer.

Within months the regime had removed from the statute book the Act of Six Articles and every subsequent anti-reform measure. Commissioners were despatched throughout the land to report on the state of the church, armed with draconian injunctions. They were to bestir the local clergy,

> that they shall take away, utterly distinct and destroy all shrines, covering of shrines, all tables, candlesticks, trindles [wax tapers], or rolls of wax, pictures, paintings and all other monument of feigned miracles, pilgrimages, idolatry and superstition, so that there remain no memory of the same in wall, glass windows or elsewhere within their churches or houses. And they shall exhort all their parishioners to do the like within their several houses . . .[16]

As if that 1547 injunction were not clear enough it was followed in subsequent years by still more specific instructions for the whitewashing of church interiors and the removal of all traces of the old style of worship. Cranmer and diocesan officers kept a close eye on parish clergy to ensure that their orders were being carried out. The government's attitude gave the green light to local zealots to take the law into their own hands. In vain the commissioners pointed out that unauthorized defacing of images was forbidden. The general impression gained by most ordinary people was that the churches were to be gutted by order of the new regime. Therefore, activists saw no reason to hesitate to vent their feelings on artefacts they found offensive. Conservative clergy and parishioners protested against this iconoclasm, but cases which came before the Council or justices of the peace were usually decided in favour of the reformers.

What cannot be doubted is the shock of the new order, felt immediately in every community. It was not just the appearance of the churches that changed. Cranmer was eagerly working on a revised liturgy. The mass was replaced by a communion service in which the sacrament was administered to the laity in both kinds and, in 1549, the first Edwardian

Prayer Book imposed historical changes. Not only was worship in the vernacular, but the congregation were expected to participate by reading or learning by heart the words of prayers, responses, canticles and psalms. For some this was liberation. For others it was sacrilege. For all it was revolution. There was a new spirit abroad in the nation, inspiring, to use Professor MacCulloch's words, 'a movement of hope and moral fervour, capable of generating a mood of intense excitement.'[17] Somerset's England was a young man's England; an England for hot-headed demonstrators and idealistic social theorists.

Prominent among the latter was John Hales, a minor Coventry landowner but a passionate commonwealth man. Having personally overcome the disadvantages of a poor education and a serious accident in youth which left him permanently crippled, he had a profound fellow feeling for the disadvantaged. The man who had taught himself to read four languages founded a grammar school for poor boys in Coventry. He achieved election to parliament in order to improve the lot of the underprivileged. Hales may have been the author of *A Discourse of the Common Weal of this Realm of England* which analysed the causes of the nation's social and economic woes and placed the rapacity of landlords high on the list. Certainly he showed himself much in sympathy with the views expressed in that book and drew himself to Somerset's attention as a promising apostle of the Protector's social gospel. In 1548 Somerset placed him in charge of a commission to enquire into enclosures. The brief given to Hales and his colleagues was to gather information in the central counties on rural depopulation and specifically to report on any violations of the statutes which limited the encroachment of pasture over arable land. Hales proved a zealous chairman of this commission and the notice he sent before him to all regional and parish authorities indicates that he had already made up his mind what the commission would discover. 'The people of this realm, our native country', he wrote, 'is greatly decayed through the greediness of a few men . . . where there were in few years [past] ten or twelve thousand people, there be now scarce four thousand.' Taking an image directly from More's *Utopia*, he went on, 'sheep and cattle that were ordained to be eaten of men, hath eaten up the men.'[18]

The area of Hales' survey included John Dudley's territory and it is hardly surprising that the two men should have come into conflict. Dudley did not like the commission's modus operandi and resented its results, as did most of his neighbours. He almost certainly had a long acquaintance with Hales, for the campaigner was born at Halden, Kent, where Dudley spent most of his early years, and had long been a prominent member of Warwickshire society. There was something of the barrack-room lawyer about Hales. He was driven by self-righteousness combined with a lack of respect for authority. As such he was the kind of man Dudley found it hardest to stomach (as his later relationship with John Knox shows). It may have been past irritations as well as present annoyance that provoked him to clash with Hales over the commission. Dudley believed that the likes of Hales, far from easing rural malaise, actually added to it. They encouraged the discontent of the lower orders, prompting them to embrace unrealizable aspirations and to be disrespectful towards their betters. His opinion seemed to be borne out in August when a minor riot flared up in Buckinghamshire. He wrote angrily to Hales, accusing him of being responsible for the outbreak. Hales was unrepentant and his reply was a direct challenge. He was, he wrote, astonished 'that those that seemed to favour God's word should go about to hinder or speak evil of this thing, whereby the end and fruit of God's word, that is love and charity to our poor neighbours, should be so set forth and published to the world.'[19] The taunt is reminiscent of the words Anne Askew threw at Dudley and points to the shallowness of his personal faith. Yet, perhaps 'shallowness' is too harsh a description. Dudley was essentially a man of action, a man of affairs. He lacked both the intellectual and spiritual apparatus which enables men to reflect deeply on issues, to steer a course through the eddies of doubt and conflicting truths and reach the certainty of which saints and martyrs are made. He lived in the day-to-day world and his study was men, rather than theories and philosophies.

Events in that real world were very soon to vindicate his rejection of Somerset's noble but quite impracticable policies. Just as government pronouncements had seemed to give sanction to religious zealots to vandalize churches, so rural malcontents, believing the 'good duke' to be on their side, took the law into their own hands and set about righting local wrongs. Five hundred Kentish villagers descended en masse on the estate of Sir Thomas Cheyney and uprooted his hedges and fences. And there were also communities opposed to the religious changes being imposed on them. A Cornish mob smashed their way into a house at Helston, dragged out the ecclesiastical commissioner, William Body, and stabbed him to death. That done, their spokesman announced that they would only obey laws promulgated in the late king's reign until Edward VI reached the age of twenty-four. All over the country local justices were anxiously assessing the mood of the people. There was nothing they feared more than the collapse of the social order. If many poorer folk were disturbed by the disruption caused by new ideas, their superiors were more so. And they, too, had sound theological arguments for resisting peasant and yeomen demands. The social order was ordained by God. True, he demanded charity and compassion from those in power but he also required the lower orders to show that obedience to their superiors that they showed to him. It was Luther who had set his face firmly against political revolution. 'If the peasants became lords,' he said, 'the devil would become abbot.'[20] The major uprising of 1536–7 was still a powerful memory and the ruling class were understandably concerned for the safety of their property, their families and their servants. But they also worried about the overthrow of their whole world.

Somerset received several representations urging caution and vigilance but he ignored them. He paid little attention to the Council, preferring, like insecure rulers in all ages, to rely on the advice of his own private 'cabinet' of partisan advisers. He preferred to believe men like Hales who told him what he wanted to hear:

> The people thank God for so good a King and perceive your zeal and love for them. If the thing goes forward – without which the country will soon be in misery – no King will have more faithful subjects. The people will embrace God's word only when they see it bears good fruit . . . I believe you, that, despite selfishness [i.e., on the part of the landowners] it will proceed to the common good and concord.[21]

There are two alternative ways of carrying through government-led revolution; by force or by gentle persuasion. The first requires political and, if necessary, military strength. The second takes time. Somerset had neither. He was doggedly alienating the powerful men on whom he would have to rely as soon as there was any trouble and by deliberately deciding against a softly, softly approach he had fuelled public unrest and so lost the initiative. Paget, now on embassy to the emperor, boldly pointed out to the Protector where he had gone wrong. Although his letter is dated July 1549, it clearly refers to discussions the two men had had months before.

> I see at hand the King's destruction and your ruin . . . the King's subjects [are] out of all discipline, out of obedience, caring neither for protector nor King and much less for any mean officer. And

what is the cause? Your own lenity, your softness, your opinion to be good to the poor. The opinion of such as sayeth to your Grace, 'Oh, Sir, there was never man that had the hearts of the poor as you have. Oh the commons pray for you, Sir; they say, "God save your life".' I know your Grace's heart right well and that your meaning is good and godly. However, some evil men like to prate how that you have some greater enterprise in your head, that lean so much to the multitude . . . society in a realm doth consist and is maintained by religion and law and, these two or one wanting, farewell all just society, farewell King, government, justice and all other virtue and in cometh commonalty, sensuality, iniquity, raven and all other kinds of vice and mischief.

Paget begged his erstwhile friend not to delude himself into thinking that current economic and social ills were the real cause of incipient rebellion. 'Are enclosures new or prices high only in England?' he demanded rhetorically. 'Victuals are twice as expensive here. Enclosures have been lived with quietly for sixty years.' No, the problem was the liberty Somerset had encouraged the people to grasp. Having disposed of the Protector's political philosophy, Paget went on to attack his legislative programme. 'Put no more so many irons in the fire at once, as you have had within this twelvemonth: war with Scotland, with France (though not so termed), commissions out for that matter, new laws for this, proclamation for another, one in another's neck so thick that they be not set by among the people.'[22]

The cup of Somerset's woes filled steadily throughout 1548 but it was not till the last days of the year that it ran over – thanks to the Protector's brother. Thomas Seymour's wild indiscretions had become more and more outrageous as his jealousy of Somerset turned to contempt and hatred. There was no system in his plans to supplant his elder sibling. He slandered Somerset without restraint. He tried to build up a party among the nobility. He made advances to all the women close to the succession, Mary, Elizabeth, Jane Grey. He bribed and cajoled members of the king's household to give him access to his nephew. And, seeking financial backing for whatever coup his overheated imagination conjured up, he drew into his schemes Sir William Sharington, vice-treasurer of the Bristol mint. By December Somerset could stand the embarrassment no longer and sent for his brother. When Thomas declined to come until a more 'convenient' time there was nothing to be done but order his arrest. Once he was in the Tower the work began of gathering evidence. Several people, noblemen, courtiers, royal attendants and servants in Princess Elizabeth's household, gave depositions to the Council and the prisoner was repeatedly interrogated. The process went on for six weeks at the end of which a bill of attainder was drawn up consisting of thirty-three specific charges. Throughout this time Lord Seymour was given frequent opportunities to defend himself or offer some explanation for his activities. Haughtily he refused to answer the charges against him. He met his fate publicly on Tower Hill on 20 March. According to a sermon preached at court by Latimer nine days later, the prisoner was scheming right to the end. Letters were found, 'sewed between the soles of a velvet shoe,'[23] addressed to the two princesses urging them to conspire against the Protector. Elizabeth's verdict on her step-uncle was shrewd, if more than charitable: Lord Seymour was 'a man of much wit and very little judgement.'[24]

Dudley seems to have taken no part in these dismal events and for much of the winter he was ill at his town house, Ely Place, perhaps with a stomach ulcer, being tended by the king's surgeon, Henry Makerell. With the passing of the years Dudley made increasing reference to poor health in his correspondence. This is only to be expected in an age when most ailments and diseases lacked really effective treatment. Dudley seems to have been very careful of his health and if there were times when he was not as poorly as he thought he was that does not necessarily suggest hypochondria. As for his occasional absences from the Council Table, he certainly had no love of committee work and could easily persuade himself that he needed bed rest or the more salubrious air of the countryside. But there was always the nagging irritation of the loss of the Admiralty. After Thomas Seymour's death Dudley might well have expected to be restored to the position which he had loved or, at least, that his friend, Edward Clinton, might be made Lord Admiral. In the event Somerset refused to oblige him. Equally, he refused to snub Dudley by appointing one of his own cronies. He simply left the office vacant, despite the fact that he was planning a resumption of war with Scotland.

That war would have provided Dudley with a more congenial occupation. At the end of May 1549 Somerset appointed him supreme commander of the army for the forthcoming campaign and he set about the necessary preparations for mustering and transporting thousands of men. But the planned expedition never took place. Devastating events closer to home compelled the duke to direct the military forces of the Crown elsewhere. The discontent which, like the slow build up of stifling airs and moody clouds in high summer had threatened storms of rebellion, finally boiled up into demonstrations throughout south and central England, some of which spilled over into violence. Most of them were dealt with promptly and effectively by the local gentry but news rippled out rapidly from the various trouble spots engendering widespread excitement and panic. John Dudley was still at Ely Place (or perhaps he had been away on military affairs and recently returned) and still complaining of ill health on 12 July, when the Protector sent for him. Somerset wanted details of the situation in the area under Dudley's control and it would seem that he questioned his loyalty for, in his reply, the earl commented 'for my meaning towards his grace, I would his grace knew it as God doth.' In the maudlin tone he not infrequently lapsed into he promised to rouse himself from his sickbed, 'though it cast me down utterly. For the body that shall not be able to strive at this present were better out of the world than in it, and so, if God should not give me health now to stir, I would me to be in my grave.'[25] He went on to explain that he had only just heard about the situation in Warwickshire. He vowed to do his utmost to restore order but expressed some doubt about whether his men would be able to hold Warwick Castle. In the event the crisis there seems to have passed because we hear no more of insurrection in the Dudley heartland. However, Somerset was not convinced either of his old friend's loyalty or ability. He obliged Dudley to agree to an exchange of lands with the Crown. Among the properties the earl had to give up was Warwick Castle and its appurtenances. That must have seemed like a slap in the face to Dudley.

By now Somerset was tightly cocooned within his own fears and suspicions. He refused to accept that his policies had contributed to the breakdown of public order. He sent out edicts spurring the local justices to swift action in dispersing the crowds who had gathered into camps for the better presentation of their petitions while, at the same time, acknowledging that the rebellious commons had genuine grievances and issuing pardons to captured ringleaders. He insisted that the crisis was a minor one and would soon pass but simultaneously made emergency arrangements for the defence of the capital. He continued to criticize the big landowners yet he imperiously demanded their help. When major military action became necessary he havered and wavered about what forces to send where and whom to put in command. He had hired foreign mercenaries, intending to use them in the latest round of his quarrel with the Scots. Now they were kept in their camps by a ruler who shrank from launching them against his own subjects. His dilemma in this regard was very real. As long as he regarded the chief men of the realm as opponents of his policies if not of his person he was loth to put them in command of large bodies of armed men within only a few days' march of London. Yet by mid-July it became obvious that royal armies would have to be despatched to the main trouble spots. It was, doubtless, anxiety about Dudley having a major power base from which to operate that prompted him to demand the surrender of Warwick Castle. To add to his problems the king of France chose this excellent moment, from his point of view, to declare war.

It is astonishing that, under these circumstances, Dudley continued to act with conspicuous loyalty. Members of the Council were, as we know, grumbling behind the Protector's back. In their private discussions and correspondence they debated how much longer they could tolerate this muddle-headed tyranny and whether the time had not come to wrest back from the Protector the power they had yielded to him. Dudley must have been brought into these debates yet neither his actions nor his extant letters betray anything other than support for the regime and the desire to re-establish order. He was appointed to supervise the removal of cannon from the Tower and their relocation at the City gates. Similarly he made arrangements for the defence of Windsor. That done, he hastened to the Midlands to lend his support to the pacification of the region. But he was not allowed to stay there long. Events were moving fast and the Protector was getting desperate.

In two places the actions of the commons had gone well beyond relatively peaceful protest. In Devon and Cornwall men rose in revolt principally against the government's religious policy. The so-called 'Prayer Book Rebellion' was so named because it was the introduction of the new liturgy that set the linstock to the powder. Led by their priests, several communities demanded the retention of the old mass, certainly a reasonable demand in some areas of Cornwall in which English was as much a foreign language as Latin. But, in reality, the reaction against Cranmer's de-papalised services was an emotional one, the heartfelt protest of the inhabitants of an introverted, remote region who felt their traditional way of life being threatened by a distant government which was indifferent to all they held dear. Like the Pilgrims of Grace a decade earlier the west country rebels united round religious symbols which appeared to give their actions spiritual sanction. Somerset and the Council had no problem about dealing with what they regarded as the anguished death throes of English papistry.

Those who resist temporal authority resist God's ordinance and those who die in rebellion are utterly damned. The rebels . . . deserve death as traitors and receive eternal damnation with Lucifer, the first rebel, whatever pretence they make of masses or holy water . . . In the order of the church and outward rites God requires humility, innocence, charity and obedience. If any man uses the old ceremonies his devotion is made naught by his disobedience . . . It is a foolish, unlearned devotion. God requires the heart rather than the outward act.[26]

So the government wrote to the recalcitrant Bishop Bonner of London against whom they were also proceeding at this time. (Within weeks he was deprived of his see and thrust into the Tower.)

The uprising in Norfolk was as ideologically distinct from that in Devon and Cornwall as the counties involved were geographically distant from each other. The rebels there were at one with the Protector's evangelical programme. Their initiative began, like other peasant protests, as a holy mission for the redress of economic grievances. As people were caught up in the fervour of the cause it took on the character of a bold, irresistible movement. At the last it disintegrated into blood-lusting mob rule devoid of any ethical *raison d'être*. It began on Monday 8 July at Wymondham, ten miles south-west of Norwich. A crowd who had gathered for a religious feast day found themselves listening to self-appointed agitators demanding to know why, a year after the announcement of commissions to enquire into enclosures, nothing had been done. Buoyed up by the enthusiastic response of the audience, the agitators turned words into actions, leading their followers in an assault on the estates of landowners in the area. Personal feuds mingled with issues of principle to produce several hours of uncontrolled hedge-ripping. This might have exhausted itself when the perpetrators grew tired and hungry and began to drift back to their homes had it not been for the emergence of a charismatic leader. Robert Kett was a man of modest means but he was a gentleman by birth and someone to whom the lower orders listened with respect. He inspired them to believe that if they were resolute and organized they could make an impact on government policy.

Kett led his rapidly growing band towards Norwich, which was then the second city of England in terms of population and mercantile wealth. As they went they continued their onslaught on the offensive boundaries of field and meadow. The local gentry, overawed by the size and temper of the crowd, melted away before them. One prominent landowner who tried to defend his property was pulled from his horse and came within an ace of being clubbed to death. Another was threatened with having his house burned down, the insurgents eventually contenting themselves with the destruction of his dovecotes. The march came to a halt at Mousehold Heath opposite the north wall of the city. Here Kett established his camp and from here he calmly took control of the region as the king's deputy! So effective had Somerset's propaganda been that Kett and his followers could really believe that they were carrying out government policy and that this gave them unlimited powers. Kett began to issue impressive-sounding edicts, such as

> We, the King's friends and deputies, do grant licence to all men to provide and bring into the camp at Mousehold all manner of cattle and provision of victuals, in what place soever they may find the same . . . commanding all persons as they tender the King's honour and royal majesty and the relief of the commonwealth to be obedient to us the governors . . .[27]

When news reached the Protector he first fell back on the tactic that had worked elsewhere. He despatched York Herald to parley with the rebels, assuring them that their grievances would be considered and offering them a free pardon. Kett was having none of this. Pardons were only granted to wrongdoers, he flung back at the royal spokesman. Since they were assembled to carry out the declared will of their sovereign it did not apply to them. This provoked the action which proved to be the turning point of the Norfolk Rising. The herald proclaimed Kett a traitor and tried to arrest him. He ended up fleeing for his life to the safety of the city. The next day (22 July) the rebels overran a large part of Norwich. The die was now cast. Confronting positions had been taken up. The outcome would be bloody. The only question was how bloody.

Somerset could not allow such defiance to go unchallenged. He was forced, against his will, into a military response. Since he could not leave the capital himself and since some of his generals were already involved in putting down the western rebellion, it would have seemed obvious to entrust the government's armed response to England's most talented and experienced field officer. Yet, instead of Dudley he chose William Parr, Marquess of Northampton, a man with virtually no campaign experience but a faithful adherent. Somerset may have underestimated the opposition. Yet it is difficult not to read into his passing over of Dudley some other motive. He had picked up the Westminster rumours that named Dudley as the most effective champion in any challenge to his own authority. It might be very dangerous to make him a present of a formidable mini-army. So, Northampton marched to Norwich through the intense late July heat. His orders were to avoid unnecessary bloodshed by blockading the city and forcing the rebels to surrender but this proved impossible because Kett had withdrawn to Mousehold Heath where he now commanded some 16,000 rebels (including non-combatants). Any competent tactician would have deployed his men in open ground and brought the enemy to battle on his own terms. What Northampton did was lead his men into the city to the rapturous welcome of the terrified people. He thus threw away the advantage his well-trained troops gave him and ensured that they would be tangled up in the narrow streets and confined riverside meadows if and when Kett's superior force decided to attack. The king's men did not have to wait long. The rebels made a sortie during the small hours of 1 August and a more determined assault a few hours later. The hand-to-hand fighting was fierce in conditions which made the rebels' makeshift weapons as effective as the swords and lances of their opponents. In the melee Northampton lost several of his best men, including his second-in-command, Lord Sheffield. He could make no impression on the enemy, who simply came against him in wave after wave. After many hours of ineffective conflict he put an end to the carnage by ordering a retreat and regrouping his men to the south of Norwich. Turning back he could see the smoke and flames rising from several fires started deliberately by Kett's vengeful host. Then he put spurs to his horse and headed south.

For Somerset this humiliation was the last in a series of disasters. His brother's treason, the abandonment of his Scottish campaign, the widespread unrest, treasonable risings launched by both Catholic and Protestant malcontents, Henri II's declaration of war, the news that Exeter was under siege and now the Norwich fiasco, all these events played into the hands of his critics. Yet, like a gambler who throws good money after bad in the frantic hope that his luck will change, the Protector refused to abandon his policies. The immediate priority was the military one. Both rebel movements must be suppressed before disaffection gave rise to widespread anarchy. Even Somerset must have now realized that the restoration of law and order would have to be accompanied by retribution against the traitors and that his own reputation among the people might not survive the sight of their heroes' bodies hanging from gibbets and church towers. They would believe that his promises were empty; that their champion had gone over to the side of their oppressors. However, there was no time for such sombre reflection. On 7 August he accepted the inevitable and wrote to John Dudley ordering him to crush the Norfolk Rebellion.

The earl received his instructions two days later. At dawn on 10 August he sat at his desk to pen a weary reply to a letter he had just received from Cecil.

> . . . seeing how we stand with the French, open war seems better than coloured friendship. I wish we had no more to deal with; as it is we must trust in the Lord. With your letter I received a commission to lead the counties of Cambridge, Bedford, Huntingdon, Northampton, Norfolk and Suffolk, for which I am bound to [the Protector] and Council but wish they might allow the Marquess of Northampton to continue in his commission or, at least, have it renewed. He has lately had enough misfortune and this might discourage him forever. I shall be glad to serve with or under him. No one should be discarded for one mischance, which may happen to us all. Explain this to [the Protector] and write again. In the meantime I will make these counties ready.[28]

William Parr, Marquess of Northampton, was a friend and Dudley must have known that he had received the rough edge of Somerset's tongue for his incompetence (perhaps Cecil's letter had contained the news). His magnanimity in pleading for Northampton was based on his experience of military command. He knew that the best way of handling an officer crushed by his own sense of failure was to show confidence by giving him a new job. This was one of many lessons the self-obsessed Edward Seymour had never learned.

Dudley's confrontation with the Norfolk rebels was brief and effective. On 23 August he arrived in the region of Mousehold Heath with 7,500 troops and with Northampton thankfully occupying the position of second-in-command. He immediately had a meeting with Kett and offered pardon in return for immediate dispersal of the host. This was refused and Dudley responded by encircling the rebel camp. On 24 August, a little after dark, he led an infantry attack on the city, broke through the flimsy defences, engaged the occupying force in street fighting and, within hours, had expelled them, though not before the enemy had captured and carried off some of his artillery. The swift execution of all prisoners gave warning to Kett and his followers that continued resistance could only have dire consequences. Having cut the Mousehold supply lines from the city and the surrounding country, Dudley waited for the enemy to make a move. Kett's superior force occupied the high ground of the Heath but would be unable to last out long without supplies. Behind them was a stretch of marshland. They were effectively trapped. Dudley's men, by contrast, were well victualled and he was expecting reinforcements in the shape of 1,400 German mercenaries.

What was obvious to Dudley was less so to the citizenry who, not unreasonably, feared a repetition of the fate that had overtaken them when Northampton had tried to hold Norwich. Their leaders came to the commander-in-chief, begging him to remove his troops to open ground and deal with the rebels at a safe distance from their homes. It was a difficult moment for Dudley. If he did not win over the townsmen it was conceivable that they would try to appease Kett by betraying Norwich to him. He decided on a dramatic, chivalric gesture. Summoning the city elders and all his captains, he told them that he had no intention of retiring. 'I will first suffer fire, sword, finally all extremity,' he said, 'before I will bring such a stain of infamy and shame either on myself or you.' Then, turning to his officers, he bade them 'kiss one another's swords, making the sign of the holy cross' and swear a solemn oath not to desert Norwich until they had 'utterly banished the enemy or else, fighting manfully, had bestowed their lives cheerfully for the King's majesty.'[29] Once again he had demonstrated the charisma and the understanding of men that makes a great leader. After this the resolve of the people held firm, though Kett launched a series of attacks in a desperate attempt to regain the city. When they failed, he knew that his only hope lay in forcing Dudley into an open battle and trusting in his greater numbers to carry the day. During the night of 26 August he moved his men down to lower ground. The place was called Dussindale.

Dudley gave the rebels no time to complete their preparations. At first light he led his cavalry out to Dussindale. He was confronted by rows of makeshift defences. The rebels had been toiling all night by the light of camp fires, digging ditches, throwing up earthworks and setting up lines of pointed stakes as a deterrent to the cavalry. They had arranged the captured artillery in what they thought to be strategic positions, though whether they had the expertise necessary to fire their pieces effectively is doubtful. But Kett had one other encumbrance to put in the path of the formidable foe preparing to storm his position. Over the previous month his men had taken several prisoners gentlemen, burgesses and servants who had remained loyal to their masters. Having prominent local figures in their power had reinforced their bitterness towards their social superiors and encouraged them to make sweeping demands, summarized in a twenty-nine-point manifesto which went far beyond the issue of enclosures. This document was an expression of class hatred which would have stripped major landowners and clergy of most of their authority and economic power. Kett now made a dramatic demonstration of his contempt for the leaders of shire society by bringing the prisoners to the battlefield, chaining them together and placing them in front of their defensive position.

If we seek a psychological moment which moved Dudley from being an unhappy but loyal supporter of Somerset to an active agent for regime change this may have been it. The fellow Englishmen he was being asked to hack down were facing him in their ramshackle, pseudo-military redoubt because of the Protector's ill-conceived policies. He had no great enthusiasm for the work he was called upon to do that day and his first action on arriving at the battlefield was to send a herald with a repeated offer of pardon to all except the ringleaders. Only when this was scorned did he send his professional warriors crashing through the enemy barricades. For the peasant soldiers, many of whom had never seen war, the thundering charge of several hundred *landsknects* must have been a terrifying sight. Their ranks broke at the first onslaught. After that the 'battle' was no more than a rout. At one point some of the rebel leaders managed to rally a contingent of their men from the scene of bloody panic and gathered them together for a last-ditch stand. Seeing this, Dudley called a halt to the action. He sent the herald once more with an offer of pardon to all who would yield themselves to the royal mercy. The peasants, understandably, thought this was a trick. To reassure them the general rode forth in person and gave his word for their safety. The remnant of Kett's army threw down their weapons. The Norfolk Rebellion was over. At Dussindale there fell some 250 of the king's men. The losses on the other side were ten times greater. No one ever made a careful count.

Dudley was true to his word: most members of Kett's mob were spared. The prime movers had to suffer. They were traitors who had risen against lawful authority and committed acts of pillage, wanton destruction and murder. It was necessary for justice to be done and to be seen to be done. Dudley ordered the traditional punishment for treason but the number of those who perished in the aftermath of battle is, again, not known. However many it was, the executions did not satisfy the burgers of Norwich. They had seen their houses burned, their business premises ransacked, their families terrorized and they wanted vengeance. Dudley refused to assuage their bloodlust. To their demand for more deaths he replied,

'There must be measure kept and, above all things, in punishment men must not exceed.' He knew [he said] their wickedness to be such as deserved to be grievously punished and with the severest judgement that might be. But how far would [the townsmen] go? Will they ever show themselves discontented and never pleased? Would they have no place for humble petition; none for pardon and mercy? Would they be ploughmen themselves and harrow their own land?[30]

Yet, whatever disappointment this may have caused the more rabid members of the Norfolk establishment, it did not spoil the overwhelming sense of relief and rejoicing in the city and its environs. On 29 August Dudley and his captains went in procession to the church of St Peter Mancroft for a service of thanksgiving. For the remainder of their stay they were feted by the wealthier inhabitants and the 'triumph' of Dussindale was marked in perpetuity by the anniversary being declared a public holiday and by Warwick's arms being displayed alongside the royal insignia on the city gates.

One member of Dudley's family had particular cause to be pleased with the brief campaign and its outcome. The earl had been accompanied by his three older sons, John, Ambrose and Robert. On their approach to Norwich the royal army camped one night on the estate of Sir John Robsart of Stanfield Hall, a relative by marriage of Robert Kett but certainly no supporter of his. Robsart was, in fact, one of the prominent gentlemen of the shire; only recently he had served a term as Sheriff of Norfolk and Suffolk. He conceived it to be his duty to speed the royal force on their way and he received the senior officers as his guests. Among those who catered for their needs was their host's seventeen-year-old daughter, Amy. Robert, more extrovert than his brothers, was immediately smitten by her and she was more than ready to be swept off her feet by the dashing cavalryman in his plumed helmet and part armour. The Robsarts and their relatives, the Flowerdews and Appleyards, were among those involved in the celebrations and the more sombre task of administering justice in the aftermath of the rising. There was, then, opportunity for the young people to become better acquainted. Whether their fathers set in hand the necessary financial arrangements then or later, Robert and Amy were married the following summer. John Dudley could have arranged to ally all his children to the leading families of the realm in order to build up a strong network, but this, it seems, was not a preoccupation of his, a further indication that the traditional assessment of him as a power-hungry schemer is wide of the mark. Robert, at least, was allowed to follow the dictates of his heart.

The alliance with an influential Norfolk family did little for Dudley at a national level but it was not without its political significance. As a reward for suppressing the rebellion he received some of the confiscated Howard lands in the county. He subsequently saw Robert established as an important member of the land-owning class in north Norfolk. Perhaps in the long term he envisaged the Dudleys assuming the eminence vacated by the Howards. In the event it was his failure to secure a following in East Anglia that proved his undoing. He may have been the saviour of the Norfolk gentry but the events of August 1549 left a bitter memory for many lesser folk. Dussindale was not and could not have been the end of mutual ill-feeling in the county between landlords and tenants. For months the authorities were having to deal with seditious preachers, unruly gangs and loudmouthed critics who railed against the gentry when they had a few jugs of ale inside them. In the fullness of time John Dudley would inherit the legacy of this ill will.

The hero returned to London on 8 September, having disbanded most of his troops but still accompanied by the hired mercenaries. The critical events of the next month were probably as complex and confusing for those involved in them as they have been for historians seeking to unravel them. By 14 October the Duke of Somerset had been removed from office and conveyed to the Tower. But how and by whom he was brought down are questions not easy to answer. All the players involved had their own game plans and the eventual outcome was the result of conflicting aims and ambitions. The simple analysis that presents Dudley returning from Norfolk to put into operation a preconceived plot, subtly using the Catholic members of the Council for his own ends, must be discarded. He moved from event to event and day to day.

The basic elements in the political situation were as follows: First, by now all the councillors realized that the nation was under

the overbearing rule of a self-centred man, greedy for private gain

while severe on the profits of others, incompetent at handling all
personal relations and disastrously incompetent in politics, well-
meaning but erratic, willing to employ drastic instruments and
ignore the basic elements of the constitution.[31]

Impervious as ever to the results of his policies, Somerset had, in recent
weeks, received news that his captains had been obliged to abandon the
Lowland forts which were supposed to keep the Scots within bounds
and to cede control to Henri II of much of the territory round
Boulogne. Heedless of his need for political allies, he had continued to
antagonize the very men who were smothering the fires of rebellion. He
wrote carping letters to Lord Russell about his conduct of the western
campaign against the Prayer Book rebels and he offered Dudley considered affronts as hurtful as they were needless. When the successful
commander of the Norfolk campaign suggested that his soldiers
deserved some extra recompense for their effective and expeditious
suppression of the rebellion, the Protector returned a curt refusal. What
was more painful was Somerset's rejection of a personal request. Young
Ambrose Dudley had quitted himself well (or so his father believed) and
he had arranged a method of rewarding him. One of his chief officers
was an old campaigning friend, Sir Andrew Flammock. It may be that
he sustained serious wounds during the fighting, for he drew up his will
on 6 September and died a few months later. He and Dudley made an
arrangement whereby Ambrose received the reversion of certain offices
held by Flammock. When Dudley wrote to the Protector on the matter
he received a reply which must have been intended as a deliberate snub.
Not only was the grant refused, it was refused on the grounds that
Somerset had decided to bestow this particular favour elsewhere, upon
one of his own secretaries. It was bad enough that the reversion was
given to a pen-pusher but what added insult to injury was the fact that
the recipient, Thomas Fisher, was a one-time servant of the Dudleys
who had transferred to the Protector's household.

Such incidents made it plain that Somerset was quite unchastened by
his increasing isolation. The only ace he held in an extremely weak hand
was his control of the king's household, and this he used in a desperate
attempt to influence Edward and his companions against his potential
rivals. Among the accusations brought against the Protector a few weeks
later was,

. . . you declared and published untruly, as well to the King's majesty as to other the young lords attendant upon his grace's person, that the lords of the Council at London minded to destroy the King; and you required the King never to forget it but to revenge it. And likewise you required the young lords to put the King in remembrance thereof, to the intent to make sedition and discord between the King and his lords.[32]

Despite all that had happened in July and August Somerset's popularity still stood high with the people and this constitutes the second element in the October crisis. They were prepared to excuse Somerset of bloodguilt arising out of the suppression of various groups of dissidents and happily heaped all the blame on local gentry and agents sent from London. In all his dealings with the encamped malcontents in various parts of east and central England Somerset had continued to show sympathy and offer concessions. One group of protestors demanded the early recall of parliament. Somerset agreed. Commotioners at Thetford told him that they did not approve the make-up of the local enclosure commission. Somerset invited them to put forward the names of those they would find acceptable. When anxious rebels in Hampshire asked for reassurance that they were all covered by the terms of the latest royal pardon, Somerset replied, 'if his majesty might gain a million of gold to break one jot of it with the poorest creature in all his realm, he would never.'[33] The 'good duke's' rhetoric impressed and encouraged the lowborn advocates of social change. Many of them shared his own belief that he was a man of destiny, a man of the people, raised up to right the wrongs of generations. Somerset believed that he had deserved well of the common man. He trusted in popular support to protect him from his powerful enemies.

The third element and one which, in their different ways, both Somerset and his staunchest opponents relied on was the disunity within the Council. Though the majority were unanimous in their desire to end the duke's autocracy they could not agree on the style of government that should replace it. The leading Catholics, Thomas Wriothesley, Earl of Southampton, and Henry Fitzalan, Earl of Arundel, hoped for and worked towards a complete reversal of the policies that had been followed since the last months of the old king's reign. They were encouraged by divisions among the progressives and by changes in the composition of the Council which had weakened the Protector's support. Sir Anthony Denny, the hugely influential evangelical councillor and courtier, died on 10 September and other changes to the Council, occasioned by death, promotion or demotion, had already brought onto the body men who

were not card-carrying reformers. The evangelical party was in disarray
and the two earls, in secret correspondence with the old fox, Stephen
Gardiner, the imperial ambassador and the Catholic network in the shires,
reasoned that, with careful planning, they could get rid of Somerset,
reinstate the Bishops of Winchester and London and the Duke of Norfolk,
offer the regency to Princess Mary and then purge the court and Council
of all remaining heretics, as a prelude to restoring the old religion. While
Dudley and Russell were absent on campaign the Catholics worked hard
on their colleagues and persuaded some (Paget, Petre and, perhaps, St
John and Rich) to change sides. Paget, writing to the imperial
ambassador, expressed the hope that even Dudley might be brought to 'a
better position regarding religion'.

It was Dudley who constituted the fourth element in the situation.
Not only was he the man of the moment with an impressive body of
soldiery at his command, he was also the only councillor with sufficient
charisma to command a following among the people who mattered, the
lords, burgesses and knights of the realm together with the progressive
intelligentsia. With Dudley's support the chances of removing Somerset
were high. Without it they were negligible. Any hope of a Catholic
revival had always rested on driving a wedge between Seymour and
Dudley. Wriothesley and Fitzalan had bided their time for two and a half
years, deliberately cultivating Dudley and sympathizing with his
mounting frustration at the Protector's frequent snubs and rebuffs. In
1547 Wriothesley had incurred a debt of gratitude by agreeing to vacate
Ely Place so that Dudley could take up the lease, thereby enhancing his
prestige. By September 1549 Dudley's patience had finally snapped and
he was ready to enter into talks with the Catholic leaders. The only
question was who was using whom.

The crisis of autumn 1549 evolved into a bloodless *coup d'état* carried
out almost in camera but such an outcome was not inevitable. The clash of
fears, ambitions and expectations extended far beyond the chambers of
Westminster, Hampton Court and Windsor. The claims and counter-
claims, the accusations and suspicions hurtled back and forth and eddied
round about so vigorously that no auditor could determine the truth of
things. To gauge the atmosphere in the tense uncertain autumn days of
1549 we need to listen to the rumours, slanders and calls to arms running
through the capital and from the capital across much of England:

To all true lords and gentlemen and us the poor commons:
Let us rise with all our power to defend the King and Lord

Protector against certain lords and gentlemen who would depose
the Lord Protector and endanger the King . . .
(Handbill circulating in London)

Henry A. to all true Englishmen:
Be loyal and not deceived by crafty traitors who aim at one target
and shoot at others. They have murdered the King's subjects and
now, fearing that the Lord Protector . . . would have redressed
things in parliament to the ease of the commons, have conspired his
death. That done, they will murder the King because of their
ambition to restore popery . . . As for London, faithless Troy,
Merlin says that twenty-three of its aldermen will lose their heads in
one day, which God grant be shortly . . .
(Handbill circulating in London)

. . . under pretence of simplicity may rest much mischief, as I fear does
in these men called 'common welthes' and their adherents . . . If words
may be treason, none ever spoke so vilely as these 'common welthes'
saying if they have no reformation before St Clement's Day (23
November) they will seek another way . . .
(Letter of Sir Anthony Aucher from Dover to William Cecil)

A conspiracy has lately risen against the King and us, as was never
seen before. It cannot be maintained without unheard of rumours.
They say we have sold Boulogne to the French and withold soldiers'
wages . . . you are to hasten here for the King's defence with such
force as you have, causing the rest to follow . . . They are not
ashamed to send posts abroad that we are already committed to the
Tower and that we would release the bishops of Winchester and
London and bring back the old mass.
(Letter of Somerset to Lord Russell and Sir William Herbert)

The Duke of Somerset, seeing his detestable treasons detected,
levied many men to achieve his devilish purpose, to the great peril
of the King and state, and also spreads false rumours against us the
King's council assembled here. Publish this in all places within your
shrievalty and allow no men to be raised or molested by any orders
not from us . . .
(The Council in London to all sheriffs)[34]

So each person interpreted events in his own way and read the signs of the confused times according to his best information.

When Dudley returned from Norfolk he received the applause of his fellow councillors but no word of official thanks in the name of the king or the Protector. In fact, there was little contact of any kind between Somerset, who spent the summer, when he was not on his estates, with the royal household at Hampton Court, and the 'Council in London'. The duke's habitual aloofness now contributed to his undoing. He had no first-hand knowledge of what Wriothesley, Dudley and others were saying and planning behind his back. He spurned negotiation and therefore could only feed off rumours of plots and suspicious troop movements.

Any 'conspiracy' was a long time in brewing. Dudley and the Catholic leaders had a series of meetings, no doubt sounding each other out very cautiously, careful not to commit themselves until they knew what reaction to expect. Van der Delft, the imperial ambassador, learned from Princess Mary that she had been approached about giving her blessing to a move against Somerset and the possibility of accepting the regency. Interestingly, in wisely declining to lend her name to a conciliar faction, she described Dudley as 'the most unstable man in England.' What she meant was that she regarded the earl as someone in two minds. She could not convince herself that he had thrown in his lot with her political friends or that he had turned his religious coat. Paget, and he may not have been alone, was trying to bring Dudley round to the old religion and Dudley seems to have encouraged them to hope by obliging his household to take up certain Catholic observances but Mary knew better than to read too much into such outward show – and so should we. Dudley had always been plagued by uncertainties when it came to his role in political affairs and he had good reason now for playing his cards close to his chest. He had convinced himself that Somerset must go but had no intention of allowing reactionaries to take his place and drag king and country back into the pre-Reformation era. In order to explore what the Catholic alliance had in mind Dudley himself rode out to Van der Delft's country residence for what might now be called a 'full and frank exchange of views'. Piece by piece he collected the information he needed about individuals and caucuses but still he kept his own counsels. In all probability he did not know himself what he would do.

It may be that these inconclusive debates would have dragged on for weeks or months had not a panicking Somerset accelerated the crisis. He planned a purge of the Council in order to fill vacant places with his own nominees. When the London men heard of this they responded by appointing, on their own authority, four new members, all Catholics. The London group had now become a rival government. Waverers were forced to choose between the ruler at Hampton and the rulers at Westminster. The councillors at court began drifting away to join their colleagues. It might still not have been too late for the Protector to open negotiations with the dissidents but, instead, he chose a trial of strength. On 30 September, he issued an order for all armed soldiers to leave the capital. He presumably intended to deprive his rivals of military backing and then march into London at the head of his own army to the cheers of the multitude. Yet critically he failed to make a move. There followed a few days of paralyzing, nail-biting indecision. At last, on 5 October, he issued what was effectively a declaration of war against the London councillors. It was an appeal, over the heads of all central and local authorities, to the common people:

The King to all subjects, to repair armed and with all haste to Hampton Court to defend the King and the lord protector, against whom a most dangerous conspiracy has been attempted.[35]

It was only the following day that Somerset sent messages to Lord Russell and Sir William Herbert, who still had armies in the field, to come to his aid.

The gloves were now off. The London councillors replied, on 6 October, with strongly worded appeals to the leaders of the shires:

The King is in danger because of the treason of the Duke of Somerset, who now has it rumoured that we of the council intend evil to his highness, hoping to deceive and be aided by the people. For the King's surety we require you to let the people know the truth; and since he already gathers force, to put yourself in order with all the power you can and repair to us for the King's service.[36]

On the same day Somerset set out for London with the king. He sent word ahead to the Lieutenant of the Tower, hoping to reach its security and overawe the city. The London councillors forestalled him and swore the guardian of the fortress to their cause. When the Protector realized that he was too late he turned and headed for Windsor Castle, the only other available stronghold. Armed contingents were already responding to his summons from a wide area of southern England and the Protector still had hopes of putting himself in a strong defensive position. He looked for the arrival of the western army within days. However, Russell and Herbert were more concerned about the ugly mood in the shires than Somerset's predicament. They brought their men as far as Andover, then halted. Somerset now reaped the harvest of his high-handed attitude towards his commanders in the field. It must have been with some relish that the generals wrote to him on the 8 October:

> . . . As long as we thought the nobility now assembled had conspired against the King, we proceeded with our company. But today we heard from the lords that they are loyal, which we believe, and that this great extremity proceeds only from private causes between you and them. We have therefore decided to levy as great a force as we may for the safety of the King and realm. Let the King not fear, and conform yourself, as these private causes produce universal displeasure. Let bloodshed be prevented by any means. *We much dislike your proclamations and bills put about for raising the commons.* Evil men will stir as well as loyal subjects . . . [my emphasis][37]

The generals spoke for the majority of substantial men in the country who by now regarded Somerset as a demagogue and a rabble rouser. The duke had boxed himself into a corner. His rivals had trained troops ranged against him and his only assets were his control of the king's person and the growing number of ordinary countryfolk converging on Windsor. But it was an illusion to believe that he could rely on these. Edward was becoming very upset at being hustled round the country and used as a shield for his uncle's protection. He was looking increasingly for advice and comfort to Cranmer and Paget, the only other councillors still in his entourage, and they were using their influence to draw Somerset back from disastrous confrontation. As for the people, to lead them against the forces of Dudley, Russell and Herbert would be to invite a bloody repetition of Dussindale. Later the same day the secretary, Sir Thomas Smith, was able to send word to London that the Lord Protector had bowed to the inevitable. Smith, one of the most honest as well as most brilliant scholars of his age, was loyal to Somerset long after others had deserted him. He told William Petre, his colleague, that the situation at Windsor had plunged him into the depths of despair. Although he disliked some of the Protector's doings, he said, 'I cannot leave the King and him who is my master, from whom I have had all.'

He informed the Council that Somerset was prepared to leave office and begged the men in London to be merciful towards him, 'that the country does not have a double tragedy in one year and become the scorn of the world.'[38]

It remained only to agree the terms of Somerset's surrender, and letters flew back and forth between Windsor and Westminster over the next few days. The once mighty duke, in genuine fear for his life and property, was reduced to grovelling. One of the messages with which riders hurried to London was a personal appeal to Dudley based on their ancient friendship:

> My lord, I cannot persuade myself that there is any ill conceived in your heart as of yourself against me; for that the same seemeth impossible that where there hath been from your youth and mine so great a friendship and amity betwixt us, as never for my part to no man was greater, now so suddenly there should be hatred; and that without just cause, whatsoever rumours and bruits, or persuasions, of others have moved you to conceive. In the sight and judgement of Almighty God, I protest and affirm this unto you, I never meant worse to you than to myself; wherefore, my lord, for God's sake, for friendship, for the love that hath ever been betwixt us or that hereafter may be, persuade yourself with truth, and let this time declare to me and the world your just honour and perseverance in friendship, the which, God be my witness, who seeth all hearts, was never diminished, nor ever shall be while I live . . .[39]

It is a moving letter, even when we take into account that it was written at a time when hearts were prone to be worn on sleeves and by a man desperate to save himself from a traitor's death. Was Dudley moved by it? He could not have accepted the writer's ingenuous plea that he had no cause to be angry with his old comrade in arms. Ever since January 1549, Somerset had consistently presumed upon and abused the 'friendship and amity' to which he now appealed. On the other hand, Dudley knew that the 'persuasions of others' were seeking to drive a wedge between him and the duke for their own purposes. Clearly, John Dudley did feel a residual affection for Edward Seymour. Their paths had run close and parallel for too long for him to be indifferent to the latter's fate. Despite all the provocations he had been offered, he only entered late into the intrigues against the Protector and all he wanted to do was reduce Somerset to the level of equality with the other executors of the late king's will. Wriothesley certainly, and others possibly, had a more drastic fate in mind for the chief enemy of Catholic truth and the landed interest, and Dudley obviously knew the hatred that motivated them. A few weeks later it was he who delivered Somerset from the wrath of his sworn enemies. So it would seem that the virtual prisoner at Windsor did not appeal in vain for sympathetic treatment.

Dudley's collaboration with the friends of Rome at this time has been variously interpreted over the centuries. Some have assumed that he was a cynical politician who lacked religious principles and would always go with the flow. Others have suggested that he was playing cat and mouse with the Catholic leaders and following a cleverly worked out plan. Both assessments cannot be right; in my opinion neither is. According to contemporaries, Dudley was a man who was difficult to 'read'. The experienced diplomat and humanist scholar, Sir Richard Morison, described him as someone who had 'such a head that he seldom went about anything but he conceived first three or four purposes beforehand.' A French communiqué placed a much more sinister interpretation on the hidden workings of Dudley's mind. Dudley possessed, said the writer, 'great acumen' and carried himself with such dignity that 'those less well acquainted with him considered him worthy to be the governor of the realm.' He was 'affable, gracious and kind in speech'. He was lavish both in his own lifestyle and in his generosity towards others. But all this outward show concealed an inner man who was 'proud, vindictive and disdainful of any who opposed him'.[40] What this comes down to is that John Dudley was secretive and politically cautious. But to be secretive is not to be duplicitous and being politically cautious is not the same as being by nature conspiratorial. In the extremely uncertain days of late summer and autumn 1549 he would have been a foolish man indeed who allowed all and sundry to know his plans and opinions. Dudley had been drawn by others into the plot against Somerset, albeit with a certain amount of grim relish. Once in and forced to keep company with ruthless men more adept than himself at political manoeuvring he was circumspect, and wisely so.

Sunday 13 October was the major turning point in the life of John Dudley and of the nation. That was the day that the Duke of Somerset yielded up the protectorate. On Monday he was conveyed to the Tower where his guards provided him with comfortable quarters and enforced a strict ban on all unapproved visitors. Dudley stepped into the vacant position of government leader by virtue of the constitutional arrangements established in Henry VIII's will. This had entrusted the new king and the realm, not to the Council, but to the executors named therein. That body was much more evenly balanced between the conservative and progressive parties than was the Council. Dudley was now the undisputed leader of the evangelicals and, with the firm support of Cranmer, constituted a formidable force. With the removal of Somerset and his adherents at court the first priority was to provide the young king's entourage with replacements acceptable to him and to the new government. Among those 'safe' courtiers appointed to the chamber staff were the Marquess of Northampton, Sir Thomas Wroth, Sir Thomas Darcy, Lord Wentworth and Sir Andrew Dudley, Warwick's brother, all friends of reform. The Earl of Arundel was the only conservative appointee. Dudley took over from Somerset as Lord Great Chamberlain and, at the earliest possible opportunity (19 October), resumed his position as Lord Admiral.

It now remained for him to gather into his hands all the reins of government. Over the next few weeks the battle was on for the control of the Council. The executors installed new members in order to outweigh the Catholics. But Wriothesley and his colleagues did not give up without a struggle and Van der Delft, for one, was confident of their eventual triumph:

> the archbishop of Canterbury still holds his place in the council, but I do not believe they will leave him there unless he improves . . . they are not yet making any show of intending to restore religion, in order that their first appearance in government may not disgust the people, who are totally infected. But every man among them is now devoted to the old faith, except the Earl of Warwick, who is none the less taking up the old observances . . . and it seems probable that he will reform himself entirely . . .[41]

But the ambassador was not the only foreign observer reading the entrails and seeing in them what he wanted to see. The Swiss reformer, John ab Ulmis, was writing home about the same time in equally gloating vein:

> I am able to write to you as a most certain fact that Antichrist in these difficult and perilous times is again cast down by the general decision of all the leading men in all England; and that not only have they decided that the religion adopted last year is the true one,

but a doubly severe penalty has been imposed upon all who neglect it. There is nothing therefore for the godly to fear, and nothing for the papists to hope for . . .[42]

Van der Delft still believed, in mid-October, that Wriothesley was the dominant figure at the Council board. However, within three weeks, he had come to realize that the balance of personalities was somewhat different. While he was encouraged that Wriothesley was lodged at court where 'a great number of lords' resorted to him, he went on to note that Wriothesley had 'most authority with the earl of Warwick', thereby tacitly acknowledging that the latter was making the running. No major household or government office came Wriothesley's way. Indeed, the responsibility he was given, for the defence of Portsmouth and the Isle of Wight, might well have been no more than a ploy to remove him from the centre of power. Parliament under the direction of the Council had begun to dismantle much of Somerset's social legislation but there was little sign that the process of religious reform was to be dealt with in the same way. Indeed, on 30 October, a royal proclamation was issued in order to scotch rumours about a reversal of religious policy. The 'old Romish service, mass and ceremonies', it declared were not about to be restored. It was becoming increasingly obvious that the English Reformation had not been halted by the change of regime.

This did not mean that tension had eased. The leading Catholics, frustrated by the failure of their bid for dominance in Council and chamber, scanned a wider horizon in their desperation to find some way of halting the evangelical bandwagon. They worked for a treaty with the emperor against the French. They renewed their intrigues with Princess Mary's household. Both avenues turned into culs-de-sac and when Sir Thomas Arundel was discovered to be in secret correspondence with Mary, Dudley responded swiftly and angrily by blocking his appointment as the new Comptroller of the Household.

In the second half of November both great rivals were confined to their homes by illness. Dudley was, apparently, troubled with a 'rheum in the head'. Wriothesley's indisposition was, if we believe contemporary reports, more serious:

. . . the earl of Southampton is ill and in danger of death. If he were to fail us now I should fear matters might never be righted . . . a good part of the council is now well disposed but would astray and follow the rest without him for there is not a man among them of sound enough judgement to conduct opposition . . .[43]

So Van der Delft mournfully reported on 26 November. Wriothesley had for some weeks absented himself from Council meetings and according to one source was suffering from consumption. However, he was well enough a few days later to ride to the Tower with some of his colleagues to interrogate Somerset and this might suggest that his malady was, in part at least, psychological. The seasoned intriguer had allowed himself to believe that he would triumph over his enemies and God's enemies and being outmanoeuvred by Dudley may have plunged him into black depression from which he was only roused by the prospect of giving Somerset the third degree. Bullying prisoners was something for which Wriothesley had a distinct flair. Several men and women had suffered questioning and, in some cases, torture at his hands when the government required information or confession, Catherine Howard, Anne Askew, the Earl of Surrey, to mention just the more celebrated. Thomas Wriothesley was a man who derived personal satisfaction from destroying careers and lives. Interrogating the hated Somerset would have been a treat he would not have wanted to deny himself, sickness or no sickness.

What emerged from this examination was a wild plot, the last desperate throw of the Catholic dice. It is reminiscent of the strikes against Cranmer and Catherine Parr, in which Wriothesley was also involved; yet another attempt to decapitate the evangelical cause. Under interrogation Somerset's defence was that he had done nothing without the approval of the Council. It occurred to Wriothesley and his co-conspirators that if the ex-Protector were put on trial and made the same claim, then his inevitable condemnation must stain the leading radical councillors who had backed him. Richard Scudamore, a London evangelical who passed on news to his friend Sir Philip Hoby at the imperial court, claimed to know what was afoot. Wriothesley planned to bring down two birds, Somerset and Dudley, with one stone:

> . . . being hot to be revenged of the both for old grudges past when he lost his office, [he] said . . . I thought ever we should find them traitors both; and both is worthy to die for by my advice. My lord of Arundel in like manner gave his consent they were both worthy

to die, and concluded there that the day of execution of the lord protector the earl of Warwick should be sent to the Tower and have as he had deserved.[44]

Wriothesley's indisposition might have obliged him to be absent from the Council. Dudley used the excuse of an attack of rheum to make the Council come to him. Frequent meetings were held in his Holborn mansion, where he could more easily dominate the proceedings. Thither the whole Council was summoned to hear the reports of Somerset's examination and to decide on the prisoner's fate. The scene in Dudley's bedchamber, even if exaggerated, carries conviction. It was coloured with that sense of theatre for which Dudley had a penchant. The members of England's executive ascended to the main chamber of Ely House and were ushered in by a servant. There they discovered the Earl propped up on cushions, with 'a warlike visage' and one hand resting on a long broadsword which lay upon the coverlet. As they stood or sat around the great bed, Wriothesley enumerated Somerset's faults and commented on his demeanour. He gave it as his judicial opinion that the duke was guilty of 'many high treasons', for which the penalty was death. Everyone looked to the sick man for his reaction. Dudley's reply was brief, blunt and unequivocal: 'My Lord, you seek his blood and he that seeketh his blood would have mine also.'[45] The message to the councillors was clear; 'whoever is not for us is against us.' From this point on it became obvious that Dudley planned to release Somerset and would probably readmit him to the Council. The Reformation would stay on track and probably gather momentum. Above all, it appeared that England had a new master.

10

The Cares that Wait upon a Crown

———⟩∘◦∘⟨———

England had a king and one who was no longer a child. At twelve years of age Edward was already showing signs, or so his tutors averred, of becoming the third great Tudor monarch. He resembled his grandfather more than his father, serious beyond his years, meticulous about taking notes and keeping records, emotionally detached almost to the point of cruelty and, above all, intensely religious. He seemed to be growing steadily into the role allotted him of England's Josiah, after the great reformist king of the Old Testament, and there was every indication that he would become an extremely capable monarch. According to Hooper the boy's devout and scholarly disposition set the tone for all the members of his household (which included at least two of Dudley's sons):

> He receives with his own hand a copy of every sermon that he hears and most diligently requires an account of them after dinner from those who study with him. Many of the boys and youths who are his companions in study are well and faithfully instructed in the fear of God and in good learning.[1]

Several of these 'boys and youths' would become the mature courtiers of Elizabeth's reign and ensure a continuity of Protestant idealism.

Historians inevitably compare Somerset and John Dudley as 'uncrowned kings' of England but the circumstances in which the two men found themselves were very different. Somerset was the closest relative of a child monarch and could never throw off the pretensions that arose from the fact that he and Edward had shared blood. He believed that this gave him a special place in the state and certainly set him above his fellow councillors. Dudley, by contrast, was very conscious that he was the first among equals, and sometimes he even eschewed that eminence in his dealings with his colleagues. As for his relationship with the king he understood that his was only a caretaker position. No one could foresee that Henry VIII's only son would die young. Everyone expected him to grow into a monarch who would achieve the same regal stature as his father and grandfather. In a little more than five years Edward would assume full control. Those years would be vitally important for king and country and Dudley saw himself as having a dual role during this period. He had to tutor the young king in all aspects of policy and that meant persuading Edward to endorse those attitudes and decisions of which his Council approved. At the same time he had to encourage Edward to develop his own ideas. He had fertile ground to work with in this respect, for the boy already possessed a determined, not to say stubborn, streak.

The fact that Somerset and Dudley exercised the same *de facto* power in government is not as relevant as the fact that they understood and used that power differently. Professor Hoak, the expert on Edward VI's Council, has succinctly pointed out the distinctive features of their attitudes. Somerset, he explains, 'called together only so many councillors as he thought it convenient to consult occasionally.' Dudley 'exercised very much the same power as the Lord President of an organised, continuously working board staffed by his supporters or appointees.'[2] On Somerset's fall the offices of Protector of the Realm and Royal Governor were abolished. Government then devolved constitutionally upon the body of executors appointed by Henry VIII. This group assumed the right to nominate members of the Council. Dudley now dominated it and was able to expel Wriothesley and Arundel from the Council and replace them with his own allies. He assumed the office of President of the Council and since he also became Lord Great Master of the Household he was supreme in the two centres of power. There was nothing novel about one man holding both these positions; it had become customary to link them. In fact, what Dudley did was restore the honour of the council presidency which had become a cypher under Somerset's regency. What was new was the transformation of prestige offices into an effective power base.

The relationship between Dudley, the king and the Council looked different from different perspectives. A French diplomat regarded the Lord President as nothing but a cynical manipulator. Dudley, he reported,

had given such an opinion of himself to the young King that he [the King] revered him as if he were himself one of his subjects – so much so that the things which he knew to be desired by Northumberland [Dudley became Duke of Northumberland in October 1551] he himself decreed in order to please the Duke and also to prevent the envy which would have been produced had it been known that it was he [the duke] who had suggested these things to the king. He [Northumberland] had placed [in the King's household] a chamberlain, [Sir John] Gates who was his intimate friend and principal instrument which he used in order to induce the King to something when he did not want it to be known that it had proceeded from himself; [it was Gates] who was to report back to him everything said to the King, for this Gates was continually in the Chamber . . . All of the others who were in the Chamber of the said [King] were creatures of the Duke. [Sir Henry] Sidney was his son-in-law and it can be said that he had acquired so great an influence near the King that he was able to make all of his notions conform to those of the Duke. When there was anything of importance which he [Northumberland] wanted to be done or said by the King without it being known that it had proceedeth by his motion, he visited the King secretly at night in the King's Chamber, unseen by anyone, after all were asleep. The next day the young Prince came to his council and proposed matters as if they were his own.[3]

This can scarcely be considered an impartial assessment and was written after Dudley's disgrace and execution. However, it was certainly true that the Lord President relied very closely on friends, relatives and clients placed about the king. This does not bear an inevitably sinister interpretation. In the immediate aftermath of the October 1549 coup Somerset's cronies in the Chamber were replaced by 'safe' men including the Earl of Northampton and Sir Andrew Dudley. Of those specifically referred to by the French observer as Dudley's 'creatures', Sir John Gates had been on the privy chamber staff during the last years of the old king and had been a close associate of Sir Anthony Denny. Henry Sidney had been a constant companion of Prince Edward from his earliest days and was one of the boy's intimate friends. Most of the young king's other companions were men in whose company he had grown up and with whom he was comfortable. They were chosen as much for their acceptability to Edward as for their loyalty to Dudley. As for those private, nocturnal audiences, they suggest the very opposite of what the French critic implied. Here was the king's 'business manager' actually meeting with his sovereign to explain the intricacies of national and international affairs and to elicit the royal endorsement. He would have been far more culpable if, like Somerset, he had attempted to run the country without reference to the titular monarch.

John Dudley had a profound respect for both king and Council. No reader of his letters can conclude that he saw himself as another Wolsey or Cromwell, determined to overawe the other advisers or come close to usurping the royal prerogative.

> Let us be ready to spend our goods, lands and lives for our master and country, and despise the flattering of ourselves with riches as the greatest pestilence in the commonwealth. Let us not be blinded and abused by those so inflicted. Though plagued in body and purse, I am rich in goodwill to serve my master and commonwealth.[4]

So Dudley protested to Cecil in December 1552 and it was not the only occasion on which he wrote in similar vein. Before we dismiss such sentiments we should measure Dudley's words against his actions.

As the months passed Edward became more and more involved with the work of government. The first indication of a new regime was the regular location of Council meetings. Somerset had usually summoned his colleagues to one or other of his own residences. Dudley decreed that the Council should meet at court and that when the king was on progress some of his councillors should be on hand to consult with him, leaving only a rump at Westminster. This was not difficult to achieve because there was no institutional gap between Council and chamber. Several of Edward's household officers and attendants also belonged to the advisory body. In other words the young king always had to hand men he trusted with whom he could discuss affairs of state. Early in 1552 the situation was formalized when the 'Council for the State' was set up. This was a body largely, but not exclusively, chosen from among the members of the Council, who were appointed to meet with the king once a week to overview the more pressing items of government business and draw up an agenda for the ensuing six days. It is not clear how much creative input Edward made to these discussions but the intention was to familiarize him with the complexities of the nation's affairs and he responded as a serious young man would to taking on those responsibilities for which he had been trained every day of his short life.

As for Dudley, he too studied to make his royal charge into a king. And not just any king but the assertive, confident heir of his magnificent father. We can see both their minds at work in a letter bearing the stamp of the royal signet which was sent to the Lord Chancellor, Richard Rich, in October 1551. Rich had returned to the Lord President a previous despatch from the Council at court on the grounds that it did not carry enough signatures. It brought an imperious response. Was the Lord Chancellor, Edward demanded, casting doubt on the king's authority?

> We think that our authority is such that whatever we do by the advice of our council attendant, although much fewer than eight, has more strength than to be put into question. You are not ignorant that the number of councillors does not make our authority. If you or any other should be of any other opinion . . . that is not convenient and might be harmful where our affairs, for lack of speedy execution for expectation of other councillors might take great detriment.[5]

Edward had discussed his stern response with Dudley but the sentiment and the sense of personal affront were his own and he recorded as much in his private journal. If he were expected to submit every decision to be endorsed by a large committee, he noted, 'I should seem to be in bondage.'[6]

The king was emerging from the chrysalis of total dependence on sage counsel and John Dudley was creating the conditions for this metamorphosis. The Lord President's letters to the Council were increasingly peppered with such comments as 'when you have showed the letter to the king, if he likes it, you may work with the rest of the lords,' 'the King has seen [this letter] and would have the man communed with', 'it is time the King's pleasure were known for the speaker of the house [of Commons].' Surviving Council memoranda prepared for Edward indicate that he was consulted on (or at least informed about) a wide range of issues from relations with foreign states to grants of land and pleas from supplicant subjects.

'Without counsel the people fall,' Dudley wrote in September 1552, quoting back to Council Secretary, William Cecil, words from Proverbs 29: 18 previously referred to by his protégé. Good government during a minority depended, both men agreed, on a body of men who were united in their objectives and effective in working towards the accomplishment of those objectives. Dudley and his colleagues had before them a heavy agenda of national recovery after the disastrous Somerset years when the kingdom was governed by a man of 'unskilful protectorship and less expertise in government'.[7] Dudley took it as axiomatic that decisions should be made by the whole Council and this is what actually happened, despite the administrative difficulties of the board often being divided during royal progresses. Does this indicate a genuine absence of faction or simply that England had exchanged the tyranny of Somerset for the tyranny of Dudley? Had he so effectively packed the Council and the chamber with his own cronies, and did his powerful personality so dominate the political life of the nation that no one dared thwart his will? It is very difficult to make the surviving records support the traditional image of Dudley as an ambitious, ruthless schemer who subordinated the interests of king and country to his own. Even the final episode of the Seymour tragedy cannot be made to serve the 'wicked Dudley' thesis. Indeed, we gather from the treatment of the fallen Protector a much more rounded view of Dudley's character.

In February 1550 Somerset was set free and subsequently pardoned. This was political expediency dictated by the ex-Protector's popular following and the need to avoid rifts in the evangelical consensus. In order to underline the restoration of amity between the old comrades, Dudley's eldest son, John, was married to Somerset's daughter, Anne, on 3 June. The lavish celebrations at the Somerset estate at Sheen were attended by the king and most of the court and Edward commented favourably in his journal on the 'fair dinner' and the dancing which followed. The only lead player to be absent from the celebrations was the groom's father, Dudley pleaded ill health as the reason for missing John and Anne's nuptials. As well as a show for public consumption, this wedding was a genuine attempt by the two men to patch up their quarrel. But that does not explain the singular mark of favour which had been extended to Somerset in April, when he was restored to the Council, where he became assiduous in his attendance. It may be that Dudley believed or wished to believe that the duke really had turned over a new leaf. He might have been persuaded by his colleagues that the support of Somerset's clientage would be valuable to the regime. He must have recognized that if the ex-Protector were left in the political wilderness he might soon be making mischief, whereas if he were tied into the government it would be much more difficult for him to dissociate himself from agreed policy. Unfortunately Dudley's generosity backfired.

What happened was that whenever Dudley was absent from Council meetings Somerset asserted his authority over the body. On several Council orders and letters it is his name that heads the list of signatures. Far from resenting this, Dudley seems to have encouraged Somerset to take on the role of deputy president. We find him instructing Cecil, 'see what Somerset, the master of the horse, you and the others resolve: send me the instrument if it needs my signature and I will sign it,' and, in order to expedite certain matters while he is absent the secretary is to gather together the appropriate documents so that 'at Somerset's coming to court you may deliver them to him.'[8] Government solidarity was at the centre of Dudley's thinking; if recent troubles were to be laid to rest the nation's leaders must be united behind a coherent agenda. He needed Someset to be and to be seen to be a committed member of the regime and he fell over backwards to accommodate the duke. That is not to say that he did not have misgivings. Within weeks of Somerset's rehabilitation he suspected that the duke was trying to build up a political following of his own. He had, on his own initiative, begun talks with Bishop Gardiner, the Earl of Arundel and others imprisoned for their parts in the recent conspiracy. On 25 June Dudley had an earnest talk with one of Somerset's closest supporters, Richard Whalley, who reported the conversation to Cecil.

> Last night Warwick . . . talked with me at great length about [the Duke of Somerset], to whom he seems a faithful friend, being much concerned about his late proceedings – his unadvised attempt to release the bishop of Winchester and the Arundels and his late conference with the [Earl of] Arundel. He told me that the whole council dislikes these things . . . They all think he aspires to have again the same authority he had as protector. He would harm himself. His late government is still disliked and he does not stand in the King's credit as he and others fondly believe. By discretion he might have the King as his good lord, and all he can reasonably desire . . . let your better wisdom consider [Somerset's] preservation. Never leave him until you persuade him to some better consideration of his proceedings, and to concur with Warwick, who will be very plain with him at his coming to court.[9]

Presumably this overture via one of Somerset's friends was followed by a direct approach. Diplomats, ever eager to detect government rifts, reported that all was well between the two old comrades in arms and throughout the summer and autumn Somerset played a leading role in the work of the Council. It is difficult to see what more Dudley could have done to maintain an honourable place for the ex-Protector in the political life of the kingdom. Unfortunately, Somerset was incapable of responding with a due measure of humility or even intelligence. He remained deaf to the entreaties of friends, the promptings of reason and even to considerations of self-preservation. Had he bided his time and concealed his intentions it might well have been that, in the summer of 1550, Somerset would have had the political field to himself, for Dudley had planned on a long absence.

He had decided to take up once more the governance of the northern border region and a patent was drawn up appointing him Warden of the East and Middle March. The Scottish problem was becoming progressively worse. England's inadequately provisioned Lowlands garrisons were picked off, one at a time, by the local Scottish magnates with help from Henri II, and French influence north of the border had never been stronger. In February Dudley realized that he could not devote sufficient attention to the guardianship of the Narrow Seas and, in February, he handed the Admiralty into the safe keeping of his protégé, Lord Clinton (who continued in that post with one brief intermission until his death in 1585) and prepared to travel north to negotiate a new agreement with the Scots and to reinforce the authority of central government in an area where the loyalty of local magnates could not be automatically relied on.

However, on 19 July, a Council minute recorded, 'it was not thought convenient that the Earl of Warwick should, according to the former order, go into the north, but rather for many urgent considerations attend upon the King's person.'[10] Plans for the border region were downgraded, the veteran soldier and lawyer, Sir Robert Bowes being sent to make a thorough survey of the territorial and political situation. Chief among the 'many urgent considerations' for the change of plan was the behaviour of Somerset. Every policy that was ill received by a substantial section of the political nation played into Somerset's hands, since he was the obvious focus for discontent. So far from associating himself with the decisions of the conciliar majority he allowed government opponents to know that they had his sympathy. One place to which he could look for support was parliament and he tried to persuade the Council to recall it. The two houses had been adjourned for Easter and members had been told to be ready to reconvene in October. Yet, despite the government's need for money and the piling up of other urgent business, Dudley insisted on further prorogations and the assembly did not meet again until January 1552.

Foreign diplomats drew their own conclusions, which certainly had some foundation in reality: Somerset and Dudley were at loggerheads in the Council; the duke intended to appeal over the heads of the government to his friends in the country; as soon as the Commons met he would accuse Dudley and the Council of pursuing their own interests rather than those of the king and the people; he was spreading sordid rumours about Dudley, including the extraordinary claim that the earl intended to divorce his wife and marry Princess Elizabeth. Dudley was acutely conscious of how unpopular he was becoming. Since young Edward was beyond criticism Dudley was the target for everyone with a grievance against the government. He was indelibly marked with the stain of having removed the 'good duke' and suppressed the common people in the interests of the wealthy elite. He was also branded as a man who came from tainted stock. Dudley knew that men murmured in corners and commented that one could expect nothing better from the son of an executed traitor. 'Had I sought the people's favour,' he grumbled to Cecil, 'without respect to his highness's surety I needed not so much obloquy for some kind of men. Though my father, after his master was dead, died for doing his master's commands, I will serve without fear, seeking God's glory and his highness's surety.'[11]

In the meantime all Dudley could do was keep a close watch on Somerset and outplay the potential rival in the game of building up alliances. But we must not exclude the personal element in Dudley's reaction to Somerset's opposition. There is no worse enemy than a betrayed friend and Dudley, with much justification, felt himself betrayed. He could truly claim that he had saved Somerset's life, that he had restored him to a place of honour, that he was continuing the religious revolution to which the Protector had been committed. There may well have been considerations of realpolitik in all this but that does not mean that Dudley felt no affection for Somerset or that the years of comradeship in court and on campaign counted for nothing.

Had Dudley been a political animal who enjoyed outwitting enemies and loved power for its own sake – in other words, had he been the Machiavellian schemer of popular legend – he would have been in his element. He was not, and he found the burden of government, the constant demands made upon him and his growing unpopularity wearying and debilitating. He frequently claimed that cares of state undermined his health. If his own self-diagnosis is to be believed his body was racked by sundry torments. In March 1550 he was 'very ill and troubled with sickness'. In September he was laid up with a fever. A few weeks later he had a throat infection (a 'falling of the uvula'). In December 1552 he excused his absence from court with the words, 'Being continually sick I cannot but talk of cure and medicine: bear with my infirmity, for I mean as well to master and country as the fittest.' And when he was not sick himself he worried about the presence of contagious disease in his own household and concluded, 'I think neither I, my son, nor any in my house should repair to the king unless he commands to the contrary or you think it without danger.'[12] How genuine were Dudley's claims to be so frequently incapacitated? There were, if a seventeenth-century chronicler is to be believed, some colleagues and close observers who declined to take the Lord President's protestations at face value.

'What,' said they, 'is he never sick but when affairs of greatest weight are in debating? Or wherefore else doth he withdraw himself from the company of those who are not well assured of his love? Wherefore doth he not now come forth and openly overrule . . . ? Would he have us imagine by his absence that he acteth nothing? Or, knowing that all moveth from him, shall we not think that he seeketh to enjoy his own ends . . . ?'[13]

Dudley's frequent absence from the centre of power does not really square with the image of an overbearing Svengali who made the juvenile king his puppet and crushed all opposition by the force of his personality and the threat of dire reprisals. However well the Lord President and Lord Great Master may have packed the Council and royal household with his own agents and supporters, he could not assert his will effectively if he was frequently away from court, particularly when Somerset and his allies were challenging his authority. It is only when we cast aside the traditional presentation of the 'bad duke' and allow his words and actions to speak for themselves, as they happened, rather than as they have become coloured by the notoriety attaching to the final crisis of his life, that we can properly understand John Dudley, his achievements and his ultimate failure.

The only known or assumed portrait of John Dudley.

Dudley Castle, showing the new lodgings constructed by John Dudley.

Queen Jane with her husband, Guildford Dudley, as
conceived by the Victorian artist C. R. Leslie, RA.

Inscription in the Beauchamp Tower of the Tower of London, carved by John Dudley while he and his brothers were imprisoned there by Mary Tudor 1553–4.

The execution of John Dudley, Duke of Northumberland in 1553, as envisaged by a 19th century engraver.

In 1575 the celebrated Italian artist Federico Zuccari paid a brief visit to England. The only fully attested works from his brush at this time were a portrait of Elizabeth and this one of Robert Dudley.

Kenilworth Castle as it appeared in 1620 – later copy of an original fresco (now lost).

Coronation portrait of Elizabeth I c.1559 by an unknown artist. This painting on panel was probably presented by the Queen to Robert Dudley or his brother, Ambrose.

This seventeenth-century print of Henry VII's new palace at Richmond gives an impression of the splendour which the first Tudor sought to project.

The Lord Leycester Hospital in Warwick was founded by Robert and Ambrose as a home for old soldiers – a function it still fulfils.

This engraving from John Foxe's *Acts and Monuments* celebrates the accession of Edward VI, the new Josiah, and his purging the realm of 'Romish superstition'.

Robert Dudley and his wife Lettice lie beneath this magnificent funerary monument in St Mary's Church at Warwick.

Sir Robert Dudley, illegitimate (?) son of the Earl of Leicester was the most talented member of the family – adventurer, ship designer, engineer, author and courtier. He settled in Florence after the accession of James I. This portrait is after a miniature by Nicholas Hilliard.

The end of the line. Because Sir Robert Dudley's legitimacy was never established, the death of Leicester's only son 'the Noble Imp' in infancy in 1584 meant that the Dudley lands and titles would be dispersed. The young child's effigy lies close to that of his parents in the magnificent Beauchamp Chapel in St Mary's Warwick.

He was a man whose head and heart were often in conflict. Like the good tactician he was, Dudley had a clear understanding of what the country needed. In political terms he was absolutely committed to two principles. He believed that England could only prosper under a strong, personal monarchy. Henry VIII was his model. He had never known any other occupant of the throne, but he had heard stories of the periodic chaos that had afflicted the realm in the days of his father and grandfather. He believed also in consensus government during a royal minority. It followed that he saw his own position as provisional and that he had no intention of emulating the *folie de grandeur* of Somerset's solo rule.

However, when it came to making consensus government work Dudley was hampered by his consciousness of his own limitations and by his impatience to get things done. He had little enthusiasm for committee work and sometimes felt disconcertingly out of his depth in debate. Called upon to give his opinion on a discussion paper prepared by the king, he ruefully confessed, 'as it is all in Latin I can but guess at it.' He asked for a private meeting with the Lord Chamberlain and one or two others who could explain clearly what was on Edward's mind.[14] Dudley held highly educated men in awe and felt keenly his own inability to converse with them on equal terms.

It was largely because of William Cecil's impeccable Protestant–humanist credentials that Dudley advanced his career and used him as his eyes and ears in the Council. In his correspondence with the secretary his frustration with conciliar procedures sometimes broke through. He found it tiresome that his colleagues thought it necessary to have his endorsement of all their decisions: '[I] marvel not a little that . . . my said Lord Chancellor hath sought me and travelled the streets on foot only to speak with me who can show him no more than others that were first privy before me.'[15] He sometimes found oppressive and even unnecessary the sheer volume of letters reaching him every day, 'a mass of matters which I return without having gathered much fruit.' He was cross when people approached him directly on government business: 'Let him and others know that those weighty offices are ruled by the whole board.'[16] Beyond strict conciliar affairs there were always at his doorstep supplicants wanting his help in disputes with neighbours, complaints against local officials, finding a place at court for a son or daughter. Then there were the ambassadors. They always gravitated towards the most influential member of the government, so it was not unusual for Dudley to receive confidential messages from diplomats who had been instructed to speak with him rather than the whole Council. Reporting such a visit from a member of the French embassy, Dudley passed on a dinner invitation issued to all the Council and added wearily, 'I answered that I was so ill that I could not promise to come.'[17] Far from enjoying his pre-eminence, he often felt like a beast of burden, thanklessly carrying the cares of the nation on his aching back.

> I am reminded of the Italian proverb that a faithful servant will become a perpetual ass . . . It is time for me to live of that which God and the King have given me and keep [away] the multitude of crawlers from his court that hang daily at my gate for money . . . What comfort may I have after my long and troublesome life? So long as health gave me leave I as seldom failed my attendance as any others. When they went to their suppers and pastimes after their travail I went to bed, careful and weary. Yet no man scarcely had any good opinion of me. Now by extreme sickness and otherwise constrained to seek health and quiet, I am not without a new evil imagination of men. Why should I wish longer life – but for my few children?[18]

Yet such self-pity was mingled with teeth-gritting determination. Dudley did not court unpopularity. He did not like it. But he did not show it. He was a conviction politician who recognized, as did every other member of the establishment, that authority had to be centred in one individual. In English political life there was no place for cabinet government. Theoretically all decisions were taken by the king in Council and Dudley was assiduous in asserting that he acted as the servant of both but everyone knew that this was a polite fiction. The Lord President might complain when he was pestered with trivia his colleagues could easily have dealt with but he knew that they would not dare sanction any important action without obtaining his approval and he would have been outraged if they had. He might grumble about his large, unwieldy postbag but he knew that he had to direct the nation's affairs and impose on them coherence and consistency. He might admire the intellectual capacity of Council members who could argue the minutiae of complex issues but he was a man of action with little patience for debates that rambled round the shire. His mental equipment was that of the soldier: in politics, as in warfare, one had to identify the problem, take stock of one's resources, and then deploy them with as much efficiency and as little delay as possible. John Dudley shouldered the governance of England for three and a half years and, because he brought to the task a combination of cool calculation and focused energy he ruled extremely effectively. 'Given the circumstances which he inherited in 1549, [Dudley] appears to have been one of the most remarkably able governors of any European state during the sixteenth century.'[19]

The primary 'circumstance' that Dudley inherited was a nation caught up in the greatest revolution it had ever experienced. The Reformation was a religious earthquake whose violent social, political and economic aftershocks vibrated through every urban and rural community in the land. The official dismantling of the old church had made a dramatic start under Cromwell, had faltered in the 1540s and accelerated again during Somerset's protectorate, with the attendant confusion and violence we have already noted. The victor of Mousehold Heath was committed to the restoration of order and we might suppose that the best way to achieve that would have been to allow England a period of calm in which to assimilate the new doctrines, church services and devotional practices imposed by statute and royal proclamation. That would have been a purely political solution and it was not the one Dudley chose to adopt. During the 1549 coup he had made clear that the deposition of Somerset did not imply a reversal of religious policy. Now he encouraged Cranmer and other reformist divines to press on urgently with the establishment of evangelical teaching and worship in every parish. More than that, as the months passed he veered further and further towards the radical end of the theological spectrum.

Dudley's adoption of extreme, aggressive evangelicalism has puzzled many historians. Why should a man whose understanding of the main issues of religious debate was so limited and who, in the last days of his life, recanted his former opinions have hustled his country along the Protestant path so rapidly that it would never be able to retrace its steps? The conventional answer is that Dudley was an unprincipled opportunist who backed the Reformation because it happened to be the best show in town. This simplistic view is not only cynical, it is also anachronistic. The detached, amoral tergiversation which it posits was not only alien to John Dudley, but to most members of mid-sixteenth century ruling élites. Religious beliefs were passionately adhered to by men and women at all levels of society and Dudley was no exception.

To explore the new ruler's relationship to religious change we might start with an event that took place on the morning of 3 August 1550. At St Andrew's, Holborn, a stone's throw from the gateway to Dudley's London residence, Thomas Wriothesley, Earl of Southampton, was laid to rest. The sworn enemy of Seymour, Dudley and religious reform had gone into a rapid decline since being deprived of office in February. A contemporary reported,

> my lord Wriothesley, seeing all his heart was opened against him . . . and [thinking] this act could never be forgiven, and [because] his ambitious mind could take no [lower] place, he killed himself with sorrow in so much as he said he would not live in such misery . . .[20]

Wriothesley went to his grave believing that he and much that he held dear had been defeated. We may assume that his loathing for his enemies remained undiminished. And that makes one aspect of his funeral seem rather strange to modern observers. Wriothesley instructed that the sermon should be preached by John Hooper, probably the greatest Protestant extremist in London and certainly its most controversial celebrity. For over a year Hooper, hot from a long sojourn among the radical evangelicals of Switzerland, had been drawing crowds by his inflammatory preaching. But it was not just the City enthusiasts to whom he appealed. Somerset appointed Hooper as his personal chaplain and the king invited him to preach at court. Dudley also approved of the Protestant firebrand and had just secured his appointment as Bishop of Gloucester.

Some historians have assumed that Wriothesley must have been among those won over in his final months to the cause of radical reform. Why else would he have chosen Hooper to speak at his obsequies? If he had still been an arch-conservative would he not have wanted to use the funeral to launch a final defiance at the regime? The answer is 'No'. It was the custom for the dying, whether facing their end on the scaffold or in their own beds, to make their peace with all men. This was important for their posterity if not for themselves. A man in Wriothesley's position would not want his heir to inherit the enmity of those in a position to blight his career. Wriothesley left his title and extensive lands to a five-year-old son, who became a royal ward. Life could have been made very difficult for the boy if he had been obliged to grow up in the shadow of his father's unpopularity. There was also the principle of *cuius regio eius religio*, the ruler's religion determining the religion of his people. For over twenty years this pragmatic solution to religious conflict had been gaining wider and wider acceptance throughout Europe. Since national unity ruled out the possibility of rival brands of Christianity co-existing within one realm, it made practical sense for the government to decree which one should be followed. There were always some devotees whose consciences were deeply offended by the state religion. For them the choice was exile or the risk of persecution. However, the vast majority, and particularly those with a major stake in their own country, accepted the fait accompli and prayed for better times.

Dudley's basic attitude to life would have been much the same as Wriothesley's, a carefully balanced relationship between his devotion to God, to the king and to his own dynasty. Had he been pressed to explain his faith he might have been disposed to answer as Cromwell had once answered: he believed as the king's majesty believed. There was no doubt about Edward's faith. The young Josiah had been too well brought up by his mentors to be anything other than a committed evangelical and one with the ardour of a zealous adolescent. His father had had a pulpit erected in the privy garden at Whitehall so that all the court could listen to edifying sermons during Lent. Edward extended the practice. The pulpit was occupied every Sunday and those who wanted to remain in the king's good books were careful to be seen there taking notes and discussing the salient points afterwards.

This predilection of the king and the Lord President for radical Christianity (the fiery Scot, John Knox, was one of Dudley's chaplains) has to be seen against the background of a 'leftward' thrust in the nation's official religion. The Edwardian establishment had a sense of a task unfinished. The doctrine and liturgy of the Church of England, they believed, both stood in need of further reformation. The usually cautious Cranmer sounded a clarion call in 1550:

> . . . many corrupt weeds be plucked up . . . But what availeth it to take away beads, pardons, pilgrimages and such other like popery, so long as two chief roots remain unpulled up? . . . the roots of the weeds is the popish doctrine of transubstantiation, of the real presence of Christ's flesh and blood in the sacrament of the altar (as they call it), and of the sacrifice and oblation of Christ made by the priest for the salvation of the quick and the dead. Which roots, if

they be suffered to grow in the Lord's vineyard, they will spread all the ground again with their old errors and superstition.[21]

Since the beginning of the reign England's sense of solidarity with the radical reform movements on the continent had been growing. A steady stream of Protestant leaders came to England, some fleeing from persecution in their own lands, others invited by Cranmer and his friends from sister churches to discuss the burning issues of the day or to take up preaching or teaching posts. Until this point the main foreign influences upon native religion had come from Lutheran or humanist centres. Now Calvinist and Zwinglian theologians were welcomed. They entered into earnest debate with Cranmer and his episcopal colleagues, while their less restrained co-religionists pelted priests in the streets with offal and stirred up iconoclastic gangs to go 'purifying' churches. Cranmer, who had come to reject the miracle of the mass and the Roman concept of sacerdotal priesthood, set about entrenching reformed teaching in a second prayer book and a new ordinal. He was now advocating sacramentarian beliefs such as those for which people like Anne Askew had gone to the stake less than four years before.

Dudley was fully in tune with this re-identifying of English religion. When a disputation on transubstantiation had been held in the Lord's chamber of parliament in December 1548 he had been among the eager participants, though his contribution seems to have largely consisted of heckling the defenders of the Catholic position. One of the first pieces of legislation his government steered through parliament was a new Act against objects of superstition. Hitherto it had been sufficient for churchwardens to see that offending articles were removed from places of worship. Now they were to ensure that all such items were utterly 'defaced and destroyed'. The object was to ferret out statues, roods, reliquaries, stained glass and other superfluous ornaments that had simply been hidden away by church authorities. It was a part of the practice Cranmer referred to of rooting up idolatrous weeds so thoroughly that none was left to sprout again into the Lord's vineyard. The next move by the reforming government was to order bishops to have all altars removed from churches. Since the sacrifice of the mass had been replaced by the 'supper of the Lord' what was required was not a stone altar but a wooden table set lengthwise in the chancel so that Christ's people could gather round Christ's board.

It would be difficult to exaggerate the visual impact of this revolution. Dim church interiors where candlelight had once been reflected from polychrome frescoes and gilded statues were now awash with light through plain glass windows bouncing back off whitewashed walls. The empty spaces where subsidiary altars and shrines had stood were being replaced by pews so that people could listen to long sermons. The 'holy of holies' at the east end where the priest had performed his mysteries in semi-obscurity was now thrown open by the removal of the rood screen, and worshippers were bidden to take their seats to watch a plain-robed minister break bread. The momentum of change, urged on by the king, the Archbishop of Canterbury, a growing number of diocesan bishops, the intelligentsia, dour members of the mercantile community, hot-headed young activists and foreign well-wishers, proceeded at a gallop.

Dudley led the charge, the champion of purified Christianity. Hooper apostrophized him as an 'intrepid soldier of Christ'. Knox lauded him from the pulpit. John Bale, another evangelical firebrand (known to his enemies as 'Bilious Bale' because of his down-to-earth style in religious controversy), dedicated to Dudley his *Expostulation or Complaynte Agaynste the Blasphemyes of a Franticke Papyst of Hamshyre* in which he inveighed against traditionalists who dug their heels in against change. Dudley continued and intensified the evangelical publishing offensive launched by Somerset and Cranmer, encouraging authors and pamphleteers to write in support of the Reformation. The printing/publishing industry expanded so rapidly that experts had to be brought over from the Low Countries to run printshops and instruct English workmen in the necessary techniques. He took every opportunity to replace hostile and lukewarm bishops by zealous radicals. The 1549 Prayer Book was out of date almost before it hit the bookshops and Cranmer soon began work on a revised edition that would reflect the latest theological thinking and, hopefully, unite as many English Christians as possible in support of a common liturgy. As he acknowledged in the preface, this was no easy task:

> . . . the minds of men are so diverse, that some think it a great matter of conscience to depart from a piece of the least of their ceremonies, they be so addicted to their old customs; and again on the other side, some be so new-fangled, that they would innovate all things, and so despise the old, that nothing can like them, but that is new . . .[22]

John Dudley became all too aware of the problem. As he tried to steer the church in the direction he believed it should go he found other hands grabbing for the wheel, hands belonging to men who could not agree among themselves. Not only did they squabble about what seemed to him to be insignificant theological trivia, they opposed his understanding of the relationship between church and state and some of them stood in moral judgement on his own actions. The honeymoon period soon passed and the 'intrepid soldier of Christ' found himself coming under fire from those he had considered his allies.

In mid-1550 a conflict with Cranmer over what Hooper should be allowed to wear at his consecreation as a bishop led to Dudley backing down. After a great deal of argument and a spell in the Fleet prison, Hooper dutifully wore the prescribed garments. But the beginnings of a rift had appeared between Dudley and the leadership of the church. What widened the gulf dramatically was his final and bloody solution of the Somerset problem.

11

Desperate Measures

———⊙⊙⊙———

By the late summer of 1551 it was clear that Somerset was quite unchastened. He opposed Dudley's policies in Council and it must have particularly rankled when the man who had given such an impetus to evangelical reform now extended friendship and support to such enemies of change as Gardiner of Winchester, Tunstall of Durham and Arundel. When Seymour sided with Princess Mary over her refusal to use the new Prayer Book in her household Dudley was furious and launched into a diatribe against the evil of the Mass. Added to this was the perpetual irritation of Somerset's vaunting behaviour round the court. He continually stressed his superior rank and his relationship to the king. And he did not restrict his disruptive activities to the household, but extended his criticisms to a wider audience. All the country's ills, he indicated to friends and sympathizers, stemmed from Dudley's seizure of power. This provoked understandable but petty responses from Dudley. When Somerset's mother (the king's grandmother) died, in October 1550, a 'royal' order was issued that she was to be buried quietly without undue pomp. Six months later Dudley removed from his rival the privilege of having his own meal table at court and in the records of the Order of the Garter he added the words 'on his mother's side' to the statement of Somerset's relation to the king. It was clear to all that friendship had turned into something akin to hatred. It was also clear that the issue of Dudley–Seymour rivalry would have to be resolved soon, if for no other reason than that the government could not put off the recall of parliament indefinitely. What was not clear was how things could be brought to a final resolution. Somerset's support in the country was still strong. Even if he did not talk about the possibility of a counter-coup some less restrained supporters did.

Everyone expected Dudley or Somerset to make a dramatic move. The diplomatic wires were abuzz with rumour: Somerset was planning an alliance with reactionary peers and would ride into the Catholic north to place himself at the head of a formidable force, such as had troubled the realm in 1536–7; Somerset was sounding out potential allies at home and abroad; Somerset was about to make a bid to restore his Protectorate by capturing the Tower and raising London. There was little or no truth in all this gossip but that did not rob it of its power to make mischief. It created such an atmosphere of expectancy that Dudley, the military tactician, at last decided on a pre-emptive strike. And it was very much 'at last'. There had been earlier provocations and opportunities to which Dudley had not responded. In February 1551 Richard Whalley had been clapped in the Fleet prison. Somerset's servant had obviously not been won over by Dudley and he had been canvassing support among the nobility for a restoration of the Protectorate.

During the summer the issue of Mary's freedom of worship provoked interference by the emperor. The princess appealed to him and he vigorously took up her cause. In a heated debate between Dudley and Charles' representative the ambassador put forth his master's claim that Edward's Council had no right to make sweeping religious changes in his name during his minority. At one point the threat was actually made that an imperial army might cross from the Netherlands in order to 'liberate' the boy king from his heretical mentors. It was a passing crisis and Charles was soon too busy elsewhere to do any more for Mary than make vague protests but it was a reminder to the government that their religious settlement was very far from being firmly established and that it had powerful enemies at home and abroad. As Professor MacCulloch has observed, 'Add to all this the undoubted evidence that Somerset was not only seeking out malcontent politicians, but was also actively using his continuing popular following to undermine Warwick's position, and the former Lord Protector could only be seen as a dangerous loose cannon in a highly alarming situation.'[1]

This was the background to a series of actions by Dudley that were morally indefensible and constitutionally questionable but politically necessary. Somerset's absence from court throughout the late summer weeks, because of sweating sickness in his household, gave Dudley the chance to confer with those who might be happy to see the duke brought low. His first act was to consolidate his own position by elevating himself to the top rank of the peerage and by distributing honours and lands to those whose support he relied on. He became Duke of Northumberland. Henry Grey was nominated Duke of Suffolk, William Paulet Marquess of Winchester, and William Herbert Earl of Pembroke. Cecil and six gentlemen of the household received the honour of knighthood.

The promotions were announced in Council on 4 October and the next day the court returned to Westminster from summer progress. Within a couple of days Dudley was locked in secret conference with Sir Thomas Palmer, a courtier and veteran soldier from an old Sussex family whom Dudley had known most of his life. From this meeting emerged a supposed plot of Somerset's to invite Northumberland and Northampton to dinner and there cut off their heads. It was a wild accusation and it is extraordinary that Dudley could not conceive anything more convincing. Had he been a true Iago he would have made a better job of it.

The arrest of Somerset took place on 16 October in a time-honoured fashion. He attended a Council meeting in the morning, then, after dinner, guards were summoned to convey him to the Tower. Over the next couple of days other supposed conspirators joined him there. According to one later account Dudley confessed that of all his acts while in power none weighed more heavily on his conscience than rigging the case against Somerset. But he was irrevocably committed. His plot proceeded jerkily. He bribed a French adventurer to claim that he had been hired by Somerset as the assassin who would do the direful deed. He covered his back by receiving a pledge of troops from the French king in the event of a popular uprising or intervention by the emperor. He prevented the Council from interfering by announcing that in future royal instructions would appear over the signature of Edward alone and would not require the counter-signature of a councillor. Since that, in effect, meant that Dudley's will had been elevated above that of his colleagues, he was now guilty of the same abuse of power for which Somerset had been deprived of office.

Most people refused to believe in Somerset's treason and credulity was further stretched when Palmer changed his story by making new extravagant revelations. Somerset, he alleged, had laid plans to call out the London apprentices (young hotheads of whom the City authorities were always wary), to secure the capital and then use the Isle of Wight as a mustering point for a large personal army. The government had to act with dispatch. Other detainees revealed under pressure words and stratagems of the incarcerated duke that were much closer to the truth. Somerset *had* discussed with the Earl of Arundel the possibility of arresting Dudley and assuming leadership of the Council and he *had* planned to marry the king to his own daughter. By late November Dudley was satisfied that he had as good a case as he was likely to get and Somerset's trial was fixed for 1 December.

The prisoner was brought out of the Tower before dawn. He 'was conveyed through London with the axe of the Tower before him, and with great preparance of bills, halberts, pikes and poleaxes, in most forcible wise; a watch also set and appointed before every man's door through the high street of London.'[2] At Westminster Hall he faced trial by his peers on sundry counts of treason and felony. The members of the jury had been well chosen but that does not mean that they were all happy to do Dudley's bidding. When it came to a choice between the two principal antagonists they felt no great warmth for either and the mood of the crowd inside and outside the hall must have induced a certain nervousness. The trial went on, with an adjournment for dinner, until late in the winter afternoon. At last their lordships retired to consider their verdict and the cavernous space was but dimly lit by flaring torches when they returned and William Paulet, the new Marquess of Winchester, asked them to declare their findings. By a majority vote the jury concluded that the Duke of Somerset was not guilty of treason. However, they found that he had contemplated harm to Dudley and other members of the Council and that was a felony.

Dudley may have allowed himself to feel relief at the outcome, for felony, though a lesser crime, still carried the death penalty. In point of fact, there was no winner in this final contest between two men whose lives had been bound up together for a quarter of a century. Somerset would lose his life but Dudley's reputation suffered just as fatal a stroke. In the aftermath of the trial he had to muster a thousand troops in Hyde Park to overawe the London citizenry and send messages to rural magistrates to deal firmly with malcontents and spreaders of seditious libels (such as the tale that a new currency was about to be issued bearing Dudley's device of the bear and ragged staff). Elaborate security precautions had to be taken on the day of the execution. The scaffold on Tower Hill was ringed by pikemen of the royal guard and their number was augmented by a thousand members of the London militia. They were certainly needed to control the emotionally unstable crowd, 'as great a company as have been seen' according to one eye witness. Somerset went to his death in a quiet and dignified fashion, extolling the people to remain loyal to king and Council.

From the end of 1551 an ever-widening gap opened between Dudley and his ecclesiastical allies. Cranmer and Ridley had both tried to dissuade him from pursuing Somerset to death. Yet what stung Dudley even more sharply was the opposition of John Knox, a man whose career he had taken a personal interest in advancing. The zealous Scot preached against the execution of Somerset in Newcastle and wrote to his patron in frank disapprobation. When Dudley got over his anger at this he brought the Scot to London to enter the debate on the new Prayer Book – and by doing so gave further irritation to Cranmer. The arrangement for kneeling to receive communion to Knox smacked of the idolatry of the old mass and Dudley backed his complaint. Cranmer and other bishops were furious at this eleventh hour intervention and declined to make a major change in the book. Deadlock was only broken by a compromise: the so-called 'black rubric' was added, indicating that no suggestion of transubstantiation or worship of the bread and wine were involved. Once again the cracks were papered over but they were becoming more difficult to disguise.

Theologians, as Dudley was acutely aware, enjoyed the luxury of a two-dimensional approach to national problems. He had to tackle several interrelated issues, relating religious affairs to every other aspect of policy and, as he was already discovering, success in one area often led to complications in another. At the beginning of 1550, the state of the kingdom had presented the appearance of the Augean stables. The Treasury was empty. Relations with France and Scotland remained unresolved. Social and economic discontent smouldered unseen in several areas, ready to break out again as it had in 1549. He had made an impressive start on dealing with all these problems before being distracted by the need to hinder Somerset's obstructiveness. In the spring of 1550 he had reached a settlement with France which had stopped the debilitating drain of men and gold. Boulogne was sold back to Henri II and an alliance drawn up involving the betrothal of Edward to one of the French king's daughters. This counterbalanced the marriage of Mary Stuart to the dauphin and paved the way for the pacification of the Scottish border.

It was a start on the process of balancing the books but the nation's financial problems were complex and not completely understood. Nevertheless, certain facts were quite clear to Dudley and his advisers.

The ruinous expenditure of Henry VIII's last years had created a situation which Somerset had not addressed and a run of bad harvests had made the economic situation worse. Crown debts, a poor reputation for repayment and repeated debasements of the coinage had pushed up prices, reduced the value of the pound on the foreign exchanges and raised the cost of government borrowing. Dudley was no financial expert but he was a clear-headed pragmatist with a good head for business and he knew that firm measures had to be taken to redress a dismal situation. Crown expenditure and income had to be made to balance. That meant making economies and finding new ways of raising revenue; reducing reliance on loans from international bankers; obtaining better credit terms for money when it was borrowed, which involved creating confidence in the stability and reliability of the regime. It meant overhauling the Crown's financial administration and cutting out bureaucratic waste; selling royal assets and, where possible, extracting money from subjects by way of taxation, forced loans and unvarnished confiscation; doing everything possible to encourage trade with the continent. The solutions adopted by the son were not the same as those of his father Edmund – but they were no less unpopular in certain circles.

He found a spectacularly talented lieutenant to help him construct and implement a programme of economic recovery. Thomas Gresham was, in his early thirties, already an astute, not to say ruthless, businessman. He came from merchant stock and his father had been Lord Mayor of London. He had extensive commercial contacts in Antwerp and had been employed on government business there before April 1551, when Dudley appointed him royal agent in the Netherlands. No one understood the international money market better than Gresham and no one was better equipped to manipulate it to best advantage. He set about restoring confidence in the English currency. In little more than a year he had repaid over £75,000 of foreign debt and by 1553 he had restored the exchange rate to the value it had enjoyed at the beginning of the reign. His tactics ranged from lavish hospitality offered to the 'right' people to downright bullying. He used government money to buy up sterling in Antwerp, thus raising its value. He badgered the Council to be more prompt in making interest payments. He impounded the property of his fellow merchants until they had made short-term loans to the government at favourable rates. On the other hand he urged the government to bring to an end the long-running conflict between London merchants and the German Hanseatic League over the privileges foreigners enjoyed to the detriment of their English counterparts. Those privileges were duly abrogated in the spring of 1552. Not all Gresham's schemes were successful. When the government took up his suggestion to establish a Crown monopoly on the mining and selling of lead there was an understandable outcry from landowners and industrialists. 'The clamour grows great and may breed more damage than can now be seen,' Dudley commented. It makes me 'sorry I was ever a meddler in it. Princes' affairs, especially touching government and trade . . . though they are full of devices with appearance of profit, they must be weighed with other consequences.'[3] Gresham was not immediately successful in persuading Dudley to abandon the debasement of the currency and a final issue of adulterated specie was made in the summer of 1551. Thereafter the practice ceased.

Borrowing, restoring confidence in sterling, boosting trade and forcing down interest rates were all very well but they were no substitutes for raising income. In the light of recent events and his own general unpopularity Dudley was chary about approaching parliament with the government's financial needs. When the houses assembled the day after Somerset's execution he did not risk asking for taxes, a wise precaution, since a bill concerning the disposition of the late duke's estate had a rough ride through the Commons. It was eventually passed and the Crown was able to appropriate the extensive property Somerset had accumulated since 1541. Dudley looked elsewhere and set in train a rigorous examination of income and expenditure. The easiest way of raising ready cash was the sale of Crown lands and the Council set up various commissions to market royal property and ensure prompt payment.

However, the source of income most favoured by Dudley for a mixture of ideological and economic reasons was the church. One of his notes to Cecil, 'scribbled in bed as ill as I have ever been' indicates how Dudley conceived 'God's service and the king's' being happily advanced by the same means. He was writing about the break-up of the vast see of Durham after Tunstall's deprivation.

> . . . if the dean of Durham is appointed bishop with 1,000 marks more than his deanery, the houses he now has in the city and country will serve honourably – so may the king receive the castle, which has a princely site, and the other stately houses the bishop had in the country. The chancellor's living to be converted to the deanery and an honest man placed in it; the vice-chancellor to be

turned into the chancellor; the suffragan . . . may be removed, being neither preacher, learned nor honest, so pernicious that the country abhors him. The living, with a little more to its value – 100 marks – will serve the erection of a bishop of Newcastle. Thus the king may place godly ministers in these offices and receive £2,000 a year of the best lands in the north . . .[4]

Secularization of ecclesiastical property was popular with those in society who stood to gain from it and also with religious radicals who believed that ecclesiastical 'fat cats' were an affront to the Gospel. The dismantling of the Church's vast territorial wealth had been going on ever since 1536. Somerset had followed Cromwell down this route and now it was Dudley's turn do the same. It was not a new policy. Nor was it necessarily hypocritical. He believed that a slimmed down church would be a more effective church. But the leaders of that church, despite their evangelical convictions, did not agree.

Cranmer was becoming increasingly disturbed by the encroachment of secular control and he was suspicious of Dudley's motives over the breaking up of the Durham episcopate. Not only had Dudley chosen the title of 'Northumberland', he had begun to build up a considerable landholding in the north and had exchanged some of his other properties in order to shift his centre of operation to the border region. He held the office of Warden General of the Marches and he became steward for all those lands confiscated from the bishopric. The removal of the Prince-Bishop of Durham looked like a cynical manoeuvre in a purely political game that had nothing to do with purifying the church and little to do with strengthening the power of the Crown. When the bill for Tunstall's deprivation came before the upper house of parliament Cranmer was one of only two peers who voted against it. This may have emboldened some of the Commons to question the legislation for they raised an amendment which the Council refused to accept and the measure had to be withdrawn. Yet again Dudley felt that he was being balked by the very man who should have been leading the assault on the last redoubts of conservative opposition and he was furious. The breach between the two men was never healed.

Dudley was coming under increasing criticism from around the country. He was sensitive to such comments but by no means paranoid. In November he ordered a reprieve for one John Borroghe who was condemned to the pillory 'for telling news of me concerning certain of the king's coffers.' The man's imprisonment, Dudley suggested, had been punishment enough. 'I trust he will amend. His brother is of the best sort for favouring the king's godly proceedings and has no heir but this young man.'[5] Attacks from the pulpit were another matter. Clergy and people were still trying to get used to the new liturgy and the unfamiliar layout of church interiors for the demystified communion service. But at least it seemed that the threat to some of their ancient treasures had been lifted. Somerset had ordered an inventory of all church goods at the beginning of the reign preparatory to confiscating everything not in keeping with the new style of worship. This had caused widespread apprehension but nothing had happened because the government did not want to provoke yet more unrest. But, in January 1553, the Council, hard pressed for money, ordered the seizure of church plate, vestments, jewels and pewter vessels. This sparked a wave of pulpit denunciation which provoked Dudley to anger.

The parliament of January to April 1552 had been largely preoccupied with religious legislation, primarily the Second Act of Uniformity, imposing the revised Prayer Book and ordering all subjects to attend church every Sunday and use the new services. The government also shouldered the Christian responsibility of motivating individuals to acts of practical charity. Alms boxes were compulsorily installed in every church and a harsh Vagrancy Act of 1547 was replaced with legislation to enforce weekly collections for the relief of the parish poor. Official encouragement was given to private acts of charity and the king set a personal example by donating the palace of Bridewell for use as a house of correction for vagabonds and harlots, founding Christ's Hospital school and endowing St Thomas's Hospital for the care of the sick. Yet, for all that Dudley could see, it was the clergy who were the main obstacles to reform, 'so sotted with wives and children that they forget their poor neighbours and all else pertaining to their calling',[6] as he put it. Commission reports indicated that the total wealth of the English church, despite fifteen years of 'redistribution', still stood at over £3,500,000, while royal revenue collectors were scratching around for every penny. And Cranmer's preachers had the gall to call him rapacious and question the sincerity of his faith!

One area of expenditure that Dudley deliberately declined to prune was defence. Having abandoned Boulogne he took care to reinforce the Calais pale. Having pulled his forces back to the Scottish border, he had all the garrisons inspected and, where necessary, strengthened. But it was his first love, the navy, that received the lion's share of available funds. There was no wholesale laying off of ships and men as had always happened in the past when the nation enjoyed a period of peace. Over £20,000 per annum was being regularly spent on the navy which, in August 1552, numbered fifty-five ships, most of which were either at sea or ready for service. The Council for Marine Causes maintained the dockyards at Portsmouth, Deptford, Gillingham and Woolwich, which had an ongoing programme of building, repairing and refitting. Crews were kept busy on escort duty with the mercantile and fishing fleets and with forays against the pirates of the Narrow Seas.

It would be stretching the evidence to claim that Dudley had a vision for overseas expansion and exploration but he certainly continued his interest in maritime developments. He looked beyond the narrow confines of Europe with the continual frustrations that war and diplomatic complications threw in the way of trade and he encouraged brave men who did have vision and the will to pursue it. One such was Thomas Wyndham. With his three voyages (1550–53) the age of English long-range exploration may be said to have arrived. This experienced mariner ranged along the Atlantic coast of Africa, was the first English captain who 'fairly rounded Cape Verde and sailed into the Southern Sea',[7] and reached the Bight of Benin. The possibilities of Wyndham's third voyage excited interest far beyond the mercantile community. Cranmer provided the captain with letters of introduction in Latin, Hebrew and Syriac to be presented to whatever exotic princes he should meet in distant lands. Though the leader of the expedition was among the many Europeans who perished from west coast fever in what later ages came to know as the 'white man's graveyard', he had blazed a trail which others followed. Wyndham represented an eager, impatient, nationalistic and avaricious maritime sub-culture that was not content to allow Spain and Portugal monopolize the riches of a world opening up to European enterprise.

Dudley put the old mariner Sebastian Cabot in charge of a floating school for navigators in the bark *Aucher*. Here the veteran passed on his vast knowledge of the sea and ships to a new generation of navy men, men like Richard Chancellor, who established regular trade with Russia, and Matthew Baker, the master shipwright who built for Elizabeth vessels that confronted the Armada and crossed the Atlantic to pester Spain's New World commerce. According to a remarkable claim Cabot made later, Dudley was the father of an Anglo-French project to establish a base at the mouth of the Amazon from which to harass Spanish settlements. Such a scheme was beyond England's resources in the 1550s but not beyond the imagining of adventurous minds. It may be no coincidence that it was precisely at this time that England's most original thinker returned from years of study and renewed acquaintance with his old patron, now the Duke of Northumberland. John Dee had been a tutor in the Dudley household before travelling to the continent, where he had studied with the leading experts of the day in mathematics, astronomy and cosmography and enjoyed a close relationship with Gerard Mercator, the cartographic genius who had given the world its most accurate terrestrial globe. Still only in his twenties, Dee was already a celebrity. His recent lecture on Euclid in Paris had been so packed that several students had to stand outside the open windows to hear him. Now he was introduced to court and awarded a pension by the king. He immediately interested himself in a new projected voyage, to sail via northern waters to the Far East, thereby opening up trade routes with China and the Spice Islands that the Iberian nations would be unable to challenge.

With Dudley's backing this venture attracted an unprecedented amount of support from councillors, courtiers and London merchants. Two hundred and forty shares were sold in a company whose unlimited remit was reflected in its title: the 'Merchant Adventurers of England for the discovery of lands, territories, isles, dominions and seignories unknown'. What was new and forward-looking about this venture, apart from the number of prominent men involved in it, was its open-ended-ness. Normally members of the cautious mercantile community committed themselves to single trading voyages and shared any profits when and if the ships came safe home. This time they were investing in a long-term project which would depend on the establishment of commercial relations with far distant princes of whom they only knew from popular myths and mariners' tales. The first of many voyages launched by this company began on 10 May 1553. It consisted of three ships under the command of Sir Hugh Willoughby, with Richard Chancellor as navigator. As the vessels were towed past Greenwich Palace,

> . . . upon the news thereof the courtiers came running out and the common people flocked together, standing very thick upon the shore. The Privy Council they looked out at the windows of the court, and the rest ran up to the tops of the towers. The ships hereupon discharge their ordnance and shoot off their pieces after

the manner of war and of the sea, insomuch that the tops of the hills sounded therewith, the valleys and the waters gave an echo, and the mariners they shouted in such sort that the sky rang again with the noise thereof. One stood in the poop of the ship and by his gesture bids farewell to his friends in the best manner he could. Another walks upon the hatches, another climbs the shrouds, another stands upon the mainyard, and another in the top of the ship. To be short, it was a very triumph (after a sort) in all respects to the beholders. But (alas!) the good King Edward (in respect of whom principally all this was prepared) he only by reason of his sickness was absent from this show . . .[8]

The young king was, in fact, dying.

Dudley's only consolation during the opening months of 1553 lay in contemplating and planning for the future. The present was fraught with mounting worries, annoyances and pressures. Despite all the financial measures put in place, the Crown was desperately short of money. This led to the unwelcome prospect of going cap in hand to a parliament that could not be expected to be sympathetic to the government. As he acknowledged to Cecil at the close of 1552, 'there is no other remedy for the king's great debt.' At the same time the assembly could not be relied upon: 'in case parliament should be summoned chiefly for that intent and then not serve the purpose, the summoning were better protracted till after harvest.' Dudley by now regarded parliament as a hostile institution. Give the members warning of the taxes required before Michaelmas, when the profits from summer farming and trading were known and recorded, and it would be easy for them and their friends too defraud the king. Furthermore, it would, 'take away every man's comfort of traffic and gain in the meantime, yet avoid little or nothing the danger of murmuring or grudging.'[9] The Council ignored this advice and set the date of 1 March for the opening of the next session. There was nothing to do, therefore, but fall back on the usual devices of influencing elections and exercising a tight control over the agenda.

While these preparations were in hand the Council came under an unprecedentedly ferocious and sustained attack from those they had always looked upon as their allies. As usual the cream of the nation's preachers were summoned to occupy the court pulpit during Lent. Almost to a man they lashed the royal advisers for their vices, 'insatiable covetousness, of filthy carnality and voluptuousness, of intolerable ambition and pride, of ungodly loathsomeness to hear poor men's causes, and to hear God's word'. Dudley and his colleagues were furious. They had given their evangelical allies free rein to attack all perceived enemies of the Gospel and now they themselves were put within that category.

Amidst these and other cares Dudley solaced himself by looking to the not far distant future. He would soon be able to lay aside his burden because Edward would be of age. To be able to retire from the thankless task of government was what he now desired above all things and he was actively preparing for his change of role. He was already keeping a lower profile in government and no longer exercising unquestioned authority over the Council. On such issues as the summoning of parliament and the urgent appointment of a new Bishop of Durham he was outvoted. He seems to have absented himself even more from court and Council and was frequently to be found, not in the magnificence of Ely Place, between Westminster and the City, but in his 'little house' in the tranquil suburb of Chelsea, where, like Thomas More before him, he found a measure of peace.

He devoted what time he could spare in 1552–3 to personal and family matters, although these were inevitably often tangled up with affairs of state. The summer months of 1552 saw him making a leisurely inspection of the administration of the Scottish Marches and his own property in the far north. It has often been assumed that the third movement of his territorial base (i.e. from Kent and Sussex to the Midlands and then to the north-east) is further proof of his personal aggrandizement and his desire for a strong power base. The reality is more complex. Had he really aimed to replace the semi-independence of the great Percy family, the 'princes of the north', he would have appreciated that such an objective would take generations to achieve. However, no one knew better than he how vital it was that the central government should be well represented in the border region and how limited was the obedience of some of the great landowners there. Several were men of Catholic sympathies and not a few had cross-border connections that were more important to them than commitment to the regime in distant London. And it may well have been that very distance that was for Dudley an added attraction. From his base at Newcastle or Alnwick he could serve the king in years to come by keeping the border region quiet and avoid involvement in the stressful daily grind of court politics and intrigue.

It was with an eye to the future that, in the latter half of 1552, he embarked on a series of dynastic negotiations which would integrate the Dudleys more intimately with families close to the throne. Edward had very few relatives on his father's side and those he did have were all female. His aunt Margaret had, long years since, married James IV of Scotland and her only descendant was Mary, Queen of Scots, currently being brought up in France as a good Catholic. His other aunt, Mary, had made a runaway marriage with her father's bosom friend, Charles Brandon, Duke of Suffolk, and she had given birth to two daughters. Frances Brandon married Henry Grey, Marquess of Dorset who later became Duke of Suffolk, in right of his wife. Of their children only three survived, Jane, Catherine and Mary. Edward's other first cousin, Eleanor Brandon, became the wife of Henry Clifford, Earl of Cumberland, and had one daughter, Margaret, before her death in 1547. All these ladies had a claim to the throne, but only after the princesses Mary and Elizabeth, who had been named in their father's will. Clifford was something of a recluse and seldom visited the court but Suffolk was a councillor, a friend and supporter of Northumberland, and a religious radical. Jane, the eldest of the Grey girls, was of age with the king and there was talk at one time of the two being wed. Those plans had been scotched by Somerset who had designed to marry Edward to his own daughter and Jane to his eldest son (something often omitted from the story of Lady Jane Grey and the wicked Duke of Northumberland).

In 1552 Dudley had two unmarried children to dispose of, Guildford and Catherine, and it was arranged that they should unite the Dudley clan with other establishment families. For Guildford his father tried, unsuccessfully, to make a match with Margaret Clifford and Catherine was betrothed to Henry Hastings, son and heir to the Earl of Huntingdon, also a councillor of evangelical persuasion. To complete this network of alliances Catherine Grey was promised to the Earl of Pembroke's son, Lord Herbert. There was nothing unusual or, by the standards of the day, untowardly calculating about this matrimonial patchwork. The heads of these aristocratic clans were placing their offspring around the throne in order to ensure their continuing prosperity and social elevation. They were also, as they saw it, providing the Tudor regime with a core of committed Protestant courtiers and Edward certainly gave his blessing to all these arrangements. The Seymours had done no less, nor the Howards before them, nor numerous other ambitious noble families for generations.

What becomes clear from these negotiations is that they had nothing to do with the succession issue. In 1552 John had no plan to put his own son on the throne by marrying him to Jane Grey, the closest female claimant after her mother. Only when Cumberland declined Guildford Dudley as a match for his daughter did Guildford's marriage to Jane become a possibility and, for reasons of state, desirable to at least some of the parties concerned. It is this which disposes, once and for all, of the myth of the scheming, ambitious 'evil duke'. Had Dudley been aiming for royal power the simplest way of achieving his objective would have been to marry Catherine Dudley to the king. The Howards and the Seymours had both schemed to place female relatives in the royal bed. Perhaps that is the point. Had Dudley seriously entertained royal pretensions he only had to think of the old Duke of Norfolk now repining in the Tower and the two Seymour brothers recently perished under the axe to conclude that such a game was not worth the candle.

Dudley was as ever bothered about his health. In December he reported mournfully to Cecil, 'neither close keeping, warm furs nor clothes can bring any natural heat to my head, and I have no hope of recovery'.[10] One concern Dudley did not have at this time was for the king's health. Edward was never robust. In 1552 he suffered from measles and also a slight attack of smallpox. But, with the resilience of youth, he threw these off and when, in the new year, he succumbed to what seemed to be a seasonal cold and cough no one took much notice. Yet, at some moment in the early months of 1553 Edward himself gave anxious thought to the implications of his dying before he could sire children. In his habitual, scrupulous way he set down his wishes for what should happen in such an eventually. And so we come to the notorious 'device' for the succession.

This document, written very clearly in the king's own hand, represents his passionate concerns and sense of responsibility for the well-being of his country. On balance it seems unlikely that he discussed his ideas with Dudley, Gates, Cecil or anyone else at this stage. Succession issues were matters of royal prerogative and Edward would have believed that it was in his power to name his successor. He would have seen no need to consult his advisers about something that might never become a reality. What Edward wanted and what he believed the realm needed was a male, Protestant ruler. Male because that was the divinely appointed order of things. England had never been ruled, unchallenged, by a queen and could not possibly be secure in female hands. Edward's father, as he knew, had gone through hell and high water to provide himself with a male heir and Edward was determined, if need be, to do no less. Protestant because the English Reformation was not complete.

Evangelical truth was a tender plant which still had not sent down deep roots into the native soil. It was the king's responsibility to see that it was nurtured, even if he was no longer present to tend it personally. He was passionately determined that England should not fall back into Roman bondage. That would certainly happen if his half-sister Mary succeeded to the Crown. He had personally remonstrated with her, face-to-face and by letter, and knew how stubbornly she was addicted to the old religion. As for Elizabeth, Edward had no reason to doubt her commitment to the reformed faith but she would probably marry some foreign prince and he, by the law of averages, was highly likely to be Catholic. Edward therefore planned meticulously for a future which, God willing, would never materialize.

The king's problem was that among the possible claimants to the Crown there was not a single male contender. All he could do was what he did do. Setting aside the claims of Mary and Elizabeth (who, in any case, despite Henry VIII's will, were still technically bastards, their mothers' marriages having been annulled), he devised the Crown to the future male offspring of his only living first cousin, Frances Brandon. In default of Lady Suffolk giving birth to a boy (and she was now thirty-six) Edward nominated as next in line the possible sons of her daughters, Jane, Catherine and Mary. If they failed to oblige, and if their mother had, meanwhile, given birth to another daughter, then that daughter's sons were to be brought into the account. In the event of all the Suffolk line failing for want of a male heir, attention was to switch to the potential sons of Margaret Clifford. The thorough Edward had not yet exhausted all the possibilities. Next in line were to be 'the heirs male of the Lady Jane's daughters . . . the heirs male of the Lady Catherine's daughters . . . and so forth till you come to the Lady Margaret's daughters' heirs male.'[11] Nothing could illustrate better than this genealogical treasure hunt the slender thread on which the English Reformation hung and the king's determination to protect it come what may.

It is impossible to regard this device as springing from any mind that was in touch with political reality. It was the work of an adolescent zealot who saw matters in black and white and who believed that he had the autocratic power to bend people to his will. Edward's councillors would have blenched if they had known the details of the document which it might fall to them to execute. It would have involved maintaining themselves in power as a regency council for some king who might at some future time be conceived. The device could very well become a testament, not for ensuring a peaceful succession, but for plunging the nation back into the dynastic chaos of the fifteenth century. If Edward did show it to Dudley or any of his colleagues they would probably have regarded it as one of those intellectual exercises the king enjoyed. Nor had it anything to do with bequeathing the Crown to one of the leading noble families. Even if it had been possible to put the device into effect it would have bypassed the husbands of all the king's female relatives. Edward knew about the forthcoming marriages arranged by his councillors and, therefore, that all the unborn infants indicated in his device would be brought up in good evangelical homes. Nominating these phantom children was the only way that he could see of achieving that objective closest to his heart. It is also worth noting, in passing, that Edward's elaborate scheme to ensure the Protestant succession is not unique in British history. The protracted negotiations which brought George, Elector of Hanover, to the English throne in 1714 were far more extreme. They passed over, purely on the grounds of religion, no less than fifty-four Catholics who had much stronger claims.

Whether or not the king had some intuitive recognition of the fact, he was seriously ill with a chronic pulmonary condition, probably tuberculosis. Through the early months of the year he experienced typical symptoms of that disease, persistent coughing, fatigue and general debility. There were also, as is common, temporary respites in his steady deterioration, which tended to give hope to those who anxiously watched his condition. No one watched more anxiously than John Dudley. For all the leaders of the regime everything depended on Edward's survival. That meant that they required daily bulletins from the royal physicians and had to decide what to do with the information received. The first priority was secrecy. Any hint of concern about the king's condition had to be kept away from the diplomatic community and from rumourmongers who might spread the idea that the government was on the point of collapse. Council members tried to give the impression of business as usual. Edward attended some meetings, his decisions were sought and petitions were presented to him. He fulfilled his public duties whenever he was up to it, although he was too unwell to open parliament, and the customary removal of the court to Greenwich in April had to be postponed for two weeks.

This understandable nervousness about the king's health and the political consequences of its deterioration renders even more worthy of note that Dudley was scrupulous over keeping Elizabeth and Mary informed of their brother's condition. In early February, at a time when Edward was actually too ill to receive visitors, a message was sent to the elder princess. She came immediately and was escorted to court by an honour guard led by Dudley's eldest son. At Whitehall Dudley and his wife received her with a great display of respect and affection. Was this the behaviour of a man cynically indifferent to religion and hedging his bets in order to remain on the winning side? Or was it the behaviour of a politique, lulling Mary into a sense of false security as a prelude to ousting her from the succession and ensuring the continuance of a Protestant state with himself at the helm? One thing is clear; it cannot have been both, as popular legend has suggested. In point of fact, it was neither. The prospect of Mary's accession was certainly anathema to him but not because it presented any threat to his own well-being. He had done nothing to merit reprisals from the future queen. Indeed, he had always made a point of treating her with the courtesy due to her station. The worst that could happen to him at the inauguration of a Catholic regime would be his expulsion from the political limelight and that, as we know, would not have struck him as an unmitigated disaster. As the spring passed, Dudley was not carefully calculating all his options; he was waiting on events, ready, as he doubtless would have said, to leave the future in the hands of the Almighty. Any other interpretation of his state of mind makes a nonsense of his complete failure to deal with the crisis that was about to burst upon him.

Our understanding of that crisis is hampered by insufficient evidence of the exact sequence of events during May and June. During these weeks there was an acceleration of activity, culminating in frenzy as the king's death became imminent and his passionate determination to alter the succession became known. If we could be in no doubt about who knew what and when we would be better able to judge the motives of the lead players in what has become known, erroneously, as the tragedy of the 'nine days' queen'. There will always be room for disagreement about who was the driving force behind the plan to change the succession and who actively supported it. After its failure there was, inevitably, a rush of councillors and courtiers to extricate themselves from any taint of treason by insisting that their heartfelt loyalty to Mary was overridden by Dudley. In most cases it suited the new queen to accept these asseverations but there was a world of difference between what men did in June and what, in July, they claimed they had done in June. Actions, opinions and emotions during King Edward's last days were confused and we are left to unravel them as best we may.

Hopes and fears ebbed and flowed during May as king-watchers detected, or thought they detected, improvements or deteriorations in

Edward's condition. Some of the key players were absent from the centre of affairs during the month. Cranmer's relationship with Dudley had completely broken down in April and he had gone off in a huff, not to return till 6 June. He was, in any case, busy doing his utmost to hasten the process of reform by publishing and disseminating religious propaganda. Dudley's attendance was, as always, erratic and he was present at less than fifty per cent of full Council meetings (though he was probably more assiduous about participating in sessions of the 'council for the state', the inner 'cabinet' where the real decisions were made). In May some of his energy was devoted to organizing the biggest social event of the year, the multiple weddings which took place on Whitsunday (21 May).

On that day, crowds gathered outside Durham Place, one of the most magnificent waterside mansions in the environs of London (commandeered by Dudley after Tunstall's deprivation) to watch the 'quality' assembling for the celebration of weddings involving the families of Dudley, Grey, Hastings and Herbert. The celebrations continued till 25 May and during these days were joined in holy matrimony, as had been painstakingly arranged over recent months, Henry Hastings and Catherine Dudley, and Henry Herbert and Catherine Grey. There were two changes to the planned unions. The Clifford negotiations having broken down, Guildford Dudley was fatally united with Jane Grey. But the Clifford connection was not lost. Young Margaret's father, who had balked at seeing her married to Guildford, was happy to betroth her to the young man's uncle, Sir Andrew Dudley, who was thirty years her senior (the marriage never took place). This event occurred three weeks before Edward's amended plans for the succession were revealed. The questions that need to be resolved are: When did Dudley become party to the king's intentions? To what extent did he influence Edward? And did he deliberately try to grab the Crown for his own family?

Whoever occupied the throne, the Grey girls were fated to be significant pieces in the game of dynastic politics. It was important to the Edwardian regime to have them married off to 'safe' husbands who would not try to mount their own claims (Mary Grey, barely into her teens, was, at the same time, betrothed to Lord Grey de Wilton). They could not be left single to become prey to ambitious suitors or rebellious cabals. There is no evidence that anyone, even Dudley's bitterest enemies, saw anything in the ceremony at Durham Place beyond a prudent tidying-up of the dynastic situation. Edward, as we know, had his own reasons to be very satisfied with the marriages but no one outside his inner circle knew or even guessed what was in his mind. As late as 12 June Scheyfve the imperial ambassador reported a rumour that Dudley had some scheme in mind to keep Mary from the throne but he did not know what that scheme was. It seems that, for all his well-paid spy network at court, all he could do was repeat vague gossip, most of which was unreliable. He even reported, at one stage, that Dudley was poisoning the King. If there was no leak of the plan to disbar the princesses from the succession it seems very unlikely that many people knew about it, particularly as the secret of Edward's terminal illness was out in early June. On 6 June a substantial grant of land was made to Princess Mary, which suggests that the Council were already looking to the future and seeking to ingratiate themselves with the lady who would soon be their mistress.

On the balance of evidence and of human psychology it seems right to deduce that Edward did not reveal his device until he had accepted the fact that he was dying. This happened in the first week of June. Dudley was informed by the royal doctors that the king had suffered a fatal relapse and either he or some other confidant broke the news to Edward. The devout young man now had nothing to do but render his account to God, who would want to know how he had used his steward-ship of England to advance the Gospel. It was, therefore, a matter of the most intense personal importance to the dying boy that he would be able to lay before the judgement seat a realm delivered once and for all from the coils of Antichrist. Having accepted that his days on this earth were severely numbered, Edward had to make his will and it was in connection with that that he revealed to his closest advisers, probably for the first time, his intentions for the succession.

The emotional impact must have been both devastating and complex. The device presented Dudley and his colleagues with several problems. In its existing form it was utterly unworkable. Even if it could, somehow, be made into a practical arrangement for passing on the crown would Edward's will be accepted as legal? The political nation might reject it on two grounds: it was the work of a minor and it sought to set aside by mere royal fiat the line of succession laid down by Henry VIII and endorsed by parliament. In view of these valid objections, were the councillors grouped around Edward's deathbed in that stuffy, closed chamber reeking of medicaments going to tell their royal master that they could not or would not deliver what he demanded of them with all the passion his wasted frame could muster? Only Cranmer ventured to express doubts in the king's presence and he received a sharp dressing down for his temerity. Edward demanded to know whether his archbishop 'would be more repugnant to his will than the rest of the Council were'.

As usual everyone looked to Dudley to give a lead and he cannot have found it easy to decide what to do. The simplest course of action would have been to promise to obey the king's dying commands while secretly arranging for the peaceful transfer of power to Mary. Simple but not very honourable – and Dudley had a strict code of honour. Obedience to the sovereign was the basis of his political code, and Edward, though a boy, was still his anointed king. Duplicity had a strong smell of treason. Then, as he ruminated on what it was that Edward was proposing, it may well have struck him that it could be made to work. With a very slight change to the wording of the device the Crown could be handed to a living relative rather than some nebulous future infant. All that was necessary was to replace the phrase 'the Lady Jane's heirs male' with 'the Lady Jane and her heirs male'. Up to this point Dudley had faced the prospect of a Catholic, pro-imperial succession that would overturn all his work, the peace with France, the transfer of ecclesiastical wealth into the royal coffers, the bringing of the Reformation to a state of near completion. But now there was an alternative, and a very attractive one. England would have an intelligent young queen of impeccable evangelical convictions. Jane was young and healthy and, presumably, capable of bearing a new generation of royal princes. She would, of course, being a mere woman, need the guidance of an experienced politician, and who more obvious for that role than her father-in-law?

It may or may not have been Dudley who thought of this compromise, although people would assume, as many have assumed since, that he was the brains behind it and that his objective all along was to establish a Dudley royal dynasty. Whoever was responsible, the king still had to be persuaded to accept the qualification of his original device. It gave him an assured Protestant succession but at the cost of placing a woman on the throne. However, it was the religious issue that weighed more heavily with him and, on 17 June, he approved the complete draft of his will. In its final form it included additional clauses requiring the executors to defend the settlement of the church as it existed at the death of the testator.

But this was far from dealing with all Dudley's doubts. There were still huge obstacles to be overcome. The duke was under no illusion about how the transfer of the Crown from Mary Tudor to Jane Dudley would be received. The princess had always enjoyed widespread public sympathy because of the way Henry VIII had treated her and her mother and it was by no means only Catholics who would be outraged at the thought of her claim being set aside. The Protestant courtier, Sir Nicholas Throckmorton, spoke for many when he observed,

> And, though I liked not the religion
> Which all her life Queen Mary had professed,
> Yet in my mind that wicked notion
> Right heirs for to displace I did detest.[12]

Even Bishop Hooper, who had once hailed Dudley as an 'intrepid soldier of Christ', took sides with Mary. The king's will would have to be sold first to enough members of the political elite to provide the new regime with a secure base. Then, the government would have to be sure of the regional authorities and local JPs who would have to be on the alert for any expressions of pro-Mary sentiment. John Dudley, as we know, was painfully aware of his own unpopularity. It was likely, therefore, that the change of dynasty would have to be firmly imposed on the nation. There might have to be military action. Certainly the princesses would have to be kept under secure guard to prevent them becoming figureheads for internal revolution or foreign intervention.

How carefully he weighed up all the pros and cons we can only speculate, but the disastrous aftermath of his decision to back the king's will to the hilt can only be explained with reference to what was going on in his mind. Why did his usual tactical skill desert him at the critical moment? All observers believed that the 'coup' he attempted after Edward's death would be successful. He controlled the capital and he only had to bring the princesses there to prevent any rising. Yet he not only failed, but failed miserably. This suggests a degree of confusion leading to fatal inertia. The sort of man who could have carried the day would have been a ruthless, clear-headed, determined, Machiavellian schemer, something John Dudley never was. Emotion and reason became fatally mixed in him during those awful days when he had to watch his royal protégé wasting away to death.

First there was the family motto, *droit et loyal*, that he had been brought up to live by. In his letters Dudley frequently protested his utter devotion to the Crown. 'You and others may witness of my care for all that pertains to his highness . . . I trust I shall be found ready to serve the king, whatever his pleasure, with my life.'[13] So he had written as late as January and we should not be so sceptical as to dismiss such asseverations. He was certainly about to prove his willingness to do Edward's bidding, whatever his pleasure, and to stake his life upon it. He – and the same is true for most of his Council colleagues – had formed the habit of obedience to the king's will. They had spent years grooming him to take important decisions. It was difficult now to defy their monarch in his last pitiable extremity.

Something else that will certainly have influenced Dudley was the dazzling prospect of becoming the progenitor of England's ruling dynasty. The more the ancient nobility looked down on him as an *arriviste*; the more the rumours spread that his father was only the son of a Midlands carpenter; the more sniggering critics reminded each other that Edmund Dudley had died an ignominious traitor's death, the more satisfying it was to Northumberland to show that he had climbed to the very top of the heap. He had never been warped by ambition but now, with the greatest of all prizes dangling before him, it would have taken gargantuan self-denial to refuse it.

Then there was the desire to preserve all that had been achieved since the death of the old king. He might have fallen out with Cranmer and some of the more outspoken evangelical preachers but in all the essentials they were still on the same side. Moreover the task of creating a godly commonwealth was still unfinished and Dudley was as aware as the archbishop of work yet to be done. It would not have been difficult for him to persuade himself (as probably the king also attempted to persuade him) that his endeavours had the blessing of God, blessing he might well forfeit if, having put his hand to the plough, he should now turn back. Nor was religion the only area of national life where there were government programmes to be seen through to completion. The Council had just begun to turn around the financial situation. They had sponsored overseas ventures which might open exciting commercial prospects. Dudley had provided England with a standing navy that would change the conduct of foreign affairs as well as mercantile endeavour. Finally, the realm had been given a period of peace and he must have been looking forward to building on this foundation. So there was much to play for in attempting to carry Edward's will into effect.

All these rational and emotional weights tipped the scales in favour of action but the legal difficulties and the knowledge that the majority of right-thinking people were against him still weighed heavily on the other side of the balance. These considerations were urgent enough to prod that self-doubt to which Dudley was always prone and to stir confusion in his mind. The aggression, even violence, he displayed in his attempts to create a consensus suggests a man as desperate to convince himself as others. In mid-June a series of meetings took place involving leaders of government, Church and judiciary. Most of the Council were with Dudley but others had to be bullied into compliance. The lawyers, led by Sir Edward Montague, pointed out that they could not draw up the will the king wanted because it went counter to the existing statute. Dudley flew into a rage, threatening the penalties of treason for refusing a royal command. For him this seemed like yet another example of pernickety quibbling over details. The lawyers were as bad as the theologians; always ready to indulge the luxury of arguing over niceties when there was action to be taken. The law men left in confusion, only to be ordered back by the king a few days later and instructed to come in a more amenable frame of mind. They set to work on the document, Montague comforting himself with a nice legal sophism: to draw up a document on which one had no intention of acting could not be construed as treason. Cranmer, also, as we have seen was unhappy about the will. He asked for permission to reason with Edward in private but this was denied him and, faced by a determined and reproachful king, he gave way. On 21 June all the notables of court and capital were summoned to Greenwich to set their names to a document confirming the change to the succession. Several of them must have had their fingers firmly crossed behind their backs as they did so.

At the end of June everyone who was at all informed knew that their sovereign was dying and that the princesses had been dispossessed. The men who mattered were carefully giving the impression of unity and making preparations for the proclamation of Queen Jane. But by no means were they all doing so with enthusiasm. There were many who nursed misgivings and even more who were secretly resolved to wait upon events. Mary, in her residence at Hunsdon, near Hertford, received almost hourly news about her brother. Dudley, moving up and down river between Chelsea and Greenwich, was, of course, even better informed. He had dismissed the royal doctors and installed his own physicians at the royal bedside. Thither he made frequent visits, mesmerized by the steady evaporation of this young life. The crisis moment was coming nearer and those most closely concerned did – nothing.

There was a hush of inactivity which lasted almost a week. Dudley did not muster his military forces. He did not send troops to guard Mary or bring her to court or have her moved to a more secure lodging. He completely failed to take the initiative. The reasons are not difficult to determine. They existed, as it were, on two levels. The first and most obvious was at the legal and constitutional level. He was unwilling to take decisive action without the authority of the king. Every decision he had taken since 1550, every order he had issued, theoretically at least, had always had royal warrant. Now the only person who could issue such a warrant was beyond concerning himself with affairs of state. Fighting for breath, racked with pain and kept from delirious stupor by stimulants, Edward longed only for his heavenly reward. Given time Dudley would have legitimated the change in the succession by Act of Parliament and plans were already in hand to recall the assembly. But time was the one commodity he lacked. Once again we have to make the point that the Dudley of legend would have efficiently and effectively filled the power vacuum and issued orders on his own authority. He would certainly have brought some of his crack troops from their border garrisons to protect Queen Jane and her court in her and its first, vulnerable days and weeks. At the lower level the reason, therefore, lies in his inner motivation. I believe he was still uncertain about what action to take. The moment he made a move against the princess would be the moment he was irrevocably committed. He always preferred to proceed by peaceable consensus rather than by violent confrontation. This was what he had done in October 1549, and the way he had resolved his conflict with Somerset then indicated his dislike of extreme measures. The evidence points to Dudley desiring some accommodation with Mary, hoping for some honourable position for her in the new order. That was why he hesitated until the last possible moment and why the first move that he did make as soon as he knew for certain, on 4 July, that Edward only had hours to live was to send for the boy's half-sisters.

This procrastination enabled Mary to grasp the initiative. While Elizabeth pleaded illness, her sister obeyed the summons to Edward's bedside, setting out to ride southwards on 5 July. But, wary of what might be awaiting her, she travelled slowly, sending messengers on ahead to bring her the most up-to-date intelligence of events in the court and the capital. By the evening of 6 July she and her suite had covered only five miles and were lodged at Hoddesdon. It was late that night that she received the news that Edward had died a few hours earlier. The king had breathed his last in the embrace of his close friend Sir Henry Sidney (Dudley's son-in-law), who recorded the event in his memoirs:

This young Prince, who died within my arms, had almost caused death to penetrate his dart even into my own soul, for to behold him and how like [a] lamb he departed this life, and when his voice had left him, still he erected his eyes to heaven, it would have converted the fiercest of papists if they had any grace in them of true faith in Christ. He would call upon none saving his Saviour. He prayed that God would be pleased to bestow the Gospel on his subjects, for his glory and their salvation. He also in his sickness made a prayer to God to deliver this nation from that uncharitable religion of popery, which was the chiefest cause for his election of the Lady Jane Grey to succeed before his sister Mary . . . out of pure love to his subjects, that he desired they might live and die in the Lord, as he did.[14]

The news galvanized Mary into action. Immediately she ordered her people to prepare for instant departure and in the small hours she set out at a greatly increased speed. To put as much distance as possible between her and the rival regime, she rode northwards, travelled by side roads to avoid detection and, by nightfall had reached Sawston, south of Cambridge, where a kinsman of one of her attendants gave her refuge.

By this time Dudley had bestirred himself. He sent his sons John and Robert with an armed escort to bring Mary to court. This was still no more than courteous convention; the young men had not been despatched to arrest the princess. This is evidenced by the complete confusion into which they were thrown when they reached Hunsdon to discover that the bird had flown. If their orders had been to bring Mary in come what may they would have immediately set out in hot pursuit and would probably have caught up with her before she had plunged deep into East Anglia. In fact, they separated, Robert riding on to seek out the princess and John returning to Greenwich for fresh instructions. Robert took the highway (the present A10) and, stopping for neither food nor sleep, clattered into Cambridge before dawn on 8 July. There he learned that he had overshot his mark and he immediately turned back towards Sawston. Once again he was too late; Mary had set off on the Newmarket road scarcely an hour before. Now the twenty-year-old Robert gave vent to his anger and frustration. He was tired and humiliated by failure. Not only that, he was worried. The mood of the people he met along the road was distinctly hostile and some of his own men had deserted during the hours of darkness. He was hearing stories of local gentlemen flocking to join the fleeing princess. So, instead of pressing on with his pursuit, he ordered his men to set fire to Sawston Hall while he rode back into Cambridge. This was the vital turning point. Had Robert followed Mary, resolved to complete his mission, there was a good chance that he would have succeeded. It was what his father, the seasoned campaigner, would have done. But the situation had changed drastically since he had been given his instructions. To have pressed on in the face of growing opposition would almost certainly have involved an attempt to seize Mary by main force. Because he shrank from this, the smoke and flames that rose into the fenland sky became a beacon marking the failure of Dudley hopes and pretensions.

John rejoined his brother in Cambridge on 8 July. He brought the news that Jane had been publicly proclaimed queen, that she and Guildford and their court would shortly be moved to the Tower and that orders had gone out for loyal nobles and gentlemen to repair to London with their forces ready to defend their sovereign. The word was being disseminated that Catholic Mary was in flight to the coast in the hope of crossing to the continent to raise an army of invasion. This was almost certainly what Dudley believed. It may even have been what Mary had originally had in mind when she fled from Hoddesdon but, if so, her plans changed completely when she observed the delirious joy with which she was greeted along the way. What was encouraging to her had the opposite effect on the Dudley brothers. With new orders to follow the princess and promises of military reinforcements from their father, they set out along the Newmarket road. Every mile brought more depressing news. Mary's entourage had swollen dramatically. In Bury St Edmunds the corporation had given her a civic reception. She was headed for Kenninghall Castle, the centre of her extensive East Anglian estates, where she could count on the support of her considerable tenantry and most of her gentry neighbours. As for the reception accorded to the pursuers, sullen looks and shouted insults left them in no doubt about the unpopularity of their father's regime. It was particularly unfortunate for Dudley that his showdown with Mary should have occurred in the eastern counties. Here people had vivid memories of the suppression of Kett's rebellion. Many families had lost sons or husbands in its bloody aftermath and in the private reprisals carried out by the chief men of the shires. Partisans for social and religious change, of whom there were many in this part of the country, felt betrayed by the 'murderer' of Somerset. Thus radicals, Catholics, sympathizers with the rejected princess, supporters of the legitimate succession, tenants of the dispossessed Howards and people who simply hated the 'upstart'

Dudley found common cause in rallying to Mary's support. By contrast, this was not a part of the country where the Dudleys had substantial landholdings and, therefore, tenants and agents upon whose support they could rely. (Robert did his best but could only raise a modest force.) As soon as she arrived at Kenninghall Mary sent a strongly worded letter to the Council in London declaring that she was now their lawful queen and demanding their allegiance.

In London matters did not yet look hopeless. Assuming that Mary was bent on escape, Dudley despatched ships to patrol the east coast on the lookout for imperial vessels. Queen Jane and her Council were secure in the Tower and the government held London. Bishop Ridley and other preachers were advocating the new regime and denouncing Catholic plans for an overthrow of England's godly Reformation. News from the provinces was mixed but some nobles and substantial gentlemen were reported as mustering forces to support Jane. Several East Anglian town corporations had declared for her. Once again, prompt and decisive action on Dudley's part might have resulted in victory before the princess was able to organize an effective military strategy. As always in these situations, most men of consequence waited to see which way the wind was blowing before committing themselves. But once again Dudley hesitated. His colleagues urged him to take the field in person against the rebels, reminding him of his success at Dussindale. However, their very insistence was part of Dudley's problem. He knew that some of his 'supporters' had mixed motives. If he took up arms against Mary and was unsuccessful, they would fall over themselves to dissociate themselves from him. Once they had changed sides the City would be lost to him and his retreat cut off. The alternative would be to throw down the gauntlet to the princess, let her march on the capital and hope to energize the citizenry in their own defence. But frequent reports came in asserting that Mary's force was growing by leaps and bounds. In order to show herself as all things to all men she assured local evangelicals that she would enforce no religious changes (a promise she spectacularly broke as soon as her throne was secure). Thanks in part to Dudley's earlier hesitation, everything was now happening too quickly for him. Given time, he could have brought his mercenaries back from the border. He might even have been able to reinforce them with troops from France, for he had sent his kinsman Henry Dudley to Paris asking the king for aid. Eventually there was nothing for it but for Dudley to leave the capital with whatever forces he could muster.

He set out on 14 July, having first urged the Council to remain united and firm in their resolve, a message which had about it more than a hint of desperation. But he never put his cause to the trial. He arrived in Cambridge with some 1,500 men and a small artillery train. The word that reached him there was that Mary had moved to the nigh-impregnable Framlingham Castle and could call on 20,000 supporters. This was certainly a wild exaggeration but Dudley could not know that and more reliable news of various defections added to his depression. Even the crews of ships he had sent forth to frustrate Mary's supposed emigration plans mutinied and went over to her side. Yet, it was not the military imbalance that decided the issue. Lord Clinton arrived with reinforcements and other contingents were expected. Really determined leadership (something which Mary's army lacked) and clever tactical planning might still have made a contest. The reason why Princess Mary's rebellion succeeded without a shot being fired was that the opposition imploded. Several of Dudley's allies simply did not have their hearts in the enterprise, and probably the same may be said of Dudley himself.

Back in London it took very little time for nerves to crack. The first person to give way under the strain was someone Dudley had thought he could rely on but who now showed himself a time server par excellence. William Herbert, Earl of Pembroke, one of the principal dynasts involved in the marriage negotiations back in May, now made common cause with one of Dudley's old enemies, the Earl of Arundel, who had been recently rehabilitated. The two men called a Council meeting at Pembroke's town house on 18 July and persuaded most of their colleagues that Mary's claim could not be set aside. This was exactly what Dudley had feared; without his energizing presence the Council lacked backbone. The following day the Duke of Suffolk himself informed his daughter that she was no longer queen. London, we are told, exploded in a spontaneous festival of rejoicing. Bonfires were lit in every street, church bells were rung, cheering, laughing crowds gathered and, according to one report, money was thrown from windows. This release of pent-up emotion had many elements. People were jubilant that justice had at long last been done to Mary, that Somerset's blood was avenged, that the Tudor dynasty had been saved. Many, doubtless, were simply relieved that an unpopular government had been overthrown without the shedding of blood. No regime, they assured each other, could be worse than Dudley's. Not for the first or last time in history such malcontents were soon to learn how wrong they were.

Dudley advanced as far as Bury St Edmunds before conceding that the game was up. He returned to Cambridge and there, on 20 July, proclaimed Mary the rightful Queen of England. Four days later Arundel arrived to arrest him. By the 26th John Dudley, and all his sons were prisoners in the Tower. Earlier in the year the duke had commented in one of his many letters to Cecil, 'I trust I shall be found ready to serve the king, whatever his pleasure, with my life.' He cannot have known then how prophetic his words were.

The last days of John Dudley were a drab, dispirited coda to an exciting and spectacularly successful life. On 18 August he was brought to Westminster Hall where the newly released Duke of Norfolk presided over the formality of his trial. The prisoner, who can have been under no illusion about the verdict, conducted himself with dignity and pointed out that, throughout his days in power, he had always acted with the support of the Council, some of whom were now looking down on him from their jury seats. Such veiled accusations can only have been counter-productive. All members of the political elite were united in their need for a scapegoat and fully intended to keep Dudley isolated. He and he alone was to be branded as guilty, not only for the Jane Grey plot, but for all the ills that had beset the realm since 1549, however one might define them. Gardiner, Bonner, Howard and other religious conservatives concocted the official story that Dudley had seduced the boy king into heresy. Former allies distanced themselves from responsibility for government acts by claiming that they had been pressured by Dudley into doing his will. Above all, Queen Mary could not afford to start her reign with an orgy of blood-letting. Her security in a society fractured along so many fault lines depended on the support of the political class, and of men of all persuasions within that class. As Scheyfve observed, Mary 'cannot possibly . . . punish all who have been guilty of something; otherwise she would be left without any vassals at all.'[15] So it was in everyone's interest to give the populace what it wanted, the severed head of the 'bad duke'. Dudley was found guilty and his execution fixed for two days time.

However, the eager crowd that gathered on Tower Hill on 21 July were disappointed. Time was made for a different ceremony, one which set the seal on Mary's triumph. A distinguished congregation, including the fresh clutch of prisoners, gathered in the chapel of St Peter within the Tower. Bishop Gardiner entered, vested in full Roman paraphernalia and accompanied by acolytes to perform the full canon of the mass. At its climax Dudley and his associates knelt to receive the consecrated bread. At the end of the service he stood up to make a brief speech.

Truly, I profess here before you all that I have received the sacrament according to the true Catholic faith; and the plagues that is upon the realm and upon us now is that we have erred from the faith these sixteen years. And this I profess unto you all from the bottom of my heart.[16]

For the new regime this propaganda coup was intended both to discredit Dudley in the eyes of all who were stubbornly addicted to evangelical religion and to symbolize that England's clock was to be put back to its pre-1527 setting. In the first of those objectives it succeeded spectacularly. Upholders of the reformed faith would never, after this, be able to revere Dudley as a religious martyr.

Dudley's total capitulation has been habitually cited as evidence of his lack of religious conviction. A man who, perhaps in the hope of gaining a reprieve, could renounce those things he had always declared himself to believe passionately must have lacked any spiritual depth. From there it is but a short step to asserting that he was motivated throughout his life by nothing but ambition and greed. However, the eleventh hour conversion of a man condemned to suffer a humiliating public death is an ill-constructed cross upon which to crucify a man's whole reputation. If Dudley is to be accused of cynicism and cowardice for changing his coat others must stand in the dock with him. William Cecil, ardent Puritan at heart, wriggled his way into Mary's counsels and played a part in reconciling England to Rome. Thomas Cranmer recanted his 'errors', though he famously recanted his recantation at the stake. The Marquess of Northampton, brother of the pious Catherine Parr, Sir Andrew Dudley and Sir John Gates, the Vice-chamberlain, discovered that they had really been Catholics all along. The members of the Council who hoped to be retained in office ostentatiously attended mass in Mary's chapel. The queen was not a little astonished at the squabbling and mutual recriminations of the old guard, whose members, as she told the imperial ambassador, changed their opinions more often than their shirts in order to protect their reputations. And Princess Elizabeth had no hesitation in conforming to her sister's type of worship. For all these people the Latin tag that enabled them to square their consciences was *cuius regio, eius religio*. As long as Edward was their anointed king they had obediently followed his lead in matters of faith. Now that God had placed Mary on the throne they could do no other than accept her religion.

There can be no doubt that Dudley hoped for a commutation of sentence and that this lay behind his acknowledgement of his offences and his grovelling pleas for mercy. On the same day that he attended mass in the church of St Peter ad Vincula he wrote in desperation to Arundel and Gardiner, begging them to intercede for him with Mary. Only a transcript version of his letter to the earl has survived but there seems little reason to doubt its genuineness.

> . . . O my good lord remember how sweet life is, and how bitter ye contrary. Spare not your speech and pains, for God I hope hath not shut out all hope of comfort for me in that gracious, princely and womanlike heart . . . Once your fellow and loving companion but now worthy of no name but wretchedness and misery, JD.[17]

It reads like the emotionally unrestrained self-abasement of a man who has lost the last shreds of dignity, but we should not judge it by the standards of a later age. For someone in Dudley's position it was the convention to throw oneself on the royal clemency. Cromwell in a similar situation had begged Henry VIII for 'mercy, mercy, mercy'. Dudley could, morally, lay claim to some consideration. Though he had had rivals imprisoned and fined, he had never pursued any of them to death, with the exception of Somerset, and, during his last days in the Tower, he had made his peace with the late duke's sons. Arundel had reason to be well aware of Dudley's forbearance. Despite his intrigues with Wriothesley and Somerset, he had suffered nothing worse than some months' incarceration in the Tower. His fine had been remitted in full and he had been restored to the Council. There is no evidence that he was now prepared to lift a finger to help Dudley.

Thus it was that, on the morning of 22 August, John Dudley was led out to Tower Hill and there given into the charge of the Sheriff of London who presided over the gruesome business of his execution. As was the convention, he made a speech to the throng gathered round the scaffold in which he confessed his offences, reiterated his resolve to die in the true Catholic faith and exhorted the people to remain loyal to their lawful sovereign. He spent some moments in prayer with Bishop Nicholas Heath, then knelt to place his head on the block.

It was forty-three years almost to the day since his father had perished on the same spot and there must have been some in the crowd who had witnessed that earlier execution. They will have compared the two events and, perhaps, murmured to themselves 'like father, like son'. If Dudley reflected on these things from his different perspective, as surely he must have done during his last days, he might well have come to the same conclusion, though for different reasons. Edmund had loyally served his royal master. He had made a valuable contribution to the government of the Tudor state. In doing so he had drawn upon himself that universal loathing which could not be directed at the monarch. The next incumbent of the throne had found it expedient to brand him as the source of all the government's unpopular policies and to punish him for the constitutional schemes of his sovereign. Like father, like son.

IV

THE LOVER

12

De Profundis

In a first floor room of the Beauchamp Tower within the Tower of London visitors can still see, among the various carved graffiti which generations of prisoners left for posterity a panel more elaborate than the rest. It represents the Dudley heraldic devices, the bear and ragged staff, and the double-tailed lion, and, beneath them, the name of the artist, 'IOHN DVDLI'. With patient care the Duke of Northumberland's eldest son inscribed this memorial and displayed his learning with a charming conceit: he encircled the legend with a border of leaves and flowers whose significance he explained in a verse carved below:

Yow that these beasts do wel behold and se
May deme with ease wherefore here made they be
With borders eke wherein [there may be found]
4 Brothers names who list to serche the grounde'

John affectionately represented his siblings by carving roses for Ambrose, gillyflowers for Guildford, oak leaves for Robert (Latin *robur* = oak) and honeysuckle for Henry. Robert, less ambitiously, chiselled an oak spray into the granite together with his initials. But perhaps the most moving memorial is the one word 'IANE', carved, we may assume, by seventeen-year-old Guildford.

He and Suffolk's daughter had been thrown together in a loveless marriage and, during their very brief time together, Guildford had found it humiliating to be treated as a mere consort to his wife, for Jane had resolutely refused to bestow on him the title of 'king'. As a result of this unwanted match the young man now had to endure cramped prison quarters, was separated (most of the time) from his bride and had the threat of execution hanging over him. He had every reason to resent those who had entangled him in their political coils. Yet such evidence as has survived indicates that Guildford wasted no time in bitter brooding. During Jane's first days in captivity the earnest, young ex-queen wrote a short devotional treatise which later came into the possession of the Lieutenant of the Tower. Guildford added a brief prayer to it, in which he asked God to grant long life to his father.

The unity and solidarity of the Dudleys in adversity is really quite remarkable. They did not seek to distance themselves from their father's disgrace and the family did not fall apart in mutual recrimination. The Duchess of Northumberland devoted all her energies to achieving her sons' release and constantly petitioned friends at court to use their influence on the prisoners' behalf. As men of social standing, they were able to command certain privileges, servants to attend them, food provided for their common table, furnishings sent from home for their comfort, books and even pets brought in for their amusement. Robert's wife, Amy, had permission to visit him at 'any convenient time'. Sometimes the brothers were invited to dine at the Lieutenant's table and they were allocated periods for exercise on the leads between the Beauchamp and Bell Towers. Yet no alleviations of the harshness of their incarceration could lift from them the gloom of the complete reversion of their fortunes and the stress of not knowing what the future might hold.

Mary started her reign cautiously. She was wise enough and, perhaps, compassionate enough not to pursue everyone suspected of involvement in the plot to keep her from the throne. She did not parade her triumph over Northumberland by having his head stuck on a pole and displayed to the public gaze. She granted the petition of one man who was not ashamed to remain loyal to John Dudley:

John Cork, Lancaster Herald, sometime servant to this Duke, begged of Queen Mary to bury the head of his old master in the Tower of London, which was granted him with the whole body and performed accordingly. In remembrance whereof the said Lancaster did ever after bear for his crest *a bear's head silver, crowned gold.*[1]

John Dudley's corpse, united with its head, was buried before the altar in St Peter ad Vincula, beside the remains of the Duke of Somerset, thus imposing in death a fitting symmetry on the destinies of the one-time friends who had fallen out over their desire to rule Edwardian England. She set at liberty Suffolk, Northampton and other prominent members of Dudley's faction. It was as she ran into opposition and discovered that the loneliness and rejection of her earlier years were as nothing compared with what she had to endure as queen that her attitude hardened. Her obsession with forcing her will upon her people grew and she ended shedding more innocent blood in five years than her father had in thirty-seven. Having been welcomed so enthusiastically, she must have been surprised by the speed with which the mood changed and by the animosity displayed by many of her subjects. The demonstrations began within weeks.

As early as 13 August the queen's chaplain narrowly escaped death from a hostile crowd when he preached at St Paul's Cross. Parliament, when it met in October, proved unco-operative about repealing old statutes. When, towards the end of the year, the news was published that the queen was negotiating a marriage with Philip, heir to the throne of Spain, national pride and hatred of papists merged in a general outcry. Country priests were manhandled. Scurrilous pamphlets were distributed. A dead dog with a 'tonsured' crown was thrown in through one of the palace windows. Mary was obliged to double her personal guard and Bishop Gardiner received so many assassination threats that he was forced to take up residence in the royal household.

All this disturbance was bad news for the Dudley brothers. The fact that they were obliged to share their prison quarters was the result of the Tower rapidly filling up with fresh batches of detainees. Yet more worrying was the possible impact of unrest on the queen and her councillors. Mary was urged to demonstrate her resolve by making short work of all traitors. John Dudley, Earl of Warwick, was the only one of the brothers who actually stood condemned of treason, having been tried along with his father (Sir Andrew Dudley, Northumberland's brother had been arraigned on 19 August) but, as the autumn set in, the shadow of the axe fell across the younger Dudleys. On 13 November, Ambrose, Henry and Guildford were arraigned at the Guildhall, along with Jane and Thomas Cranmer. Robert was temporarily spared because it was difficult to gather evidence concerning his activities in distant Norfolk. However, he too was taken to the Guildhall on 22 January for his show trial. But the City's mood had changed and the prisoner must have been aware of it. Few citizens braved the cold to indulge the pleasure of shouting curses at the last of the detested Dudleys on his way to justice. Only a couple of weeks before some of them had, however, turned out to pelt Spanish visitors with snowballs. At the end of the dismal proceedings the pre-ordained sentence was read out. On a date as yet unspecified the convicted traitor was

> to be brought through the middle of London to the gibbet at Tyburn, and there be hung and quickly brought down to the ground, and his entrails taken out of his body, while he was still alive, and burned, and that he should then be beheaded and his body divided in four parts, and that his head and his quarters should be taken and displayed at such places as the queen should assign . . .[2]

Still Mary stayed her hand and still there was hope. That hope suffered a severe blow within days. Several anti-Spanish gentlemen and noblemen had been planning a demonstration ever since they heard of the proposed royal marriage. Poor communication and faint hearts undermined the rising that erupted in February – but not before it had come within a whisker of success. While other participants failed to raise their promised forces, the hotheaded Thomas Wyatt, son of Northumberland's old friend, raised 3,000 men in Kent and marched on London. Mary sent the aged Duke of Norfolk to confront the rebels at Rochester but when the royal troops came face to face with the enemy most of them threw down their weapons and the remnant fled back to London, 'their coats torn, all ruined, without arrows or string in their bows'.[3]

Whatever information reached the Dudleys, they cannot have failed to be aware of the bustle and confusion around the Tower. Cannon were trundled out for the defence of the City, the castle's own ordnance being trained on the south side of the river along which the rebels were advancing towards Southwark. Wyatt's impetus came to a halt when he failed to capture London Bridge. He was obliged to move upstream to cross the Thames at Kingston. His forces were dwindling as they made their way back along the north bank. The critical moment came when some of Wyatt's followers put to rout the royal guard at Whitehall, but were too few in number to follow up their advantage. Wyatt plunged on and the outcome eventually depended on the response of London's citizens. Most remained inert. Few came out to join him but few also declared wholeheartedly for the queen.

The Dudleys became aware that the rebellion had fizzled out soon after dawn on 8 February when they heard the shouts and jeers of the garrison as Wyatt and hundreds of his bedraggled supporters were marched into the Tower. They saw the captives divided into groups and distributed among the overcrowded prison quarters, the majority being herded into the crypt below St John's Chapel, the only space left, and conveniently close to the chamber where the rack was housed. The watchers could not but be fearful of the outcome. They knew that Mary would be forced to make her throne more secure. The only question to be answered was, how many heads would fall in the process. They were not kept wondering long. That very day the queen ordered the executions of Jane and Guildford. Neither had been implicated in Wyatt's rebellion but Mary, like her father before her, considered it necessary to remove possible rival claimants. The unfortunate couple were ordered to prepare themselves for death the following day, although the date was subsequently moved to 12 February. By then the Duke of Suffolk had been re-arrested and a spate of hangings of rebellious lesser fry had begun. Gallows were set up at every London gate, one at the end of London Bridge, four in Southwark, one at Leadenhall, two in Cheapside, six or eight in Fleet Street and more at Charing Cross. The prisons were so full that some offenders had to be locked in churches, forty or more at a time.

Contemporary accounts report that Jane and Guildford faced death with quiet dignity. Not for them any grovelling last minute conversion. They shamed their elders by affirming their Protestant faith to the end. Jane, indeed, was openly contemptuous of her father-in-law's apostasy when she told a visitor

> . . . like as his life was wicked and full of dissimulation, so was his end thereafter. I pray God I, nor no friend of mine, die so. Should I who am young . . . forsake my faith for the love of life? Nay, God forbid! Much more he should not whose fatal course, although he had lived his just number of years, could not have long continued . . .[4]

Guildford was taken to the scaffold on Tower Hill, where he refused the ministrations of a Catholic priest before kneeling for the headsman. Jane was spared a public execution. She died, as was becoming customary for English queens, on Tower Green. She did not, as later moralizers insisted, rail against her father-in-law. She had more important things on her mind.

Good master Lieutenant, . . . I shall as a friend desire you, and as a Christian require you, to call upon God to incline your heart to his laws, to quicken you in his way, and not to take the word of truth utterly out of your mouth. Live still to die, that by death you may purchase eternal life . . . For, as the preacher saith, there is a time to be born and a time to die, and the day of death is better than the day of our birth. Yours, as the Lord knoweth, as a friend,

Jane Dudley[5]

Thus Jane wrote in the prayer book she handed to Sir John Bridges, the Lieutenant, during her last moments on earth. In point of fact, none of the younger Dudleys deserted the evangelical faith they had espoused during the heady days of radical fervour at the Edwardian court, although repeated assaults were made upon their religion by priests sent to draw them back into the Catholic fold.

The killings continued. On 23 February it was Suffolk's turn to take the short walk out to Tower Hill. Less than a month later the one who posed the greatest potential threat to Mary's security joined the Tower prisoners. Fickle public favour had by now transferred itself from Mary to Elizabeth. The unwed Protestant princess had a swelling crowd of sympathizers, some of whom were ready to plot and scheme on her behalf. It was on Palm Sunday, 18 March, that Princess Elizabeth came by barge to the Privy Stairs (not the grim portal of Traitor's Gate, as legend would have it) and was escorted to lodgings prepared for her in the ancient palace complex adjacent to the White Tower. The princess was terrified of this place where her mother had been executed and now lay buried. She had pleaded not to be sent here but Gardiner had persuaded the queen and bullied the Council. So, briefly, Elizabeth shared incarceration with the Dudleys.

At the beginning of the next century the chronicler, William Camden, at a loss to explain Elizabeth's attraction to Robert Dudley, pondered,

Whether this proceeded from any virtue of his, whereof he gave some shadowed tokens, or from their common condition or imprisonment under Queen Mary, or from his nativity and the hidden consent of the stars at the hour of their birth, and thereby a most straight conjunction of their minds, a man cannot easily say.[6]

This may be the origin of the romantic legend which proposed clandestine assignations between Robert and Elizabeth in some grim corner of the Tower as the breeding ground of their lasting love. There is no evidence for any such meetings. But nor is there any proof that they did not take place. The strictest security surrounded the princess; she was not supposed to set foot outside her quarters without being guarded by five attendants. This does not mean that there was no contact at all between the two prisoners. They may have met as guests at the Lieutenant's table. Robert may well have smuggled messages conveying loyalty and encouragement to Elizabeth. It is not beyond the bounds of possibility that the two young people may have been able to snatch a few moments' conversation together. Despite the sternest injunctions, guards were always open to bribes. Only nine years later the Earl and Countess of Hertford found themselves in the Tower under royal displeasure. They were in separate lodgings and forbidden to meet. Yet during their captivity they managed to produce a baby.

In reality there is no need to imagine any stolen moments of mutual consolation in order to explain the emotional commitment of these two young people. Their relationship reached far back into childhood. Elizabeth had paid periodic visits to her father's and brother's courts. Thus their relationship such as it was in the frightening spring weeks of 1554 rested on a shared normality, the happy memories of better days. Whether or not they ever met in the Tower, the bond between them was now strengthened by their participation in a common fear. And to whom else but the last Tudor could Robert and his family show genuine admiration and devotion? As for Elizabeth, she needed friends, and friends who would not compromise her safety. While in the Tower she had to submit to harrowing hours of interrogation about her contact with malcontents and plotters. The experience was doubly difficult for her because she *had* received overtures from Wyatt's friends and if the rising had been successful she would have been prepared to have the crown thrust upon her. Elizabeth was a survivor and she valued the support of discreet people who understood her predicament and behaved accordingly. If it seems, on the surface, strange that she should have given her affection to the son of John Dudley, the man who had sought to exclude her permanently from the succession, we might reflect that there were similarities between the princess and the duke. Elizabeth also knew what it was to be caught between a rock and a hard place and to have to master the art of dissimulation. After nine weeks the princess earned a reprieve. She was taken to Woodstock in Oxfordshire, where she could be closely guarded in some comfort but well away from the political centre.

The Dudley men had to endure several more months of uncomfortable incarceration and for one of them it proved fatal. They owed their eventual release to the endeavours of their mother, their brother-in-law and the queen's husband. John Dudley's widow, Jane, lacked regular access to the court where she might plead her family's case. This was where Sir Henry Sidney came to her aid, showing himself a good friend to his wife Mary's family. In March 1554 he was chosen as one of a diplomatic mission sent to Spain in connection with the negotiations for the marriage of Queen Mary to Prince Philip. For his father, the Emperor Charles V, it was important that the reconversion of England should not be bought at the price of a fresh outbreak of religious conflict that could involve the diversion of Habsburg men and money from areas where they were more needed. Philip was, therefore, under instructions to placate the great English families and use his influence with the queen to promote harmony. Sidney seems to have made a good impression on the prince. The Spaniard stood godfather to Sidney's son, born later in the year, and gave the boy his name. As a result Jane Dudley found herself accepted at court in the summer and with many new friends among the lords of the king's Privy Chamber and their ladies.

However, there had to be more deaths before Jane's surviving boys gained their liberty. At the end of the summer the eldest brother, John, Earl of Warwick, fell ill, probably from the fever which stalked the insanitary prison during the hot months of the year. His affliction dragged on for several weeks before, as a special mark of royal clemency, he was allowed to move to the Sidneys' home at Penshurst. The scholarly twenty-three-year-old said goodbye to his brothers, and to his unfinished wall carving and set off for the more salubrious airs of Kent. Alas, his departure had been left too late and he died three days later, on 21 October.

This further tragedy may have proved more than the duchess could bear. She took to her bed at Chelsea and devoted much of her little remaining energy to writing her will in her own hand. To the very end her dominant thoughts were of her sons' rehabilitation. She wrote:

> . . . my three sons and my brother Sir Andrew Dudley stand presently attainted of high treason . . . my said will cannot take place according to my meaning in all things if I should be called out of this life before my said sons and brother have obtained the King's and the Queen's most gracious pardon . . .[7]

The duchess died on 22 January 1555 and the warrant for the release of Ambrose, Robert, Henry and Sir Andrew Dudley was made out the same day. Before the end of the month Ambrose and Dudley both appeared at court. Mary's foreign husband was making some effort to overcome native prejudice and decided to stage the kind of joust that had been so popular in 'Old King Harry's' day. He needed accomplished athletes for this demonstration and the older Dudleys were excellent exponents of tiltyard skills – though they must have been a bit rusty after more than seventeen months in prison.

Though free, the Dudleys were still attainted, which meant that the bulk of their estates remained sequestered. This was deliberate. It prevented the potential rebels attracting a following, bribing royal officials or developing those contacts necessary for stirring up trouble. Not that the Dudleys had trouble in mind. For the time being they had enough to do eking out a living. Cash was so short that Robert even had to enter a bond with the aptly named Thomas Borrowe, a London merchant, in order to meet the £20 bill of his mother's apothecary.[8]

Any possibility of the Dudleys having their lands and fortunes restored depended on their good conduct and they were careful to avoid any who might carry the contagion of rebellion. The mass was restored and the Latin liturgy once again imposed on English people. All the Reformation legislation of a whole generation was repealed, while ancient heresy laws were revived. Evangelicals were faced with very unwelcome choices. This ensured that there were enough new Wyatts around to cause the government real concern. One was Sir Henry or 'Harry' Dudley, a son of 'Lord Quondam'.

He had earlier unhesitatingly thrown in his lot with his successful cousin and become a confidential agent for him at the French court at the crucial time when John Dudley was repairing relations with France. For this service he was knighted by the duke. Regarded as Dudley's 'creature' and suspected of attempting to bring French mercenaries over in the summer of 1553, Henry was arrested and interrogated by Mary's Council. He confessed all he knew, cast himself upon the royal mercy and, after a brief spell in the Tower, was released. Pardoned but unchastened, he was back at the French court by the summer of 1554 and, together with the enemies of England, constructing a plot which was as widespread as it was potentially dangerous. In return for handing over Calais to France, Sir Henry was to have every assistance in conveying a thousand men to Portsmouth or the Isle of Wight. The scheme was very detailed and, considering the number of people involved, it was kept secret for a surprisingly long time. £50,000 was to be taken from the Exchequer to pay for the invasion. The conspirators who were to carry out this audacious robbery included an ex-Lord Mayor, the Keeper of the Star Chamber, the wife of an Exchequer teller, the customs officer at Gravesend, Henry Peckham, courtier and son of Sir Edmund Peckham, councillor and Master of the Tower Mint. The plan was betrayed. Peckham and his accomplices perished on Tower Hill in July 1555, but Henry escaped.

His newly liberated kinsmen were careful to avoid all connection with this plot. They knew that they were being carefully watched. Weeks after their release they were called before the Council and questioned about their conversations with known malcontents whom they met at St Paul's. They were ordered to take themselves off into the country and maintain a low profile. Gradually, cautiously, the restraints placed on the Dudley men were relaxed. Sir Andrew was the first to be fully pardoned and his property was restored to him in April 1555. He was a sick man and considered to be no threat. He retired to the country and died four years later. It was not until July 1556 that Ambrose and Henry were restored in blood. Robert remained under a cloud. His fortunes changed when Charles V decided to abdicate his Spanish throne to Philip in 1555. In September, the new king crossed the Channel to take up his position, having offered positions in his suite to several scions of the leading families. Robert Dudley was among their number. He was eager to demonstrate his loyalty and the government were, doubtless, just as eager to send him abroad where he could do no harm (and certainly not be in regular contact with Elizabeth). He travelled with the court through the Low Countries as, one by one, the seventeen provinces acknowledged their new sovereign and then in March 1557 he brought to Greenwich the glad tidings that Philip was on his way to pay Mary a visit.

However, it was not the prospect of marital embrace which was drawing the Spanish king back to England. He was preparing for the next round of his conflict with Henri II and he was desperately in need of soldiers. If a royal army was not forthcoming there was another way of cobbling together an English contingent. This was to appeal to Mary's more substantial subjects who might want to curry favour with the regime to by attending the king with their own levies.

Robert Dudley had already made it known to Philip that he and his brothers could raise a substantial body of men for the Habsburg cause. It was almost certainly this prospect that lay behind the issue of letters patent under the great seal dated 30 January 1557 which lifted his attainder. Now the Dudleys had to make good their promise to supply the king with men, horses and harness, no easy matter since only a fraction of their lands had been restored to them. They set in train a complex series of transactions designed to provide them with necessary ready cash. Robert took the lead. All the Dudley siblings had shares in the prime Halesowen Abbey estate. First of all Robert borrowed money to buy out the others. Then he mortgaged the whole estate with a trusted Dudley friend, Anthony Forster, for £1,928.6.8d.[9] Forster, a gentleman who was to play a crucial role in Robert's life, was a substantial and well respected member of Berkshire and Oxfordshire society and served as sheriff and on various commissions. He had served John Dudley as steward of his Midlands estates and had recently fallen under suspicion of being involved in plots against Queen Mary. But politics was not the forte of this cultured and scholarly man and he devoted much of his time to improving his attractive home of Cumnor Place, near Oxford, which he rented from George Owen, who, as royal physician and confidant of Henry VII, Edward VI, Mary and Princess Elizabeth, had prospered mightily. Forster was a discreet and loyal Dudley protégé and his financial support at this time was vital to the recovery of the family's fortunes. Robert and his brothers were able to recruit and equip a modest contingent for the 6,000 men which went over to the Netherlands in July. Robert was given charge of the artillery, presumably because he had learned about big guns from his father, who had been Master of the Tower Armoury.

The English contribution to Philip's army was led by arch-trimmer William Herbert, Earl of Pembroke. The army struck deep into enemy territory and began the investment of St Quentin, an important wool-producing centre on the Somme, not eighty miles from Paris. On 10 August the Constable of France, de Montmorency, brought a relief column up from the south. This was annihilated and the Spaniards took many prisoners including the French commander. St Quentin continued to hold out and its eventual overthrow begat appalling horrors. For the Dudleys the siege brought a personal tragedy. Young Henry, not yet twenty, was killed beneath the walls. According to Holinshed, he paused to adjust his hose and was struck by a cannon shot.[10]

England suffered a loss which was, on a national scale, as traumatic as that of the Dudleys. Instead of pressing home his advantage and marching on Paris, Philip disbanded much of his army and sent the rest into winter quarters. As a result, the French were able to recoup. They re-occupied St Quentin and, the following New Year, began an assault on Calais across the frozen marshes. On 7 January the town fell. The humiliation of losing their last continental foothold after 210 years was devastating for the nation and the government. It reinforced the opposition that radicals had expressed about the union with Spain, an opposition reinforced when Philip elected not to press for the restitution of Calais in the ensuing peace negotiations. This was only one disaster for Mary, for whom events moved from bad to worse. The marriage of Mary, Queen of Scots to the dauphin occurred in April. More troops had to be sent to the border to confront renewed Scottish belligerence and Philip continued to demand military assistance when the next campaigning season opened. Government finances were in such a mess that the queen had to consider recalling several of her ambassadors simply to cut costs. The religious policy was, literally, turning to ashes. Determined application of the anti-heresy laws, designed to make examples of recalcitrant Protestants and thus frighten the majority back into the Catholic fold, resulted in about 300 men and women going to the stake (including Cranmer, Ridley, Latimer and Hooper), and countless others dying in prison. The queen was widely reviled for vindictiveness, and then compelled to face a superb irony. Cardinal Pole, her Archbishop of Canterbury and the man on whose spiritual council she relied implicitly, was labelled a heretic by the pope and summoned to Rome. Paul IV, who received the triple crown in 1555, was a sworn enemy of Philip II and it was out of this animosity that his desire to make trouble for Pole and Mary grew. But the queen's overwhelming tragedy was her falling prey to the curse of the Tudors. She failed to produce an heir to the throne. She would cheerfully have endured all her sufferings if her ardent prayers for a son to cement the Catholic restoration had been answered. Not only were they not answered; Mary's mistaken pregnancies made her a laughing stock.

In 1558 the House of Dudley seemed to be suffering a similar blight to that of the House of Tudor. John Dudley's duchess had presented him with thirteen children. Now that number had dwindled to four and as yet there were no male heirs to carry the family name to the next generation. Ambrose, twice married, had only fathered one child, which had died in infancy. Robert and Amy, after eight years of marriage, were still waiting for children.

By now Robert had emerged as the family's leader. Ambrose, though older, was by disposition quiet, scholarly and devout. His geniality and especially his patronage of Puritans soon earned him the nickname of the 'good Lord Dudley'. Though in the next reign he performed court duties, he preferred country life and was happy to leave politics to his

extrovert, ambitious brother. Robert now sold Halesowen to a neighbour and kinsman, settled his debt to Forster and took modest accommodation in London with Amy. With cash in his purse and the risk of
further suffering in body or estate now vanished, he allowed himself a
certain braggadocio. He took to styling himself Lord Dudley of
Halesowen, despite having given up that manor.[11] The Syderstone
house was no longer adequate to his needs, as he pointed out to his
agents:

> I must, if to dwell in that country, take some house other than mine
> own, for it wanteth all such chief commodities as a house requireth,
> which is pasture, wood, water, etc.[12]

A promising residence was located on the Babingley River at Flitcham,
near Castle Rising and serious negotiations were set in hand. But in the
end they came to nothing, and the reason is not far to seek.

The queen was ill, probably terminally ill. Her physical condition was
dropsy but this was exacerbated by periods of deep depression. She had
been deserted by her husband and had to endure the gossip about
Philip's numerous amours. She had failed in her great mission, for it was
obvious that if and when Elizabeth succeeded her she would bring the
hated Protestant heresy with her. England was no more united than it
had been five years earlier. Philip and his Spanish attendants were held
in widespread contempt. In some circles she, herself, was hated as
resolutely as Northumberland had ever been. And she believed herself
responsible for the humiliation of the loss of Calais. 'When I am dead
and opened,' she famously said, 'you shall find Calais lying in my heart.'

It was a time for wily men to be looking to the future. And that future
was Elizabeth. Her status had changed from being princess in peril to
being queen in waiting. Men hastened to commend themselves to her in
her country retreat. She was now living in her own manor at Hatfield,
having eventually won the battle of wills with her half-sister and gained
her freedom. The fashion for ingratiating oneself with Elizabeth was led
by no less a person than Philip II. While ignoring his wife, the king
instructed his ambassador to convey gifts and messages of affection to
her half-sister. Where Philip led others did not hesitate to follow.

Yet Robert Dudley, in this regard, was not a follower. As we know,
his relationship with the princess stretched back over many years. For
four and a half centuries people have struggled to explain the special
bond which existed between these two young people. On 16 June 1561

the scholar and diplomat, Hubert Languet, wrote to Augustus, Duke of Saxony:

> The English leaders had made it plain to her [Queen Elizabeth] that her too great familiarity with my Lord Robert Dudley displeased them and that they would by no means allow him to wed her . . . The Queen replied . . . that she had never thought of contracting a marriage with my Lord Robert; but she was more attached to him than to any of the others because when she was deserted by everybody in the reign of her sister not only did he never lessen in any degree his kindness and humble attention to her, but he even sold his possessions that he might assist her with money, and therefore she thought it just that she should make some return for his good faith and constancy.[13]

A seventeenth-century author, Gregorio Leti, adds flesh to the bare bones of this story of Robert's financial help. He writes of a gift of £200 sent by the hand of a lady together with an exaggerated assurance of devotion from one who 'would willingly lose his life if that would be of any service to her or procure her liberty.'[14] Unfortunately, Leti was a notorious romancer, and anything from his pen must be read with the greatest caution. Yet the story bears some relation to known facts. Not until Robert's return from the Low Countries in the summer of 1557 would he have been in a position to render the princess any assistance. At that time he was raising capital by selling large parcels of land with the support of his brothers. Genuine affection and an eye to the main chance might both have prompted Robert to give the princess tangible proof of his loyalty. Robert would have been foolish not to take every opportunity to assure Elizabeth of his support and devotion. Nor was that the assurance of a time-serving courtier. Just as Edmund had been *droit et loyal* to Henry VII and John had no less sincerely served the first Tudor's son and grandson, so Robert Dudley now dedicated himself to the last Tudor.

We are not totally devoid of clues as to how he maintained regular contact with the mini-court at Hatfield. He had several friends in the princess's household. William Cecil, John Dudley's invaluable aide, was her surveyor and a man in whose skill and discretion she reposed considerable trust. Then there were Gianbattista Castiglione, Elizabeth's Italian tutor, and John Dee, her astrologer. Both were well known to Robert; both enjoyed his generous patronage in after years; both had been apprehended by Mary's officials on suspicion of plotting an Elizabethan coup. The necessary secrecy which guarded all Elizabeth's dealings at this time has prevented historians from unravelling the relationships which undoubtedly existed between the princess and her many friends at home and abroad but Robert Dudley was very prominent among them. In all likelihood he held a unique position which enabled him to form a bridge between the world of Elizabeth's fragile retreat, her friends and well-wishers in the country at large, and the court of Philip II, whose concern for her well-being advanced steadily as his wife's health decreased. Robert had deliberately cultivated members of the king's suite and was well placed to keep Elizabeth informed of official Spanish attitudes towards her. For all these reasons and because these two young people understood each other, Elizabeth had good reason to be grateful to Robert Dudley.

The autumn was oppressive with anticipation and especially so at Hatfield where Elizabeth awaited the news which never came. On 8 November Mary accepted the inevitable and nominated the princess her successor. But still she did not die. William Cecil rode back and forth along the London highway carrying news and messages. It was a highway increasingly choked with hopeful men and women travelling to Hatfield.

As soon as Mary Tudor breathed her last, just before dawn on 17 November, the lords of the Council immediately set off into Hertfordshire. In the park at Hatfield they found Elizabeth walking beneath the bare trees and knelt to offer their allegiance. The new queen's first reaction was to render thanks to God. Then, laying emotion aside, she settled down to business, sitting in conference with Cecil and some of the others to discuss immediate arrangements. There were certain people who had to be informed urgently of Elizabeth's accession. So it was that a secretary made the first memorandum of the reign. This revealing document, though damaged by fire, still survives:

> To send messengers to the Emperor, Sir William Pickering, Sir [Nicholas] Wotton; to the King of Spain, Sir Peter Carew, Lord Robert Dudley; to the King of Denmark, Sir Thomas Ch[alloner] . . .[15]

13

The Gypsy

───◦◦◦───

> The King's Majesty, about a twelvemonth past, gave a pardon to a
> company of lewd persons within this realm, calling themselves
> Gipeyans for a most shameful and detestable murder.[1]

The words are those of Thomas Cromwell and date from 1537. Gypsies
first made their appearance in England around the beginning of the
sixteenth century and like most asylum seekers who followed an
alternative lifestyle to that of good, home-dwelling, honest-working,
English people they were regarded with suspicion and, often, hostility.
Gypsies were, in the common mind, swarthy vagabonds capable of every
imaginable crime from selling poisons to horse stealing, from cut-
pursing to kidnapping children. So when people referred to Robert
Dudley as the 'Gypsy' they were not being complimentary.

The head of the remarkable Dudley clan which had somehow
bounced back from its seemingly complete destruction in 1553 was
always the object of scorn and mistrust. Partly, this was the result of his
black inheritance. His grandfather and father had both been cordially
hated and both had died as traitors, so it was inevitable that people
should believe that Dudley blood was tainted. There was, of course, an
element of jealousy involved, especially among courtiers who saw
themselves as rivals for the queen's favour. Men who began with the
assumption that Lord Robert was a 'bad lot' were genuinely puzzled by
Elizabeth's obvious regard for him. They saw him as a shallow charmer

who lacked the intellectual equipment to serve as a fitting companion for so intelligent and well educated a queen. Women were less surprised. They looked at Robert Dudley and saw an incredibly handsome, self-confident man, tall by the standards of the day (a little under six feet), dark, athletic, magnificent on horseback, always stunningly dressed and having flashing, mischievous eyes. (Elizabeth nicknamed him her 'eyes' and he kept up the intimate joke by often signing himself 'ŌŌ'.) Dudley had all the swaggering, macho, seductive arts of the accomplished courtier and, at twenty-five, he was at the height of his manly powers. He was 'dangerous' and, therefore, attractive to women.

However, at the outset of the reign, none were surprised or scandalized when Elizabeth summed the Gypsy to be a senior member of her household. His appointment as Master of the Horse was an obvious one. He was a member of a prominent family, he was a highly accomplished rider and the office had been held in Edward's reign by his eldest brother. Robert Dudley was known to be an old friend of the queen and it was perfectly reasonable that she should choose men she liked and trusted to be among her more intimate companions. If any observers were anxious about the resurrection of Dudley fortunes their fears were calmed by the fact that Lord Robert and his kin had no political power in the new regime. In the slimmed-down Council with which Elizabeth began her reign there was, pointedly, no room for Robert or for Ambrose, who was made Master of the Ordnance or for Sir Henry Sidney, who became President of the Council in the Marches of Wales. Elizabeth had had plenty of time to think about the style and personnel of her household and her government and had discussed such matters with Cecil, who immediately took up the position of Secretary. For the Council they basically recreated the kind of body that Northumberland had established in the early days of his regime: it was compact, consisted largely of like-minded men (most of Mary's advisers were either excluded or subsequently removed) and regarded itself as having a semi-tutorial role. The new occupant of the throne was not a minor but she was a 'mere' young woman and would require particularly firm guidance. The seasoned diplomat, Sir Nicholas Throckmorton, did not hesitate to play the pedagogue with his royal mistress. 'Beware of womanish levity,' he admonished, 'for where the King governeth not in severity and prudence there doth emulation and ambition sow their seeds.'[2] An attitude that to us sounds patronizing was the norm in sixteenth-century government circles. Female rule was regarded as unnatural and potentially disastrous (as the last five years had amply demonstrated) and high on the Council's agenda throughout the early years of the reign was the business of finding a suitable husband for the queen. It was frankly inconceivable that she would choose to remain single, any more than Mary had. She should, she must and she would marry and have children, thus sparing the nation fresh bouts of trauma over finding a legitimate heir.

The Privy Chamber, whose members had exercised considerable influence with Henry VIII and Edward VI, was depoliticized. This was because it was staffed largely by women but also because Cecil disliked the diffusion of power. No longer did all the great household officers have seats on the Council. The policy failed because it did not acknowledge that the monarch's closest companions *were* political figures and because this particular monarch was determined to turn for advice to whomsoever she chose. Elizabeth soon made it clear that she would not be bullied by her Council, nor would she take them fully into her confidence on every issue. Therefore, if the Queen's political advisers wanted to know what she was thinking or wanted to press home their advice they needed intermediaries: they needed the queen's friends. Thus emerged the figure of the royal favourite, the unofficial consort. And for most of the reign that position was held by Robert Dudley.

Lord Robert's new job carried considerable responsibility, the more so as Elizabeth hugely enjoyed going on progress and regularly spent three months of the year on tour, showing herself to her people and enjoying the hospitality of her wealthier subjects. The Master of the Horse was responsible for the transport of the queen and the court on all occasions, ceremonial and otherwise; for the supervision of the royal studs together with the purchase, training and equipping of horses for all purposes; for the provision of mounts for household officials and royal messengers; for the organization of the queen's annual progresses; and for the planning of ceremonial journeys. He had to provide war horses, 'great horses' for the joust and for pulling the unsprung carriages just coming into fashion, coursers for the queen's gentlemen; palfreys and amblers for the maids of honour, cobs and rouncies for lesser attendants, mules and sumpters for baggage, and a supply of hacks and hunters for the queen's sport. The stable employed a large staff of aveners, grooms, clerks, farriers, purveyors and baggage-men. The routine organization was done by subordinates but Robert maintained close personal control and much of his time was spent considering reports on horses at stud; instructing foreign agents to buy new bloodstock; planning the stages of the royal progresses; organizing tourneys and accompanying the queen in the hunting field.

It was work he found congenial and for which he was well qualified, but more important than the daily routine of stable administration was the proximity it gave him to the queen. No official had reason to be closer to Elizabeth than her Master of the Horse. Wherever she stayed Robert had his own suite of rooms. On ceremonial occasions he rode immediately behind her. He was at her side when she travelled abroad and when she went to the hunting field. Since she loved being in the saddle, these occasions were frequent.

However unremarkable Robert's appointment might have seemed originally, his relationship with Elizabeth soon set tongues wagging. People said that the queen was bent on following the example of her cousin, Frances Grey. She had carried on an affair with her master of the horse, Adrian Stokes, behind the back of her husband, the Duke of Suffolk, and as soon as the duke had been executed she had married her lover. Now royal watchers observed the body language of Robert and Elizabeth, listened to tittle-tattle about what the couple, supposedly, got up to in private and scented a delicious scandal.

If we want to understand this latest episode in the black legend of the Dudleys we, once again, have to draw back the curtain of contemporary and later prejudice. The legend goes something like this: Elizabeth was a wonder-queen of whom one should think no ill. She was also an extremely intelligent and canny woman. Yet, somehow, she became infatuated with Dudley. Since she could not possibly be to blame for this unfortunate state of affairs, obviously the Gypsy had cast his spell over her. Once again a member of this incorrigible family had set his sights on the achievement of ultimate power. Fortunately for England, Elizabeth the queen finally triumphed over Elizabeth the woman and Robert Dudley's ambitions were quashed. Such a simplistic interpretation of events fails to take account of the complexities of Elizabethan court politics. The relationship of Elizabeth Tudor and Robert Dudley evolved over three decades and was shaped by various pressures. The first traumatic and ultimately tragic twenty-two months were fashioned by the young queen's inexperience, political rivalries, the rehabilitation of the Dudleys, Robert's relationship with his wife and the conventions of courtly love.

It all started with the friendship of the queen and the courtier. They were of an age. They understood each other. They had just shared a harrowing five years. The queen compared her experience under Mary with that of Daniel in the lions' den.[3] Elizabeth faced a daunting task. She needed wise councillors but also people with whom she could relax.

She loved music, dancing, masques and plays and threw herself into court entertainments with an enthusiasm some thought unbecoming. Robert, the dashing, handsome perfect courtier was the ideal companion of her leisure hours but it was almost inevitable that he should become more than that. Within a month his closeness to the queen was common knowledge. By the following spring the Spanish ambassador, Don Gomez Suarez, Count Feria, was reporting a much increased intimacy between Elizabeth and her favourite:

> During the last few days Lord Robert has come so much into favour that he does whatever he likes with affairs and it is even said that her majesty visits him in his chamber day and night. People talk of this so freely that they go so far as to say that his wife has a malady in one of her breasts and the Queen is only waiting for her to die to marry Lord Robert. I can assure your Majesty that matters have reached such a pass that I have been brought to consider whether it would not be well to approach Lord Robert on your Majesty's behalf promising your help and favour and coming to terms with him.[4]

Another member of the diplomatic corps, ears and eyes ever open to potential scandal, hinted at libidinous goings-on but thought it prudent to exercise self-censorship:

> My Lord Robert Dudley is in very great favour and very intimate with her majesty. On this subject I ought to report the opinion of many but I doubt whether my letters may not miscarry or be read, wherefore it is better to keep silence than to speak ill.[5]

If Elizabeth knew of the whisperings and the disapproving glances around the court she did not care. Now, for the first time in her twenty-five years she could do as she liked. And she did.

For his part, Robert had deliberately set out to impress. The rebuilding of his family's fortunes depended on his maximizing the relationship he already enjoyed with Elizabeth. In 1559, he approached Baron Edward Dudley with an offer to buy Dudley Castle and its dependencies. He had a list made of all the baronial lands together with the outstanding mortgages and calls upon it.[6] But cousin Edward was no Lord Quondam; though he affirmed that 'if God does not send us issue there is no one I would rather see inherit than your Lordship,' he was not prepared to sell,[7] and by the end of 1560 Robert had been obliged to give up his plans to acquire the ancestral home.

Robert was well equipped to achieve his objectives. Not only was he handsome and charming; he was the most extrovert member of the family and had inherited the lion's share of his father's drive and ambition. It was natural to his siblings that he should become their leader. But they were not blind to his faults. Within weeks of his appointment as Master of the Horse Robert received a letter from his sister Catherine, wife of the pious Earl of Huntingdon.

> I hear God hath increased you with honour since my departure. I pray let me desire you to be thankful unto him that showeth himself so gratious unto you. I am bold to write this because I know honour doth rather blind the eye than clear it . . .[8]

Catherine knew that her brother was vain, proud and headstrong and feared that his elevation might go to his head.

Dudley was an utter spendthrift on anything that might make a show and enhance his public persona. In later years he remarked, with a ruefulness which thinly veiled boasting, 'I have lived always above any living I had.' His letters give ample evidence of his extravagance. To a colleague in Antwerp he sent an urgent commission:

> Touching the silks I wrote you about, I wish you to take up and stay for me 4000 crowns worth of crimson and black velvet and satins and silks of other colours. And if there be any good cloth of tissue or of gold or such other pretty stuff, stay for me to the value of £300 or £400, whatever the charge shall be . . .
> P.S. Make stay of as much stuff as I have written for and the money shall be sent you immediately . . . Let it be of the best sort of every kind I have written for . . .[9]

His wardrobe was immense, running, according to an inventory, to several hundred items listed under a profusion of headings:

> Night gowns, short gowns, cape cloaks, short cloaks, long cloaks, riding cloaks, riding slops, cassocks, hose paned and slops, doublets, jerkins, buttons, brooches, tags and points of gold, caps and hats, boothose and stockings, rapiers and daggers with their girdles and hangers, fawchions, woodknives, buskins, shoes,

pumps, pantophels, slippers and boots.[10]

Another list of several thousand personal possessions contained numerous exotic items ordered from leading English and foreign craftsmen:

> the portraitures of the Queen's majesty and my lord, cut in alabaster . . .
>
> a salt, ship fashion, of the mother-of-pearl, garnished with silver and divers works of warlike ensigns and ornaments, with sixteen pieces of ordnance, whereof two on wheels, two anchors on the fore part, and on the stern the image of Dame Fortune, standing on a globe, with a flag in her hand . . .
>
> A chess board of ebony, with chequers of crystal and other stones layed with silver, garnished with bears and ragged staves and cinqfoils of silver, the thirty-two men likewise of crystal and other stones set, the one sort in silver white, the other gilt, in a case of leather, gilded and lined with green cotton.[11]

Dudley's exotic showmanship has to be seen against the background of an exuberant, youthful court and the kind of behaviour that was expected of its members. In particular we need to understand the kind of love games in which the queen and her attendants were constantly involved and which affected personal and family fortunes.

The courtier's everlasting role was to make ostentatious display of loyalty and devotion to the sovereign. When that sovereign was an unmarried woman such behaviour inevitably took on the character of flirtation and even courtship. The queen had to be wooed with songs, poems, gifts and exuberant protestations of love. The overblown, amorous rhetoric of a letter from Christopher Hatton, one of her 'suitors', indicates the kind of attention Elizabeth expected and which became the convention. After Hatton had been sent away from court for his health, he wrote:

> . . . Madam, I find the greatest lack that ever poor wretch sustained. No death, no, not hell, no fear of death shall ever win of me my consent so far to wrong myself again as to be absent from you one day . . . I lack that I live by. The more I find this lack, the farther I go from you . . . My spirit and soul (I feel) agreeth with my body

and life, that to serve you is heaven, but to lack you is more than hell's torment unto them. My heart is full of woe . . . Would God I were with you but for one hour. My wits are overwrought with thoughts. I find myself amazed. Bear with me, my most dear, sweet Lady. Passion overcometh me. I can write no more. Love me; for I love you . . . Shall I utter this familiar term, 'farewell'? Yes, ten thousand, thousand farewells. He speaketh it that most dearly loveth you . . .[12]

It was all a game, with elaborate rules that every player had to abide by. But the stakes involved were so high that the sport was intensely serious. Elizabeth was wagering her own freedom and the well-being of her people. For her partners in the matrimonial charade failure to perform well could spell exile from court and social ruin. Everyone, possibly including herself at this time, believed that Elizabeth would marry. As soon as her first parliament convened in February 1559 members fell to discussing possible husbands and there was a strong feeling, in reaction to Mary's disastrous marriage, that she should seek a partner within the realm. Some of them favoured the Earl of Arundel, the Catholic peer who had survived the purge of Marian officials, retaining both his position as Lord Steward of the household and his seat on the Council. At forty-seven Arundel was urbane, cultured, a member of the ancient nobility, and recently widowed. He outranked Lord Robert in every way and he was also the Dudleys' implacable enemy. This was the man who had plotted against Somerset and Dudley, been imprisoned without trial, pardoned, restored, had promised to hold London for Queen Jane and subsequently hastened to Cambridge to arrest Dudley. What future could Robert and his family look to if Arundel became the royal consort? All this added urgency to his own efforts to dazzle the queen. Whatever his feelings for Elizabeth, it was important for him to outplay his rival in the game of courtly love. Whatever Elizabeth's feelings for Robert, she revelled in the experience of having two men vying for her favour.

These romantic manoeuvrings should not be viewed separately from their wider political implications. Arundel made no secret of his adherence to Catholicism and his contempt for 'newfangled' religious ideas. He was brusque and arrogant in Council, often expressing his opinions forcefully and, on at least one occasion, almost coming to blows with colleagues who opposed him. What he did keep secret was his network of Catholic activists. Not only was he a potential danger to the Dudleys, he was also anathema to Cecil and those councillors who were working to restore the momentum of the English Reformation. As long as Robert could dazzle Elizabeth she might be prevented from 'throwing herself away' on the likes of Arundel or some other unsuitable matrimonial candidate.

Yet, while all members of the royal household were engrossed in mock courtship rituals and while the Council were consumed with the necessity of finding an acceptable consort for the queen, Elizabeth had given her political advisers an absolutely unequivocal answer to their probing questions about her marriage. On 10 February, in response to her parliament's importunings, she had assured them that they need not fear that she would rush into an unsuitable match. 'Whensover it may please God to incline my heart to another kind of life, ye may well assure yourselves my meaning is not to do or determine anything wherewith the realm may or shall have just cause to be discontented,' she said. For herself, she declared that she had no desire for the wedded state: 'in the end, this shall be for me sufficient, that a marble stone shall declare that a Queen, having reigned such a time, lived and died a virgin.'[13]

Was she serious? Robert in later years would tell people that Elizabeth had pledged herself to the maiden state from the age of eight, but how many children and teenagers go through a phase of insisting that they will never marry, only to abandon their resolve when the hormones kick in or when, later, they become alarmed at being left on the shelf? Some biographers have made great play with the idea that Elizabeth had been put off sex by the abusive behaviour of her step-uncle, Thomas Seymour when she was fourteen or fifteen. Others suggest that she was, by nature, more intellectual than physical, that her head almost invariably ruled her heart. Such simple answers to complex personality issues will not serve.

Elizabeth was fully possessed of all the normal female instincts. She did want a lover. She did hope for marriage and she resented bitterly that her position made it difficult, if not impossible. Her talk of 'marble stones' and 'living and dying a virgin' was intended to head off her politicians and assure them that she would not stand on her prerogative and plunge into a disastrous union without their consent, which was what Mary had done. It was only in later years that her advisers made a virtue of necessity by creating the icon of the 'virgin queen'. Then she became increasingly paranoid about others who could not practise the restraint forced upon her. Nothing annoyed her more than the clandestine marriages of members of her household, and she developed a pathological dislike of non-celibate priests. The young Elizabeth was a very 'physical' woman. She loved dancing, especially the more risqué jigs from Italy and France, which involved close contact between the partners. She rode like a wild thing, preferring spirited horses and delighting in outstripping her companions (behaviour which often caused her Master of the Horse genuine alarm).

At the same time Mary's unhappy reign had made her acutely aware of the problems marriage would bring. Philip's indifference had broken his wife's heart and his involvement in government had restricted her influence. He had also divided the political nation. It was obvious to Elizabeth and to all who understood the personal and ideological rivalries at the centre of national life that no potential suitor would command universal support. Whoever Elizabeth chose, inside or outside the realm, would provoke strife.

The escape valve for all her pent up emotions and repressed desires was Robert Dudley. With him Elizabeth could allow herself to fall in love, and she did so. For the one great advantage he possessed was that he was already married. Commentators observed then and have observed since then that the queen and her Gypsy were clandestine lovers only waiting for Lady Dudley's death fully to consummate their union. Nothing could have been further from the truth, at least as far as Elizabeth was concerned. Her relationship with Robert was a bitter-sweet romance that involved no matrimonial complications. With Robert at her beck and call and Amy obliged to live in the country the queen could have her cake and eat it. There can be no other reason for Robert's wife being excluded from the court other than Elizabeth wished it to be so. Robert could then play the ardent bachelor suitor and she the object of his passionate devotion. Why else would Lady Dudley not have been allocated a privileged place in the queen's chamber? Most household officials saw their wives ensconced among Elizabeth's ladies. Ambrose's wife enjoyed that honour. So did her sister-in-law, Mary Sidney (fast becoming a favourite with the queen). The truth of the matter must have been as Feria succinctly described it in April 1559: the queen 'is in love with Lord Robert and never lets him leave her.'[14]

It must have been very hard for Amy not to be allowed to bask in her husband's celebrity or enjoy the exciting life of the court. During the winter, spring and summer of 1559, when lavish entertainments and diversions, of which her husband was a major impresario, followed hard on one another's heels, Amy was not there to share in the fun. At Christmastide the court enjoyed, among other theatricals a rabid anti-Catholic masque which offended some foreign observers who were obliged to be present

> I [have] not sufficient intellect to interpret . . . the mummery performed after supper . . . of crows in the habits of cardinals, of asses habited as bishops, and of wolves representing abbots, I will consign it to silence . . . Nor will I record the levities and unusual licentiousness practised at the court in dances and banquets . . .[15]

Amy missed it. She spent the festival quietly with friends in Lincolnshire. A few weeks later she was staying with relatives in Bury St Edmunds. With the coming of spring she went to be with her maternal kinsfolk in Camberwell. The only place she had to call 'home' seems to have been a house belonging to William Hyde, another family friend, at Denchworth, near Abingdon.[16]

Those who want to excuse Elizabeth's responsibility for Lady Dudley's exile assume that Robert or Amy herself desired it. The most obvious reasons for this would be that the couple were estranged or that Amy was in poor health. In fact, there is no evidence for either. Certainly the couple had been married for eight years and were still childless. Certainly the ups and downs of those eight years had been traumatic, and since 1553 they had enjoyed virtually no home life together. But adversity does not seem to have driven a wedge between them. A relationship which had begun as a love match still appears to have been strong. Amy had visited Robert in prison and now, amidst his pressing court duties he found time to think of her and occasionally to spend time with her. Curt account book entries reveal an attentive husband who obtained for his wife in the smart London shops 'sewing silk', '2 pair of hose', 'a looking glass' and '2 ell of fine Holland cloth' for ruffs. Frequent gifts atoned for his long absences from Amy's side.

To Thos. Jones to buy a hood for my lady	35s
To Gilbert the goldsmith for 6 doz. Gold buttons of ye Spanish pattern, and for a little chain delivered to Mr Forrest for y lady's use	£30
Delivered for my lady's charge riding into Suffolk With 40 pistoles [Spanish coins] delivered to Hogans To put into her ladyship's purse	£25.13s.4d.[17]

Other entries show that Robert paid visits to Denchworth, thoughtfully sending on ahead venison and spices so that he and his suite would not overtax his host's larder. We glimpse Robert and Amy playing cards with their friends, and losing; Robert was obliged to borrow 40 shillings from Hyde to pay his debts. On other occasions Amy visited Robert at court, though she stayed in the vicinity and not under Elizabeth's roof.

One of the only two surviving letters by Amy deals with the sale of wool from the Syderstone estate. In it she tells their agent, John Flowerdew, to hasten the business so that a debt could be discharged, 'for my lord so justly required me, at his departing, to see those poor men satisfied.' She apologized for not dealing with the matter earlier and explained, 'I forgot to move my lord thereof before his departing,[18] he being sore troubled with weighty affairs and I not being altogether in quiet for his sudden departing.' Robert's visit had obviously been brief and snatched from his courtly duties and Amy was upset that he had to hasten back so peremptorily to the queen's side.

Fortunately, we know what 'weighty affairs' were so urgent that they forced Robert to cut short his visit. Amy's letter was dated 7 August 1559. Where was the royal court from 6–10 August? Staying at Nonsuch Palace as guests of the Earl of Arundel. It was during this visit that the earl made his most determined attempt to woo the Queen, offering her expensive entertainments such as had not been seen since the days of Henry VIII and overwhelming her with the lavishness of a parting gift, a cupboard of gold plate. Small wonder that Robert had to hurry back from Berkshire, his domestic duties incomplete.

On all this evidence Robert Dudley emerges as a familiar type of man; a successful, upwardly mobile achiever, trying to balance home and job. In that case, one might have thought that he would provide Amy with a home in or near London where they could spend more time together. Norfolk was too remote and Robert had abandoned the idea of buying a house more commodious than Syderstone. In 1559 he was contemplating acquiring Dudley Castle so he must have either possessed or been able to lay his hands on sufficient funds. But for Robert to have had his wife close to the court and been constantly popping home, instead of constantly available to Elizabeth, would not have pleased his possessive mistress at all.

A lively and devoted wife such as Amy seems to have been cannot have enjoyed being excluded from the court. The gossip about her husband and the queen cannot have been easy to bear. However, she could comfort herself with the knowledge that she was married to the handsomest and most famous man in all England and he did always come back to her. If she had to share him with Elizabeth Tudor, well that was a price that had to be paid for the royal bounty that she and Robert enjoyed. And she knew better than to protest. The queen's purse, now open to Robert, could quite easily be snapped shut.

If Robert did not callously desert his wife and deliberately shut her away in the country, can we accept the contemporary gossip that suggested that Amy was kept from court by illness? Feria reported that Amy had 'a malady in one of her breasts'. The Venetian ambassador informed his government that 'many persons believe', that Amy had 'been ailing for some time.'[19] Once again, any hard evidence we have does not support the idea of Amy Dudley as a reclusive semi-invalid shut away in the country. We have to forget what we know or think we know about Amy's early death and try to establish the sort of woman she was in 1559. We have already seen that she was capable of dealing with estate business and confident enough to act on her own authority. And if we refer back to the Dudley account books, they do not support the image of someone in decline who had lost all interest in worldly vanities. On the contrary they reveal a woman very interested in the latest fashions. One extensive and detailed account from William Edney, a London tailor, lists gowns, petticoats, bodices, kirtles, sleeves, ruffs, collars, lace trimmings and materials ordered by Amy over several months.[20] Then we have to ask ourselves how likely it is that a lady in rapidly declining health would have spent her days travelling the rutted winter highways and dusty summer byways on a constant round of visits to friends. Would she not, rather, have gone to live among her kinsfolk in Norfolk?

In fact, Syderstone was too far away. Had she stayed there she would have seen even less of her husband and have had virtually no contact whatsoever with his glamorous life at court. Denied a home in the capital, she passed her days as agreeably as she could visiting friends and relatives in the home counties. And the person responsible for imposing this peripatetic life upon her was the queen.

Elizabeth threw caution to the winds in her impulsive and very public amorous behaviour with Dudley. By her actions she defied anyone to challenge her. And no one dared to do so – except one. In August 1559 her longest serving and most faithful attendant, Katherine ('Kat') Ashley, threw herself on her knees before the queen and implored her to break off her affair with Dudley and to find a husband. Katherine upbraided her mistress for his shameful conduct and even went so far as to say that had she been able to see into the future she would have strangled the infant Elizabeth in her cradle. Katherine was right. The situation was serious. The libertine queen and her paramour were setting an appallingly bad example. Was this to be the style of the new reign? Elizabeth and Robert were being widely slandered in bawdy ballads and alehouse gossip. Goodwives in the marketplace assured their neighbours that they had it on good authority that the queen had given birth to a daughter, subsequently smuggled out of the palace and placed in a distant foster home. English diplomats abroad were embarrassed to have to rebut salacious rumours and listen to lewd jokes about their sovereign, and the emperor sent a special envoy to make careful enquiry about the truth of the relationship between the queen and Lord Robert. Elizabeth did not demean herself by responding to the smear campaign but she did react to Kat Ashley's protestation and her words are significant. She categorically denied that there was any impropriety about her relationship with Lord Robert but, then, petulantly added that even if there was, 'she did not know of anyone who could forbid her'.

Elizabeth made the running in this relationship. It could not be otherwise, for she was queen. It was for her to command and, by opening or closing the royal cornucopia, to make or break those in her service. It was for Dudley, as it had been for his forebears, to remain *droit et loyal* to the sovereign and to give the queen whatever she wanted. In return he received very tangible proofs of Elizabeth's love. He was admitted to the select Order of the Garter on the first St George's Day of the reign. During 1559 he received various parcels of land in different counties: Knole in Kent, Burton Lazar Manor and hospital, Leicestershire, Beverley Manor, park and borough, Skidby and the site of Meaux Abbey, all in Yorkshire. On 24 November letters patent were issued appointing Dudley Lord Lieutenant of Windsor Castle and Park, a post made vacant by the death of William Fitzwilliam. At the same time Sir Francis Eaglefield was obliged to surrender to Robert his life constableship of Windsor Castle.

What most people at the time saw and what many historians since have seen was an irresponsible clandestine relationship between a headstrong queen and an over-ambitious subject. To outsiders everything about Lord Robert – his extravagance, his princely bearing, his arrogance, his monopoly of the queen's affections – proclaimed a king in waiting and they would have remembered that, back in 1553, a Dudley had been husband to the proclaimed queen of England. Most observers believed that all the evidence pointed to yet another member of this accursed family grasping for the ultimate prize. Most, but not all. The seasoned diplomat, Sir Thomas Chaloner, who knew Robert well, rejected the gossip about his soaring ambition as 'most foul slander', and suggested that Elizabeth should be circumspect in displaying her gratitude and affection: 'a princess cannot be too wary what countenance of familiar demonstrations she maketh more to one than another . . . No man's service in the realm is worth the price of enduring such malicious tales.'21

But for the couple at the centre of national life the situation was much more complicated and, at times, dangerous. The new Spanish ambassador, Alvarez de Quadra, explained in one of his first reports that Thomas Howard, Duke of Norfolk (grandson of that other Thomas Howard who had spent all of King Edward's reign in the Tower)

> is the chief of Lord Robert's enemies, who are all the principal people in the kingdom . . . he said that if Lord Robert did not abandon his present pretentions and presumptions, he would not die in his bed . . . I think his hatred of Lord Robert will continue, as the Duke and the rest of them cannot put up with his being king.22

In November, Howard almost came to blows with Dudley whom he accused of introducing himself into the government of the realm. Within days the duke found himself 'promoted' to a new job – Lieutenant General in the North. Very reluctantly he was obliged to set out for Newcastle to do battle with the Scots and to abandon the campaign at court.

Norfolk was right in identifying Dudley as a significant player in the political life of the nation. The royal favourite was no mere court exotic, fopping around the queen's chambers. He may not have been a brilliant, original thinker but he did have clear religious and political convictions and he did discuss the issues of the day with his royal mistress. His potential importance had been recognized as early as November 1558 when Feria had made the incorrect assumption that Robert was a member of the new Council. Cecil's policy of depoliticizing the chamber was now rebounding on him. Instead of depriving the queen's household of any influence in state affairs it had created the circumstances for the emergence of a favourite who could, and did, discuss matters of moment with the queen without being at all answerable to the Council. This provoked some fresh thinking as early as May 1559. A memorandum circulating in government circles and headed 'for redress of the state of the Realm' recommended that all the senior officials of the household and the chamber should be members of the Council. For the time being, however, Dudley had to content himself with being an unofficial politician.

Unofficial but active, and never more so than in the tense foreign situation which confronted England after the sudden death of Henri II in a jousting accident in July 1559. Since Mary Stuart, wife of the new fifteen-year-old king, Francis II, was the Scottish queen the crowns of England's closest enemies were now brought together. With France and Spain enjoying one of their rare interludes of peace and Mary vigorously asserting her claim to the English throne, the foreign situation was grave indeed, but the Council was divided on the advice they gave. Cecil and his supporters, who saw international affairs in terms of a Catholic conspiracy against the Protestant nation, were for launching a pre-emptive military strike against Scotland in order to forestall an anticipated Franco–Scottish invasion. Others were disposed to proceed by diplomacy. By forging an alliance with the Protestant Lords of the Congregation they hoped to create a strong bond between the neighbouring nations and force Mary to grant religious freedom to her subjects. This was the policy Elizabeth preferred and she was supported in it by Dudley. He now headed a group in the chamber to whom the queen turned for advice more readily than the full Council. Lord Robert enjoyed his own political network thanks to his clients in various parts of the country and his contacts abroad. During the Scottish crisis he often corresponded with Maitland of Lethington, the leader of the Scottish Protestant nobles. What frequently drove Mr Secretary to distraction was not a disagreement with Dudley over policy fundamentals; they shared an ardent Protestant nationalism. It was in their attitude to the queen that the two men differed. To Cecil, Elizabeth was a headstrong young woman who ought to leave the serious business of government to older and wiser heads. For Dudley she was queen. She should be supported in her determination to rule effectively. Cecil grumbled that, if his advice was to be constantly ignored or rejected, he might as well not be there and the threat of resignation became for him a favourite ploy. The Council thought it prudent to strengthen the border garrisons and this was one reason why Norfolk was dispatched northwards at the end of the year. In May 1560 Elizabeth was vindicated when Norfolk's attempt to seize Leith turned into an expensive flop which resulted in a thousand English fatalities. The queen was furious. She berated Cecil and immediately sent him to Edinburgh to patch up the best treaty he could.

This really worried the Secretary. He knew that Dudley had been opposed to his aggressive policy and suspected that the favourite was behind the decision to send him away from court. It is highly unlikely that Robert Dudley wanted to remove Cecil from his trusted position as the Queen's principal adviser or that Elizabeth would have dismissed him but he certainly made the most of the councillor's absence to settle a few old scores and nudge religious policy in a radical direction. Several deprived bishops and Marian officials who had been allowed to live in semi-retirement or had their movements only slightly restricted were now thrust into prison. On 10 June Nicholas Heath, late Archbishop of York, was sent to the Tower. He was swiftly followed by John Boxall, Mary's secretary, the erstwhile bishops of Exeter and Bath and Wells, and others.[23]

Meanwhile, thanks largely to the French court being distracted by a crop of domestic problems, Cecil was able to achieve what, under the circumstances, was a very reasonable settlement with the Scots. That was not how the queen perceived it. On his return the Secretary was hauled over the coals for his 'failure', which plunged him into black despair as he explained in a letter to the Earl of Bedford.

> The court is as I left it and therefore do I mind to leave it, as I have too much cause, if I durst write all. As soon as I can get Sir Nicholas Throckmorton placed [as Secretary] so soon I purpose to withdraw myself, which if I cannot do with ease I will rather adventure some small displeasure for so have I cause rather to do than to continue with a perpetual displeasure to myself and my foolish conscience.[24]

Rightly or wrongly, Cecil now believed that he was fighting for his political life against the evil machinations of Robert Dudley. But he was not seriously contemplating retirement from public life. Mr Secretary Cecil had not yet played his last card. Nor had fate.

14

Death and Transfiguration

———❦———

Edney, with my hearty commendations, these shall be to desire you to take ye pains for me as to make this gown of velvet, which I send you with such a collar as you made my russet taffeta gown you sent me last and I will see you discharged for all. I pray you let it be done with as much speed as you can . . .[1]

These, the last words of Amy Dudley that have survived, were written to her dressmaker on 24 August 1560. They deal with trivia, but trivia that were important to Amy. She loved fine clothes and was impatient to receive the latest addition to her wardrobe. They are not the words of a young woman contemplating death. A few weeks later one of her servants claimed that she had often heard her mistress pray that God would deliver her from her desperation but, on being pressed, the girl denied strenuously that Lady Dudley harboured any thoughts of harming herself. Her desperation may have been caused by physical pain or by feelings of inadequacy as a wife or by the malicious gossip she had to endure about the queen and her husband – or by any combination of these distressing circumstances. However resilient she was, it would be remarkable if her unusual married life did not result in occasional mood swings.

Amy wrote her letter from Cumnor Place, near Oxford, which had become her principal residence at the beginning of the year. It was altogether more suited to her needs than Mr Hyde's house at

Denchworth. The move had been arranged by Dudley in collaboration with his old friend and steward, Anthony Forster. This substantial fourteenth-century house built round a square courtyard had been designed as a summer residence for the Benedictine abbots of Abingdon and was acquired by the royal physician Dr George Owen at the Dissolution. Forster now leased it from William Owen, the doctor's son. Here the cultured and congenial Forster provided a home for his own family and for three single ladies who either did not choose or could not afford to run their own establishments. They included Dr Owen's elderly widow, Elizabeth Odingsells, a widowed sister of William Hyde and Lady Dudley. It may not have been the most stimulating company for a lively young woman but it was commodious and comfortable. And it was close enough to the court for Robert to be able to visit whenever he could escape, especially when the court was on summer progress west of the capital.

At the beginning of September the court arrived at Windsor, a morning's ride away from Cumnor. William Cecil was there and he was still suffering the frustration of the bureaucrat who has lost control of events. His access to the queen was limited and he was convinced that policy was being made by Dudley and his friends, who outranked the Secretary and had their own private political networks. He must have been desperately worried about his own future as well as the state of the country for he now did something utterly disreputable, if not akin to treason. The Spanish ambassador, de Quadra, arrived at Windsor on Friday 6 September and one of the first people to seek him out was Cecil. The diplomat was not a natural confidant; he mistrusted the Secretary and loathed his ardent Protestantism. However, he was on good terms with Dudley and was respected by the queen and it may have been that Cecil was using him as a conduit to convey his message to the royal ear. This is how de Quadra reported to his master the dramatic interview:

> . . . after my many protestations and entreaties that I would keep secret what he was about to tell me, he said that the Queen was going on so strangely that he was about to withdraw from her service . . . he perceived the most manifest ruin impending over the Queen through her intimacy with Lord Robert. The Lord Robert had made himself master of the business of the state and of the person of the Queen, to the extreme injury of the realm, with the intention of marrying her, and she herself was shutting herself up in

the palace to the peril of her health and life. That the realm would tolerate the marriage he said he did not believe. He was, therefore, determined to retire into the country although he supposed they would send him to the Tower before they would let him go. He implored me for the love of God to remonstrate with the Queen, to persuade her not utterly to throw herself away as she was doing, and to remember what she owed to herself and to her subjects. Of Lord Robert he said twice that he would be better in paradise than here . . . Last of all, he said that they were thinking of destroying Lord Robert's wife. They had given out that she was ill, but she was not ill at all; she was very well and taking care not to be poisoned. God, he trusted, would never permit such a crime to be accomplished or so wretched a conspiracy to prosper.[2]

This slanderous tittle tattle was the kind of talk for which lesser people were being examined by local magistrates and stood in the pillory. But Cecil's repetition of gossip was not the spontaneous outburst of an irresponsible official to the representative of a foreign and potentially hostile, Catholic power. It was a deliberate leak by a master politician. It also became the prologue to the most notorious episode in Robert Dudley's life. For, on Sunday 8 September, his wife did die, and she died suddenly and violently.

According to the reconstruction of the fateful day by Lord Robert's agents, it began with an argument. It was the first day of Abingdon Fair, a highlight of the Berkshire social calendar, and Amy seemed intent that the entire Cumnor household should go off and enjoy it. When Mrs Odingsells demurred, on the grounds that it was beneath her dignity to rub shoulders with servants, Lady Dudley became petulant and the two women exchanged harsh words. Elizabeth Odingsells went off to her room and Amy to hers. The bulk of the household then set out for the fair, leaving Cumnor Place almost deserted. A few hours later Amy dined alone with old Mrs Owen, who was the last person to see her alive. That evening the servants returned, presumably in high spirits, and resumed their various duties. It was, perhaps, as one of them was going through the hall with a lighted taper for lamps and rushlights that he made the dreadful discovery of Lady Dudley sprawled at the foot of the shallow staircase leading to her first floor chambers. Her clothing was undisturbed but her neck was broken.

These are the bare facts of one of the most celebrated mysteries in

English history. The details of Amy's death and the subsequent investigation have been pored over by historians and fiction writers ever since. The consensus of scholarly opinion is that Lady Dudley died as the result of a tragic accident and this agrees with the findings of the coroner's jury. That verdict has never satisfied conspiracy theorists or sensation seekers. Until well into the twentieth century local legend spoke of the poor lady's unquiet ghost wandering Cumnor Park before being exorcised by no less than nine Oxford clergy. It was the common perception, rather than the factual details, which was of greatest concern to those most closely involved. Robert's immediate reaction bears this out. He sent the following message to his chief household officer, Sir Thomas Blount, on 10 September.

> The greatness and the suddenness of the misfortune doth so perplex me, until I do hear from you how the matter standeth, or how this evil should light upon me, considering what the malicious world will bruit, as I can take no rest. And, because I have no way to purge myself of the malicious talk that I know the wicked world will use, but one which is the very plain truth to be known, I do pray you, as you have loved me, and do tender me and my quiet-ness, and as now my special trust is in you, that [you] will use all the devises and means you can possible for the learning of the truth; wherein have no respect to any living person.[3]

Elizabeth, also, was thrown into dismayed confusion. That same day she told de Quadra that Lady Dudley was 'dead or nearly so' and begged him to keep the news secret. It was a couple of days, however, before she could bring herself to acknowledge what everyone at court already knew: 'Si ha rotto il collo [literally, "she has broken her neck", the reflexive verb implying accident, rather than the agency of another]. She must have fallen down a staircase.'[4] The queen was in shock, at first not wanting to believe the worst (Amy might be only 'nearly' dead) and then anxious to make it clear to everyone that there was nothing suspicious about Lady Dudley's fatal misadventure. For the moment she was bearing the brunt of the tragedy. Robert had plenty to occupy him; giving instructions for the summoning of an impartial coroner's jury to get at the truth, sending messengers to Amy's relatives and beginning to make arrangements for the funeral. Elizabeth could only fret and pine and fume and worry about the fallout from this event which had turned her life upside down. She was pale and irritable and kept herself shut up in her private apartments most of the time. One of her few positive acts in the immediate aftermath of the Cumnor affair was to distance herself from it. She dispatched Robert to a house at Kew she had recently given him, with instructions to stay there until the coroner's verdict was known. De Quadra accurately assessed her distracted state: 'I am not sure if she will marry the man at once, or even if she will marry at all, as I do not think she has her mind sufficiently fixed.'[5]

With the shock waves of the affair still reverberating no one could assess its political implications and the wildest speculation was rife. De Quadra, who, of course, saw English events in terms of their international implications, was far from dismayed at the prospect of Cecil leaving office but prophesied a period of dire confusion:

> These quarrels among themselves and Cecil's retirement from office will do no harm to a good cause. We could not have to do with anyone worse than he has been. But likely enough a revolution may come of it. The Queen may be sent to the Tower and they may make a king of the Earl of Huntingdon [Francis Hastings (father-in-law of Robert's sister Catherine) may have been seen as a candidate by a few Protestant extremists, as was his son later], who is a great heretic, calling in a party of France to help them.[6]

The ambassador's words reflect the dislocation of the moment rather than any well-considered view of the situation but they do reveal the extravagant ideas which were being openly discussed.

The only person to profit from the chaos was William Cecil. Within days Elizabeth sent him to Kew with messages for the 'prisoner' there. All thought of resignation was abandoned but the Secretary was careful to avoid any triumphalism. He was far too clever to risk making an enemy of the queen's favourite, as Dudley's thank-you letter clearly reveals:

> Sir, I thank you very much for your being here, and the great friendship you have shown towards me I shall not forget. I am very loath to wish you here again but I would be very glad to be with you there. I pray you let me hear from you, what you think best for me to do. If you doubt, I pray you ask the question [i.e. if you do not know what to advise me ask the queen if she will permit me to return], for the sooner you can advise me [to come] thither, the more I shall thank you.[7]

Robert and Elizabeth waited tensely for the coroner's verdict but must have known that they had already been tried and convicted by the jury of public opinion at home and abroad and that that conviction would not be altered by mere facts. Through Blount, Dudley urged the twelve good men and true of Cumnor and district to reach an impartial decision and they eventually declared that Lady Dudley had met her death by misadventure. The queen received Robert at court and declared the matter closed. Of course, it was not closed. The scandal vibrated along the diplomatic wires and Nicholas Throckmorton in Paris was not the only ambassador to find his job made almost impossible. Mary and Francis were making the most of Elizabeth's discomfiture and Throckmorton reported that he could not bring himself to repeat the vile calumnies current in the French capital. His prognostication of what would happen if Elizabeth were to marry the newly widowed Dudley were as alarmist as de Quadra's: 'God and religion . . . shall be out of estimation; the queen, our sovereign, discredited, condemned and neglected; our country ruined, undone and made prey.'[8] Throckmorton wrote via Cecil and directly to the queen in this trenchant vein until the secretary warned him off. Such language, he told his colleague, was counterproductive. Elizabeth's response was fiercely unequivocal. She said that 'the matter had been tried in the country and found to be contrary to that which was reported, saying that [Robert] was then in the court and none of his [people] at the attempt at his wife's house, and that it fell out as should neither touch his honesty nor her honour.'[9]

Elizabeth was turning this way and that to avoid a reality she did not wish to face: the event which had made her marriage to Dudley possible had also made it impossible.

The game of love that Elizabeth had been able to play with Robert precisely because he was unavailable was over. Now she had to face up to marriage issues in real earnest.

Was Amy's death at this precise time purely fortuitous or should we look for a more sinister explanations? Suicide has always been ruled out. No one at the time suggested it as remotely likely, nor would anyone contemplating self-slaughter fling herself down a flight of shallow stairs with two landings. Accident then? Are there any circumstances which could have made a simple slip fatal? Modern theorists have come up with two medical conditions which could have produced such a result. One is breast cancer. It is a painful and emotionally disturbing disease and there was no means of combating its inexorable encroachment. A woman suffering from such a malady might well become 'desperate' and be prone to bouts of irrational anger. Furthermore, as the disease develops, cancerous deposits are built up in the bones. If the cervical spine is affected in this way, the slightest jolt (such as would arise from simply walking down stairs) is enough to cause a fracture (in other words a broken neck). A slightly less convincing theory, but one which adequately takes account of the available medical evidence, is that Amy was suffering from an aortic aneurism, a morbid enlargement of the great artery of the left ventricle of the heart. The symptoms of this condition are pains in the chest, sometimes accompanied by a swelling on the chest wall, and a secondary complaint known as ischaemia. This is mental instability caused by insufficient blood reaching the brain. The patient would certainly be given to fits of rage and depression. Again any slight sudden pressure can burst the aneurism, whereupon death is instantaneous. If such a death had overtaken Amy, even near the foot of the staircase, she might well have pitched forward awkwardly and struck the floor with sufficient force to break her neck.

Such suggestions have been advanced because no evidence of foul play was brought forward in 1560. The third possibility is that, as most contemporaries believed, Lady Dudley was murdered. Some assassin, acting on instructions, entered the deserted Cumnor Place, attacked Amy, whose cries would not have been heard, and arranged the body to make death appear accidental. This cannot be ruled out but what can perhaps be ruled out is that Dudley and/or the queen were the agents of Amy's death. Whether or not they wanted to be free to marry, they knew the rumours that were current and that any suspicion attending Amy's death would rebound upon them. Their reactions on hearing the news from Cumnor make it quite clear that they were genuinely dismayed by it and understood its implications.

In any modern investigation of a suspicious death one question that would be asked would be 'Who stood to gain from it?' If we pose the same question about the Cumnor mystery, the answer has to be 'certainly not Robert Dudley.' There was only one person who gained anything from the sudden death of the favourite's wife. That person certainly had motive. He was facing ruin in the summer of 1560 and he believed that his own and the nation's ills stemmed from Elizabeth's infatuation for her Master of the Horse. He was, by his own confession, in a desperate state of mind. His behaviour prior to the incident was highly suspicious, for he deliberately spread the story that the Queen and her lover were plotting Lady Dudley's death. No one has ever made out a case for Cecil as a calculating murderer but he is just as plausible a candidate as Robert Dudley.

Elizabeth hated having decisions forced upon her. She knew inwardly that marriage with Robert was impossible – more so now than ever – but she was not going to give the appearance of being pushed into a corner by public opinion or by the preaching of outraged diplomats. She ostentatiously resumed her support for Robert. In October she decided to grant him an earldom. This was to be a further public acknowledgement of her regard but, inevitably, those around her saw it as a move to make him more acceptable as a potential husband. It was not well-advised. If the Dudleys were to have some of their father's honour restored to them, Ambrose should have been the first to be ennobled. It was an act which could only exacerbate jealousy and ill-feeling. If her advisers protested, Elizabeth simply went ahead with more determination. The patent was drawn up. Then, at the last moment, in a fit of rage, Elizabeth took a penknife and cut the document to shreds. Yet again, her inner turmoil became externalized and was painfully obvious to all.

Life could not continue indefinitely at this high pitch and over the following months everyone settled down. Cecil and Dudley found a modus vivendi which recognized that Mr Secretary was the Queen's principal agent in state affairs but that Robert was definitely a lead figure in the political process. At Christmastide 1561 the Dudleys took a major step towards their former pre-eminence. The earldom of Warwick was restored to Ambrose and he and his brother both received significant grants of land that had reverted to the crown on their father's attainder. In the following months Robert's political stature increased. He began taking initiatives in the international field and he gathered round him a group of thinkers, statesmen and religious leaders which can be called a 'party'.

The launch platform for this Protestant imperialism was an attempt to intervene in the internal affairs of France. The stability of that country had collapsed in a religious war between the Catholics led by the Guise family and the Huguenots whose champions were the Prince of Condé and Admiral Coligny. Throckmorton urged Elizabeth to come to the aid of her co-religionists and his appeal was echoed in English Protestant circles. The queen was not interested in confessional conflict but she did see the possibility of achieving something very close to her heart – the regaining of Calais. This was one reason why she abandoned her usual dislike of military activity and agreed to commit troops to a French campaign. The other was that it was enthusiastically sponsored by Robert Dudley. Most of the Council were sympathetic but it was Dudley, not of their number, who assumed the lead. Cecil was forced into a subordinate role. He tried and failed to commend a policy of conciliating the rival parties in France. After that he could do nothing but implement the policy of his colleagues. The Secretary wrote the letters, sent the messengers, passed on conciliar instructions but it was Lord Robert who initiated those instructions. In May he sent his brother-in-law, Henry Sidney, to France as his personal representative. It was Sidney who won over Nicholas Throckmorton. No longer did the ambassador regard Dudley as a political disaster. Now, he saw the queen's favourite as a knight commander of the true faith and a valued ally in the struggle against Antichrist.

It was a sentiment many radical Protestants shared. By October all was ready for the military expedition. Six thousand troops were ready for embarkation and their leadership was given to the Ambrose Dudley. Then everything was put on hold as heart-stopping news came from Elizabeth's privy chamber: 'The queen is nigh to death.'

1562 was a bad year for smallpox. Hundreds of people of high and low degree succumbed. Soon after arriving at Hampton Court Elizabeth developed a fever and became delirious. Her physicians gathered round but could do little except encourage the disease to reach – and pass – its crisis. But the crisis did not come; the pustules were slow to develop and the queen grew weaker. She would only allow her favourite maids to attend her. Her most constant attendant was Mary Sidney who paid for her devotion by contracting the disease herself and becoming hideously scarred by it.

Panic seized court and Council as the prospect of a third short reign in succession, with all its attendant dislocation, stared them in the face. Everyone fell to discussing and planning for the succession. Support was divided between the claims of Catherine Grey, currently in the Tower for marrying without royal permission, and Henry Hastings, the new Earl of Huntingdon (he had succeeded to the title in 1561), the choice of those religious rigorists who from about this time began to be called 'Puritans'. The Council was paralyzed by divisions. The queen lapsed into unconsciousness and was unable to make her will known. Then, thanks perhaps to the ministrations of a German doctor brought in by Lord Hunsdon, Elizabeth began to show signs of recovery. Her advisers hastily congregated round her bed, more interested in what would happen if she died than in doing what they could to help her live. The queen came out of her delirium and spoke with total clarity and, for once, without equivocation. What she had to say stunned the hearers and dismayed most of them. In the event of her death, she ordered, they were to appoint her beloved Robert Dudley as Protector of the Realm with a salary of £20,000. She went on to tell them of her trust and love for Robert – love she assured them which had never involved them in any impropriety.

This is the moment at which we can take full measure of Elizabeth's feelings for Robert Dudley. *In extremis* she declared, not only her love for him, but also her confidence in him as someone of political weight. More than that, Robert she firmly believed, was a man who had the skill and the charisma to lead the nation. It was the second occasion on which a Tudor had looked back from death's door to deliver a political bombshell. Had Elizabeth died at this point and had Robert, like his father, attempted to carry out the wishes of his late sovereign, the consequences must have been even more serious than in 1553. It was an intense relief to everyone, including, one imagines, Dudley, when the queen's improvement continued. But she did not allow her advisers to dismiss her remarks as the outpourings of a fevered brain. On 20 October she appointed Robert to the Council. The only concession she made to his opponents was nominating the Duke of Norfolk at the same time. This was a turning point, not only for Dudley, but also for the reign. Elizabeth kept her Council fairly small and only nominated men whose judgement she valued and respected. Robert had worked hard to merit a place in her government. He had interested himself in every aspect of national and international affairs. He had given advice when called for. He had provided the queen with snippets of information gleaned from his own sources. He had negotiated on her behalf with councillors, diplomats and local officials. When given the chance he had initiated policies of his own and shown himself skilful in carrying them into effect. He deserved his place at the Council table, he valued it, and to the end of his days that place was seldom empty.

Elizabeth said something else when her body was racked by fever, something seemingly inconsequential but, in fact, the only statement she ever made which might provide a clue to the degree of her intimacy with Robert. Having assured her hearers that nothing improper had ever passed between them, she ordered that one Tamworth, Dudley's body servant, was to receive an enormous pension of £500 per annum. Was this hush money? Tamworth slept in Robert's bedchamber and kept the door of his inner sanctum. He was the only person who had regularly witnessed the comings and goings between the apartments of the queen and her favourite. He had stood guard at the door while they indulged in sweet dalliance. He was the keeper of their secrets. He was the man best able to confirm or deny the innocence of their relationship. Was Elizabeth's unexpected bequest to him the result of prudence or a guilty conscience?

Once Elizabeth was on the mend the French campaign dominated the government's agenda. It failed because the commander in the field and the commander-in-chief in her distant palace had conflicting objectives. Ambrose Dudley, whose suite included several Puritan enthusiasts who preached to the soldiers the glory of this Protestant crusade, crossed to Le Havre (then called Newhaven). His objective was to break out from there to assist the Huguenots, currently being hard pressed in their other strongholds of Dieppe and Rouen. Elizabeth did not see her role as liberating foreign Calvinists. She intended her troops to hold on to Le Havre so that it could be traded for Calais in the ensuing peace negotiations. She therefore ordered Ambrose to stay and defend his position come what may. For weeks he and his troops held on bravely even when contrary winds prevented supplies being brought in. Ambrose urged the government to sanction a larger military commitment. If the queen would not allow him to move onto the offensive while French affairs were still in some disorder, he argued that, with more arms and men, he might still be able to make important gains which would give England a good bargaining position. Robert strongly supported his brother's professional assessment of the military situation but the queen would have none of it. She would not even provide sufficient funds for repairing the defences of Le Havre. She made a token demonstration of her confidence in Warwick by admitting him to the Order of the Garter in April but that was the extent of her commitment. Meanwhile plague struck the besieged garrison. In July, with his men dying in large numbers every day, Ambrose was forced to seek Elizabeth's permission to surrender. The queen agreed and he offered to discuss peace terms with the attackers. It was while standing on the wall and parleying with his opposite number that he was shot in the leg by a French musketeer. The wound never healed properly and for the rest of his life he was lame and had to use a stick. Though feverish and in pain he remained at Le Havre until he had concluded arrangements for the honourable withdrawal of his army. Within months two members of the family had been marred for life because of their unquestioning devotion to the queen. Loyalty to the Tudors was still proving costly to the Dudleys.

Of course, there continued to be material compensations. In June, perhaps as some acknowledgement that she was in part to blame for the

Le Havre fiasco, Elizabeth agreed to support the Dudleys' territorial ambitions in the Midlands. Ever since the beginning of the reign Robert had been seeking to reconstruct the family's position as leading landholders in the region. He had failed to acquire Dudley Castle but his brother had received Warwick Castle and between them they now controlled much of their father's former territory in the area. What Robert lacked was an impressive seat of his own. The only really suitable building under royal ownership was Kenilworth. This castle-palace complex was five miles from Warwick and was reckoned by John Leland in his *Itinerary* (1546) as the only other habitable castle in the shire. For a century and a half it had formed part of the Duchy of Lancaster lands, the only interruption being a few months in 1553 when John Dudley had appropriated it. Robert longed to reclaim it for his family and thus establish that the Dudleys were great in the land. At last, in the summer of 1563, the queen yielded to his importunings.

Kenilworth Castle had what Lancelot Brown would undoubtedly have called 'capabilities'. William Dugdale, in the seventeenth century, reckoned that it should be 'ranked in the third place, at least, with the most stately castles of England', but this was after Robert Dudley had got his hands on it. What he found when he took possession was a twelfth to fourteenth-century fortress in a spectacular situation. It was surrounded on three sides by a great mere which had originally been its principal defence but which now could be used for pleasure. Its massive Norman keep reared up over the landscape and to it John of Gaunt had added a resplendent hall and other spacious chambers overlooking the lake. But thereafter its royal owners had done little more than maintain it. Leland recorded, 'King Henry VIII did of late years great cost in repairing the castle,'[10] but it was still an antique building which did not afford the comforts a sixteenth-century owner and his guests would look for. Within days of receiving his letters patent Dudley was on the road north with grandiose plans in mind. Soon he had an army of masons, carpenters, glaziers, tilers and labourers at work transforming Kenilworth Castle into an Elizabethan great house. It became the architectural expression of his exuberant yet cultured persona.

Kenilworth also became almost an obsession. Whenever he could escape from court for two or three days he was to be found on site, checking details and, as like as not, changing his workmen's instructions. Dudley constructed a new gatehouse, a 600-foot causeway which doubled as a tiltyard, up-to-date domestic offices and stables, and laid out a large formal garden. But his main contribution was Leicester's Building, a large guest block on the south side of the outer court, balancing the ancient keep (known as Caesar's Tower). This never failed to impress the honoured visitors for whom it was created. One of them described it glowingly as a

> rare beauty of building that his Honour hath advanced . . . every room so spacious, so well belighted and so high roofed within; so seemly to sight by due proportion without; in daytime on every side so glittering by glasses; at nights, by continual brightness of candles, fire and torchlight transparent through the lightsome windows.[11]

We need to put this building spree into perspective. All over the country courtiers, merchants and substantial landowners were studding the landscape with status symbols in the latest style. Cecil, for example, was already at work transforming his family home near Stamford into the magnificent Burghley House, and he was able to play host to the queen on progress in his Hertfordshire estate at Theobalds long before Dudley was in a position to offer her hospitality. Elizabeth actively encouraged her wealthier subjects to vie with each other in building great houses within easy reach of the capital. It provided her with more places to stay cheaply during her summer tours and it encouraged rivalry in devotion which she found flattering. Thus Sir Christopher Hatton took advice from Cecil in order to create Holdenby House, Northamptonshire, the largest country house in England, specifically in the hope of entertaining Elizabeth there. It was all part of the routine of preferment, for lavish generosity was not all one way: hosts set out to make an impression on the queen in order to enhance their standing and obtain a favourable response to their own petitions for marks of royal favour.

If Dudley was to stay ahead of the field in Elizabeth's estimation he had no alternative but to compete in making a display. Yet, lavish he may have been; foolhardy he was not. The agents he dispatched to find furnishings for his homes had to be cost conscious, as we know from his correspondence. To his 'loving servant Anthony Forster' Robert sent very specific instructions:

> . . . I willed Ellis to speak with you and Mr Spinola again for that I perceive that he hath word from Flanders that I cannot have such hangings thence as I looked for for my dining chamber at Kenilworth. Yet, he thought there would very good be had at this

present in London and as good cheap as in Flanders . . . deal with Mr Spinola hereabout for [he] is able to get such stuff better cheap than any man and I am sure he will do his best for me.[12]

Dudley spent a massive £60,000 on new building and refurbishment at Kenilworth but the splendours of Burghley House, Longleat and Hardwick Hall swallowed up greater fortunes and, a generation later, Thomas Howard would expend £200,000 on Audley End.

The queen's close encounter with death had badly shaken the establishment and had made the succession issue yet more urgent. Edward VI, like his father, had discounted the Stuart line, descended from Margaret Tudor. Since then the choice of possible non-Catholic heirs had narrowed and Mary, Queen of Scots was noisily trumpeting her claim to be the senior heir to the English throne. Many politicians were now ready to set aside their squabbles about whom the queen should marry. The House of Lords bluntly petitioned 'that it would please your Majesty to dispose yourself to marry, where it shall please you, to whom it shall please you, and as soon as it shall please you.'[13] Most peers had apparently decided that even King Robert was better than no king at all. We might have expected Elizabeth to be greatly encouraged by this but there is no evidence that she responded at all positively to the plea. In her speech at the closing of parliament in March she assured her listeners that if they thought she was opposed to marriage they should 'put out that heresy'. As to the succession she hinted mysteriously that 'other means than ye mentioned have been thought of, perchance for your good as much, and for my surety no less.'[14] The startling plan Elizabeth had devised, but did not reveal for several months, was that Mary Stuart should marry Robert Dudley.

This might, at first sight, suggest an act of immense self-sacrifice on Elizabeth's part: not only was she prepared to give up any idea of marriage to her 'sweet Robin', she was also prepared for him to be taken from her side and sent into almost permanent exile in Edinburgh. This was not her idea at all. She was not a whit less possessive of Robert than she ever had been. When he had begged to be allowed to lead the army in France she had refused point blank. When Ambrose Dudley returned, a sick man, from Le Havre and Robert hurried to Portsmouth to see him the queen was outraged. She sent a message after him, berating him for his sudden departure from court, accusing him of putting himself in danger of contracting the plague and punishing him with a brief banish-

ment. It was not in her plan at all to be deprived of Robert's daily attendance upon her. She believed that she had come up with a scheme that
would solve several of her problems at a stroke. That scheme involved
Robert Dudley making sacrifices, not Elizabeth Tudor.

Francis II of France had died in December 1560 and his nineteen-
year-old widow had returned to Scotland in August 1562. From that
point Anglo-Scottish relations turned as much on Mary's choice of
husband as on Elizabeth's. Having an unmarried queen in Scotland as
well as England was a further dislocation of international relations.
Mary's main concern was to be officially recognized as her cousin's
successor and she was wary of contracting a marriage which would
jeopardize that. From the English point of view it was important to see
the northern queen united with a Protestant husband well disposed
towards England. Then, in the event of Elizabeth's continuing to eschew
matrimony, Mary's succession and the Protestant succession could both
be assured. It was Elizabeth who took this line of reasoning a stage
further. She would make Mary a present of the man she trusted above
all others. When politicians on both sides of the border had recovered
from their surprise at this suggestion and Elizabeth's determination they
acknowledged that, on the surface at least, it had diplomatic advantages
and, with varying shades of conviction, they tried to make it work.

Its appeal for Elizabeth went much deeper. Since the shock of
Cumnor her disinclination to marry had become a mounting obsession.
Her spinsterhood was the single most destabilizing factor in English
politics but the more councillors and parliaments pointed out this truth
to her the more obstinate she became. She spoke of being 'married to
her people' but that was a smokescreen laid to cover her refusal to be
manoeuvred into performing that primary duty demanded of all
hereditary monarchs, the generation of heirs. So she wriggled and
squirmed and came up with whatever alternatives she could devise. The
Dudley–Stuart marriage was an ill-considered policy she promoted
because it suited her book, but to Elizabeth at the time it seemed like a
political masterstroke. It would stop the clamour of her advisers for her
to choose a husband. This one act would solve the succession issue and
Anglo-Scottish conflict, for, in the fullness of time, a Dudley son would
inherit the crowns of both countries. Meanwhile, the Scottish threat
would be removed because Robert would remain, first and foremost, *her*
servant. And it would not deprive her of 'sweet Robin', for she did not
think in terms of his being permanently banished to Edinburgh. There
was no reason why Mary should not spend at least part of her time in

her husband's country (as she had when married to the dauphin). In her wildest flights of fancy Elizabeth seems to have imagined a royal *ménage à trois* in which the three of them lived together at her own expense. At one point she even joked that Mary might like to have Ambrose, while she would wed Robert, thus sealing a true sisterly covenant. Seen from Elizabeth's viewpoint the proposed arrangement had an unassailable logic and she was determined to implement it.

The main disadvantage to Elizabeth's master plan was that it took no account of the wishes and feelings of the two people most closely concerned. Neither Mary nor Robert had any enthusiasm for the proposed match. The Scottish queen was not going to allow her husband to be chosen for her by a foreign monarch and she certainly had no intention of being fobbed off with Elizabeth's discarded lover. She also knew that the English queen would always be the first woman in Dudley's life and she was not prepared to become a cypher. She had experienced real authority as the first lady of France during her seventeen-month marriage to Francis II and then, after his death, had been swiftly pushed into the wings by her imperious mother-in-law, Catherine de Medici, now regent for her young son, Charles IX. Mary was not about to be sidelined by yet another powerful woman. For his part, Dudley was thrown into confusion by the stratagems. He recoiled from being paired off with Mary for reasons of state and his dynastic ambitions did not run to placing a son on the combined thrones of England and Scotland. He had no desire to live in Edinburgh and he considered bizarre and alarming the prospect of becoming the rope in a tug-o'-war between two queens. He seems to have found it difficult to read Elizabeth's mind on this issue. He told his intimates that he was sure that it was a test imposed by the queen to prove his personal loyalty. He suggested to Mary herself that it was a delaying tactic intended to stop the Scottish queen rushing into an 'unsuitable' marriage. And on yet another occasion he asserted that it was a ploy devised by his enemies to remove him from the centre ground of English politics. He had been neatly snared. He was damned if he agreed to marry Mary and damned if he did not. All he could do for the present was play along with Elizabeth's scheme while looking for some way of escape.

Elizabeth's plan took another step towards maturity in September 1564. She decided to grant Robert the earldom she had denied him in 1560. Her main (perhaps her only) intention was to render her Robin more acceptable to the Scottish queen. Cecil hinted in a letter to Maitland of Lethington that Elizabeth would be prepared to advance him still further in order to bring the marriage plans to a successful conclusion. Perhaps there was another purpose: it may have been a further bribe to induce Robert to accept his destiny. He was becoming increasingly restless as the months passed, and was seeking around for allies. When the new Spanish ambassador, Guzman de Silva, arrived in June, Dudley hastened to make friends with him and promised his support in return for de Silva's influence against the Scottish marriage.

The ceremonies of ennoblement were fixed for the end of September and took place at Westminster. On 28th September Robert was created Baron Denbigh. The next day he received the title that had been suggested for his father seventeen years before, the earldom of Leicester. Among the spectators thronging the court was Sir James Melville, Mary Stuart's representative. When Elizabeth entered the Presence Chamber she was preceded by a sword bearer whom she had specially chosen for the occasion. It was eighteen-year-old Henry Stewart, Lord Darnley, a tall, handsome young man, who was a grandson of Margaret Tudor and, therefore, another potential claimant to the throne. Robert knelt to receive his new honour and the queen fastened the ermine-lined mantle around his shoulders. As she did so she could not restrain herself from tickling his neck. Elizabeth turned to Melville. 'How like you my new creation?' she asked. The ambassador made a polite reply. The queen pointed suddenly to Darnley. 'And yet you like better of yonder long lad,' she said. It was a barbed remark intended to show that she knew exactly what was in Melville's mind.

Darnley was a braggart with an eggshell-thin charm covering a massive ego. His conceit had been bolstered from an early age by his pathologically ambitious mother, the Lady Margaret Lennox, who planned that her son would marry his cousin, the Queen of Scots, thus strengthening her claim to the English crown, and restore the old religion to both kingdoms. Margaret's intrigues had even included presenting Henry to Philip II as the figurehead who could unite English Catholics in a rebellion against Elizabeth. All this was well known to the queen and, in 1561, she had the boy and his parents brought from their Yorkshire estate to London, where they were placed under virtual house arrest. It was only after much pulling of diplomatic strings that they secured their release fifteen months later but their freedom only extended to becoming 'guests' at Elizabeth's court. Then, at the end of August 1564, Lord Lennox received permission to return to Scotland, ostensibly on urgent business connected with his Scottish estates. It cannot have surprised Elizabeth to receive intelligence that he immediately set about raising support for his son's cause among the Catholic nobility. This was the situation as it existed at the time of Dudley's elevation to the peerage and it explains Elizabeth's *bon mot*.

She also intended Robert to hear and take note of the comment because she realized that he was hoping that Darnley would provide his means of escape from the Scottish marriage, thwarting Elizabeth's plan without Robert having to declare his opposition to it. Over the ensuing months he cautiously added his voice to those of others who were interceding on behalf of the young exile and urging the queen to allow him to return to his own country. In February Elizabeth yielded to these blandishments. Darnley sped northwards and immediately began paying ardent court to his cousin. It is small wonder that his first act on reaching Scotland was to dispatch a letter of thanks to Dudley for pleading his case with Elizabeth. By April 1565 it became clear to the Council that Mary would marry Darnley and in July the secret ceremony took place in Mary's chapel. But little escaped Elizabeth's agents and when she heard the news she was furious and lashed out against those whom she claimed had duped her. She had Margaret Lennox dispatched to the Tower and openly blamed the failure of her grand strategy on Dudley.

Commentators have always been puzzled at Elizabeth's sending Darnley to Scotland, a decision almost guaranteed to shoot her own policy in the foot. Did she miscalculate either Mary's duplicity or Darnley's sexual attraction? She knew what a shallow, callow youth Lennox's son was and her comment about Melville and his mistress preferring 'yonder long lad' may have been an expression of incredulity. Surely Mary could see that there was no comparison between a dissolute teenager and the elegant, cultured earl kneeling before her in all the finery of his new station. Yet, if any woman could understand how another could fall for a dashing, wild young man who had the advantage of being widely considered as 'wrong' for her that woman must surely have been Elizabeth Tudor. She was painfully aware of the power of sexual magic and cannot have been surprised to receive reports of how Mary had become totally besotted with Darnley. Perhaps she gave her sister queen the benefit of the doubt. When she, herself, had become aware of the political impossibility of marriage to Dudley she had put her own desires behind her. She may have assumed that Mary Stuart could do the same.

My own belief is that this episode is one of many that reveal Elizabeth's double-mindedness. Having decided on the Scottish marriage she convinced herself of its practicality and set out to convince others. When doubts and objections were expressed (and particularly those of Dudley) she overrode them. Yet, while bending her agents to her own will, she pondered, and gradually came to accept, the contrary arguments. However, rather than admit to changing her mind, she released her hold on Darnley and let matters take their own course. It might be that the Lords of the Congregation would prevent Mary rushing into an unsuitable marriage and some of the intelligence coming from across the border suggested that a plot was afoot to seize the Scottish queen and her lover. It would be preferable if the Scots themselves plucked Elizabeth's chestnuts from the fire. On the other hand, she could always insist that other people were to blame: she had been plotted against; her agents had failed her; her Council had not kept her properly informed. Among those blamed for undermining her strategy the new Earl of Leicester figured prominently. She castigated him for his ingratitude and let it be widely known that he had declined the magnificent destiny she had devised for him.

There was a cruel streak in all the Tudors. In Elizabeth it did not yet display itself, as it had done in her father and sister, in callously consigning large numbers of subjects to painful death, but it was there. Robert Dudley suffered from her refined spitefulness on a number of occasions and this was one of them. For two and a half years Elizabeth had threatened her favourite with a forced marriage, content for him to know what it felt like to be propelled for political reasons towards a loveless union. And at the end of it all Dudley was among those chiefly blamed for the frustration of the queen's plans. Elizabeth Tudor was growing into a queen who was hard to serve and a woman who was hard to love.

15

Politics, Puritanism and Patronage

———✦———

Elizabeth was in one of her petulant rages. 'I would have thought that, if all the world abandoned me, yet you would remain loyal,' she stormed at Robert Dudley, Earl of Leicester. And he was not alone in facing the queen's wrath. She denounced Norfolk as 'a traitor or conspirator, or words of a similar flavour'. To Pembroke she snapped, 'You talk like a swaggering soldier.' She taunted Northampton with his chequered matrimonial career. When Pembroke and Dudley stoutly protested their undying devotion she ordered them out of the presence chamber, not to return until summoned. Later, she insisted in self-pitying anguish that everyone was against her. It was late October 1566 and the four peers were doing what it was their duty to do; they were advising their sovereign. But what they were saying was not what Elizabeth wanted to hear. The topic was by now well worn – royal marriage and succession. The recently summoned parliament had once again pressed for action but this time the Commons had said they would not pass a vote of taxes until they were satisfied. They clearly meant it. There were ugly scenes on the floor of the chamber and some members had been distributing handbills in the London streets in order to stir up popular support. Elizabeth was outraged that she, Henry VIII's daughter, could be thus blackmailed by her own parliament. She looked to the upper house to bring pressure to bear on their colleagues. She looked in vain. Their lordships sent a four-man delegation to ask the queen to give her gracious consideration to parliament's legitimate anxieties. It was to this little posse of her closest attendants that Elizabeth reacted so violently.[1]

From about this point the conflict at the centre of English politics begins to become clear. It is not a conflict between Cecil and Dudley or between rival conciliar factions. Certainly such rivalries existed and foreign diplomats were eager to detect and magnify every suggestion of friction in their dispatches, but we should be wary about taking such reports at face value. At about the same time that Dudley and his colleagues were suffering their dressing down, Cecil was describing the atmosphere in court and Council: 'I feel myself . . . wrapped in miseries and tossed . . . in a sea swelling with storms of envy, malice, disdain, suspicion . . . What discomfort they commonly have that mean to deserve best of their country!'[2] There were personal animosities and clashes over detail but the members of Elizabeth's Council were united by a common politico-religious culture. Any disagreements over nuances of policy were slight in comparison with the fundamental problem facing the government. That problem was their clash of interests with the queen.

Later in the reign the opinion formers would learn to make a virtue of necessity. They would project the image of the virgin queen, associating with Elizabeth something of the devotion the Catholic generations had directed towards the Virgin Mary. Elizabeth would become, through the propaganda of painted canvas, heroic verse, public appearance and popular pamphlet, the resplendent wife and mother of her people. But in the 1560s and 1570s she was a woman occupying the position God intended only men to occupy. It was axiomatic to her circle of close advisers that she could not grasp the complexities of national and international affairs, that she was temperamental, that she needed the guidance of wise male advisers. Mary Tudor, for all her faults, had always paid close attention to the counsel she received from her husband, her chosen councillors and her parliaments. The problem with Elizabeth was that she did not follow this pattern. Not only did she jealously guard her prerogative rights in such issues as the succession and relations with foreign princes, she also restricted the Council's freedom of action in a range of other matters. Fundamentally, the queen did not share her councillors' understanding of her own and her country's position in the world vis-à-vis religion and overseas expansion. Robert tried desperately to maintain his personal loyalty but it clashed more and more with his religious and political principles. He and his colleagues saw the inevitability of eventual conflict with Spain but all Elizabeth's instincts caused her to shy away from confrontation. War was expensive.

She had little sympathy for religious extremists. And she was appalled at the thought of aiding rebels against their divinely appointed sovereign. Elizabeth tried to keep a balance among her advisers, so that Dudley, Cecil, Sir Francis Knollys and the Earl of Bedford were counterpoised by Arundel, Norfolk and Thomas Radcliffe, Earl of Sussex, but, thanks to Dudley's building up of a formidable progressive 'party' and to Catholic sympathizers destroying themselves in plots and intrigues, power and influence moved inexorably towards those who advocated further religious reform and intervention in Europe on behalf of fellow Protestants.

In April 1567 the Spanish ambassador de Silva reported 'Lord Robert is a strong heretic' and asserted that he had brought Pembroke round to his point of view,[3] something reiterated by the French ambassador a few months later when he declared that Leicester was 'totally of the Calvinist religion'.[4] From the mid-1560s he became the leading patron of the extremists. When zealots eager to bring the English church into line with the biblicist theocracies they had experienced on the continent sought appointments in their homeland they found in Dudley a ready patron. His service to the Puritan movement increased in direct proportion to his wealth and power. Many clergy received their livings at his hands and were regarded as his chaplains. As his landed wealth grew so did the number of benefices in his gift and his influence over tenants and neighbours responsible for other parochial incumbencies. The religious influence of such great landowners as Dudley, Warwick, Bedford and Huntingdon cannot be exaggerated. Thanks to their patronage large swathes of the country became 'hotbeds' of radical reform. Nor were parish clergy the only recipients of Dudley's encouragement and bounty. There were many men who felt themselves called to an itinerant preaching ministry, like the friars of an earlier generation. Such propagandists were paid by individual benefactors or town corporations to give instruction in private houses, public buildings and churches. Such 'lectureships', as they were called (Dudley instituted at least one, at Warwick, and the Earl of Huntingdon established another at Leicester), were entirely outside episcopal control. Inevitably certain charismatic individuals attracted enthusiastic personal followings and the bishops became increasingly alarmed by the influence they were wielding and by the breakdown of traditional authority.

These Puritans were essentially Anglicans who objected to some aspects of official liturgical practice, such as the use of vestments and the 1559 Prayer Book (a slightly modified version of Cranmer's second

Prayer Book of 1552), and who refused to conform in such matters. In the 1570s and 1580s there emerged a smaller group, called the Presbyterians, who carried their protest still further. They wanted to do away with episcopal government and introduce a system which gave greater autonomy to the local congregations. Church leaders were not slow in protesting about the activities of such radical activists, often exaggerating their 'anarchic' tendencies, and in Elizabeth they found a sympathetic supporter. She was temperamentally opposed to the severe simplicity of worship advocated by the Calvinists. The metrical psalms with which Puritans replaced the elaborate liturgical settings of the old church she dismissed contemptuously as 'Geneva jigs'. And she was worried about variations in religious observance which threatened good order. Basically her attitude differed little from her father's: English men and women should believe what their sovereign told them to believe. Addressing Convocation a few years later, she demanded that the bishops impose unity and that they should not be overawed by powerful local magnates.

> Again, you suffer many ministers to preach what they list, and to minister the sacraments according to their own fancies – some one way, some another – to the breach of unity . . . I have heard of there be six preachers in one diocese the which do preach six sundry ways. I wish such men to be brought to conformity and unity, that they minister the sacraments according to the order of this realm and preach all one truth.[5]

The extent of Dudley's personal involvement in the careers of religious extremists and the trouble he went to for them was sometimes quite remarkable. In 1570, Percival Wiburn was invited by local gentry to establish a Presbyterian model of church government in Northampton. Wiburn was a minister who had already been deprived of his London benefice for refusing to wear the surplice and who had recently returned from Geneva and Zurich. The experiment was soon successful and Northampton was the setting for the most complete example of Genevan polity that England ever saw. Clergy and magistrates jointly ruled a society of enforced morality where the citizens were compelled to attend worship, hear sermons and receive regular instruction in the scriptures. Ministers met regularly for prayer, study and mutual criticism and breaches of discipline were firmly punished. The diocesan bishop Edmund Scambler, could not allow Wiburn's church within a church to continue. However, as soon as he took action Dudley rose to the defence of the godly assembly in an earnest, protracted correspondence with the bishop. Wiburn was eventually cited before the Council and his preaching licence was revoked.

Dudley became increasingly worried by the activities of the Presbyterians who were endangering the progress of further reformations, splitting the radical wing of the church and making it difficult for him and his friends to fight for the cause at government level. Matters came to a head at Southam, Warwickshire, in 1576. One of the most important aspects of the Puritan movement was the 'exercises' or 'prophesyings': meetings of local ministers for mutual exhortation and Bible study, sometimes accompanied by public sermons. They were anathema to the queen and when complaints reached her about the behaviour of the Presbyterian ministers and gentlemen in Warwickshire, Elizabeth referred the matter to Dudley – Warwickshire was, after all, 'his' county. Dudley passed on Elizabeth's protests to Archbishop Grindal and the Southam exercise was closed down. Dudley now found himself obliged to offer a defence to Puritan activists who accused him of deserting the cause.

> . . . for the exercises which I have known and heard of in many places, there was never thing used in the Church that I have thought and do think more profitable both for people and ministers, or that I have more spoken for or more laboured in defence of, even from the beginning, especially where they are used with quietness to the conversation and unity of the doctrine established already and to the increase of the learned ministry . . . I fear the over busy dealing of some hath done so much hurt in striving to make better . . . that which is . . . good enough already that we shall neither have it in Southam nor any other where else.[6]

His fears were soon realized. Within weeks Elizabeth summoned Edmund Grindal, Archbishop of Canterbury, to court and ordered him to see that all the Puritan exercises were suppressed. The primate's sympathies lay very much with his Southam brethren and he could not in conscience obey the queen. It was Dudley who suggested a compromise solution – that the exercises be allowed to continue without lay participation – but the archbishop would not yield ground. Nor would the queen. Elizabeth insisted that her orders be carried out and demanded the deprivation of the archbishop. In the spring of 1577 Cecil sent out orders in the queen's name to all bishops authorizing the suppression of the exercises. But over Grindal she did not get her way. The old man's friends laboured hard on his behalf and Elizabeth was persuaded to allow the archbishop to carry out his spiritual functions but no others. She was absolutely obdurate and until his death in 1583, blind but still firm of purpose, Grindal was not restored to royal favour.

Dudley was a vital component of the forces which produced the 'big bang' of the Elizabethan Renaissance and the new, vibrant nationalism. This had many causes but it could never have expressed itself in so many exuberant ways without patrons, men who encouraged, inspired and, crucially, funded the wielders of pen and sword. In the 1570s and 1580s Dudley was the mighty Maecenas that made it all possible.

Dudley had a network of hundreds of scholars, mariners, literati, linguists, intelligence agents, artists, lawyers, personal ambassadors and younger sons of the nobility anxious to serve the favourite on their travels abroad or to receive more permanent employment. There were painters such as Zuccaro and Marcus Gheeraerts the Elder; writers of treatises on chess, military strategy, the rearing of horses, politics and philosophy; translators of original works in Latin, Greek, French and Italian; and musicians. Dudley was a supporter of progressive techniques in the field of medicine and an encourager of scientific studies. Thomas Gale, one of the first surgeons to undertake a close study of gunshot wounds, made his knowledge available to Ambrose Dudley's camp doctors at Le Havre. His first major treatise, *Certain Works of Chirurgery*, was dedicated to Robert in 1563. William Clowes was another physician who went on campaign with Ambrose and who later accompanied Robert Dudley to the Netherlands. In *A Proved Practice for all Young Chirurgians* he acknowledges the help the Dudleys have given to the dissemination of practical medical knowledge. John Jones revived interest in the natural properties of healing springs. As a result of his advocacy Buxton became fashionable as a place for taking the waters. Dudley and other members of his circle frequently resorted there.

Dudley carried on his father's interest and involvement in all matters maritime. William Cunningham, dedicating to him *The Cosmographical Glass, Containing the Pleasant Principles of Cosmography, Geography, Hydrography and Navigation* (1559) affirmed that Lord Robert had given science 'within your breast a resting place' and that he had encouraged the author 'both in words and most liberal rewards'. In 1570 John Montgomery addressed to Dudley his treatise, *On the Maintenance of the Navy*. Herbert and Dudley headed the list of subscribers who chartered a royal vessel, the *Jesus of Lubeck*, at a charge of £500, and this became Hawkins' flagship when he sailed from Plymouth, for the West Indies, theoretically closed to all except Spanish ships, on 18 October 1564. In 1566 Dudley received his share of the profit – £301.16s.6d. – which probably represented a return of at least 300 per cent on his capital.

Robert and Ambrose Dudley were the principal backers of Frobisher's first search for the North West Passage in 1576, though their stake (£50 each) was modest. The following year saw Robert more enthusiastically pledged to Francis Drake's expedition, which went on to circumnavigate the globe. His connection with the greatest mariner of the age probably began in 1566 when Drake and John Lovell led one of Hawkins' ventures to the New World. By the end of the 1570s the Spanish ambassador was reporting 'Leicester and his party are those who are behind Drake,' and also complaining that the favourite was an enthusiastic patron of privateers. Dudley followed Drake's career closely, and entertained him in his London house. He possessed at least two maps of the circumnavigation voyage and an inventory of his goods also included 'a fine Turkey bow' given to him by 'the Turk that came with Sir F. Drake.'

In 1581 Robert bought a fine forty-gun armed merchantman which had been built by Matthew Baker, the leading shipwright of the day, and renamed it the *Galleon Leicester*. He planned to send it on a journey to the Spice Islands to take up the concessions gained by Drake from the Sultan of Ternate. Drake contributed £663.13s.4d and the *Bark Francis*. Other backers included the Earl of Shrewsbury, the Muscovy Company and the Levant Company but, with £2,200 at stake, Dudley was by far the largest shareholder. Unfortunately, the expedition, led by Edward Fenton, collapsed within weeks of its departure because of disputes among the captains. The *Galleon Leicester* sailed later on a number of privateering trips, at least once (1585) under Drake's command.

Dudley frequently shared in expeditions under the auspices of the Muscovy Company and the Merchant Adventurers. He was the driving force behind the foundation of the Barbary Company in 1585 after years of fruitless negotiation with the rulers of Morocco, aimed at obtaining saltpetre. However, it failed to show a profit.

When the Spanish ambassador referred to 'Leicester and his party' he had in mind a formidable caucus of men with a very well-defined philosophy, one that was anathema to the Catholic world. The Dudleys, the Sidneys, Henry Herbert (Earl of Pembroke from 1570) and Francis Walsingham (Secretary of State from 1573) devised policies and maintained a vigorous correspondence with foreign Calvinists. The guru of this circle was Dr John Dee.[7] The Faustian mathematician, astrologer, alchemist, cabalist and all-round seeker after knowledge, engendered fascination and/or fear, or both, in all who knew him. On the one side he had been closely examined for heresy under the Marian regime and, on the other, the Protestant writer, John Foxe, expunged all reference to Dee from later editions of his martyrology. In 1583 a London mob would ransack his house at Mortlake to destroy his library of arcane books, his alembics and crucibles, his divining glass and all the paraphernalia he employed for communing with spirits. For Dudley and his circle of advanced thinkers Dee was their key to understanding the nation's past and their beacon shining towards a glorious future.

It was Dudley and Pembroke who brought Dee to court as soon as Elizabeth was acclaimed and she was captivated by this multi-talented scholar. In his *General and Rare Memorials Pertaining to the Perfect Art of Navigation* (1577) he represented the queen as having an inescapable destiny, arising from her supposed descent from King Arthur and the great heroes of imperial Rome. This destiny was a politico-religious crusade. Elizabeth would carry the standard of reformed religion into Europe and, through the development of the navy and mercantile enterprise, into lands beyond the seas.

Dudley's contribution to the development of the imperialist programme included encouraging chroniclers, poets and dramatists to give it expression. In 1563, the printer and publisher Richard Grafton, who had enjoyed John Dudley's patronage, dedicated to his son the *Abridgement of the Chronicles of England*. Raphael Holinshed likewise dedicated to him his *History of Scotland*, part of his massive *Chronicles of England, Scotland and Ireland* which brought him instant and then, through the historical plays of Shakespeare, lasting fame. John Stow dedicated to Dudley his *Summary of the Chronicles of England* (1565) and the longer *Chronicles of England, from Brute unto this Present Year of Christ* (1580). In later years the author looked back to the early 1560s and affirmed that it had been Lord Robert who set him on the trail of 'famous antiquities'. These chronicles were not 'history' as we understand it. They were panegyrics, pageants of characters, some mythical, some real, linking the House of Tudor to chivalric heroes of legend, and particularly to Arthur, a native king who, significantly, had stopped paying tribute to Rome, to classical emperors and to a biblical genealogy reaching back to the sons of Noah.

Edmund Spenser joined Dudley's entourage in 1579. At Leicester House he wrote his first major work, *The Shepherd's Calendar*, and dedicated it to Sir Philip Sidney. Its extolling of love, its flattering praise of the queen, its Puritan sentiments and its overall charm made it an elegant vehicle for the principles and ideals of his patron's circle. It was while he was living under Dudley's roof that Spenser began his great work, the long verse allegory, *The Faerie Queene*. One of its themes was the praise of his great patron and the policies for which he stood. Under the guises of King Arthur and Gloriana the poet told again the love affair of Robert and Elizabeth. According to Spenser no other suitor was, or ever could be, worthy of so great a lady.

> And you, my Lord, the patron of my life,
> Of that great Queen may well gain worthy grace,
> For only worthy you through prowess priefe [proved],
> If living man might worthy be to be her liefe [darling].

In the (now lost) *Stemmata Dudleiana* he praised his patron's ancestry. In *Colin Clout Come Home Again* he upbraided ungrateful colleagues who disparaged Dudley's memory. In 1590 he wrote an elegy on his patron in *The Ruins of Time* and, as late as 1596, he was still lamenting his death in *The Prothalamion*.

Robert Dudley was a crucial figure in the development of pre-Shakespearean drama. Before Elizabeth's reign was more than a few months old he formed his own company of players, later known as the Earl of Leicester's Men. He was not alone among noblemen and courtiers in keeping a troupe of actors but his prominence meant that he could always attract the best performers. In 1574 he obtained from the queen a royal patent, the first ever issued to a company of players. It authorized them to perform throughout the realm, without hindrance from local authorities, any play which had been approved by Elizabeth's Master of the Revels. The importance of this develop-ment for the history of the English theatre can scarcely be exagger-ated. As well as giving a company of actors permission to ply their craft anywhere they could obtain an audience, it bestowed a new dignity on their profession. It was, furthermore, a step away from reliance on noble patronage towards complete independence. Within a decade it was followed by two more significant events, the forming of the queen's own company and the building of the first permanent English theatre.

When Leicester's Men claimed the immunity given by the royal patent and organized performances in London, they found that the Lord

Mayor and aldermen refused to recognize royal jurisdiction within the City. Acrimonious exchanges ensued between the Puritan burghers on the one hand, and Dudley and his actors on the other. At length, Burbage, the leader of the company, thought of a scheme to thwart the enemy. With Dudley's approval, if not with his backing, he obtained a twenty-one-year lease on some land outside the city in the parish of Shoreditch, scarcely half a mile beyond Bishopsgate. There he built the Theatre and thither, by the middle of 1577, the citizens were flocking to see Dudley's actors and to enjoy the novelty of their very own playhouse. It was a great financial success and, within months, a second theatre (perhaps also built by Burbage), the Curtain, appeared nearby. It may be wishful thinking to link Shakespeare with Robert Dudley and his players. The playwright's appearance in London preceded Dudley's death by only a few months. The connection, however, is not entirely fanciful. Stratford-upon-Avon is a mere fifteen miles from Kenilworth and a stage-struck lad would scarcely have missed any opportunity to gaze upon the finest actors of the day or to watch the public perform-ances their patron permitted them to put on in local inns and barns. By 1586 or 1587 Shakespeare was working at the Theatre or the Curtain and within a few years he was a member of the Lord Chamberlain's Company, the successor to the Earl of Leicester's Men.

The two most celebrated comedians of the age certainly began their careers in Dudley's employ. Richard Tarlton was a Shropshire swine-herd until one of Robert's servants found him and, impressed by Tarlton's native wit, introduced him to his master. He became a jester and, probably, one of Leicester's Men. Soon he made himself the reputation of being one of the funniest men on the London stage, famous for his playing of clown parts, his dancing and his extemporizing of jokes and rhymes. He was one of the actors taken over into the Queen's Company on its formation in 1583. His death five years later was a great loss, for, but the gap was largely filled by Will Kemp, a colleague of Shakespeare, later to attain a bizarre fame for his dance from London to Norwich. Kemp was a member of Dudley's company by 1585. Perhaps he was employed when Tarlton left to join the Queen's players. He accompanied Dudley when he went as Elizabeth's representative to the Netherlands and received payments for such antics as 'leaping into a ditch before your Excellency and the Prince Elector as you went a walking at Amersfoort.'

Elizabeth was surrounded by image makers and she knew the impor-

tance of iconography, she certainly did not see herself as a warrior
queen, an identity increasingly projected for her by the Dudley circle as
the reign wore on. Wherever they looked around the political horizon
they saw angry clouds and lightning flashes. Scotland was in turmoil.
Mary's marriage to Darnley in 1565 and the birth, eleven months later,
of her son James did not bring peace and security to her realm. The
boorish and jealous Darnley had his wife's secretary, David Rizzio,
hacked to death on suspicion of being the queen's lover and himself was
assassinated within the year. Mary rushed into another disastrous
marriage with her protector, James Bothwell. Scotland plunged back
into war between aristocratic factions, Mary was deposed, imprisoned,
escaped and in May 1568 fled across the border to seek Elizabeth's
protection. For the next eighteen years she was a prisoner who could
only find any meaning in life by plotting her restoration and encouraging her devotees to help turn the tables on her jailer. Meanwhile,
north of the border anarchy and religious strife resumed their devastating work.

At the same time Anglo-Spanish relations progressively worsened.
Elizabeth and her councillors entertained Habsburg suitors for the royal
hand but the reign of Mary and Philip had left a lingering, unpleasant
aftertaste and public opinion was against any such match. Dudley had
originally supported the suit of the Archduke Charles, which was on and
off between 1559 and 1570 but eventually fell in with the common
view. Inevitably, his enemies believed or affected to believe that the only
reason for his opposition was his own ambition to marry Elizabeth

In the Spanish Netherlands Protestant and nationalist fervour had
grown steadily over the years and by 1567 outrages against Spanish
officials and Catholic churches were frequent. Faced with a breakdown
of law and order, Philip resolved upon a reign of terror. He sent the
fanatical Don Fernando Alvarez de Toledo, Duke of Alva, with an army
of 10,000 men (soon increased to 50,000) to suppress the rebellious
provinces.

Alva's savagery shocked the whole of Europe. He had around 9,000
people convicted of heresy or treason, at least 1,000 of whom were
executed. Most leaders of Dutch Calvinism were disposed of, the duke
having a penchant for grisly, public spectacles of vengeance, but William
of Orange, the nationalist ringleader, escaped to Germany. The outrage
of English Protestants, who had tasted something of counter-
Reformation atrocities during Mary Tudor's reign, can easily be
imagined. The current best seller was John Foxe's *Actes and Monuments*

(The Book of Martyrs), a catalogue of men and women who had suffered for their faith from earliest times. First published in 1559, it went through six editions, each larger than its precursors as the author added yet more tales of Christian heroism. In 1570 the government ordered every church to buy a copy, which was to be accessible for all to read. It was a masterpiece of politico-religious propaganda and it influenced English attitudes for generations. No one could fail to see the relevance of this mammoth catalogue of past atrocities to contemporary events and few doubted that England should stand shoulder-to-shoulder with persecuted saints abroad.

The Council was divided, not on their attitude towards events in the Netherlands but on what should be done about them. In 1567 de Silva lamented that there were no Catholics left among Elizabeth's senior advisers and he was in no doubt as to the identity of the arch-apostate:

Lord Robert is now a strong heretic, and I am told is very sorry that affairs in Flanders are prospering, speaking evil of the Prince of Orange and saying that he has deceived the sectaries by promising them help and then abandoning them.[7]

Dudley was all for going to the aid of his co-religionists. Elizabeth was more cautious. Although worried about the existence of a massive Spanish garrison just across the Narrow Seas, she remembered the expensive fiasco of the Le Havre venture. For the moment she contented herself with formal protests.

Matters were no better in France. The 1560s were years of sporadic warfare between the forces of the Huguenots, at first under the Prince de Condé and, after his death in battle, Admiral Coligny and Henry of Navarre, and the army of the young King Charles IX and his indefatigable mother. Catherine de Medici was constantly being pressed by Philip II of Spain to deal firmly with the Protestants but the royal position was too weak and the political life of the nation lurched from open war to truce to treaty and back to open war. Dudley continued to advocate military aid for the Huguenots but Elizabeth refused to have her fingers burned again.

Thus on every hand the forces of the old religion and the new were locked in deadly combat. Dudley, Cecil and the majority of their colleagues were right in seeing this ideological conflict as one from which England could not remain aloof. In February 1570 this was made crystal clear. A fanatical reforming pope who had expelled prostitutes from Rome, forbidden citizens to enter taverns and outlawed bullfighting throughout Europe (the Spaniards simply ignored the instruction) turned his attention to the queen of England. In the bull *Regnans in Excelsis* he excommunicated Elizabeth and declared that 'the lords, subjects and peoples of the said kingdom and all others who have sworn allegiance to her are perpetually absolved from any oath of fidelity and obedience.' The previous year he had supported with money and papal benedictions an attempt to remove Elizabeth by force. Although it had failed, it had come far closer to success than any document sealed with his *bulla*.

The northern rebellion of 1569 came about through a mingling of Catholic disaffection, muddled policy towards Scotland and personality clashes at court. Dudley became embroiled in the confused sequence of events and was hard put to it to extricate himself and regain the queen's favour. He and Thomas Howard, Duke of Norfolk, had continued to clash. Elizabeth persisted in believing that the two rivals balanced each other but their mutual hostility was a blight on the smooth running of court and Council. Early in 1565 the well-known 'kerchief incident' occurred. Howard and Dudley were playing tennis before the queen in one of the Whitehall courts built by Henry VIII. After a while Robert went across to Elizabeth and borrowed her napkin to mop his sweating brow. At this Howard lost control of himself. He raged at Dudley for his presumption and 'swore that he would lay his racket upon his face.' The queen was naturally angry with Howard, who now hated Dudley even more for giving rise to his public humiliation.

Petulance was a characteristic of Thomas Howard. He was a man tortured by the conviction that his talents and his position as England's premier peer had not brought him the political eminence he believed to be his due. He readily made common cause with his cousin Thomas Radcliffe, Earl of Sussex. Both men loathed Dudley and this coloured their view of the wider political scene. To them anything seemed preferable to the possibility of Dudley's marriage to the queen and they rejected the Protestant interventionism of the Leicester circle. They were convinced that England could not stand alone and must seek a matrimonial alliance either with the Habsburgs or the Valois.

Radcliffe had but recently returned from nine years as Lord Lieutenant of Ireland, where his government had been marked by vigour, ferocity and failure. He knew that Dudley was his sternest critic and he easily convinced himself that Elizabeth's favourite was the main agent of his loss of favour. By midsummer 1565 the rival earls and their followers were carrying arms at court. Six months later the two factions were wearing coloured favours: yellow for the Howard–Radcliffe alliance, purple for Dudley. There were occasional brawls between groups of supporters and Radcliffe complained directly to the queen that his life was in danger.

Elizabeth found the macho posturings of the rival courtiers tiring in the extreme and made more than one attempt to reconcile the fractious earls. When Charles IX of France expressed a desire to confer the Order of St Michael on two of the queen's subjects, she selected Dudley and Howard. At the time appointed the two peers met in the 'great closet' at Whitehall and embraced each other before proceeding to the investiture. Then, magnificently arrayed in white and russet velvet, tricked out with fur, lace, gold and silver, they proceeded to the chapel to receive their chains of office from Charles' deputies. The reconciliation was as hollow as the honour. Soon afterward Dudley and Howard both absented themselves from the court. Although Robert was back before the end of March, he confided to Cecil that he would gladly have stayed away longer.

Like his father before him, he was going through a period of depression and disillusionment. He was trapped in the cage of Elizabeth's possessiveness and the fact that he had walked into it with his eyes wide open did not make his fate any easier to bear. What rankled with him most was the implication for the Dudley dynasty. In a very frank letter to a friend he pointed out that Elizabeth's monopoly of his time and affections

> . . . forceth me . . . to be [the] cause almost of the ruin of my own house. For there is no likelihood that any of our bodies of men kind [are] like to have heirs. My brother you see long married and not like to have children. It resteth so now in myself, and yet . . . if I should marry I am sure never to have favour of them that I had rather yet never have wife than lose . . . yet is there nothing in the world next that favour that I would not give to be in hope of leaving some children behind me, being now the last of our house. But yet, the cause being as it is, I must content myself . . .[8]

There is no evidence that Dudley was wildly promiscuous but he certainly had affairs. When criticized by one of his own protégés he conceded he was 'a sinner and flesh and blood as others be . . . I may fall many ways and have more witnesses thereof than many others who perhaps be no saints either.'[9] Elizabeth knew, but chose not to know, that her 'eyes' sometimes wandered. The game of courtly love permitted discreet infidelities. She flirted with other men about the court as well as encouraging formal suitors. Yet always she expected Robert to stick to the convention of being her amorous slave. Only once did he defy this convention by paying court to one of the ladies in waiting so openly that Elizabeth could not ignore it. This was at the time that the match with Archduke Charles had been revived and Robert actually advised the queen to accept the Habsburg's offer. He was fairly confident that, for political reasons, she would not do so and he was totally opposed to any alliance with the royal house of Spain but he saw this as an opportunity to discover whether Elizabeth would loosen the cords which bound him to her. He painfully discovered that she would not. There was no volcanic outburst of royal wrath. Instead Elizabeth grew cold towards her favourite. In conversation with others she lamented that she had wasted her time on Robert Dudley. She refused him favours, such as his request for a Council place for his close associate, Nicholas Throckmorton. Cecil cryptically noted in his diary that the queen 'wrote an obscure sentence in a book at Windsor' which was, presumably, a private expression of her displeasure which only Dudley would understand. Not until he had left the court again to attend to estate business in Norfolk did Elizabeth unburden herself of her deep anger in a letter that threw him into utter despair, as he told Throckmorton:

> Time has been when my doings should never have been worse taken than they were meant, nor my meaning so scanned as [to] stretch . . . an unwilling stepping aside to a wilful slipping away . . . Foul faults have been pardoned in some; my hope was that one only might have been forgiven – yea, forgotten – [in] me. If many days' service and not a few years' proof have made trial of unremovable fidelity enough, without notable offences, what shall I think of all that past favour [when] my first oversight [results in] an utter casting off of all that was before? . . .[10]

It was not only the queen's disfavour that worried Dudley. Like his father and grandfather before him, he was painfully aware that loyalty to the regime almost inevitably carried with it unpopularity. The role of favourite was synonymous with the role of royal scapegoat. When the government made decisions that people liked, they praised Elizabeth. When royal policies were resented, they blamed Dudley.

Dudley suffered in extreme measure the ambitious courtier's constant dilemma. When attending the queen he was embroiled in feuds with jealous rivals. When absent from court those rivals had the freedom to work all manner of mischief. While Robert was away in 1566 Howard's agents were assiduously digging up whatever dirt they could with which to besmirch the favourite. They found a willing accomplice in John Appleyard, Amy Robsart's half-brother. This malcontent, who believed he had not benefited sufficiently from Lord Robert's rise to fame and fortune, was heard to mutter that he knew things about Lady Dudley's death that had not come out at the inquest. Howard had Appleyard summoned to a secret meeting with one of his dependants, who proceeded to offer him a down payment of £1,000, with more to follow, in return for any evidence that would implicate Dudley in Amy's death. Significantly, the paymaster also asked what Appleyard knew about Dudley's attempt to thwart plans for the queen's marriage to the Archduke Charles. Dudley got to hear about it, confronted his kinsman and obtained an apology. But the activities of Appleyard and his backers did not cease. It was a year later that the troublemaker was confined to the Fleet and subsequently examined by the Council, to whom he confessed that he had acted out of malice and in hope of reward for accusing Dudley of murdering his wife, sending Lord Darnley into Scotland, and advising the queen not to contract a foreign marriage.

In 1568 the Archbishop of York, President of the Council of the North died. Sussex was appointed in his stead, so by the closing weeks of 1568, and with Mary Stuart lodged, unwillingly, in Bolton Castle, all the lead players were in place for the greatest crisis of the reign. The trouble had actually begun in November when storms and French pirates forced a number of Spanish ships to take refuge in Plymouth and Southampton. They were carrying about £85,000 to pay Alva's troops in the Netherlands. On the shallowest of pretexts the English government decided to seize the money. Alva was furious at this serious blow to his suppression of the Dutch rebels. He retaliated by seizing the goods and ships of Elizabeth's subjects in the Netherlands and closing the markets to English merchants. The pro-Spanish element in the Council were scarcely less outraged than Philip II's regent. They believed, probably correctly, that Cecil had ordered the seizure on his own initiative. Urged on by the Spanish ambassador de Spes, Norfolk and Arundel set about recruiting support for the overthrow of the Secretary. The first man they had to recruit was Dudley. That was not easy, and Robert only joined them after several weeks of persuasion. They presented their argument in terms of the necessity of restoring true

conciliar government and preventing overpowerful individuals controlling affairs of state. Dudley agreed that Sir William had overstepped the
bounds of his authority and that it would be good for him to be taken
down a peg or two. Apart from anything else he was the major obstacle
to the policy which a group of councillors and noblemen had decided to
adopt towards Mary Stuart. This plan seems to have originated in the
Dudley circle, although Howard and his allies readily fell in with it for
their own reasons. It involved marrying Mary to the Duke of Norfolk
and restoring her to her throne on condition that the Protestant religion
was maintained north of the border and a permanent alliance entered
into between the two nations. This was far from being the ultimate
objective of the Howard clique.

The real plans of Norfolk and Arundel were much more sweeping. In
collusion with some of the northern magnates they intended to purge all
'heretics' from the Council, reintroduce Catholicism with Spanish (and
perhaps French) help, and restore Mary Stuart to her throne without
conditions. When Robert realized how he had been duped by his old
enemies, he was appalled and at a loss to know how he could expose the
plot without taking his share of the blame. His opportunity came when
the court was on progress at the Earl of Southampton's house at
Titchfield, Hampshire. There Robert took to his bed with a diplomatic
illness. He implored the queen to come and comfort him – a plea he
knew she would not ignore. As she sat at his bedside he poured out the
whole story, assuring Elizabeth that he had been a reluctant conspirator
(this was true of his attitude in recent weeks though not of his initial
involvement in the marriage plan), had only supported Howard because
he knew of his mistress's concern for Mary Stuart's restoration (there
was certainly some truth in that) and had never deviated from his loyalty
to her majesty. Of course, Elizabeth forgave him and preserved all her
spleen for Howard. Rather than wait to see what action she would take,
the duke fled to Kenninghall.

The planned court coup was stillborn but unfortunately Howard's
party had awaked the sleeping giants of the north, traditional
Catholicism and the feudal power of the great noble clans. The earls of
Westmorland and Northumberland remained in close contact with
Howard and looked to him for leadership. But he was in a state of
complete confusion. At first he encouraged them to be ready with arms
and men. Then he decided to call the whole thing off and throw himself
on Elizabeth's mercy.

Elizabeth, however, was feeling far from merciful. Men close to her had betrayed her trust, conspired together with foreign agents, the Scottish queen and dissident subjects. Well might she be angry and not a little fearful. She sent guards to arrest the duke and escort him to the Tower. Then she insisted that he be tried for treason. She had Mary Stuart moved farther south to the damp and draughty Tutbury Castle in the Dove valley, north of Burton on Trent. As for the northern earls, she sent instructions via Radcliffe that they were to repair to court immediately to give an account of themselves. When they refused to come she ordered Radcliffe to proceed against them with armed force, something he was inadequately equipped to do. Believing now that they had nothing to lose and bolstered by promises of foreign aid and gold and also by the crowds who daily flocked to join them, Westmorland and Northumberland rode to Durham and set their men to an orgy of Catholic iconoclasm. Bibles, communion tables and everything that smacked of Protestantism were destroyed before the rebels turned southwards. An attempt to free Mary was foiled when she was moved yet again, this time to Coventry. Elizabeth now turned to the men she knew she could trust. Ambrose Dudley and Edward Clinton were dispatched to confront the traitors.

In the event her generals were not called upon to show their mettle. By the end of November 1569 the great northern rebellion was petering out. Only able to face Elizabeth's disciplined troops with what was no more than an ill-armed rabble, the dissident earls beat a retreat. In mid-December they disbanded their men and fled into Scotland. Elizabeth's reprisals were savage in the extreme. She fixed arbitrarily upon the number of 700 rebels to be executed – enough to display dramatically in every town and village the price of treason. Then she dispatched Radcliffe across the border to destroy 300 villages and 50 castles. Elizabeth's captains moderated the harshness of their instructions but, nevertheless, this Tudor monarch proved to be more draconian in her pursuit of vengeance than any other. Beside her punishment of the northern rebels Henry VIII's retribution after the Pilgrimage of Grace and Mary's harrying of Protestants pale into insignificance.

As is often the case, it was the rank and file who paid the price of the crime into which their betters led them. Although Northumberland was sold by his Scottish friends and executed in August 1572, Westmorland made good his escape to the Netherlands and Howard was pardoned. He remained in the Tower through the winter and spring and it was partly due to Dudley's supplications that he was released from the plague-infested prison in August 1570. (Robert had also helped to get

Arundel freed from house arrest in March.) However, the duke's bitter experience had taught him nothing: he was soon involved in the machinations of Roberto Ridolfi, an Italian banker who drew Howard, Mary Stuart, de Spes and Catholics at home and abroad into a plot to change, by force, the government and religion of England. Howard went back to the Tower on 5 September and it was Dudley who wrote to break the news to Arundel. The old earl professed profound shock at the news and prayed Dudley to use his good offices once more. But Howard was now beyond the help of even the queen's favourite. Dudley was among the peers before whom the Duke of Norfolk was tried and indicted for high treason in January 1572. However, it was five months before the queen could bring herself to sign his death warrant. He perished beneath the axe on 2 June.

These disturbing events seemed to prove what Dudley and Cecil had always insisted: England and England's queen were encircled by the forces of Antichrist and must frame their policies accordingly. The following years would see Elizabeth shouldering, if unwillingly, the burden of Protestant champion that her closest advisers pressed upon her.

16

Love's Labours Lost

———— ≈◦◦◦≈ ————

It was a prophetic tableau.

For three consecutive nights in late March 1572 Queen Elizabeth lay, sleepless and pain-racked, in her bedchamber. Her ladies attended to her needs. Her physicians fussed to and fro with their nostrums and bleeding bowls. Only two other men were allowed in the sickroom and they maintained a constant watch over the recumbent figure. These three people – Elizabeth, William Cecil, recently raised to the peerage as Baron of Burghley, and Robert Dudley, Earl of Leicester – had emerged from the reign's first thirteen years as the triumvirate which would rule England for the next sixteen. Other royal advisers and trusted confidants had come and gone. New men would join the political establishment. But Cecil and Dudley were the only ones who provided continuity.

Arundel had not been able to clear himself satisfactorily of involvement in the Ridolfi Plot and was obliged to spend his remaining years in retirement. The Earl of Pembroke had died in 1570 and Sir Nicholas Throckmorton on 12 February 1571. The new figures of weight who now emerged from the shadows included Christopher Hatton, who fulfilled the need Elizabeth had for being attended by beautiful and intelligent young men. Like Dudley his skills were those of the courtier. He excelled in the tiltyard and court entertainments.

From Dudley's point of view a more significant newcomer was Francis Walsingham. Dudley found in the sombrely dressed, sad-eyed administrator an ally who shared his own political and religious views and whose talents were even more formidable than Throckmorton's. Francis Walsingham was the specialist in espionage and intelligence who had uncovered Ridolfi's activities. Between 1570 and 1573 he was employed as a diplomat in France, and in December 1573 he became Secretary of State in succession to Cecil, when the latter was appointed Lord Treasurer.

By 1572 Cecil and Dudley had come to the realization, doubtless not expressed in as many words, that they needed each other. If either had succeeded in expelling the other from government the delicate balance on which the regime depended would have been upset. We rely for knowledge of their rivalry and feuds on the statements of others, primarily foreign ambassadors. Were we to have only the letters of Cecil and Dudley themselves on which to base an assessment of their relationship we should have to conclude that they were much more kindly disposed to each other. In November 1568 the Secretary could inform Sir Henry Sidney: 'At the writing hereof my Lord of Leicester is in my house at dice and merry, where he hath taken pains to be evil lodged these two nights. And tomorrow we return both to the court.'[1] In February 1573 Leicester was using his influence on Cecil's behalf when the latter had incurred Elizabeth's temporary disfavour.

> God be thanked, her blasts be not the storms of other princes, though they be very sharp sometimes to those she loves best. Every man must render to her their due and the most bounden the most of all. You and I come in that rank, and I am witness hitherto [to] your honest zeal to perform as much as man can.[2]

When, in later years, their relationship went through periods of strain, Dudley was wont to remind Cecil of their 'thirty years friendship', to insist that his colleague had 'not found a more ready friend for you and yours than I have ever been', and to remind him that his obligation to the house of Dudley went back to the days when John Dudley, Duke of Northumberland first employed a young, ambitious lawyer.[3]

Love and war were the two dominant themes in Dudley's life during these years. He was a sexually active man who found relief from the frustration of his relationship with Elizabeth in other liaisons. However, he had always avoided serious entanglements. The first firm linking of his name with any woman appears in a letter written by the twenty-year-old Gilbert Talbot to his father, the Earl of Shrewsbury, in May 1573.

My Lord Leicester is very much with her majesty and she shows the same great good affection to him that she was wont. Of late he has endeavoured to please her more than heretofore. There are two sisters now in the court that are very far in love with him, as they have been long; my Lady Sheffield and Frances Howard. They (of like striving who shall love him better) are at great wars together and the Queen thinketh not well of them, and not the better of him. By this means there are spies over him.[4]

If these amours had only just come to light the participants had been exceedingly discreet, for Robert and Lady Sheffield had been carrying on an affair for months, if not years.

Indeed, in that very same month – May 1573 – they were married. Lady Douglas Howard, by repute a great beauty, was the daughter of William, first Baron Effingham, councillor and great-uncle of the queen. She was married young to Lord John Sheffield and widowed in 1568, when she was twenty. She was distantly related to Robert by marriage, for her sister, Mary, was the third wife of Edward, Baron Dudley. She was not far into her widowhood when, thanks to various court contacts, she won a place as a lady of the bedchamber. She soon fell under Dudley's spell. As their relationship deepened Douglas began to press her lover for the security and respectability of marriage. Gossip insisted that at one point she became pregnant and secluded herself at Dudley Castle until after the birth of a daughter (who died within a short time).

Robert, of course, resisted her importunings, explaining, doubtless on more than one occasion, why his unique position ruled out matrimony. Just as the queen had entered on a spiritual marriage with her people, so she expected her Sweet Robin to keep himself pure and faithful for her alone. But Douglas persisted and, eventually, Robert was indiscreet enough to explain himself in writing. It was not a very gallant letter. He set down the reasons why it was impossible for him to offer her marriage. He assured her of his continuing affection. He told her that he realized how unsatisfactory her situation was and he offered her two alternatives, either of which would have his blessing: she could continue their relationship on the present basis or she could seek a suitable husband. This was the decision he had reached, he said, after having 'thoroughly weighed and considered both your own and mine estate' and with Douglas' best interests in mind: '. . . albeit I have been and yet am a man frail, yet am I not void of conscience toward God, nor honest meaning toward my friend, and, having made special choice of you to be one of the dearest to me, so much the more care must I have to discharge the office due unto you.'[5]

It is unlikely in the extreme that Elizabeth knew nothing of her favourite's latest liaison. However, she elected to turn a blind eye to it and matters could have gone on much as before if Douglas had been prepared to bow to the inevitable. She was not. Probably egged on by her relatives she urged her lover to do the honourable thing. She employed emotional blackmail, at the least. He valued his reputation as champion of the Puritan cause and had already had to defend himself against accusations of licentiousness from his own devotees. Douglas had it in her power to embarrass Dudley with his own coterie, as well as providing his enemies with ammunition.

Robert lacked the ruthlessness to break with Douglas, or even to stand by the firm decision he had made in his letter. So he compromised. What he offered Douglas was a secret marriage. On a May evening in 1573, at a house in Esher, Robert Dudley was married for the second time. It was a clandestine ceremony attended only by close friends and servants of the couple. Honour was apparently satisfied. Douglas experienced the kind of existence that Amy had once experienced, unable openly to enjoy her husband's affection, although, unlike the first Lady Dudley, she was not confined to the country. The queen was tolerant of Dudley's 'affair', even after a son was born to the couple on 7 August 1574. Dudley acknowledged the baby Robert and referred to him as 'my base son' and 'the badge of my sin'. Elizabeth seems to have forgiven her favourite's 'lapse' (a far from unusual one in Tudor high society); the Countess of Leicester seemed content to enjoy her new station in the seclusion of Esher and Leicester House; and everything went on much as before. Or so it seemed. In fact, this clandestine episode was to have momentous repercussions for the Dudley dynasty. Robert now had the son and heir he had longed for but by insisting that young Robert was a bastard he was actually disinheriting him. If his son should ever try to make good his claim to Leicester's titles and social position (as he did), he would find it very difficult.

The blame for this complication of Dudley's life might reasonably have been shared by Elizabeth. If she had not kept him on the tight leash of her jealousy he would not have been driven to a subterfuge which eventually put an end to his hereditary line. But the further difficulties he ran into were entirely the result of his own libidinousness.

In the summer of 1575 he made a final bid to clarify Elizabeth's intentions towards him. It took the form of a stupendous, eighteen-day entertainment at Kenilworth at which, under the guise of masque, pageant and drama his protégés made an heroic presentation of the subject of marriage in all its aspects. Elizabeth's visit to Kenilworth Castle in July 1575 was the social event not only of the year, but of the decade; perhaps even of the reign. She had been there twice before, in 1565 and 1572, but Dudley made her last visit so memorable by the incredible extravagance of the entertainment he provided that it became a talking point for years afterwards.

On 9 July Robert Dudley rode out from his fine castle, having satisfied himself that all the last-minute preparations for the queen's coming were in hand. He met the royal party at Long Itchington and dined them sumptuously in an enormous pavilion. By the time he had brought Elizabeth and her court back to Kenilworth it was eight o'clock in the evening, and the castle, twinkling with the light from thousands of candles and torches, looked like a fairy palace rising from the lake. To heighten the illusion, as the visitors approached the outer gate, 'appeared a floating island on the large pool there, bright blazing with torches, on which were clad in silks the Lady of the Lake and two nymphs waiting on her, who made a speech to the Queen in metre of the antiquity and owners of that castle . . .'[6]

Throughout the following days Dudley, the great impresario, presented a series of entertainments as varied as they were lavish, making the most of Kenilworth's spectacular buildings, lake and park. When Elizabeth went hunting, a savage man and satyrs appeared to recite flattering verses. Returning on another day to the castle, she was 'surprised' by Triton who emerged from the lake, dripping weeds and water, to make another oration. Even at her departing she found Sylvanus running at her stirrup and urging her to stay for ever. There were masques and pageants in plenty, banqueting and bear-baiting. There were games arranged for the townsfolk in the tiltyard so that the queen could see her ordinary subjects and be seen by them. There were mummers and a troupe of actors from Coventry who came to present traditional plays. There were tumblers and jugglers, and firework displays. There were picnics and minstrelsy on the lake. And everywhere 'magic' surprises – bushes that burst into song, pillars that grew fruit and gushed wine, trees decked with costly gifts. To achieve this effect Dudley and an army of servants bustled behind the scenes, ready to change the programme at a moment's notice in accordance with the whim of the queen or the weather.

Elizabeth and her court were only too well aware of the serious purposes behind all the play-acting and buffoonery. Marriage was the constant theme. An actual rustic wedding was staged in the grounds with all its attendant, homely celebratory rituals. A local couple had been chosen and they came with a host of family, friends and neighbours to perform their nuptials before the 'quality'. Rather like the 'rude mechanicals' in *A Midsummer Night's Dream*, they took their roles very seriously while their superiors looked on with patronizing amusement. The ceremonial entry of the bride drew many superior laughs:

> God wot, and ill-smelling was she: thirty years old, of colour brown-bay, not very beautiful indeed, but ugly, foul, and ill-favoured; yet marvellous fond of the office, because she heard say she should dance before the Queen, in which feat she thought she would foot it as finely as the best: Well, after this bride there came, by two and two, a dozen damsels for bride-maids, that for favour, attire, for fashion and cleanliness, were as meet for such a bride as a tureen ladle for a porridge-pot.[7]

In an outdoor pageant the Lady of the Lake was presented as a maiden imprisoned by Sir Bruce sans Pitié who tried to force her to marry and who had the support of the gods, a transparent reference to the attempts to propel Elizabeth into a foreign marriage against her personal inclinations. In a masque Diana's nymph Zabeta was shown stubbornly maintaining her virgin state and transforming her suitors into fish, fowls, rocks and mountains. Frequent references were made throughout the queen's stay to the noble descent and manly virtues of her host. Most interesting of all the Kenilworth entertainments was the one which was not performed. George Gascoigne's diversion about the contest of Diana (goddess of chastity) and Juno (goddess of marriage) for the allegiance of a nymph was probably set aside because the allegory was too threadbare. In it one of the characters advised Elizabeth:

> . . . give consent, O Queen,
>   to Juno's just desire,
> Who for your wealth would have you wed . . .

Whom should she wed? The answer was more than hinted at:

. . . where you now in princely port
   have past one pleasant day:
A world of wealth at will
   you henceforth shall enjoy
In wedded state . . .
O Queen, O worthy Queen,
Yet never wight felt perfect bliss,
   but such as wedded been.

The multi-layered allegories made varied statements and allusions but Dudley's playwrights were basically saying two things: the queen should marry or release her suitors from their bondage. And not only her suitors; the suggestion was being made that the country and the queen herself were being held in thrall by her vow of perpetual maidenhood. Elizabeth's apparent inability to abandon the courtship game, whether with her courtiers or foreign princes was a source of almost unendurable personal and political frustration for all her advisers but most of all for Robert Dudley.

His own love life was getting in a tangle. If he had been able to restrict his amorous activity to Douglas things would not have been quite so bad but even before his marriage he had been stalking other game. Five months after the Kenilworth festivities de Guaras was passing on court gossip:

As the thing is publicly talked about in the streets there is no objection to my writing openly about the great enmity which exists between the Earl of Leicester and the Earl of Essex in consequence, it is said, of the fact that while Essex was in Ireland his wife had two children by Leicester . . . great discord is expected in consequence.[8]

The affair referred to by the ambassador had been running for a couple of years. Lettice, Countess of Essex, was thirty-five in 1575; no flighty young maid of honour on the lookout for amorous adventure. Her magnificent portrait at Longleat (painted some ten years later) reveals a lady with even, pretty features, auburn curls and a determined set to the mouth. She was the daughter of Sir Francis Knollys, Dudley's colleague and supporter on the Council. She was married to Walter Devereux, Viscount Hereford (later Earl of Essex) when they were both about twenty. For some years the couple lived quietly in the country, but it seems there was little domestic harmony and it may well have been a relief to Lettice when Walter volunteered to lead a colonizing force to

Ireland in 1573. It was probably while her husband was over the water conducting himself with conspicuous bravery and total ruthlessness against the ever-troublesome Irish that Lettice began her affair with Dudley. Devereux died of dysentery in September 1576. Rumour concerning Dudley's relationship with Lettice was sufficiently well established for there to be gossip about poison. Sir Henry Sidney, the Lord Deputy of Ireland, immediately ordered a post-mortem. His detailed report to the Council intimated that nothing during Devereux's last days nor in the subsequent examination suggested foul play. This was supported by a private account written by the late earl's secretary. Early in 1578 the inevitable happened: Lettice told her lover that she was pregnant. Robert's immediate reaction was the stratagem that had succeeded with Douglas. In the spring he married Lettice in a secret ceremony at Kenilworth. She was not satisfied. The role of deserted wife was one she had played before and had no intention of playing again. Dudley made another concession: he bought the house and manor of Wanstead, Essex, and the neighbouring manor of Stonehall and set up Lettice on this pleasant estate near the capital.

But still Lettice was not satisfied: her position was essentially no better than Douglas Sheffield's. Her husband was free to decide which, if either, of his two marriages he would acknowledge. Neither she nor the child in her womb had any security. She insisted that Robert disembarrass himself of the 'other woman'. His visits to Douglas had already become infrequent and he had probably grown tired of a lady who had little to commend her save her youth and her beauty. It was at a meeting in the gardens of Greenwich Palace that Dudley told his secret wife that she was freed from her obligations to him. He took with him two friends to witness the transaction. There, among the hedges and spring flowers, Robert offered his discarded mistress £700 a year to disavow their marriage and yield up custody of their son. According to Douglas' account given many years later, she rejected his offer tearfully and he began to shout at her angrily. Then, after mature reflection, she decided to bow to the inevitable because no practical purpose would have been served by doing other-wise and she was afraid of the reprisals Dudley might take if she resisted his will. In 1578, as he had promised five years before, he found a husband for his discarded mistress. There was, just emerging into prominence, a young man of the same age as Douglas. His name was Edward Stafford, he was a distant relation of the dukes of Buckingham and the barons Stafford, and his mother was Elizabeth's

Mistress of the Robes. Edward's first wife, Robserta Robsart, a close relative of the first Lady Dudley, had recently died. Through his family connections Dudley was able to bring Edward and Douglas together.

Robert's behaviour throughout this sordid matrimonial muddle was shabby in the extreme. Lettice thought as much and, more to the point, so did her father. Sir Francis Knollys was a senior royal councillor and a dyed-in-the-wool Puritan. He was one of the determined Protestants who had gone into exile during Mary Tudor's reign rather than compromise his faith. Now, although a friend and supporter of the favourite, he was determined that Leicester should make an irreversible commitment. Therefore, a second marriage ceremony took place at Wanstead on 21 September 1578. There, in the presence of Sir Francis Knollys, Ambrose Dudley and the Earl of Pembroke, Robert and Lettice were joined in matrimony by Humphrey Tindall BD. This seems to have satisfied the bride's family for the time being but, on 18 February 1580, Tindall was required to make a sworn deposition to the fact that he had performed the rite and copies of this statement were kept by all parties concerned. This must have been to safeguard the legitimacy of the couple's child. Lettice's first baby by Robert did not long survive, but at the end of 1579 she was delivered of a boy who was christened Robert and known affectionately by his parents as the 'noble imp'.

This marriage having taken place and being impossible to hush up, it only remained to break the news to Elizabeth. Dudley used a stratagem which had succeeded before, the confession from the sick-bed. A few days after this interview Dudley thought it wise to absent himself and travel to Buxton to take the waters. He was genuinely ill; his physical health and also his spirit were seriously undermined. These matrimonial exploits had occurred at a time when he was throwing himself whole-heartedly into political activities and experiencing mounting frustration in his attempts to handle the queen. The result was that increasingly he took his own initiatives and went behind Elizabeth's back. This inevitably brought reprisals which contributed to his estrangement from her. This in turn plunged him into depression and he felt he had to get away. He was absent from court for an unusually long time, not returning until late July. He missed much of the summer progress and had to ask Philip Sidney, his nephew, to deputize for him when the queen visited Wanstead in mid-May. This unprecedentedly long absence may well have been engineered in order to make Elizabeth's heart grow fonder. An exchange of letters between Dudley and Hatton certainly suggests some such design, and that it was successful. Sir Christopher reported on 18 June that Her Majesty had fallen to brooding about matrimony:

> Since your Lordship's departure the Queen is found in continual great melancholy. The cause thereof I can but guess at, notwithstanding that I bear and suffer the whole brunt of her mislike in generality. She dreameth of marriage that might seem injurious to her, making myself to be either the man or a pattern of him. I defend that no man can tie himself or be tied to such inconvenience as not to marry by law of God or man, except by mutual consents, as both parties, the man and woman, vow to marry each to other, which I know she hath not done to any man and therefore by any man's marriage she can receive no wrong.[9]

It is little wonder that Hatton was bewildered: the 'marriage that might seem injurious to her' was, surely, not one that she herself was thinking of contracting but one already entered into by another.

Robert rejoined the court in Suffolk during the days of high summer. The tour of East Anglian great houses was not going well. Transport arrangements had run into difficulties without the Master of the Horse around to organize and chivvy. The queen was annoyed at his absence and was showing her petulance to everyone. Elizabeth usually enjoyed her progresses but few members of the court shared her enthusiasm. The queen's moodiness made the dusty travelling, the packing and unpacking and the finding of new quarters at every halt almost intolerable. Hatton wrote to tell Dudley that everyone was waiting for his return to breathe some life into the dreary routine of the itinerant court. Dudley arrived to discover that Elizabeth was genuinely glad to see him but, inevitably, their relationship had changed. The queen seems to have coped with Robert's marriage by choosing to ignore it. She banished Lettice from the court and never re-admitted her. She had never acknowledged that there was any other woman in her favourite's life and she did not do so now.

This domestic drama was played out contemporaneously with the long-running comedy of Elizabeth's marriage negotiations and there were several points of contact between the two. In the mid 1560s one of her suitors had been Henri, Duke of Anjou, a brother of Charles IX. That had foundered on the rock of religious incompatibility but Catherine de Medici had never given up the hope of an Anglo–French alliance. She chose to revive it, in favour of her youngest son, Francis, Duke of Alençon, in the summer of 1572. Her timing could hardly have been worse. On 23/24 August she and Charles had unleashed the St Bartholomew's Day Massacre. This was the government's 'final solution' to the Huguenot problem. The slaughter began in Paris, where 3,000 Protestants were put to the sword, and spread to the provinces where tens of thousands perished. Walsingham, who as ambassador had been working to achieve a treaty, was forced to take refuge in the embassy where he gave asylum to as many fleeing Huguenots as he could accommodate. A month later Elizabeth wrote to him there, 'the King to destroy and utterly root out of his Realm all those of that Religion that we profess, and to desire us in marriage for his brother, must needs seem unto us at the first a thing very repugnant in itself.'[10] If Elizabeth had seen Alençon, repugnance might also have existed on a personal level. The prince, once handsome, graceful and athletic, had emerged from a bout of smallpox badly scarred in body and spirit. His face was bloated and dotted with lesions. His eyes were bloodshot. He skulked around the court, aware of the covert glance and the snigger behind the hand. Gradually self-pity turned to resentment and resentment to opposition to his brother, the king. That opposition increased after May 1574, when Charles IX died and the crown passed to the fanatically Catholic Anjou. Alençon, determined to make his own individual mark in the world, flirted with Protestantism and pursued with ardour his suit for the hand of Elizabeth Tudor. For twelve years this match was seldom absent from the Council's agenda, creating divisions among its members and violent arguments between them and the queen.

Elizabeth had never wanted to acknowledge that religious conflict was the main determinant in foreign and domestic affairs, as Dudley, Cecil and their allies had always urged, but the northern rebellion, her excommunication and the St Bartholomew's Day Massacre forced her to acknowledge the truth. Emotional reaction to these events throughout the country was turning England into what it had not hitherto been, a Protestant nation. Her Council were now, almost to a man, devotees of the Reformed faith, many of them aggressively so. The Dudley–Walsingham caucus pressed ever more vigorously for her to intervene unequivocally on the side of their co-religionists. The revolt of the Netherlands was the focal point of ideological conflict. Alva's bloody repression had failed and Philip II's policy veered between partial toleration and further outbreaks of repression. Spain was gradually losing its grip on the Calvinist northern provinces (which would eventually become the Dutch Republic) and there was no prospect of peace between the colonial power and the nationalists. In France the atrocities of 1572 had only driven the Huguenot minority to more determined defence of their religious liberties. If any lingering doubt remained in Elizabeth's mind it was dispelled when Catholic troops were sent to Ireland in the hope of using the province as a launch pad for the reconversion of England. At the same time zealous Jesuits were smuggled into England, a canker eating away at the Protestant nation from within. But she was warned by continental events against harsh government measures towards fanatics. Warfare she continued to hate as both bloody and expensive. Diplomacy, preferably between crowned heads of state, was always to be preferred to military conflict.

The result was growing tension between the queen and her councillors, who frequently pressed her to be proactive. The most notable fact about life at the political centre in the 1570s was the edginess of everyone concerned. At times there was an almost complete breakdown of working relationships. Elizabeth was impossible. She refused to make decisions herself and frequently silenced those who urged her to action. At length, only Dudley and Hatton were permitted to broach affairs of state. Then she forbade even them to present suits. On at least one occasion Robert had to resort to his old stratagem of begging the queen to come to his sickbed in order to have a few hours of serious discussion with her. Council members squabbled among themselves. The delicate relationship between Dudley and Cecil was endangered. In September 1578 Robert wrote a tetchy letter to the Lord Treasurer:

> . . . we began our service with our sovereign together and have long continued hitherto together. And, touching your fortune, I am sure yourself cannot have a thought that ever I was enemy to [it] . . . [Yet] if I have not both long since and of late perceived your opinion . . . better settled in others than in me, I could little perceive anything. Yet this may I say and boldly think, that all them never deserved so well at your hands as myself, except in such secret friendship as the world cannot judge of . . .[11]

The fact was that the 'balance of power' within the Council had shifted drastically. Dudley, now enjoying the wholehearted support of Secretary Walsingham, had adopted the role of virtual 'prime minister'. Mendoza accurately analysed conciliar mechanics when he reported:

. . . the bulk of the business depends upon the Queen, Leicester, Walsingham and Cecil, the latter of whom . . . absents himself on many occasions, as he is opposed to the Queen's helping the rebels [in the Netherlands] so effectively and thus weakening her own position. He does not wish to break with Leicester and Walsingham on the matter, they being very much wedded to the States [Netherlands] . . . They urge the business under cloak of preserving their religion, which Cecil cannot well oppose, nor can he afford to make enemies of them as they are well supported. Some of the councillors are well disposed towards your Majesty, but Leicester, whose spirit is Walsingham, is so highly favoured by the Queen, notwithstanding his bad character, that he centres in his hands and those of his friends most of the business of the country and his creatures hold most of the ports on the coast.[12]

The routine procedures by which the board worked were few and simple: the Council handled day-to-day matters and made recommendations. Dudley was the main link with the queen. By and large he represented her wishes and liaised with her, particularly on sensitive matters. His colleagues might resent Robert's hold on the queen's affections but they relied on him when there were unpleasant facts or uncongenial decisions to be placed before Her Majesty, or when she had to be cajoled into endorsing their decisions. Dudley understood what another flamboyant politician, Benjamin Disraeli, observed three centuries later, that queens need to be wooed. His charm was a vital lubricant in the political mechanism. Walsingham, by contrast, Elizabeth found irritating (as Victoria found Gladstone irritating) because he was a religious enthusiast who tended to lecture her.

Nothing more clearly demonstrates the clandestine nature of government activity and, more specifically, Cecil's non-involvement in some important decisions than his deliberate exclusion from the most exciting maritime exploit of the entire reign, Francis Drake's circumnavigation of the globe (1577–80). When the expedition was in the planning *El Draco* was straitly charged that 'of all men my Lord Treasurer should not know if it.'[13] This was because he would have been firmly opposed to the concealed objective of the voyage. The official story was that Drake was bound for Alexandria, like some of Dudley's other ships, to take on a cargo of currants. Only his backers, the queen, Dudley, Hatton, Clinton, Walsingham, John Hawkins and Sir William Winter, knew that the real destination was the Pacific coast of South America, where Drake proposed to make a piratical raid on the silver bullion route from Peru to Panama. The promoters waited till Cecil was away taking the waters at Buxton before finalizing their plans.

However, there was no question of Dudley exercising a controlling influence over the queen. As often as she supported his recommendations, she rejected them. Even more often she did neither. A new tension had entered their relationship, resulting from the worrying complexities of state affairs, their differences of political viewpoint and Dudley's 'betrayal' of Elizabeth by marrying Lettice. There was often a coolness in her attitude towards her 'Eyes' now that had seldom been present before. Certainly there were times when they seemed as close as ever. In October 1578, for example, it was Robert who sat up all night with her when she had toothache. Certainly none of the handsome young men, like Hatton, who seemed to be following in Dudley's footsteps, were ever admitted to the same degree of intimacy. Yet the estrangements were more frequent. Dudley more often felt the sharp edge of Elizabeth's tongue or had some suit refused. They did not now share secret laughter or send each other messages couched in terms of cheerful, intimate banter. And, undoubtedly, Elizabeth's emotional reaction to Robert's amorous adventures coloured her conduct of the marriage negotiations with Alençon. In its early stages the official courtship of Elizabeth and her 'Frog' followed a familiar pattern. By never saying 'yea' or 'nay' and by instructing politicians and diplomats to raise a succession of 'points of order' she kept the French ever hopeful of an eventual alliance and this had distinct advantages for England. It acted as some sort of brake on Philip II's ambitions: he was less likely to resume war with France or provoke increased opposition to his Netherlands policy as long as there was a real prospect of England joining a league against him.

Dudley knew exactly what game Elizabeth was playing. While men like Walsingham took the queen at face value and complained 'no one thing hath procured her so much hatred abroad as these wooing matters',[14] he warmly supported the Alençon courtship, appreciating its diplomatic importance and knowing that nothing would ever come of it. He had personal motives for encouraging the proposed match. No one could accuse him of pursuing his own matrimonial ambitions with the queen when he was known to be pushing her towards Alençon's waiting arms. Predictably the scheme fizzled out in 1576. However, two years later it was energetically revived and this time Dudley was firm in his opposition to it.

He had several reasons for wishing to deflect Elizabeth from this alliance. His political concern was that the foreign situation had become much more unstable. Alençon (since the death of Charles IX he had actually become the Duke of Anjou), in defiance of his brother, had blundered into the Netherlands' situation as a friend and champion of the rebels. It was feared that, if unchecked, he might initiate a Franco-Spanish conflict which could only end in one or other of the major European powers gaining control of the Low Countries. Tying England to an aggressively Catholic power would be unpopular with the people and dynastically pointless since Elizabeth was now past the age of safe child-bearing. Dudley and his friends were wedded to a very different strategy – the formation of a Protestant League in which England would be a major player. But the queen really seemed to be in earnest about the Anjou match. She talked excitedly about her French lover, carried his tokens about with her, sighed like an infatuated teenager and remarked what a splendid institution marriage was. Her comments about the blessed state of holy matrimony were pointed, if not barbed. Dudley had deserted her for the arms of another, she implied, so why should she not do the same? To that he could give no answer. But what worried Robert most of all was the queen's secrecy. She carried on her own correspondence with the French court and refused to take him or anyone else into her confidence. She deprived him of his privileged role as consort/first minister/inter-mediary. Like other councillors, he found himself groping for an under-standing of her true intentions. Like other councillors, he had to handle the French affair with kid gloves, as he advised Walsingham:

> You know her disposition as well as I, and yet can I not use but frankness with you . . . I would have you, as much as you may, avoid the suspicion of her majesty that you doubt Monsieur's love to her too much, or that you lack devotion enough in you to further her marriage, albeit I promise I think she hath little enough herself to it. But yet, what she would others think and do therein you partly have cause to know . . . You have as much as I can learn, for our conference with her majesty about affairs is but seldom and slender . . . For this matter in hand for her marriage, there is no man can tell what to say. As yet she hath imparted with no man, at least not with me nor, for ought I can learn, with any other.[15]

In January 1579 Anjou sent Jean de Simier, a close friend and accom-plished ladies' man, to conduct his wooing. Simier, whom Elizabeth christened her 'monkey', was handsome, charming and audacious and captivated her completely. He showered her with gifts, was ever ready with flattering speeches and 'stole' personal items such as kerchiefs and nightcaps for his master to keep as treasured keepsakes. In short, he totally eclipsed Dudley in the arts of courtly love. For six months Elizabeth had eyes for no one but Simier. She luxuriated in his company and flaunted her affection for him before the court, just as she had openly revelled in Robert's attentions twenty years before. Part of this display was, undoubtedly, for Robert's benefit. He responded by doing everything he could to prevent the French match.

In the summer Anjou begged to be allowed to come in person. Casting caution and diplomacy aside, Robert pleaded with Elizabeth day after day not to see the Frenchman. He urged all the obvious objections. He prostrated himself at her feet. Not, apparently, without some effect: 'she hath deferred three whole days with an extreme regret and many tears before she would subscribe the passport, being induced thereunto and almost forced by those that have led this negotiation in despite of the said Leicester.'[16]

Anjou came and stayed for twelve August days. It was a private visit, kept secret from a hostile populace. Those who were obliged to be about the court apparently shared Leicester's embarrassment and revulsion at the dalliance between the ill-matched lovers;

> The councillors themselves deny that Anjou is here and, in order not to offend the Queen, they shut their eyes and avoid going to court, so as not to appear to stand in the way of interviews with him, only attending the Council when they are obliged. It is said that if she marries without consulting her people she may repent it. Leicester is much put out and all the councillors are disgusted except Sussex.[17]

The same reporter stated a few days later: 'A close friend of Leicester's tells me he is cursing the French and is greatly incensed against Sussex, as are all of Leicester's dependants.' Two of his 'dependants' certainly demonstrated their loyalty. When, in July, Robert withdrew from court, his sister Mary, still a great favourite with the queen, also left. Her son, Philip Sidney, addressed to Elizabeth a long letter advising against the marriage and calling to mind such proofs of French treachery as the St Bartholomew massacre. He suffered a severe scolding for his pains.

By now public alarm at the proposed marriage was widespread but the more others protested, the more determined Elizabeth became.

When a certain Oliver Stubbs published a diatribe against the French prince the queen ordered his right hand to be publicly severed. In October she had petulant tears in her eyes when she told the whole Council that she was resolved to marry and that she looked to them to make all the necessary arrangements.

Despite these brave words inconclusive letters and embassies passed to and fro for another two years. Elizabeth continued to struggle with competing thoughts and emotions. She longed for the strong support of a devoted consort, the role Dudley had vacated. She was determined to assert her own sovereign will. Yet, however much she forced her Council to keep silent on the matter, she could not ignore the mounting disapproval of her court, her advisers and her people at large at the prospect of a French marriage. Meanwhile, foreign affairs did not stand still. The unstable Anjou, determined to demonstrate that he was a person of consequence who would not live in his brother's shadow, was ambitious for a crown of his own – any crown. He accepted the position of Sovereign Defender of the United Netherlands. Thereafter, he became bogged down in difficult campaigning against Philip II's forces – difficult and expensive. He turned to Elizabeth for financial help. Nothing could have been more calculated to cool her ardour.

In November 1582 Elizabeth's Frog was back, protestations of love on his lips and a begging bowl in his hand. Once more the couple behaved in public like lovesick youngsters, while her advisers lamented the political complications into which the queen seemed to be rushing with a headstrong man of little substance who could only become an embarrassment. As one of his own relatives said of him, 'I cannot persuade myself that he will ever perform anything that is great, nor preserve those honours which are now heaped upon him.'[18] The prince stayed three months. It was too long. Elizabeth gave no outward sign of anything other than continued affection but the reality was that she tired of her ardent and importunate suitor. She was now in her fiftieth year and love games had begun to lose their fascination. So, she was actually relieved when, on 8 February 1582, having seen him on his way as far as Canterbury, she eventually took her tearful leave of him. She detailed Dudley to see the prince safely across the Channel. From the Netherlands he wrote to report the successful accomplishment of his mission. He could not restrain himself from a contemptuous observation: 'The Duke of Anjou is already like an old boat gone aground on the sand and waiting for the wind and tide to release it.'[19]

Dudley's scorn for Elizabeth's Frog was genuine and profound and had a great deal to do with Alençon's posturing as champion of the Dutch Protestants. It suited the queen to let the prince fight her battles for her. Providing occasional financial aid was far cheaper than sending her own army across the North Sea as the Leicester–Walsingham clique wanted. It also enabled her to keep a diplomatic distance between her and Philip's rebellious subjects. However, with every passing year her role of pseudo-neutrality became increasingly difficult to sustain. The national mood was becoming more belligerent and Dudley was more in tune with it than his mistress. The political nation was now in favour of England's Protestant identity being unambiguously asserted. In 1581 parliament called for a public fast, with preachings to that end and passed a bill demanding more rigorous reprisals against Catholic fifth-columnists. Both were resisted by the queen but she was trying to keep the lid on a pot which was boiling ever more furiously.

Two events in September 1580 pushed England and Spain much closer towards inevitable conflict: Spanish troops under the Duke of Alva overran Portugal and Drake came home. Alva's success gave the Spanish king the entire Iberian peninsula, the port of Lisbon, command of the Straits of Gibraltar, a large military and mercantile fleet and a colonial empire in the east to be added to his own in the west. Philip now claimed naval supremacy over all the shipping lanes from the Narrow Seas to Magellan's Strait, from the Main to the Moluccas. Yet the *Golden Hind*'s arrival in Plymouth, laden to the gunwales with Peruvian silver and Indonesian spices, raised a large question-mark over any such claim. Francis Drake had rifled Philip's supposedly secure treasure houses, sailed across his supposedly private lake – the Pacific Ocean – and traded in his supposedly reserved markets. He returned with breathtaking wealth. After paying himself and his crew and making lavish presents to the queen and chosen courtiers he was able to pay his backers £47 for every £1 invested. When accounts were settled Robert Dudley was the richer by many thousands of pounds.

The reaction of Elizabeth's government to these two incidents was a clear pointer to the future trend of events. Mendoza protested at Drake's piracy in the strongest possible terms, demanding punishment and restitution, but the queen was more impressed by the wealth Drake had brought back and the enormous popularity he now enjoyed. She, there-fore, welcomed her corsair to court, had his ship placed on public exhibition and, upon its deck, she knighted him. Subtly she involved France by having Anjou's representative, Marchaumont, perform the dubbing ceremony (despite all the later representations of the event in genre paintings and films). A few months later the Portuguese pretender, Don Antonio, was also welcomed to England. At Dudley's instigation he was installed in Baynard's Castle, which belonged to the Earl of Pembroke. Dudley was much in the company of both Drake and Don Antonio. He had the famous mariner elected to the Inner Temple and he helped to plan an expedition to be led by Drake to seize the Azores in the name of Don Antonio. Preparations for the proposed attack were put in hand: men and ships were mustered, backers were found, but, in August 1581, Cecil managed to sway the majority of the Council and the queen against the enterprise. The voice of caution was not yet entirely silent.

Throughout the 1570s Dudley had been mentally and emotionally involved with the politico-religious struggle convulsing Europe. He consistently backed a policy of active intervention in the Netherlands and his own agents were much involved in discussions with anti-Habsburg activists abroad. Soon after the freedom fighters began their revolt in 1572 he had proposed the sending of an expeditionary force led by Ambrose Dudley, but from this the queen had recoiled in horror. When Walsingham was in Paris he had acted as Dudley's envoy in liaising with various Protestant princes for a joint invasion of the Spanish Netherlands. There he was later joined by Dudley's nephew, Philip Sidney. The young man became an important link between Dudley and the leaders of the Dutch revolt. In Frankfurt he met William of Orange's brother, Louis of Nassau. Dudley established a close link with William of Orange's circle and messages passed frequently back and forth between them. His principal agent was the long-serving Dudley protégé, Thomas Wilson, who went over to the Low Countries as Elizabeth's representative in November 1574 and whose anti-Spanish activities were so vigorous that he was suspected of instigating a plot to kidnap the Regent of the Netherlands. The selection of such a man as official representative between 1574 and 1577 was a major triumph for the radicals and prevented the adoption of any accommodation between England and Spain over the Netherlands. Wilson was rewarded with a Council seat in 1579.

Throughout the middle years of the decade Elizabeth made efforts to mediate between the Regent of the Netherlands and his rebellious subjects. Dudley was closely involved in these diplomatic activities and the emissaries reported back to him as well as to the queen. Clearly they were committed to separate agendas by their principals. The man sent to the court of the Regent, Don John of Austria (who nursed his own ambition of marrying Mary Stuart and displacing Elizabeth), in 1576 was Dudley's intimate, Edward Horsey. For the queen, Horsey tried to bring the two sides to the negotiating table. For Dudley he probed Don John's military strength. At the same time Thomas Wilson proposed to William of Orange that Dudley should personally lead an army to come to the aid of the Dutch. The idea was warmly received but a change in the diplomatic climate prevented it being acted upon. However the seed had been sown. On Horsey's return he, like Wilson, was admitted to the Council.

Dudley now sent a more exalted emissary to William's court. This was Philip Sidney who arrived at Gertruidenberg to stand proxy for his uncle at the christening of William's daughter. The two men took to each other immediately and afterwards kept up a lively correspondence. Philip was particularly impressed by the depth of William's religion and the way it permeated all his political actions. The prince thought equally well of his guest and was disposed to a greater affection for his guest's uncle. There was even a rumour in diplomatic circles that Sidney would marry William's daughter and become the future ruler of Holland and Zeeland (he actually married Walsingham's daughter, Frances, in 1583).

Philip had scarcely returned to make his favourable report before Netherlands politics took another violent turn. In July Don John seized the fortress of Namur and, using it as a rallying point, summoned King Philip's subjects to join him in battle against William of Orange and his supporters. This summons was a tactical blunder: it reunited the Dutch against him and reopened negotiations between the States General and the English court. Now it was the Netherlanders who wanted Dudley to cross the Narrow Sea with an army. The Marquis of Havrech, who headed the Dutch delegation, told the queen that he knew Dudley to be a great leader of men. In fact, he had another reason for favouring Dudley's generalship: 'If he is in command the queen will take care to provide him with all that may be needful.'[20] Dudley feted Havrech during his weeks in England and made detailed plans for the proposed campaign. He was much encouraged by news from William Davison, who had succeeded Wilson in Antwerp:

> You have made a good beginning with the Prince and States of Holland, where, by the report of all men, your name is as well known and yourself as much honoured as in your own country. The same effect cannot but follow here, if you list to march with the like zeal.[21]

But Dudley was unable to 'march'. The States General dithered, Elizabeth held back and eventually put her faith in Anjou. The final collapse of his plan early in 1578 plunged Robert into a pit of despair, frustration and embarrassment. As he confided to Davison, 'I have almost neither face nor countenance to write to the Prince, his expectation being so greatly deceived.'[22]

When Anjou left England for the last time in February 1582 he was accompanied, as we have seen, by Dudley, who was delighted to be travelling in person to the Netherlands and to be meeting the country's leaders. He was warmly received by Prince William and the two men rode side by side in the magnificent procession which brought Anjou into Antwerp.

As long as the fiction of Anjou's rule could be maintained Elizabeth could resist the inevitability of Dudley's Netherlands policy but in January 1583, the duke departed, discredited, from his principality and eighteen months later he was dead. In the south Parma's strength steadily increased and the United Provinces looked once more to William of Orange as their saviour. Then, on 10 July 1584, William was gunned down in the Prinsenhof in Delft by a fanatical Catholic.

In England, public anxiety and conciliar desire for action now coalesced in universal alarm. On the very same day that William was assassinated Francis Throckmorton suffered a traitor's death at Tyburn. This nephew of Dudley's former intimate had, under torture, revealed a devastating plot involving Philip II; Bernardino de Mendoza; Mary, Queen of Scots; the Guise faction in Paris; Philip Howard, Earl of Arundel; Henry Percy, Earl of Northumberland; and other prominent Catholics in a plan to invade England, enforce religious toleration and have Mary proclaimed as Elizabeth's heir. This was a threat on an altogether different scale to the fevered schemings of zealots such as John Somerville who had travelled to London the previous year with a pistol, intent on shooting Elizabeth, the 'serpent and viper'; whether from international intrigue or crazed individuals, the queen could no longer be considered safe.

These events changed – permanently – the mood of the country and the conduct of the government. Robert Dudley took it upon himself to direct both. In May he had written to Elizabeth urging her to abandon the policy of seeking security by means of a foreign alliance. The major powers were all in thrall to Rome and, therefore, could not be relied upon. The practice of playing off the Habsburgs against the Valois that had governed foreign policy ever since her grandfather had come to the throne almost exactly a century before had been rendered obsolete. Now the 'empire of England' needed no alien crutch on which to lean. Elizabeth could rely on 'the mighty and assured strength you have at home'.[23] He had his protégés pour forth a flood of Puritan and patriotic propaganda. One of them, Thomas Digges, wrote a pamphlet entitled *Humble Motives for Association to Maintain Religion Established*. It was a plan for a formal bond to be entered into by all English Protestants for the protection of their queen. It was this project which the whole Council took up months later when they drew up the Bond of Association. This provided for a body of twenty-four councillors and peers who should enquire into all plots against the queen and prosecute not only those responsible but those in whose name they were devised. In the event of a successful attempt on Elizabeth's life they were to assume control and to ensure that the claimant in whose interests the assassination had been carried out did not succeed to the crown. The Bond was ratified by parliament and copies circulated to all parts of the country where thousands flocked to sign them, thereby committing themselves to 'pursue as well by force of arms as by all other means of revenge all manner of persons of what estate so ever they shall be . . . that shall attempt . . . the harm of Her Majesty's royal person,' and 'never [to] desist from all manner of forcible pursuit against such persons to the uttermost extermination of them.'[24] With public paranoia fed by proof of plots at home and rumours that Philip II was preparing an invasion fleet, Elizabeth could no longer dismiss what Dudley, Walsingham, Cecil and others had been telling her for years, that she and her people were embattled against the awesomely powerful forces of Antichrist.

17

Fair Means and Foul

———✦———

It may be difficult for us to understand the intensity of the religious and nationalistic emotions that divided Europe in these years. By 1584 a vicious propaganda war was raging. Hundreds of anti-papal tracts were in circulation, some dedicated to Dudley, carrying the bear and ragged staff on their title pages and eulogizing the piety of their patron. Many of them focused on the sins and crimes of Mary Stuart, castigated in Protestant diatribes as a wanton creature who had instigated the horrendous murder of her second husband, Lord Darnley, in order to marry her lover, James Bothwell. Catholic controversialists hit back. Needing to find a counterweight to Mary in infamy and unable to vilify Elizabeth, they characterized her closest friend as a debauched monster. In this summer of 1584, from a secret press in Paris or Antwerp, there emerged what may be the vilest libel ever printed, commonly known as *Leicester's Commonwealth*. The English version of this diatribe was set forth under a much more innocent sounding title: *The Copy of a Letter Written by a Master of Arts at Cambridge*. Its central thesis was that Dudley was an accomplished, amoral conspirator set upon a Machiavellian scheme to remove, one by one, all rightful claimants to the throne until Elizabeth stood alone, and then to assassinate her. He would then back the Yorkist claim of his brother-in-law Huntingdon, but only as a step to his own ultimate assumption of supreme power. Stated thus baldly, the scheme seems too absurdly far-fetched to attract any credence and had it been declared in such simple terms few contemporaries would have paid it any attention. The anonymous author's skill was shown in the way he dressed up his central argument with titillating gossip, half-truths, innuendoes and fearful suspicions.

His personal attack on Robert had three elements: he impugned Dudley's ancestry, his morals and his policies. In reminding the reader of the treasons of Edmund and John the author was on safe ground. Both men had been unpopular. Both had ended their lives on the scaffold. It was easy to draw attention to their cunning, deceitfulness, disloyalty and manipulation of the sovereign and to suggest that these traits had been inherited by the third generation of their accursed house.

When he shifted his aim to Dudley's private life the author had an even more substantial target to hit. Dudley's failings were well known and commonly exaggerated, an embarrassment to his friends and a comfort to his enemies. He was a celebrity and could not avoid the attentions of the Elizabethan equivalent of the tabloid press. *Leicester's Commonwealth* added hugely to the old stock-in-trade of gossip. It credited Dudley with an impressive list of assassinations, murders and attempted murders. Thus, he killed his first wife, the husbands of his mistresses, Douglas Sheffield and the Countess of Essex, Cardinal de Chatillon, Sir Nicholas Throckmorton and Lady Lennox, and made an unsuccessful attempt to dispose of Jean de Simier, Anjou's agent. On his orders William Killigrew tried to murder Lord Ormonde. He employed 'cunning men' to keep him supplied with 'secret poisons', and his patronage of Italian scholars was regarded as being particularly sinister in this connection. As far as women were concerned, the book asserted that 'no man's wife can be free from him whom his fiery lust liketh to abuse . . . kinswoman, ally, friend's wife or daughter, or whatsoever female sort besides doth please his eye . . . must yield to his desire . . . There are not (by report) two noble-women about her majesty . . . whom he hath not solicited.'[1] There were pages more of the same sort of muck-raking nonsense.

Leicester's Commonwealth was only one item in what became almost an anti-Dudley literary sub-genre in the 1580s. Elizabeth responded by ordering local authorities to suppress such scurrilous canards. She identified them for what they were; attacks on herself in the guise of attacks on her closest adviser:

as though her Majesty should have failed in good judgement and discretion in the choice of so principal a counsellor about her, or be without taste or care of all justice and conscience in suffering such heinous and monstrous crimes (as by the said libels and books be infamously imputed) to have passed unpunished.[2]

As for Dudley, he treated these diatribes with the contempt they deserved, but they went on to provide an excellent example of how vigorous but unsubstantiated testimony can colour the historical record. The book did not see the light of day again until 1641. In that year Charles I's favourite, Thomas Wentworth, Earl of Strafford, was on trial for treason. His enemies rediscovered *Leicester's Commonwealth* and published a new edition. In that totally different context it seemed to provide a telling object lesson about the corrupting influence of an overmighty subject. Seventeenth-century readers, knowing nothing of its origins and coming to the calumnious pamphlet as a moralizing tale, accepted its assertions uncritically. And thus was put in place the coping stone of the black legend of the Dudleys.

The suggestion in *Leicester's Commonwealth* that Dudley was bent on the destruction of Mary Queen of Scots was quite wrong. He had no interest in plotting Mary's death for two very good reasons. The first is that Elizabeth would not for a moment have contemplated such a dire act. She had a stubborn regard, if not for the person of the Scottish queen, certainly for her status. Mary was a royal person and, therefore, bound to her by steel-strong, mystic ties. It was Elizabeth's dearest wish to allow Mary's return to her own country, if only the political situation there would permit it. Dudley supported the queen in this until the late 1580s, when the atmosphere in international relations deteriorated drastically as a result of Catholic attempts at subversion. The second was that he had an eye to the future. It was by now obvious that the Tudor dynasty his family had served so faithfully was coming to an end. The next occupant of the throne would almost certainly be a Stuart and he wanted to make sure that his son and his son's son enjoyed the favour of that future regime. As we have seen, he had his own contacts among the Scottish rulers and he maintained good relations with them.

This included, as far as possible, getting on with Mary. He was well placed to achieve this, for Mary was in the guardianship of his old friend George Talbot, Earl of Shrewsbury. This amiable peer was the henpecked husband of the notoriously ambitious Elizabeth Talbot, commonly known as Bess of Hardwick. Through the Talbots Robert came into personal contact with their unwilling guest. Robert spent some time with Mary on at least one occasion, in June 1577. This tête-à-tête between two of the great sex symbols of the age must have been fascinating. Although little of political import passed between them, the meeting itself was sufficient to make William Cecil request permission to visit the royal prisoner a few weeks later. The request was denied.

Any mutual respect or admiration between Mary and Dudley had, by 1584, been destroyed by the worsening international situation and in the spring of that year Mary tried to make serious mischief for Dudley. A coded letter she sent to the French ambassador was intercepted by Walsingham. It contained the following passage:

> I would wish you to mention privately to the Queen that nothing has alienated the Countess of Shrewsbury from me but the vain hope which she has conceived of settling the crown of England on the head of her little girl, Arabella, and this by means of marrying her to a son of the Earl of Leicester. These children are also educated in this idea, and their portraits have been sent to each other.[3]

Do we have here real, solid evidence of a plot to replace the Tudor dynasty with the house of Dudley? Bess Talbot's daughter by a previous husband had, to the queen's great displeasure, been married to Charles Stuart, Earl of Lennox, brother of the murdered Lord Darnley. Lennox had died (December 1576) but not before siring a daughter, Arabella Stuart, now in the care of her domineering grandmother. This little girl, a great-granddaughter of Henry VII, stood high in the succession to the English throne besides being of the Scottish blood royal and her scheming grandmother energetically advanced Arabella's claim over that of Mary's son James on the grounds that the former was securely Protestant and was being brought up in England. Bess even tried to persuade Elizabeth to contribute to the household expenses of her 'princess'. Elizabeth, of course, rejected these pretensions but she kept a close eye on little Arabella, as she did on all potential claimants. All this is undisputed fact but was Dudley an active partner in these dynastic schemes?

The first point to make is that Mary's claim has to be seen in the context of the domestic situation at Sheffield Castle and Chatsworth, the Shrewsbury homes where she was incarcerated. The married life of the Talbots had degenerated to the point at which they could not bear the sight of each other. Mary was caught in the middle and for years had to endure the jibes and insults thrown by Bess who had taken it into her head that her husband was having an affair with his royal prisoner. The Countess of Shrewsbury deliberately spread unpalatable rumours about Mary and even wrote to Elizabeth to complain of her conduct and attitude. It was to this constant goading that Mary responded in kind in 1584. She listed all the countess's schemes, ambitions and disloyal comments about the queen and sent them to the French ambassador (and perhaps, also, to Cecil). They included the supposed marriage agreement made by Bess and Dudley. We can trace this 'agreement' no further back. It would have been wholly in character for Bess to have dreamed it up, but she might have discussed such a proposal with Dudley. It is quite likely that she hinted to Mary that a deal had been struck which would forever debar her and her son from the English throne. However, none of this proves Dudley's active involvement in the scheme.

It would, in fact, have been very much out of character for him to have been snared. If the queen had learned that he was interfering in the succession issue, that he was making plans about what would happen after her death, it would have been the one sin she would have found impossible to forgive. Dudley knew full well how hypersensitive she was on this matter and would not have been so stupid as to risk her wrath. Also, he would not have wanted to alienate his friends at the Scottish court by giving his backing to any rival claimant to James. Whatever rumours or half-rumours Mary may have heard while under the Shrewsburys' roof, there can have been no truth whatsoever in her claim. Had there been, or had the story been widespread among Leicester's enemies they would not have failed to make maximum use of such splendid propaganda material. The suggestion that once again, as in the days of Jane Grey, the Dudleys were reaching out for the Crown would have been a gift they could not refuse. Yet the author of *Leicester's Commonwealth* made no mention of it, nor did any other Catholic pamphleteer.

However, within weeks any speculation became academic. In July the noble imp fell suddenly ill at Wanstead and died a few days later. Robert was devastated. As well as the natural grief of a father for a dead son he was now experiencing the extinction of all his dynastic hopes and plans. He was on progress with the court when the news arrived. Without waiting for royal permission he left Nonsuch suddenly in order to be with Lettice. He asked Hatton to make his excuses to Elizabeth. The letter he wrote to Hatton a few days later is reminiscent of the world-weary reflections his father had penned in the early fifties:

I must confess I have received many afflictions within these few years, but not a greater, next her Majesty's displeasure: and, if it pleased God, I would the sacrifice of this poor innocent might satisfy; I mean not towards God . . . but for the world. The afflictions I have suffered may satisfy such as are offended, at least appease their long hard conceits . . . I beseech . . . God to grant me patience in all these worldly things, and to forgive me the negligences of my former time, that have not been more careful to please Him, but have run the race of the world.[4]

This sad misfortune was a turning point in the life of Robert Dudley. It came as the last of a series of blows which had sent his spirit reeling. Like his father he felt more deeply than he was prepared to show his widespread unpopularity. The queen continued to be estranged from Lettice; his religious policy was being overthrown; his influence was waning; he had recently become the object of a particularly vicious libel and now the legitimate Dudley line had come to an end, for Lettice was beyond childbearing. Well might he despair of human aid and pray for 'patience in all these worldly things'. He chose a magnificent restingplace for his four-year-old son. The Beauchamp Chapel in St Mary's, Warwick had been built in the mid-fifteenth century at enormous expense as a chantry chapel for Richard Beauchamp, Earl of Warwick, and remains to this day one of the glories of Perpendicular church architecture. Robert had already designated the chapel as the final resting place for himself and others of his family so that there would be a permanent reminder of their descent from one of the great aristocratic families of the fourteenth and fifteenth centuries and it was there, close to the altar, that his son, the infant Baron Denbigh, was buried and an affecting monument raised over him. After this tragedy there was little that brought Robert Dudley any joy. His remaining years were ones of frustration, failure, anxiety and ill-rewarded service to the queen.

Many of Robert's letters reveal how keenly he felt the queen's antagonism towards Lettice and how he sought the aid of friends and colleagues in assuaging it. After their son's funeral Robert and Lettice spent a few days at Cecil's house, Theobalds. Apparently even a mother's grief had not softened Elizabeth's heart. Leicester wrote to thank his absent host: '. . . that it pleased you so friendly and honourably to deal in the behalf of my poor wife. For truly, my Lord, in all reason she is hardly dealt with. God must only help it with her majesty . . . for which, my Lord, you shall be assured to find us most thankful to the uttermost of our powers . . .'[5]

It was to check the erosion of his influence that Dudley now advanced his stepson, Robert Devereux, to royal favour. The eighteen-year-old Earl of Essex was all that Dudley had been at his age, athletic, vigorous and flamboyant. Dudley brought him to court to be a leader of the coterie of young gallants supporting his own vigorous radical policies, and also to be one of Elizabeth's 'lovers'. For the queen was not allowed to grow old. While advancing age took its obvious toll of her attendants, cosmetics and determined vigour maintained for Elizabeth an aura of eternal youth. Still she commanded the attentions of beardless, smooth-cheeked men young enough to be her own sons. Unable himself to compete any longer, Robert had no alternative but to put forward his own champion.

Only those in the innermost circle of royal intimates could be aware how profoundly, if subtly, the relationship between Elizabeth and Robert was changing. To most men Dudley must have seemed as secure as ever. By 1584, if not before, he was officially designated as Lord Steward, thereby enjoying in nomine as well as de facto the central place at the court. He continued to be Elizabeth's closest adviser and to convey messages to and from the Council. He was still permitted to advocate policies and courses of which the queen did not approve. Indeed, he did so more energetically as the years passed. Now, however, Robert was not so much a romantic consort as an old friend.

Life at the political centre was also changing as death removed former colleagues and foes from the scene. In 1583 Thomas Radcliffe, Earl of Sussex had died. This left Dudley and his allies with no effective opposition in the Council but it was also a reminder, to a man conscious of his own declining health, that his own days and his ability to make a real contribution to the well-being of his queen and country were diminishing. Radcliffe had remained hostile to the last. It is said that he warned those gathered round his deathbed, 'beware of the Gypsy, for he will be too hard for you all. You know not the beast so well as I do.'[6] Death must have been a welcome relief for Archbishop Grindal who passed away a month after the earl. He had never been summoned back to the warmth of royal favour and Elizabeth was glad to see the back of him.

In his place she appointed John Whitgift, a man much more to her taste. Whitgift was the worst kind of ecclesiastical martinet, pompous, prejudiced and stubborn. Macaulay labelled him, 'a narrow-minded, mean and tyrannical priest', a judgement with which it is difficult to disagree. He appealed to the queen because of his pathological hatred of Puritans as well as Catholics and his determination to uphold episcopal authority and impose uniformity on the English clergy. Dudley and the majority of the Council had worked for ecclesiastical unity rather than uniformity. Whitgift began dismantling what it had taken almost three patient decades to build up.

In December 1584 Robert tried, before it was too late, to reconcile the Puritans and the episcopal rigorists by holding a conference at Lambeth but the two-day event generated more heat than light. Dudley and the Archbishop were soon at loggerheads, and in March 1585 Dudley delivered a blistering attack on Whitgift's policies in the House of Lords. Cecil too protested, 'This kind of proceeding is too much savouring of the Roman Inquisition and is rather a device to seek offenders than to reform any.'[7]

The Archbishop's intransigence and the queen's support largely and permanently checked Dudley's ecclesiastical patronage. For the first time in years he lost control of an important area of government policy. His appointees were not presented to benefices. Puritan sympathizers on the episcopal bench were replaced, on death or retirement, by Whitgift's men. Some radicals were driven into separatism, though the majority resentfully conformed. Early in 1586 Whitgift was appointed to the Council and he was joined there by Lord Buckhurst, both of whom were enemies of Dudley. Another unfriendly influence was Sir Walter Raleigh, who had engaged Elizabeth's fancy in 1581 and was soon well established as one of her favourite gallants.

With his prestige in the court and the country generally waning, and with the queen pursuing policies he could only regard as disastrous, Dudley might well have concluded that the time had come to withdraw from public life. He was no longer the man he had once been. He was heavy of build and had the high colour which suggests soaring blood pressure. In addition, he suffered from an intestinal disorder which brought frequent bouts of pain. He was obliged to diet often and to take the Buxton waters whenever he could. The complaint, gleefully described in *Leicester's Commonwealth* as 'a broken belly on both sides of his bowels whereby misery and putrefaction is threatened to him daily,' may have been severe stomach ulcers or the beginnings of a malignant growth. Whatever his ailment, it combined with his frustrations and anxieties to change his character. The easygoing extrovert now became prey to bouts of bad temper. He resented anything that appeared like criticism, could not tolerate opposition, saw enemies and back-stabbers everywhere and pursued those who offended him with quite uncharacteristic persistence and spite. The change was noticed by one of his old friends, John Aylmer, in November 1583. Writing to patch up a quarrel, he remarked:

> I have ever observed in you such a mild, courteous and amiable nature, that you never kept as graven in marble, but written in sand, the greatest displeasure that ever you conceived against any man. I fear not, therefore, my good Lord, in this strait that I am in to appeal from this Lord of Leicester . . . unto mine old Lord of Leicester, who in his virtue of mildness and of softness . . . hath carried away the praise of all men.[8]

If Robert became tetchy in his fifties, Elizabeth was more so. Events at home and abroad were forcing her into a corner and she hated the reality of not being fully free to choose her policies. Philip II had once again gone on the offensive in the Netherlands, now under the Regency of Alexander Farnese, Duke of Parma. If he succeeded in establishing his mastery there and continued to enjoy his dominance at sea there would be nothing to stop him launching an invasion across the Narrows. Although all her instincts still opposed aiding rebels against their rightful sovereigns, the logic of sending military aid to the Low Countries to thwart Parma's advance was inescapable. That did not prevent Elizabeth trying to escape it. Her indecision and her tantrums when pressed threw her councillors into despair. In the summer of 1585 she finally agreed to send an army.

Dudley begged permission to lead it. Active support for his co-religionists was a cause he had always argued but he had his own reasons for desiring this office. It would be, he must have sensed, his last chance to make a real contribution to the global struggle against Antichrist. It would also give him a reason for prolonged absence from court where he found the atmosphere increasingly oppressive and uncongenial. It was his misfortune that he overestimated his own ability and under-estimated the intricacies of Dutch politics and the infinite capacity of the queen for tergiversation. It was twenty-nine years since he had been on campaign and he had never held field command of a large army. The United Provinces were far from united. Their representatives squabbled among themselves, and Parma was accomplished in dividing the rebels by promise of gold as well as threat of military action. As for Elizabeth, not only was she an unwilling principal in all this, but she was at odds with her general as to the purpose of his expedition. Dudley was setting out as a Protestant champion leading a crusade. Elizabeth was sending a force to defend the Dutch from further Spanish encroachment. Her allies wanted, not a mere condottiere who could be withdrawn at a moment's notice, but a powerful permanent leader and were prepared to trade their sovereignty for it. Elizabeth was only prepared to offer limited support and had no desire to be lured into provocative acceptance of permanent authority in the Netherlands.

The enterprise on which Dudley embarked was, thus, doomed from the start. His difficulties began before he even left England. As soon as he received his commission he dictated letters to 200 friends and dependants asking them to meet him with men and harness ready for embarkation at the end of October. He raised a loan from a consortium of London merchants, then went with Ambrose to the Tower to requisition armour and weapons. Two days were thus filled with hectic activity. He had scarcely tumbled into bed around midnight on 26/27 September when his servants admitted a messenger bearing a depressing letter from Walsingham: 'My very good Lord, her majesty sent me word . . . that her pleasure is you forbear to proceed in your preparations until you speak with her. How this cometh about I know not. The matter is to be kept secret. These changes here may work some such changes in the Low Countries as may prove irreparable. God give her majesty another mind and resolution.'[9] Dudley sat up in bed to scribble a reply. 'What must be thought of such an alteration! For my part, I am weary of life and all. I pray you let me hear with speed.'[10]

It was 4 December before he was able to march his 7,000 men out of London. Even then he had grave misgivings, expressed in a letter of farewell to Cecil.

> Her majesty I see, my Lord, often times doth fall into mislike of this cause . . . but I trust in the Lord, seeing her highness hath thus far resolved and grown also to this for execution as she hath and that mine and other men's poor lives and substances are adventured for her sake and by her commandment, that she will fortify and maintain her own action to the full performance of that she hath agreed upon . . . I beseech your Lordship have this cause even to your heart . . . for this I must say to you, if her majesty fail with such supply and maintenance as shall be fit, all she hath done hitherto will be utterly lost and cast away and we

her poor subjects no better than abjects. And, good my Lord, for my last [appeal], have me thus far only in your care that in these things which her majesty and you all have agreed and confirmed for me to do, that I be not made a metamorphosis, [so] that I shall not know what to do . . . no men have so much need of relief and comfort as those that go in these doubtful services. I pray you, my Lord, help us to be kept in comfort, for we will hazard our lives for it.[11]

Dudley was received rapturously by the States General and the people of the United Provinces. Immediately the Dutch leaders pressed him to accept a title implying supreme rule. He was eager to accept but wrote home for instructions. Contrary winds prevented him receiving Elizabeth's firm 'No' and on 25 January 1586 he allowed himself to be invested with 'highest and supreme commandment'. The messenger entrusted with the report of these events was the seasoned diplomat, William Davison. Davison was one of the most unfortunate of men. He seems to have suffered from a personality trait which made him veer from hesitancy to rashness. He had, or so Dudley would claim, actively encouraged him to accept the Dutch offer. But he then delayed his return to England with the news. The result was that Elizabeth heard about her general's elevation from one of her ladies who had the information in a private letter from the Hague. It was embellished with malicious rumour: Lettice Dudley was about to go to her husband 'with such a train of ladies and gentlewomen, and such rich coaches, litters and side-saddles as her majesty had none such' and she would establish 'such a court of ladies as should far pass her majesty's court'.[12] It is little wonder that Elizabeth flew into a rage. She immediately dictated a blistering letter to Dudley:

How contemptuously we conceive ourself to have been used by you, you shall by this bearer understand, whom we have expressly sent unto you to charge you withal. We could never have imagined had we not seen it fall out in experience that a man raised up by ourself and extraordinarily favoured by us above any other subject of this land, would have in so contemptible a sort broken our commandment, in a cause that so greatly toucheth us in honour; whereof, although you have showed yourself to make but little accompt, in most undutiful a sort, you may not therefore think that we have so little care of the reparation thereof as we mind to pass so great a wrong in silence unredressed: and, therefore, our express pleasure and commandment is, that all delays and excuses laid apart, you do presently, upon the duty of your allegiance, obey and fulfil whatsoever the bearer hereof shall direct you to do in our name: whereof fail you not, as you will answer the contrary at your uttermost peril.[13]

The depth of Elizabeth's anger took all her people by surprise. Dudley did not hesitate to write grovelling letters but, as Ambrose reported in March, the queen's rage seemed to increase rather than diminish. He suggested that if she summoned him home Robert should 'go to the farthest part of Christendom rather than ever come into England again'.[14] Cecil remarked that in all his years as a councillor he had not seen the queen so completely out of control. She threw sudden tantrums. For days on end she refused to receive reports from the Netherlands or to allow the Council to discuss the situation there. It was high summer before she came to a calmer frame of mind and that was only after Cecil had persistently pointed out that she was being unreasonable. It was news that Robert was ill which finally brought a return of her old affectionate concern.

Elizabeth's changeable conduct was not the only difficulty he had to deal with. The States General were equally impossible. He described that body as 'a monstrous government where so many heads do rule', peopled by men for whom he had nothing but contempt. They were, he said, mere 'churls and tinkers'. They refused to meet their financial obligations. They opposed his policies and appealed behind his back to the queen. Yet, instead of being able to dominate them as their sovereign, he was obliged 'to use flattery to those that ought to have sought me'.[15] The quarrels among the representatives of the states were of many kinds, political, religious and economic. Nor could they agree among themselves on the extent of Dudley's authority. At a popular level there were frequent altercations between the English soldiers and the citizenry. There were so many conflicting interest groups involved that every major decision Leicester took was almost bound to offend somebody. When he banned the export of grain to the Spanish-held southern states the merchants of the coastal towns protested. When he backed the Calvinists of Utrecht more moderate Protestant groups accused him of favouritism.

The kind of frustration Dudley and his men experienced may be illustrated by the exigencies they were forced to in order to garrison

Deventer. The local council, lacking confidence in their allies and frightened of giving offence to Parma refused to allow English troops into the town. Sir Henry Killigrew, of Dudley's diplomatic staff, had to devise a ruse to gain possession of the town. He kept the town council busy with protracted discussions for the space of two days while Edward Stanley sent his men into the town in groups disguised as citizens. When some 300 soldiers were concealed within the walls, Dudley's personal representative, Sir William Pelham, addressed the council with a final demand for the new garrison to be installed. He requested an answer by eight o'clock the following morning. The panic-stricken burghers immediately made preparations to resist their allies: they trebled the watch and threw chains across the streets. But long before the appointed hour Stanley's troops were assembled in the market place, and at 7.00 a.m. Pelham burst in upon the council. One of the Dutchmen tried to slip away to raise the alarm. At this Pelham unleashed his fury. 'Do you think,' he shouted, 'you have a people that are come over to spend their lives, their goods, and leave all they have, to be thus used of you and to be betrayed amongst you?' He ordered the guard to be disbanded and the gates of the town surrendered. 'This done, he sent them to prison, appointed new officers, and brought this stubborn town in one day to a good safety.'[16]

Such high-handed actions by his captains won them no friends but it was only by coercing his hosts that Dudley was able to put the early months of stalemate behind him and go onto the offensive. Parma moved cautiously northwards during the summer, choosing to garrison towns rather than offer pitched battles, because he knew that Leicester's force was ill-equipped for siege warfare. But the English proved to be more determined than he had expected and the campaigning season of 1586 ended with him withdrawing and leaving several captured towns to their fate. So far the war had not produced brilliant generalship on either side but the Spanish conquest of the northern provinces had been halted. English losses had not been heavy but one loss in particular was a serious blow to morale and to Dudley personally. Sir Philip Sidney, courtier, soldier, poet, the 'very flower of chivalry', was fatally wounded before the walls of Zutphen. He lingered several weeks, tended by his wife, who had a miscarriage shortly afterwards. This was another severe blow to Dudley's dynastic plans. He had designated and groomed Philip as his heir, an arrangement only set aside during the brief life of the Noble Imp. Now he had been deprived of both his legitimate son and also the young man who might have continued his policies even if he did not bear the family name. It was more than conventional condolence that Dudley expressed when he wrote to Walsingham. 'For my own part I have lost, beside the comfort of my life, a most principal stay and help in my service here, and, if I may say it, I think none of all hath a greater loss than the queen's majesty herself.'[17]

Dudley was now anxious to return home for the winter and his conciliar colleagues were no less eager to have him back at court to help them handle the latest crisis. Davison, now joint Secretary with Walsingham, wrote on 4 November, 'Your lordship's presence here were more than needful for the great cause now in hand, which is feared will receive a cold proceeding than may stand with the surety of her majesty and necessity of our shaken estates.'[18] The 'great cause' was ridding the realm of Mary, Queen of Scots.

For most of the time that Dudley had been away Walsingham had been operating a very successful 'sting' which tricked Mary into exchanging letters with the French ambassador who acted as a staging post for the members of a new conspiracy against the queen and her government. This correspondence was intercepted by Walsingham's agents, decoded, then sent on its way. What emerged from this operation was the details of the so-called Babington Plot, which entailed the assassination of Elizabeth, Dudley, Cecil and others and the placing of Mary on the throne with the help of foreign troops. By mid-August Walsingham was ready to pounce. Anthony Babington, the principal agent in the conspiracy, was arrested and most of his accomplices rounded up. It was a major coup for the Secretary. The evidence he had gathered clearly involved the Queen of Scots in high treason and, in the view of most of the Council, demonstrated beyond a peradventure that Elizabeth could not be secure as long as Mary lived. At the end of September the royal prisoner was moved once more, this time to Fotheringay Castle, Northamptonshire, described by Leland as 'meetly strong with double ditches and hath a keep very ancient and strong. There be very fair lodgings in the castle.'[19] Set in open, low-lying, marshy ground it made a comfortable but very secure jail. Here it was that Catherine of Aragon had spent her last unhappy years. And here it was that thirty-six commissioners gathered for Mary's trial which began on 14 October.

Dudley was kept fully informed of all these developments and he made his position very clear. He had come round to a hard-line opinion on Mary. The Babington business was, in his view, a plot too far. As a field commander he had seen brave men die defending the true faith against the advance of the Counter-Reformation. He himself had had a providential escape before the walls of Doesberg at the end of August. He had been inspecting some trenchwork with Sir William Pelham when they came under sniper fire. Pelham happened to be standing in front of the earl and took a bullet in the stomach. Fortunately the wound did not prove fatal but Dudley was, understandably, moved by the incident and was not prepared to see such sacrifices invalidated by Catholic intrigue at home. His chief concern was that Elizabeth would find reasons to delay the necessary dispatch of the Queen of Scots. The Council had decided to call a new parliament to show wider support for Mary's death. Dudley thought this a mistake: the government should proceed to trial and execution without delay. To stiffen their resolve he wrote to Elizabeth and all the leading councillors:

> . . . if you shall defer it, either for a parliament or a great [Council] session, you will hazard her majesty more than ever, for time to be given is [what] the traitors and enemies to her will desire . . . I do assure myself of a new, more desperate attempt if you shall fall to such temporising solemnities [ie. the summoning of parliament], and her majesty cannot but mislike you all for it. For who can warrant these villains from her if that person live, or shall live, any time? God forbid: And be you all stout and resolute in this speedy execution or be condemned of all the world forever. It is most certain if you will have her majesty safe it must be done, for justice doth crave it besides policy . . .[20]

Dudley set out for home on 23 November. He returned to find the queen desperate for his company and support. Never had she been more alone and under pressure. Political England clamoured for her to shed Mary's blood – a thing utterly repugnant to her. Catholic Europe and the Scottish king urged her to resist her people – a course of action she could not take. The Netherlands campaign was draining the treasury and making havoc of her careful finances. The international peace she had worked so hard to preserve was on the point of being shattered: Philip was known to be mustering his fleet for an invasion of England. As she tried to turn back the inevitable tide no one stood beside her or sympathized with her predicament. As she wrestled with her doubts, fears and moral dilemmas and possibly came close to a breakdown, Elizabeth had advisers in plenty: preachers reminding her of her duty; parliamentarians urging her to be revenged on her enemies; councillors steeling her arm for battle, but there was no one who understood her or realized that the policy she was being urged to pursue represented for her a deep personal failure.

Parliament *had* been summoned and the Council hoped that their entreaties would galvanize the queen into action but she lingered at Richmond, refusing to come to Westminster, 'being loath to hear so many foul and grievous matters revealed and ripped up'. By 12 November Lords and Commons had ratified the death sentence which had, ultimately, been passed upon the Queen of Scots. On the 24th a parliamentary deputation urged Elizabeth to issue a proclamation concerning the execution of Mary. She returned them an 'answer-answerless' and with that they had to be content. Then Dudley arrived. What passed between the two old friends as they supped alone that evening we do not know. But we do know that Elizabeth's doubts were overborne. She scrawled a note to the Lord Chancellor ordering him to make the proclamation. Her resolve, however, did not survive the withdrawal of Robert and the ensuing sleepless night. Before dawn another message was on its way to Westminster rescinding her order and adjourning parliament for a week. During that week, Dudley, firmly reinstalled in his favoured place, used all his powers to bring Elizabeth to the point of no return, while Cecil and other councillors passed back and forth between Richmond and the capital with messages and draft proclamations. On 4 December the queen's determination to execute her cousin was made known to her subjects.

Now all that was needed was the signed warrant for Mary's death, and Elizabeth's advisers expected that it would follow rapidly upon the proclamation. They should have known better. The queen resisted every attempt to urge her to immediate action. For Elizabeth's advisers day followed frustrating day and not one passed without Dudley discussing the crisis with his colleagues or with the queen directly. No one was more assiduous in urging the queen to positive action than William Davison and, on 1 February, she handed him the signed warrant, only to summon him back to her presence to receive fresh instructions. The Bond of Association had pledge her supporters to take any action to ensure her safety. Very well, let someone, without the queen's knowledge, go to Fotheringay and assassinate Mary. Davison was appalled and so was Mary's guardian, Sir Amyas Paulet. Elizabeth was brought face to face with the unpalatable truth that she could not evade personal responsibility for dealing with her rival. She wriggled to the very end. Poor Davison did not know what to make of the quicksilver changes of her tortured mind and sought the advice of Hatton and Cecil. A Council meeting was called and it was that body which took the decision to proceed without further delay. On 8 February Mary, Queen of Scots was beheaded. When Elizabeth received the news she exploded in a tirade of Tudor wrath. She persuaded herself that she had been betrayed and lashed out at the culprits. Hatton and Cecil were banished from the court. Davison was once again the fall guy. He was sent to the Tower, fined 10,000 marks and even threatened with summary execution for disobedience. Although he was released after eighteen months and his fine remitted, he was never taken back into favour and was, in effect, ruined. For months a paralysis gripped the government. 'The present discord between her Majesty and her Council hindereth the necessary consultation that were desired for the prevention of the manifold perils that hang over the realm,' Walsingham complained.[21]

The one person Elizabeth wanted beside her at this time was her Sweet Robin. Forgiven and forgotten was his disgrace of the previous year. The situation at court was like a rerun of the first months of the reign, when Cecil and his colleagues had bitterly resented their exclusion and Dudley's monopoly of the queen. They resented them again now. The new men were particularly annoyed. During Dudley's absence Hatton, Whitgift and others had enjoyed a greater degree of access to Elizabeth. It had seemed to them that the favourite's political power was at an end. Now he had stepped back into his old position and they were once more reduced to courting his favours and asking him to intercede with Elizabeth on their behalf. It is small wonder that his colleagues were eager for his return to the Netherlands.

The situation there had deteriorated rapidly since his departure. In January the military gains of the previous season were wiped out at a stroke. Sir William Stanley, whom Leicester had left in command of Deventer, was a Catholic and a man with a grievance (he believed that his long service in Ireland had not been adequately recompensed). He conspired with Sir Rowland York, captain of the Zutphen fort, to yield their positions to the enemy. Parma accurately assessed the impact of this defection in a letter to his master: 'The Zutphen fort . . . and Deventer which was the real objective of last summer's campaign and is the key to Groningen and all these provinces are thus Your Majesty's at a trifling cost. But what is better; the effect of this treason must be to sow great suspicion between the English and the rebels, so that hereafter no one will know whom to trust.'[22] Parma could have capitalized on his good fortune with a vigorous northward thrust but he now received

different orders from Spain. Philip II, incensed by the sentencing of
Mary Stuart to death, encouraged by a treaty with the pope and
defections from Dudley's army (William Stanley had arrived at the
Spanish court offering his assistance for an invasion of Ireland) decided
that the time was right to launch his long-contemplated 'Enterprise of
England'. He instructed Parma to concentrate his efforts on securing
ports and coastal garrisons so that he could embark his army on the
Armada which would shortly arrive. The Spanish commander, therefore, settled down to besiege Sluys on the Scheldt estuary.

Dudley was eager to return to his command but not on the same
conditions that had led to the previous difficulties. He demanded more
troops, the making good of all pay arrears and a war chest of £10,000.
(He had been obliged to dig deep into his own pocket to meet the
expenses of the earlier campaign.) For her part, Elizabeth was loath to
throw good money after bad and could not make up her mind to be
deprived of Robert a second time. Midsummer had come and gone
before Dudley was able to head back across the North Sea.

He discovered to his chagrin that nothing had changed in the allied
camp. The old arguments and misunderstandings repeated themselves.
In order to thwart Parma's coastal preparations Dudley was reliant on
the Dutch navy but their admiral simply refused to acknowledge his
authority or fall in with his tactics. This lack of co-operation showed
itself to lamentable effect when Dudley launched a waterborne attempt
to relieve Sluys. The plan was for a fireship to go ahead and destroy the
floating bridge Parma had thrown across the channel. The Dutch
warships would then bear through and Dudley would personally lead
the attack. They would make an entry for the supplies and reinforcements, carried by flyboats and barges. It was an exacting manoeuvre,
demanding fine timing and accurate manipulation of many vessels
through the shallows of the estuary. There was very little room for error
or mishap. On the evening tide the fireboat was steered towards its
target. It was a fearsome sight. Against inexperienced troops and
timorous commanders it would probably have been very effective.
Parma simply gave the order for part of the bridge to be unfastened and
swung out of the way, allowing the 'hellburner' to pass through and
exhaust itself harmlessly in the inner basin. The attacking fleet was,
necessarily, coming up at some distance from the fireship. Seeing the
failure of his stratagem, Dudley went from ship to ship in his barge,
ignoring small arms fire from the Spanish positions, ordering more sail
and full speed so as to reach the bridge before the enemy had time to

close the gap. The Dutch captains and pilots simply refused to co-operate. They, too, had observed Parma's cunning, and were afraid of running their ships into a narrow, closed channel where they would have no room to manoeuvre. While his allies argued and Leicester fumed, Parma repaired his breach, the tide slackened, the wind changed direction and the opportunity was lost. Sluys capitulated soon afterwards and, though Dudley stayed at his post until November, determinedly trying to impose his will on his fractious and obstructive allies, he eventually admitted himself beaten.

Dudley's governorship of the United Provinces has usually been represented as a failure but since there was no agreement about what he was trying to achieve, it is difficult to evaluate his contribution. In territorial terms he certainly had nothing to show for the expenditure of blood and treasure. Diplomatically the English intervention was a disaster. No common Protestant front had been established. The Dutch states were even more at loggerheads with each other than they had been in 1585 and Dudley left behind a general feeling that the rebels had been betrayed. Yet in the longer term the English inter-vention in the Netherlands proved crucial. In Alexander Farnese, Duke of Parma, Dudley faced one of the finest generals of the age, a strategist who had, by 1585, turned the tide of rebellion. He had captured Brussels and Antwerp and consolidated the southern states. He was poised to press on into the northern territory when the appearance of Dudley's army made him pause. Crucially his advance was slowed in 1586 and, in the following year, he was ordered to divert his attention away from reducing the whole country to its allegiance and prepare for the Armada. The grind of siege warfare inflicted a heavy toll on his army (the capture of Sluys alone cost him 700 men) and matters grew worse when the Armada was delayed and his men faced disease and famine. Farnese never regained his momentum. When he turned his attention once more to the United Netherlands he found himself confronted by a more formidable foe, Maurice of Nassau. Easy victories eluded him and when, in 1592, he died in the field he had already been summoned back to Spain in disgrace. There was nothing glorious about Dudley's governorship of the United Provinces but it was one episode in the long struggle for the survival of the Dutch Republic.

By the time he reached home Robert Dudley was yesterday's man. The privileged places around the queen were being filled by the next generation of courtiers and councillors. Walsingham had already warned him of this state of affairs as early as August: 'I find there is some dealing underhand against your lordship which proceedeth from the younger sort of our courtiers that take upon them to censure the greatest causes . . . a disease I do not look to be cured in my time.'[23] The future was in the hands of these brash young men – Raleigh, Essex; John Harrington, who kept the queen amused with his sophisticated poetizing; Robert Carey, who trumpeted his accomplishments at tilt, tourney, barriers, masques and balls; and that other Robert Dudley, Leicester's 'base son' who, before the age of twenty, would fit out his own voyage of exploration. With the arrogance of inexperienced youth some of them mocked 'Old Leicester's' coming home with his tail between his legs. They did so with impunity knowing that the queen was displeased that, given a second chance, her general had failed to turn the tide of war. She did not summon him immediately to her side and he spent much of the winter at Wanstead.

In truth Dudley was in no hurry to return to court. He was tired, humiliated and unwell. One of his first acts was to resign the Mastership of the Horse to his stepson, Robert Devereux. He had deliberately introduced young Essex into the queen's circle as a kind of personal proxy, a man who would remind Elizabeth of the Dudley she had once loved so passionately, who would maintain something of the family presence. The plan worked excellently. The queen was enchanted with her new beau. It was Essex who sat late into the night with her playing cards; it was he who rode with her in Windsor Great Park; it was he who delivered private, intimate messages from his stepfather and effectively negated the activities of Dudley's opponents. And when Dudley was absent from the court Elizabeth insisted that Essex should occupy his stepfather's chambers.

Dudley had certainly not been cast aside. There was still a place for him in the queen's counsels and that place grew more important as it became obvious that England was facing the threat of imminent invasion. Philip's delayed Armada would be setting sail this summer and effective defence had to be organized. That meant raising the largest army England had seen in half a century and appointing veterans of the Irish and Netherlands wars to knock raw recruits into shape. There never seems to have been any doubt about the general who was to be in overall command of land forces. Dudley might have failed in the Netherlands. There might be several young bloods competing for death or glory jobs but Elizabeth still had faith in her old friend. Dudley's appointment as 'Lieutenant and Captain General of the Queen's armies and companies' was not formally ratified until 24 July but before that date he had thrown himself energetically into the complex preparations for fending off invasion.

It was obvious that if Spanish troops landed in strength their first objective would be London. Dudley, therefore, gathered his main force at Tilbury on the Thames estuary, as the first line of defence. Concentrating men and supplies was no easy task. On 22 July he travelled downriver to examine the fortifications at Tilbury and Gravesend. He found them sadly lacking in powder, ordnance, implements and provisions and doubted whether either could be rendered impregnable. He supervized the construction of a boom across the Thames but (correctly, as it turned out) doubted its adequacy. Mustering sufficient troops was a major headache. All the men of substance preferred to pledge their contingent to serve under Hunsdon whose army was stationed on the outskirts of London. The men of Essex and the surrounding country, who might be presumed to be most interested in repelling the invader, were slow to come in. On 25 July, by which time the Spanish fleet was already off the Isle of Wight, Dudley had only 4,000 men in camp and still had inadequate officers to train his soldiers. The following day it was shortage of victuals that exercised his mind. He had personally had to order 100 tuns of beer and had instructed 1,000 reinforcements from London to stay where they were unless they were bringing their own provisions with them. He had had town criers out in all the surrounding boroughs appealing for food for the troops but found East Anglian farmers and victuallers reluctant to trust the royal quartermasters. He hurried back and forth between Tilbury, Gravesend, Chelmsford, Harwich and other towns in an effort to stir up patriotism or, failing that, self-interest and could, with some justification, claim that he was expected to 'cook, cater and hunt' for his army.[24]

Gradually order emerged from chaos. On 27 July Robert felt that he could urge the queen to pay a personal visit to Tilbury. Elizabeth had written to ask his advice. He responded by suggesting that the queen should keep about her a small force of picked men and that she should establish her headquarters at Havering, some ten miles distant from the main camp at Tilbury. From there, he hoped, Elizabeth would come to spend two or three days 'in your poor lieutenant's cabin' to inspire her troops. Elizabeth did not accept his advice about Havering, preferring to entrust her person to the security of the capital and Hunsdon's bodyguard but she did agree to review her troops at Tilbury on some appropriate day. On 5 August she sent to inform Robert that she would come the following Monday.

In the midst of all his purely military preparations Dudley now had to organize a gaudy demonstration of loyalty and defiant nationalism. By the morning of the 8th he had created what may have been little more than an illusion of military might and bold defiance. Within neat palisades and ditches the tents and pavilions stood in orderly rows, those of the officers gay with heraldic flags and bunting. The foot soldiers were drawn up in their squadrons, breastplates gleaming and a semblance of uniformity about their dress and weapons. The mounted troops made a more impressive display with their proud plumes and immaculately groomed chargers. It was Robert's last and greatest piece of stage-management, the apotheosis of all the court tournaments he had organized over the years. Everything was ready for the appearance of the principal performer.

And Elizabeth knew exactly how to respond. Leaving all her bodyguard before Tilbury fort she went among her loyal subjects with an escort of six men. The Earl of Ormonde walked ahead with the Sword of State. He was followed by a page leading the queen's charger and another bearing her silver helmet on a cushion. Then came Elizabeth herself, all in white with a silver cuirass, and mounted on a grey gelding. She was flanked by the two men who represented her past and her future: on her right Robert Dudley, portly and bare-headed but still an impressive figure on horseback, on her left the intensely handsome Earl of Essex. Sir John Norreys brought up the rear. It had all been arranged to perfection, just as the queen's speech had been carefully prepared and rehearsed. The spectacle did not fail to achieve its effect. The cheering soldiers saw their sovereign come among them as 'your general, judge and rewarder' and believed that she would 'lay down for my God and my kingdom and for my people, my honour and my blood'. Those who had eyes to see might also discern that the Dudley interest was still paramount in the circles closest to the queen. It was in his camp and not in her own capital that she delivered her rousing 'heart and stomach of a king' speech. And, in the concluding words (which are rarely quoted), she commended her soldiers to the leadership of her lieutenant-general, 'than whom never prince commanded a more noble or worthy subject'.[25]

After the review the queen dined with Dudley and her officers and slept that night in the lodging Robert had requisitioned for her. The next day she was back at Tilbury again, enjoying the bustle of camp life and watching the troops at their drill. But news arrived that Parma was now ready to cross the Channel. Dudley, who had urged Elizabeth to come downriver, was now among those who begged a reluctant queen to remove herself from possible danger. On the evening of Friday 9 August Robert handed Elizabeth into her barge and watched as she was rowed towards London.

In fact, the danger was now passed, although this was far from clear from the confused reports reaching Tilbury from coastal watchers, returning captains and foreign envoys. While Robert was entertaining the queen, Philip's admiral, the Duke of Medina-Sidonia, was desperately trying to hold his fleet together and moving northwards up the Flemish coast. During the hours of darkness Admiral Howard's fireships had forced him from his anchorage in Calais Roads. Like a pack of hounds the English fell upon the scattered fragments of the Armada, engaging several ships in running battles off Gravelines.

Now the true value of Dudley's inglorious Netherlands campaign could be appreciated. Parma's failure to overrun the United Provinces meant that he had not gained command of the ports of Holland and Zeeland and had not neutralized the United Provinces' navy. As a result his invasion barges remained pinned down in Nieuport and Dunkirk and Medina-Sidonia's harassed ships could find no haven in which to repair, revictual and regroup. The Spaniards found themselves running before a gathering storm and between two alien shores.

This did not mean that Leicester's work was done. He was responsible for the defence of the realm. Medina-Sidonia or Parma might yet succeed in getting men ashore somewhere. Catholic dissidents at home, anticipating Spanish aid, might raise the standard of revolt. Dispatches poured in and had to be responded to. On 9 August there came a report of a rumoured Spanish landing at Dungeness. On 12 August, the Earl of Huntingdon wrote from Newcastle deploring the lack of preparedness in the North

'. . . if there be doubt of the enemy his looking this way, I trust the defences will soon be repaired. If I thought otherwise my mislike of my case here would be greater than yet it is, though, in truth, it is such as, happily, your Lordship would not think it to be . . .'[26]

He even received appeals from the Netherlands where Dutch and English garrison commanders still looked to him for help. Sir William Russell at Flushing reported his continual altercations with the States

General who were trying to undermine his authority and asked Dudley 'by all means to frustrate their purposes' or else arrange his own replacement by 'someone more plausible and more agreeable unto their honours'.[27]

Not for another week was it clear that the threat of invasion had passed. Just as earlier Dudley had been pressed to gather together and equip his force at great speed, so now he was instructed by money-conscious politicians to break up his camp without delay. He was not reluctant to comply. The strain of the last weeks had taken its toll. His old stomach ailment was troubling him again and he was running a temperature. This did not stop him returning to court in triumph. His army had not fired a single shot in anger but he might well feel vindicated. Elizabeth's England had at last, as he had always advocated, stood defiant and alone against the might of the Catholic tyrant, trusting only in the stout hearts of the people and the protection of the Lord of Hosts. As he rode back through London at the head of a contingent of picked soldiers and received the cheers of the relieved citizens lining the streets and leaning from upper windows it seemed that his unpopularity had, temporarily at least, been put aside and he was welcomed as a hero. At the height of the crisis Elizabeth had once again contemplated raising Dudley to a position of pre-eminence under the Crown. She had letters patent drawn up naming Dudley Lieutenant Governor of England and Ireland. In the event she was only dissuaded from signing them by the fervent arguments of Cecil and Hatton. It was a return to events of 1562. Their relationship since then had gone through violent ups and downs but still in Elizabeth's eyes there was only one man who could govern the country in the event of anything happening to her. That man was Robert Dudley.

Dudley was not well enough to stay more than a couple of days at court. Elizabeth readily gave permission for her Robin to take the waters at Buxton and gave him some medicine prescribed by her own physicians. Robert and Lettice left Wanstead on 26 August to make their way by easy stages to the Midlands spa. On the 28th they were guests of Lady Norreys at Rycote and from there, the following morning, Dudley wrote one of those many inconsequential letters to Elizabeth, enquiring after her health, assuring her of his loyalty, thanking her for a 'token' just received. Whatever this 'token' was, it was yet further proof that even in the press of affairs following on the defeat of Spain, he was not far from the queen's thoughts. He assured her majesty that 'I continue still your medicine and find that [it] amends much better than any other thing that hath been given me.'[28]

He was putting a brave face on it for he was now very ill. He managed to travel another twenty-five miles, perhaps with an overnight stay in Oxford, and reached his lodge at Cornbury. There he took to his bed. After several days and nights of pain he died on 4 September.

V

THE EXILE

18

Tudors and Dudleys

⸎

Elizabeth was heartbroken by the death of her old friend and constant companion, so much so that she was incapacitated by grief. Three days later Walsingham reported 'she will not suffer anybody to [have] access to her, being very much grieved with the death of the Lord Steward.'[1] According to the, perhaps exaggerated, story that reached Bernardino de Mendoza in Paris, Elizabeth went into purdah until Cecil ordered the doors to her privy apartments to be forced open. The ex-ambassador's informant added the comment that if the queen was distraught by Dudley's death she was quite alone in experiencing such an emotion. He was wrong. Many people mourned Robert Dudley's passing. It was an immense loss to the Puritan movement, to his many protégés and to his wide circle of friends. His widow had him buried in the Beauchamp Chapel at Warwick and raised over his remains one of the most spectacular, polychrome monuments of the age. The Latin inscription on the tomb listed all his offices and ended with the words that 'his most sorrowful wife' had raised the memorial 'to the best and dearest of husbands'. Despite being thrice married, Lettice elected to be interred beside Robert when she died. The Beauchamp Chapel became a Dudley mausoleum rather than, as had been originally intended, a chantry chapel for Richard Beauchamp, the great warrior baron. Thus linked in death with a chivalrous past, the Dudleys through this magnificent memorial still compel our attention.

Over the next few years numerous tributes were written to Dudley's memory by men who had nothing to gain from flattering the dead. The popular dramatist, John Lyly, eulogized Dudley in his play, *Endimion, The Man in the Moon*, which was acted before the queen at New Year 1591, told the Robert and Elizabeth story under the allegorical guise of a love-sick shepherd's devotion to Cynthia, the moon goddess. The piece ends with Endimion being admitted to immortality by a kiss from his chosen deity. One wonders if it brought a tear to the royal eye. Elizabeth's continuing devotion to the memory of her Sweet Robin is well known, as is the story that she kept among her dearest treasures 'his last letter'.

Elizabeth was no proto-feminist who insisted that anything a king could do she could do better. 'This kingdom hath had many noble and victorious princes,' she conceded. 'I will not compare with any of them in wisdom, fortitude and other virtues but . . . in love, care, sincerity and justice I will compare with any prince you ever had or ever shall have.'[2] It was to represent the masculine qualities she lacked that, for thirty years, she kept Robert Dudley beside her. Just as Victoria felt incomplete without her Albert, so for Elizabeth Robert's death left a gap in her life that could not be filled. She had looked to him for emotional support and to give expression to those aggressive aspects of governance that did not come easily to her. She did not always accept his advice and she was wary about allowing him to be thought of as her master but he was always a part of that phenomenon that was Elizabeth Regina.

Notwithstanding the queen's profound affection for Leicester, it was she who inflicted on him the cruellest disaster – the dashing of his dynastic hopes. Her all-consuming jealousy had obliged Robert to disavow one marriage and to suffer the distress of having his second (or third) wife denied her place among the social elite. But, not only did Lettice have to endure this perpetual snub, she also experienced the painful failure of being unable to fulfil her first wifely duty. She was forty-four when her only son by Robert died and there was no realistic possibility of her producing further heirs. There is, therefore, an underlying sadness about the magnificent Dudley tombs in the Beauchamp Chapel at St Mary's Warwick. Ambrose's monument is also here. He survived his brother by only seventeen months. The wound which he had sustained in the 1563 campaign had never fully healed and, in February 1590, he had to endure a gruesome leg amputation. He did not survive the operation. His body was brought to the chapel where Robert and the 'Noble Imp' were already interred. The 'Good Lord Warwick' had no children by any of his three wives. Therefore, what we witness today in the Beauchamp Chapel is the end of a dynasty. The legitimate line of descent from Sir John of

Atherington, after providing the Tudor crown with a remarkable succession of loyal and talented servants, had come to an end.

Or had it?

Leicester did leave behind him a son, another Robert Dudley. The 'base son', born of Lady Douglas Sheffield, was a lively stripling of fourteen when his father died. He inherited the bulk of his father's estate and, shortly afterwards, his uncle's. Young Robert was now one of the richest men in England. He was also the most talented member of the family. He displayed all his father's charm, athleticism and showmanship and early developed the courtly graces necessary to commend him to the queen. But, beneath such surface attributes, lay a keen intellect and an enquiring mind. Robert studied at Oxford where Leicester hired Thomas Chaloner as the boy's tutor. Chaloner was one of the leaders of a new generation of philosopher-scholars, fascinated by travel and the natural phenomena. No one could have been better suited to train the mind of a young man of catholic tastes, eager to experience everything life had to offer. Robert was naturally excited by the events of 1588 and, though too young to see action, he was well placed to experience something of the thrill of those anxious and stirring months. Not only was his father in charge of the queen's land forces, but his maternal uncle, Charles, Lord Howard of Effingham, was the Lord Admiral who saw off Spanish Philip's invasion attempt. Robert was present at Tilbury when Elizabeth reviewed her troops there and his father commissioned him as colonel of a regiment of foot. The ardent teenager who had been brought up in awe of his cousin, Sir Philip Sidney, was determined to follow in the hero's footsteps and show that he, too, had inherited a full measure of the Dudley spirit.

When Robert was subsequently welcomed at the royal court it was as much for his own sake as in memory of his father. He was of course, only a minor figure in Elizabeth's entourage and extant records make little mention of him. However, such references as do exist suggest that the young man was being watched – doubtless to see if he was a chip off the old block. One gossip recorded with glee that Dudley had suffered a period of banishment for kissing one of the queen's maids of honour in full view of her majesty. However, Robert did have an excuse for such wanton behaviour: the lady in question, Margaret Cavendish, was his wife. The match must have had royal approval, for otherwise the groom's punishment would have been much more severe. Perhaps Margaret's father had obtained the wardship of this wealthy young man of such prestigious stock. The

Cavendishes themselves were a long-established Suffolk family with strong court connections but they were not socially of the first rank. Whatever his feelings for his young bride, Robert may well have had very specific reasons for welcoming the match. It brought him into close contact with Margaret's cousin, Thomas Cavendish, the hero of the hour.

On 10 September 1588, Cavendish added a cherry to the cake of national triumph when he sailed his storm-battered ship, the *Desire*, and its exhausted crew into Plymouth and became the second captain to make a successful circumnavigation of the globe. When, in 1591, Cavendish set sail again on an expedition to follow up the commercial contacts he had already made in the Orient, he took with him two ships provided by his seventeen-year-old cousin, the galleon *Leicester* and the smaller *Roebuck*. Meanwhile Robert set himself to study all he could about shipbuilding, navigation, marine warfare and everything to do with mastering the sea and establishing England's place among the leading maritime nations. Cavendish's new venture proved to be a lamentable failure and the admiral himself was among those who did not survive. That did nothing to deter his cousin from committing his energies and more of his fortune to trans-oceanic adventure.

The first fruits of this enthusiasm and industry took the form of a voyage to the West Indies, which set sail in December 1594. For this venture Robert had not only gathered his own charts and rutters and handpicked his officers from among England's most experienced mariners, he had also designed his own flagship, proudly dubbed after the heraldic device of Warwick – the *Bear*. The original plan had been for a joint expedition with Sir Walter Raleigh to search for the fabled El Dorado but the other leader could not assemble his ships and men in time and Dudley eventually departed without him. In doing so he made a worrisome enemy. Raleigh later claimed that Dudley intended to steal a march on him and could not be content to be guided by a more experienced partner. How much truth there was in this we cannot now know. It seems likely that a shared venture would not have been a happy one. Both captains were strong individualists and disagreements at sea might have had more disastrous consequences than the quarrels which later broke out between them.

Historians are rightly wary of highly-coloured tales about Elizabeth's bold, romantic, adventure-loving, Spaniard-bashing 'sea dogs', more suited to Hollywood spectaculars than sober historical analysis, but it is difficult to read the accounts of Dudley's voyage, which appeared soon afterwards among the collection of 'principal navigations' made by Richard Hakluyt, without being seduced by the patriotic and chivalric braggadocio displayed by this young English conquistador. Here he claims the island of Trinidad for his queen:

> . . . we caused the trumpets to sound solemnly three
> several times, out company trooping round. In the
> midst marched Wyatt, bearing the Queen's arms
> wrapped in a white silk scarf edged with deep silver
> lace . . . having the General's colours displayed . . .[3]

He fastened to a tree a lead plaque proclaiming that Robert Dudley had taken possession of the land in the name of her sacred majesty and swearing, 'with his sword' to defend this claim 'against any knight in the whole world'.

During the six-month voyage, Dudley dispatched a party of men several kilometres up the Orinoco to see what could be discovered of the land of gold, took some Spanish merchant prizes, sank nine other vessels and picked a fight with a larger man-o'-war. He then returned to great acclaim at court. A eulogistic, not to say sycophantic, account of the voyage was written by one of Robert's captains, Thomas Wyatt. Its objective seems to have been to commend the young admiral to some prominent member of the government and the author omitted no opportunity to paint Dudley in the most heroic of colours. Thus, when trying conclusions with the Spanish warship, Dudley, 'came forth unarmed, having only his leading staff in his hand, saluted, and took his standing on the open deck, where he might best see and be seen of his enemies'. In the thick of battle round shot and wooden splinters were flying all round him but he stood his ground unflinching even when a missle 'struck the very blade of his leading staff into many pieces, going within a handful of his head, having before torn the sails, cut the shrouds, and pierced the ship very near the place of his standing'.[4]

We live in an age that tends to be cynical of such tales of heroism and views with suspicion any idealism that expresses itself in terms of national pride or colonial ambition. John Guy has written, 'Although eulogized as naval commanders, strategists and imperial pioneers, the Elizabethan "sea dogs" were motivated by greed not altruism'.[5] Such black and white judgements obscure the mindset of a man like Robert Dudley. His motives were mixed. While he undoubtedly looked for financial return in his quest for prizes and new sources of commercial wealth, there can be no doubt of his intense national pride and his passionate interest in maritime adventure. The defeat of the 1588 Armada was very far from being the end of the conflict with Spain. The navy, augmented by privateers and hired merchantment, was the realm's first line of attack and defence. Robert Dudley was eager to serve prominently in its ranks.

The next campaign in the sea war with Spain was planned for the summer of 1596. Howard of Effingham was given command of a vast Anglo–Dutch fleet of well over a hundred ships (sources number the force at between 110 and 150 vessels) which was to convey to Spain 10,000 troops under the command of the Earl of Essex, Robert's step-brother. The expedition's objective was to destroy as many of Philip's ships as possible and frustrate his invasion plans. In this great national endeavour Dudley was given command of the 500-ton *Nonpareil*. He was in the thick of the action when the invaders fell upon Cadiz, fired the town and destroyed twenty-six men-o'-war as well as several smaller vessels. At Faro, on the Portuguese coast, the outward-bound Indies fleet was burned at anchor by its own leaders to prevent it falling into enemy hands. All in all, the English captains could congratulate themselves on a successful piece of work, especially those who profited handsomely from the plunder of Cadiz. Dudley's full satisfaction had to wait until the triumphant return to Plymouth. There he was publicly knighted, 'in the open street, when the Lords General came from the sermon'.

Returned to his estates, Sir Robert now gave his mind to establishing himself as a figure of consequence in English society. His wife, Margaret, had died of the plague while he had been away in the Caribbean and he now married Alice Leigh, the daughter of Sir Thomas Leigh, a Warwickshire neighbour. Throughout the remaining years of the dying reign he divided his time between court and county, largely pursuing his maritime interests. Most of his energies were absorbed in fitting out a new and more ambitious enterprise; a trading venture to exploit the contacts that Cavendish had made in the Orient. Having dispatched his three ships at the end of 1596, he waited impatiently for their return as the century drew towards its close. But no news of their fate ever came, and Robert never discovered what a later generation was able to piece together from Portuguese records, that his sailors had all perished from storm, disease and enemy action in the Indian Ocean. Further misfortune awaited him at home. In 1601, the Earl of Essex fell from favour and, gathering around him a motley band of malcontents and hotheads impatient with the regime of the aged queen and her greybeard advisers, attempted an armed coup. When it failed, the earl and his closest confederates were executed. Several others spent shorter or longer terms in prison. Still more found themselves under the cloud of suspicion and royal disfavour. Dudley was among this latter group. Whether he had taken any part in his step-brother's foolish plotting or whether he simply fell foul of the anti-Essex faction (of which Raleigh was a prominent member) we do not know.

As the aged queen went into her last decline in March 1603. Sir Robert, now in his thirtieth year, was among the many hopefuls who aimed to achieve prominence in the service of the new king. Dudley considered that the first thing he needed to do was lay claim to the family titles. In this he, not unnaturally, had the eager support of his father-in-law, Sir Thomas Leigh. Before James reached his new capital Robert wrote to the Archbishop of Canterbury asking him to hear evidence that would prove that his father and mother had been lawfully married and that, therefore, he was the rightful holder of the earldoms of Leicester and Warwick. He knew that this action would distress several people and would prove particularly painful to his step-mother, whom he had no wish to annoy and would embarrass his mother. When he approached his mother Douglas Sheffield (now Lady Stafford) for evidence that he had been born in lawful wedlock she, understandably, did not want to rake up painful memories or testify in court that she and her current husband, Sir Edward Stafford, had lived for years in what was technically an adulterous relationship.

Other social and emotional barriers stood between Robert and the establishment of his legitimacy. On the deaths of his father and uncle their peerage titles had fallen into abeyance and some of the lands attached to them had escheated to the crown. The nearest claimant, failing the appearance of a male heir, was Robert Sidney, the only surviving brother of the hero of Zutphen. The two Roberts were the only living grandsons of John Dudley, Duke of Northumberland. Robert Sidney, like his late brother, was a courtier-soldier, actively involved in campaigning in the Low Countries throughout the 1590s. Had he perished in the war against Spain (something Robert Dudley might secretly have hoped for) there would have been no obstacle to his cousin's ambitions. Not only did Sidney not conveniently get himself killed, he proved himself a far more effective intriguer than Dudley. The possibility of reviving the Dudley titles had been virtually non-existent during the lifetime of the old queen. Elizabeth was extremely niggardly when it came to handing out peerages. When Sidney had approached her with a petition for the Lisle barony (appended to the Earldom of Warwick) she had returned him a cold answer. Therefore, like Dudley, he fastened his hopes on James Stuart. In 1588 he had been sent as an envoy to the Scottish king and had, thereafter, worked assiduously on James's behalf at the English court. The tactics worked perfectly. The over-emotional James embraced him as a friend and treated him generously in the flurry of grants which marked the beginning of the reign. On 13 May, Robert became Baron Sidney of Penshurst and within weeks Queen Anne had appointed him her chamberlain.

Technically such displays of royal favour to a potential rival claimant should have made no difference to Dudley's action in the ecclesiastical court. Matrimonial issues fell within the purlieus of canon law and Robert had received permission to present his evidence before Dr Zachary Babington, the archbishop's chancellor in his Court of Audience. The proceedings were, essentially, very simple: the court would hear sworn depositions from witnesses and decide whether or not they proved that a lawful wedding had taken place in May 1573. If the decision was in Robert's favour it would then have been a matter for the heralds to examine the legitimacy of his claim to the family honours. An unusually virulent outbreak of plague delayed the sitting of the court, which was eventually moved – significantly – to the Consistory Court of Lichfield, Dudley country. Sir Robert, however, did not wait in idleness throughout the summer months. He instituted a civil proceeding against one of his own servants for calling him 'bastard'. This was almost certainly a contrived case, since once the taunt of illegitimacy was adjudged slanderous, it logically followed that Sir Robert had been born in wedlock. The Court of Audience was convened on 27 September.

By now the confrontation between the two Roberts had become a *cause célèbre*. Court and capital were buzzing with gossip about this deliciously sensational case. Dudley's opponents matched his energy, their activity being largely taken up with securing the support of king and Council. The main thrust of their argument was that Dudley had been guilty of lese-majesty in assuming a title which it was in the king's prerogative alone to grant. They accused him of publicly calling himself Earl of Leicester and providing his servants with livery incorporating the bear and ragged staff badge. All this formed the basis of a charge of criminal conspiracy brought against Dudley, Leigh and Babington, as a result of which an order in council was issued on 18 October for the staying of the case in Lichfield and the impounding of all documents.

Three months later Lettice, Countess of Leicester, followed this with a charge of defamation against her stepson. Robert Dudley, whose only offence was trying to prove something that, if true, was inconvenient to some members of the Stuart establishment, now found himself on the defensive, his initial claim indefinitely shelved. It was all turning very nasty.

The trial of Dudley and his assoociates did not begin until 22 June 1604, the vitriolic Attorney-General, Sir Edward Coke leading the prosecution. Coke's personal agenda consisted of two items: he wished to further his own career by energetically pursuing those identified by the king as his enemies and he was determined to assert the supremacy of the common law over canon law. On the first day of the trial he did little but harangue the defendants and disparage their witnesses. Then the case was adjourned – for eleven months.

As week followed frustrating week Robert became increasingly despondent. He was being outmanouevred and he knew it. But it was not just the blatant manipulation of justice that upset him. Everything he saw and heard about the new regime was depressing. James dispensed with the services of some of Elizabeth's most able servants, replacing them with accomplished sycophants or his own countrymen. The manners of the king and his Scottish cronies seemed uncouth to those who had been trained in the household of the Virgin Queen. Council members and court officials complained that James paid little attention to business and more to the pleasures of the chase. In his dealings with parliament he was insensitive in the extreme. Gone were the well-practised, honeyed speeches with which Elizabeth had wooed or bamboozled her Lords and Commons. James harangued them and made it clear that he expected them to do his bidding. The deterioration seemed to be symbolized by the new king's treatment of Sir Walter Raleigh. Robert can have taken no plesure from the news that this accomplished Elizabethan had been arrested on a trumped-up treason charge, violently denounced in the courtroom by Coke and condemned to death, only to have the sentence commuted in a melodramatic last-minute show of royal clemency. The injustice and indignities that Dudley was suffering seemed to be symptomatic of the misfortunes being visited on the country.

It is likely that, by the time his trial was resumed in May 1605, he had abandoned any hope of a fair outcome and already had in mind the course of action he would take if the case went against him. His defence was that since he had evidence of his parents' lawful marriage he was within his rights to test that evidence in court. Coke ensured that the substantive issue was never considered. He devoted his energies to denouncing Dudley for bribing men and women to testify on his behalf and to branding the witnesses as rogues and jail fodder. If there remained any shred of possibility that the Council and the king were remotely interested in the truth it was shattered during the course of the trial by a royal act of breathtaking, cynical disregard for the proprieties. In a display of support for his friend and a deliberate snub of Dudley, James bestowed upon Robert Sidney the title of Viscount Lisle. Days later, when the Lord Chancellor handed down his verdict, he left no doubt as to what the entire proceedings had been about. The principal defendants were acquitted but Dudley's witnesses were fined and denounced as perjurers who were to be permanently debarred from ever giving evidence in a court of law. All the documents in the case were to be seized and suppressed at the king's pleasure.

Among those who risked loss of royal favour by supporting Sir Robert in court were Lord Howard of Effingham, Baron Dudley and Edmund, Lord Sheffield (Douglas's son). This stain on the reputation of James I was eventually acknowledged by his son. In 1644 Charles I felt bound to do what he could by way of recompense. Kings, like modern politicians, are not prone to apologizing for their blunders and misdemeanours, which makes Charles's letter patent a remarkable document:

> our dear father, not knowing the truth of the lawful birth of the said Sir Robert (as we piously believe), granted away the titles of the said Earldoms to others . . . we having a very deep sense of the great injuries done to the said Sir Robert Dudley, and the Lady Alice Dudley, and their children; and that we are of opinion that in justice and equity these possesions so taken from them do rightly belong unto them . . . [we hold] ourselves in honour and consicence obliged to make them reparation.[6]

It is easy to imagine the sense of outrage and alienation Robert must have felt, after all that he had done for the Crown and all that his family had done over four generations. He immediately applied for permission to spend three years in foreign travel. On July 2 he left England with a small entourage. For his enemies at court this only sweetened their triumph. Leicester's base son, the presumptuous upstart, was crawling away from England with his tail between his legs. It was several days before news arrived from Calais that put a wholly different – and scandalous – complexion on his flight.

On his departure Dudley had been attended by a smooth-faced young page. Once clear of the country this young 'man' was revealed to be Elizabeth Southwell, the nineteen-year-old granddaughter of Howard of Effingham. More than that, she was one of Queen Anne's maids of honour. Worse was to come. When the king dispatched officials to demand that the French return them he was informed that Robert and Elizabeth had declared themselves Catholics and claimed sanctuary. The French king refused to send them back to face inevitable persecution in their own country and they were allowed to continue their journey. Dudley had successfully cocked a snook at James Stuart by dramatically rejecting all the new regime stood for.

How much of all this was a spontaneous reaction and how much had been planned? Robert's love affair with Elizabeth was genuine. The couple remained together until Elizabeth's death in 1631, by which time she had borne thirteen children. Their relationship took everyone by surprise but is unlikely to have been a whirlwind romance. They had known each other for several years for they were distant cousins and Elizabeth was the daughter of Sir Robert Southwell, a seasoned mariner and one of Dudley's old comrades in arms. She was obviously as spirited as her lover and ready to renounce everything for him. The elopement meant, of course, that Dudley was abandoning Alice, his wife, and the four daughters she had given birth to in their seven years of married life. When the runaways reached Lyon they obtained a papal dispensation to marry, on the highly dubious grounds that Robert's union with Alice was voided by a previous contract. Robert's relationship with his wife had gone sour during the recent time of stress and may have been undermined by the 'pushiness' of the ambitious Leigh family, who unremittingly nagged and pestered Robert to claim his ancient rights. (Alice's campaign continued unhampered by her husband's defection and, in 1644, her persistence was rewarded by a royal licence granting her permission to style herself 'Duchess Dudley'.) The extent to which religion played a part in Robert's decision to quit Protestant England may be doubted. He later claimed that he had long been a covert Catholic but this did not prevent him advising James, in 1612, to increase his revenues by stringent fines imposed on stubborn Catholics. Claiming the protection of the Roman church was a clever way of ensuring that diplomatic efforts to secure his arrest and forcible return to England would be unsuccessful. We must conclude that Dudley's flight in July 1605 was well prepared. It certainly achieved the result he had intended. Every scrap of news of the celebrity outlaws was eagerly snapped up in England and the widespread sympathy expressed for them added to the discomfiture of the Sidneys and their allies.

Dudley had no doubt about his eventual destination. Florence was a magnet for men of refinement and talent. The miraculous days of the High Renaissance were past but they left a long radiant afterglow and no capital in Europe was more cultured and civilized under the rule of the enlightened and immensely wealthy Medici grand dukes. The current incumbent was Ferdinando I, an exuberant and conscientious governor and a generous patron of the arts and sciences. It was he who gave employment to Galileo and he who commissioned the first opera, Jacopo Peri's *Daphne*. No one threw a better party than Ferdinando. The celebrations of his marriage in 1589 had gone on for three weeks and were reckoned as the most sumptuous that had ever been seen in any European court. This was the kind of heroic spectacle that would certainly have appealed to the son of the man who had masterminded the grand Kenilworth entertainments, of which people still spoke. The grand duke was an avid collector and builder – and not just for his own, private satisfaction. The Boboli Gardens and the Uffizi as well as the extended Pitti Palace were just some of the projects upon which he lavished enthusiastic attention.

But it was not as an expert in state showmanship that Dudley sought the patronage of Ferdinando I. The grand duke was assiduously strengthening Tuscany's political and commercial position. To achieve his goals he was willing to buy the best brains in Europe. Scholars, businessmen and technical experts came from many lands to the city which was governed by a remarkably welcoming, tolerant and broadminded regime. Two of Ferdinando's projects in particular attracted Dudley. One was the development of Livorno (Leghorn). The grand duke's father had begun the transformation of this fishing village on the Tyrrhenian coast into a major port in order to provide Tuscany with its own commercial and military outlet to the Mediterranean and Ferdinando energetically continued the building of the Porto Medicio. As Tuscany emerged as a major player in Mediterranean maritime endeavour it needed protection from the scourge of the shipping lanes – the Barbary corsairs. Ferdinando determined to build up a formidable navy for this purpose. Robert Dudley offered his undoubted expertise and experience in this area. The Grand Duke Ferdinando agreed and warmly welcomed the runaway couple from England. They never returned. Robert Dudley lived out the rest of his life as a servant of the Medicis and died at his villa just outside Florence in 1649.

It is at this point that our story – though not the Dudley line – comes to an end. It does so in a spectacular fashion, for Robert Dudley's life at the court of a foreign prince provides the final irony in a family saga replete with ironical twists and turns. Put very simply, Robert was the most talented member of the dynasty. Had the first Stuart had the intelligence to recognize, as each of the Tudors had recognized, that the Dudleys were a loyal and gifted family, there is no doubt that Robert would have achieved great things for his native country. A list of his accomplishments in Italy strikingly makes the point:

He oversaw the development of Livorno.

He drained the Pisan marshes which gave the city access to the sea and Livorno.

He wrote the three volume *Dell 'Arcano del Mare*, a magnificent treatise covering all matters to do with navigation and shipbuilding.

He designed and supervised the building of several new ships for the Tuscan navy.

He invented new navigational instruments.

His highly innovative mind turned itself to subjects as varied as training gundogs to retrieve and publishing a collection of herbal remedies.

He enjoyed a reputation as a leading member of the Tuscan intelligentsia.

Dudley's achievements and qualities were openly recognized and rewarded in his adopted land. The Grand Duchess Maria Maddelena appointed him her Chamberlain. The pope enrolled him among the papal nobility. In 1620, the Emperor, Ferdinand II, recognizing Robert's 'singular integrity of life and morals, his prudence, knowledge of affairs and rare ingenious inventions' proclaimed him Duke of Northumberland and Earl of Warwick in the Holy Roman Empire, making it clear that this was not a new creation but an acknowledgement of Dudley's hereditary rights.

This made no apparent impact on James I. Nor did various approaches essayed by Robert Dudley. Between 1612 and 1614, when his reputation was firmly established and his popularity in Florence much spoken of on the diplomatic network, he wrote a clutch of pamphlets aimed at drawing himself to the attention of the English king. Most of them related to naval matters but the most remarkable was a highly Machiavellian treatise entitled, *How to Bridle the Exhorbitances of*

Parliament. In it Dudley gave various items of advice designed to appeal to a monarch who had fallen out with the Commons, which James described as the 'house of hell'. The writer recommended the strategic placing of manned royal forts throughout the kingdom as a means of nipping in the bud any signs of disaffection. This and other measures might be funded by an annual land tax to be collected by royal officials without parliamentary ratification. Among the various other financial levies Dudley recommended to enhance government revenue were a series of imposts on Catholics as payment for adherence to their religion. All subjects should be required, on pain of death, to swear an oath of allegiance. The king, Dudley advised, should normally rule by proclamation, 'without further consent of a Parliament, or need to call them at all in such cases, considering that the Parliament in all matters . . . ought to be subject unto your Majesty's will.'[7] Such advice, assuming James ever read it, would have reinforced his own divine right prejudices. They did not, however, remove the prejudice he entertained about the man who had so insolently snubbed him seven years before. Six years later he drew a final line under the exile's hope by reviving the earldom of Leicester in favour of Robert Sidney. The rift was complete and neither Robert Dudley nor his progeny would ever pledge themselves to be 'droit et loyal' to the Stuart line as they had to their Tudor predecessors. Robert and Elizabeth's thirteen children included five strapping sons who survived into adulthood. We may regard this as the last reproach of fate to the shrivelled Tudor dynasty.

As David Starkey has remarked, 'The history of the Dudleys and the Tudors was intertwined – like a tree and, Dudley's many enemies would have said, its parasitical ivy.'[8] The simile would certainly have appealed to several sixteenth-century observers and has broadly been sanctioned by the judgement of later historians. In fact the analogy is too simple. Not only does it do no justice to a remarkable family; it distorts our understanding of the age in which they lived. How then should we characterize the relationship of the two families? Is it helpful to think in terms of symbiosis, two organisms supporting and sustaining each other? This does not work because the relationship was fatal to the Dudleys. It seems that, surprisingly, the image that fits best *is* that of the tree and the ivy. With this difference: it is the Tudors who sucked life from the Dudleys and not vice-versa.

History has variously judged the ruling house which controlled the nation's destiny during its most tumultuous and formative century. Henry VII and Henry VIII are granted a grudging admiration.

Elizabeth retains the Gloriana image so carefully created for her by her managers. Mary may invoke a degree of sympathy among readers of her story but is unlikely ever to escape the epiphet 'Bloody'. As for little Edward, he remains an enigmatic might-have-been. About the Dudleys, however, there has traditionally been a unity of opinion. The leaders of the dynasty have all been allotted their share in the black legend. Edmund has habitually been represented as, at worst, the instigator of harsh and unjust financial policies and, at best, the willing tool of a rapacious regime. John has gone down in popular legend as a villain second only to Richard Crookback; an ambitious schemer who made a bid for the Crown by trying to foist his daughter-in-law, Jane Grey, upon an unwilling nation. Only in recent years have historians begun to re-valuate Northumberland's positive contribution to the political life of mid-sixteenth century England. As for Robert, the ludicrous libels of his enemies have enjoyed a vigorous afterlife. Historians routinely disapprove of court favourites but Leicester deserves better than to be dismissed with such scornful comments as, 'England, indeed, was well rid of him'[9] and 'Leicester represented all that was worst in the politics and culture of the English Renaissance.'[10]

What I have tried to show in these pages is that the Dudleys were remarkable for two attributes – their talent and their loyalty. Their gifts varied. The family produced administrators, politicians, courtiers, patrons, soldiers and mariners. Yet, what they had in common were verve and imagination, the ability to think creatively and act decisively. Such people were vital to the Tudor regime. What the men and women who wore the crown understood was power – how to gain it and how to keep it. The Tudors – all of them, even Edward VI – were monsters. They had to be. Wielding despotic power was the only way to save England from falling back into anarchy. Between 1485 and 1603 the Crown survived frequent aristocratic rebellions, popular uprisings, plots and assassination attempts. In doing so it relied on state control of the judiciary, concentration of landed wealth in royal hands, trampling on the liberties of subjects and regimenting their religious beliefs. Such a regimen was seldom popular, never universally. It was inevitable, therefore, that the servants the rulers relied on to devise and execute the policies which kept them in power would bear the brunt of common criticism. The Dudleys accepted this – not, to be sure, with the same eagerness that they accepted the rewards of loyal service, but they were realists enough to know that unpopularity went with the territory.

The perquisites of high office were potentially enormous. Descended from the second son of a middling baronial family, the Dudleys rose to be among the wealthiest individuals in the land. They had no reason to apologize for that and nor has their biographer. The Dudleys, like their colleagues, had to play the game of Tudor politics by the established rules. They did so for personal and dynastic advantage. They also did so because there was no alternative. The four adult Tudors who reigned between 1485 and 1603 were strong-minded individuals who allowed their advisers very little latitude. Henry VII could keep councillors and privy chamber staff in line with an icy glance or sharp word. His son resorted to the knock on the door in the middle of the night. Elizabeth threw tantrums.

But Dudley loyalty was also based on conviction. All members of the family believed in the right of hereditary rulers to expect total obedience from their people. That belief even held firm when the monarch was a minor. It was Northumberland's tragedy that he could not and would not back his own judgement against the fervently expressed will of an anointed king. The principle of strong monarchy was one that Sir Robert upheld in the advice he gave to James I, even though he had, personally, suffered appallingly from the exercise of royal will.

Each generation of this remarkable family gave one hundred per cent loyalty to their Tudor sovereigns. And the Tudors, ivy-like, absorbed for their own purposes everything the Dudleys had to give. Edmund Dudley, his son and grandsons stood at the right hand of royal power, and were tireless in supporting it. When regimes changed they were swept aside. Yet always the family returned to prominence, commended to their sovereign by their talents and their personal dedication. They sacrificed their health and, in some cases their lives, to preserve the Tudors in power. In the end they sacrificed not only their own dynasty but also their reputation. For generations to come the Dudleys were branded as malicious, treacherous, murderous, licentious, overweening, avaricious schemers. It is important to set the record straight.

When we put aside malice and prejudice and draw as close as we can to these remarkable people, the story that emerges is quite extraordinary. Two constant themes appear: the Dudleys were intensely loyal to every one of the Tudor autocrats. They exercised semi-regal power and came incredibly close to succeeding the Tudors as rulers of England. But it is not the might-have-beens of history that matter. The real value of studying the Dudley story lies in understanding what happened to them during the most formative century in our history. No other family survived utter degradation to rise to the summit of power, not once but twice. It is the ups and downs of the Dudleys that provide us with a new perspective on England's most creative and destructive ruling dynasty. And no other family's story reveals just how costly it was in the sixteenth century to remain

Droit et Loyal

References

The place of publication is London unless otherwise specified

Chapter 1 – Broad is the Path and Wide the Gate

1. D. R. Guttery, 'The Two Johns: Patron and Parson', in *County Borough of Dudley Library, Museums and Arts Dept., Transcript No. 13* (1969), p. 4.
2. E. Hall, *The Union of the Two Noble and Illustre Families of Lancastre and Yorke*, ed. H. Ellis (1809).
3. No university registers exist for the years Edmund is supposed to have been there but Anthony Wood, the seventeenth-century historian of Oxford, in *Athenae Oxoniensis*, ed. P. Bliss (Oxford, 1813), I, p. 11, asserted that Edmund was a student (though he got the date wrong) and this is more likely to be true than otherwise.
4. *Cal.S.P. Span.*, I, 178.
5. Ibid.
6. Edmund Dudley, *The Tree of Commonwealth*, ed. D. M. Brodie (Cambridge, 1948), p. 38.

Chapter 2 – Notoriety

1. Edmund Dudley, *The Tree of Commonwealth*, ed. D. M. Brodie (Cambridge, 1948, p. 101).
2. Ibid., p. 35.
3. E. Hall, *The Union of the Two Noble and Illustre Families of Lancastre and Yorke*, ed. H. Ellis (1809), pp. 499–500.

4. *The Complete Works of St Thomas More*, III, pt 2, ed. C. R. Thompson (New Haven, 1980), pp. 101–3.
5. Ibid., IV, E. Surtz, et al, eds., 1970, pp. 19–2.
6. Polydore Vergil, *Anglica historia*, ed. D. Hay, Camden Society, new series, LXXIV (1950), p. 147.
7. G. R. Elton, *The Tudor Constitution* (Cambridge, 1960), p. 18.
8. Francis Bacon, *History of the Reign of Henry VII*, ed. J. R. Lumley (1876), p. 217.
9. Francis Bacon, *History of the Reign of King Henry VII*, ed. J. Weinberger (1996), pp. 183–5.
10. J. Stow, *A Survey of London*, ed. C. L. Kingsford (Oxford, 1908), I, p. 224.
11. *Letters and Papers of Henry VIII*, I, I, 146.
12. S. J. Gunn, 'The Courtiers of Henry VII' in J. Guy, ed. *The Tudor Monarchy*, 1997, p. 179.
13. Dudley, op cit., p. 6.
14. Ibid, p. 6.
15. *Letters and Papers of Henry VIII*, I, pt 2, 3408 (28) (hereafter 'L and P'); D. Knowles, *The Monastic Orders in England* (Cambridge, 1959), pp. 74–5.
16. Dudley, op. cit., p. 21.
17. *Letters and Papers of Henry VIII*, Add. I, i, 92.

Chapter 3 – A Tree and its Fruit

1. Niccolo Machiavelli, *The Prince*, trans. W. K. Marriott (1992), p. 108.
2. Ibid., p. 108.
3. F. Grosse and T. Astle, eds, *The Antiquarian Repository*, 1807–9, II, p. 316; S. J. Gunn, 'The Courtiers of Henry VII', in J. Guy, ed., *The Tudor Monarchy* (1997), p. 165.
4. *L and P of Henry VIII*, I, 231.
5. C. J. Harrison, 'The petition of Edmund Dudley', *English Historical Review*, 87 (1972), pp. 82ff.
6. E. Hall, *The Triumphant Reign of King Henry VIII*, ed. C. Whibley (1904), I, 1.
7. Ibid.
8. S. J. Gunn, op cit., p. 170.
9. Ibid., p. 2.
10. *L and P of Henry VIII*, I, pt 2, pp. 1548–9.

11. Harrison, op. cit., p. 86.
12. Ibid., p. 87.
13. J. E. B. Mayor, ed., *English Works of John Fisher*, Earl English Text Society, extra series XXVII (1886), pt 1, p. 270.
14. Lord Herbert, *History of Henry VIII* (1719), I, p. 6.
15. Dudley, op. cit., p. 21.
16. Ibid., p. 39.
17. Ibid., p. 37.
18. Ibid., p. 25.
19. Ibid., p. 65.
20. Ibid., p. 24.
21. Ibid., p. 31.
22. Hall, *The Triumphant Life . . .*, I, p. 19.
23. J. Guy, *Tudor England* (Oxford, 1988), p. 81.

Chapter 4 – **Connections**

1. See Muriel St Clair Byrne, ed., *The Lisle Letters* (Chicago, 1981),I, p. 139. There can be no complete certainty about the early years of Arthur Platagenet. Edward IV sired more than one bastard son. Miss Byrne has looked into all the evidence and makes a good case for identifying him with a son born to Elizabeth Lucy, the king's mistress in the 1460s.
2. Ibid., p. 149.
3. D. M. Loades, ed., *The Papers of George Wyatt*, Camden Society 4th series, V (1968), p. 5.
4. *Calendar of State Papers,* Spanish (hereafter '*Cal. S.P. Span*'), II. p. 71.
5. E. Hall, *The Triumphant Reign of King Henry VIII*, 1908, I, p. 43.
6. *L and P of Henry VIII*, I, 3903.
7. Byrne, ed., *The Lisle Letters* (Chicago, 1981), II, p. 571.
8. J. G. Russell, *The Field of Cloth of Gold* (1969), p. 2.

Chapter 5 – **Crises and Calculations**

1. Simon Fish, *A Supplication for the Beggars*, see G. R. Elton, *The Tudor Constitution*, (Cambridge, 1960), pp. 322–3.
2. A. A. Dollason, *History of the Owners of Dudley Castle* (Dudley, n.d.), pp. 46–7.

3. *L and P of Henry VIII*, X, 1045.

4. Ibid., XIII, App. 6.

5. Ibid., V, 1834.

6. R. Morison, *A Discourse . . . Shewing the Godly and Vertuous Resolution . . .*, in J. G. Nichols, ed., *Literary Remains of Edward VI* (1857), I, ccxxiv.

7. *L and P of Henry VIII*, VII, 309.

8. Ibid., IX, 886, VIII, 882.

9. Ibid., IX, App. 6.

10. G. R. Elton, *The Tudor Constitution* (Cambridge, 1960), p. 62.

11. Preamble to the Dissolution Act, 1536, Cf. Elton, op. cit., p. 374.

12. We know the date but the year is a surmise. It was certainly either 1532 or 1533. In later years it seems to have been assumed that Robert and Princiess Elizabeth were of an age and there is not good reason to doubt this.

13. P. F. Tytler, *England Under the Reigns of Edward VI and Mary* (1839), II, p. 155.

14. The National Archives, *S.P. 15/4*, No. 3.

15. *L and P of Henry VIII*, XIII, I, 337.

16. HMSC, *Report on MSS Magdalene College, Cambridge*, II, no. 729, pp. 1–2.

17. *L and P of Henry VIII*, X, 837.

Chapter 6 – **The Pendulum and the Pit**

1. *L and P of Henry VIII*, XI, 854.

2. *Cal. S.P. Span*, I, pp. 463–4.

3. *L and P of Henry VIII*, VIII, I, 995.

4. Ibid., XI, 816.

5. Ibid., XI, 909.

6. R. B. Merriman, *Life and Letters of Thomas Cromwell*, II, p. 95.

7. Ibid., p. 125.

8. *L and P of Henry VIII*, XIV, I, 1271.

9. Ibid., XIV, I, 1267.

10. R. Rex, 'The friars in the English Reformation', in P. Marshall and A. Ryrie, eds., *The Beginnings of English Protestantism* (Cambridge, 2002), p. 41.

11. R. B. Merriman, op. cit., I, p. 279.

12. W. Tyndale, *The Obedience of a Christian Man*, ed. R. Lovett (1888), pp. 91–2.

13. T. Hatcher, *G. Haddoni Legum Doctoris, S. Reginae Elizabethae a supplicum libells* . . . (1567), p. 419.
14. J. Foxe, *Actes and Monuments*, ed. J. Townsend and S. R. Cattley (1838), V, p. 260.
15. H. Brakspear, 'Dudley Castle', *Archaeological Journal*, LXXXI, p. 12.

Chapter 7 – King's Knight and God's Knight

1. *L and P of Henry VIII*, XIV, ii, 572.
2. E. Hall, *The Triumphant Reign of King Henry VIII*, ed. C. Whibley (1904), p. 835.
3. R. B. Merriman, *Life and Letters of Thomas Cromwell*, II, p. 223.
4. Muriel St Clair Byrne, ed., *The Lisle Letters* (Chicago, 1981), V, 1435.
5. J. Stow, *Survey of London* (Oxford, 1908), II, pp. 100–101.
6. *L and P of Henry VIII*, XVI, 1138.
7. Ibid., XVI, 101.
8. J. Foxe, *Actes and Monuments,* ed. J. Townsend and S. R. Cattley, V, pp. 515–6.
9. C. Sturge, 'Life and Times of John Dudley, Earl of Warwick and Duke of Northumberland', University of London Ph.D. thesis (1927), p. 23.
10. *Letters and Papers of Henry VIII*, XVII, 1221.

Chapter 8 – Tempestuous Seas

1. *Hamilton Papers*, ed. J. Bain (1890–92), I, pp. 286–7.
2. *State Papers of King Henry VIII* (1830–52), I, pt 2, cxciii.
3. E. Hall, *The Triumphant Reign of King Henry VIII*, ed. C. Whibley (1904), p. 346.
4. Ibid.
5. Ibid, II, p. 347.
6. *State Papers*, V, cccxciii.
7. *L and P of Henry VIII*, XIX, ii, 338.
8. *Cal S.P. Span.*, XXI, i, 289.
9. *Chronicle of the Grey Friars of London*, ed. J. G. Nichols, Camden Society, 1st series, LIII, 1852, p. 55.
10. J. Bale, *Select Works*, ed. H. Christmas, Parker Society (1949), pp. 196–7.

11. J. Foxe, *Actes and Monuments*, ed. J. Townsend and S. R. Cattley (1838) V, p. 565.
12. Hall, op. cit., II, p. 359.
13. *Cal S.P. Span.*, VIII, p. 557.

Chapter 9 – Feast in the Morning

1. S. Alford, *Kingship and Politics in the Reign of Edward VI* (Cambridge, 2002), p. 174.
2. J. Foxe, *Actes and Monuments*, ed. J. Townsend and S. R. Cattley (1938), V, pp. 691–2.
3. Ibid., VI, pp. 164–5.
4. Peter Heylyn, *A Table or Catalogue of All the Dukes* . . . (1680), p. 511.
5. Calendar of State Papers Domestic (hereafter 'Cal. S.P. Dom.') *Edward VI*, 28.
6. *Cal. S.P. Span. IX*, pp. 340–41.
7. Alford, op. cit., p. 99.
8. *Cal. S.P. Dom. Edward VI*, 182, 188.
9. Ibid., 109, 128, 113.
10. Ibid., 111.
11. Ibid., 113.
12. Ibid., 123.
13. Ibid., 217.
14. Hugh Latimer, 'Sermon on the Plough,' in *Sermons by Hugh Latimer*, Parker Society (Cambridge, 1845), pp. 64–5.
15. S. Brigden, *New Worlds, Lost Worlds* (2000), p. 184.
16. See M. Aston, *England's Iconoclasts* (Oxford, 1988), p. 256.
17. D. MacCulloch, *Tudor Church Militant* (1999), p. 126.
18. J. Strype, *Ecclesiastical Memorials* . . . (1816), II, ii, pp. 362–4.
19. Ibid., II, i, p. 151.
20. *Works of Martin Luther* (Weimar, 1883), IV, p. 280.
21. *Cal. S.P. Dom. Edward VI*, 133.
22. British Library Cotton MSS, Titus F.3, ff277–9v; Strype, op. cit., II, ii, 429–37.
23. Latimer, op cit., p. 162.
24. *Dictionary of National Biography (DNB)*.
25. The Seymour papers at Longleat, Wiltshire, II.
26. *Cal. S.P. Dom. Edward VI*, 333.
27. See J. Cornwall, *The Revolt of the Peasantry* (1977), p. 147.

28. *Cal. S.P. Dom. Edward VI*, 335.

29. British Library Harleian MSS 1576, p. 8208.

30. A. Neville, *De Furoribus Norfolcensium Ketto Duce* . . ., trans. A. Wood (1615), pp. 18–19. Neville wrote his account of the rebellion in 1575, when Warwick's son Robert Dudley was the leading figure at court, and presented his father in a favourable light. However, the words attributed to Warwick here are very much in character and there seems no reason to doubt that Neville had them from an eye witness, perhaps Robert Dudley himself.

31. G. R. Elton, *Studies in Tudor and Stuart Politics and Government* (Cambridge, 1974), p. 237.

32. Foxe, op. cit., VI, p. 291.

33. See D. MacCulloch, op. cit., pp. 45–7.

34. *Cal. S.P. Dom. Edward VI*, 378, 379, 356, 373, 387.

35. Ibid., 368.

36. Ibid., 377.

37. Ibid., 390.

38. Ibid., 396.

39. J. Stow, *Annales, or a General Chronicle of England* (1631), p. 598.

40. 'Quelques particularitez d'Angleterre du temps du roi Edouard . . .' Bibliothèque Nationale de France, MS Ancien Saint-German Français, 1588, folios 212–3.

41. *Cal. S.P. Span.*, IX, 462–3.

42. See D. MacCulloch, *Thomas Cranmer* (1996), pp. 448–9.

43. *Cal. S.P. Span.*, IX, 477.

44. British Library Additional, MS 48126, fol. 15a; D. E. Hoak, *The King's Council in the Reign of Edward VI* (Cambridge, 1976), p. 255.

45. BL, Add. MS 48126, fol. 16a; Hoak, op. cit., p. 256.

Chapter 10 – **The Cares that Wait upon a Crown**

1. *Zurich Letters*, Parker Society (1842–5), III, pp. 81–2.

2. D. E. Hoak, *The King's Council in the Reign of Edward VI* (Cambridge, 1976) pp. 267–8.

3. 'Quelques particularitez d'Angleterre du temps du roi Edouard . . .', Bibliothèque Nationale de France, MS Ancien Saint-Germain Français, 1588, folios 214b–215b.

4. *Cal. S.P. Dom. Edward VI*, 781.

5. Ibid., 555.

6. J. K. Jordan, ed., *The Chronicle and Political Papers of King Edward VI* (Ithaca, 1966), p. 85.
7. *Cal. S.P. Dom. Edward VI*, 789.
8. Ibid., 465, 466.
9. Ibid., 442.
10. See D. Loades, *John Dudley*, p. 177.
11. *Cal. S.P. Dom. Edward VI*, 779.
12. Ibid., 465, 630, 732, 789.
13. J. Hayward, *Life and Raigne of King Edward VI*, ed. B. L. Beer (Kent, Ohio, 1993), pp. 122–3. Hayward saw plots and conspiracies around every corner and he certainly invented some of the speeches that he put in the mouths of historical characters but he did make use of contemporary documents some of which are now lost.
14. *Cal. S.P. Dom. Edward VI*, 801, 802.
15. See C. S. Knighton, 'The principal secretaries in the reign of Edward VI', in C. Cross, D. Loades and J. J. Scarisbrick, *Law and Government under the Tudors* (Cambridge, 1988), p. 172.
16. *Cal. S.P. Dom., Edward VI*, 711, 722.
17. Ibid., 750.
18. Ibid., 800.
19. D. Hoak, 'Rehabilitating the Duke of Northumberland', in J. Loach and J. Tittler, eds., *The Mid-Tudor Polity, c1540–1560* (1980), p. 51.
20. See D. Hoak, *The King's Council*, p. 257.
21. See D. MacCulloch, *Thomas Cranmer*, p. 469.
22. 1552 *Book of Common Prayer*, Preface 'Of Ceremonies'.

Chapter 11 – **Desperate Measures**

1. D. MacCulloch, *Thomas Cranmer*, (Yale, 1996), p. 496.
2. J. Foxe, *Actes and Monuments*, ed. J. Townsend and S. R. Cattley (1838), VI, p. 292.
3. *Cal. S.P. Dom. Edward VI*, 749.
4. Ibid., 747.
5. Ibid., 762.
6. Ibid., 799.
7. Wyndham's achievements are narrated in R. Hakluyt, *The Principal Navigations, Voyages and Discoveries of the English Nation* (1589), I, pp. 85ff.
8. Ibid., I, p. 245.
9. *Cal. S.P. Dom. Edward VI*, 789.

10. Ibid., 773.

11. Petyt MSS, Inner Temple, xlvii, f. 316.

12. J. G. Nichols, ed., *The Chronicle of Queen Jane and of Two Years of Queen Mary*, Camden Society, old series., xlviii (1850), p. 272.

13. *Cal. S.P. Dom. Edward VI*, 809.

14. J. G. Nichols, ed., *Literary Remains of Edward VI* (1857), I, ccliv.

15. *Cal. S.P. Span., XI*, 189.

16. J. G. Nichols, ed., *Greyfriars' Chronicle*, Camden Society, old series, XLXIV, p. 83.

17. British Library Harleian MSS, 787, fol. 61v.

Chapter 12 – **De Profundis**

1. R. Brooke, *Catalogue of Nobility* (1619), p. 150.

2. *Le Report de un Judgement done en Banke*, 1578.

3. J. G. Nichols, ed., op. cit., p. 39.

4. British Library Harleian MSS, 194.

5. J. G. Nichols, ed., op. cit., pp. 56–7.

6. W. Camden, *The History of the Most Renowned and Victorious Princess Elizabeth*, ed. W. T. MacCaffrey (Chicago, 1970), p. 53.

7. A. Collins, ed., *Letters and Memorials of State* (1746), I, p. 35.

8. Longleat, *Dudley papers*, III, f. 66.

9. This was the sum repaid to Forster in 1558 and may have included interest. Society of Antiquaries MS 139, folios 129, 131: Lyttelton MSS (Birmingham Reference Library), 351613; Public Record Office: 054/546, m.16 con.

10. Holinshed, *Chronicle* (1557).

11. Longleat, Dudley papers, III, f. 67.

12. Harleian MS 4712. Printed in G. Adlard, *Amye Robsart and the Earl of Leycester*, pp. 16–17.

13. Quoted by F. Chamberlin in *Elizabeth and Leycester* (1939), App. IX, pp. 92–3.

14. *La Vie d'Elizabeth, reine d'Angleterre traduite de l'Italien* (1696), pp. 444–5.

15. *Cal. S.P. For. Elizabeth, I*, 3.

Chapter 13 – **The Gypsy**

1. H. Ellis, ed., *Original Letters, Illustrative of English History* (1824–6), 1st series, p. 101.
2. See S. Alford, *The Early Elizabethan Polity: William Cecil and the British Succession Crisis, 1558–1569* (Cambridge, 1998), p. 34.
3. L. S. Marcus, J. Mueller and M. B. Rose, eds., *Elizabeth I Collected Works* (Chicago, 2000), pp. 54–5.
4. *Cal. S.P. Span.*, I, 27.
5. *Cal. S.P. Ven*, VII, 71.
6. Longleat, Dudley papers., III, f.31. The total value is given as £5,070.
7. Ibid., I, f.172.
8. Ibid., I, f.14.
9. *Cal. S.P. Dom. Elizabeth, Addenda*, XXVI, 9.
10. Longleat, Dudley papers, XIII.
11. Ibid., V, XI.
12. H. Nicolas, *Memoirs of the Life and Times of Sir Christopher Hatton* . . . (1847), pp. 25–61.
13. British Library Lansdowne MS 94, fol. 29.
14. *Cal. S.P. Span.*, I, 57.
15. *Cal. S.P. Ven.*, VII, 10.
16. See G. Adlard, *Amye Robsart and the Earl of Leycester*, pp. 16ff: N. Fourdrinier, 'Amy Robsart' (MS MC5/29 in Norfolk Record Office), pp. 143ff; J. E. Jackson, 'Amye Robsart', in *Wiltshire Archaeol. Magazine*, XVII, pp. 61ff.
17. Longleat, Dudley papers, XIV, XV, account books of Dudley's stewards, William Chaucy and Richard Elles, *passim*.
18. British Library Harleian MSS 4712.
19. *Cal. S.P. Ven.*, VII, 69.
20. Longleat Dudley papers, IV, f.7.
21. *Cal. S.P. For. Elizabeth*, II, 387.
22. *Cal. S.P. Span.*, I, pp. 113–4.
23. J. Nicholas, ed., *Diary of Henry Machyn* (1848), pp. 238–41.
24. British Library Stow MSS, f.180b, quoted by Conyers Read, p. 199.

Chapter 14 – **Death and Transfiguration**

1. N. Fourdrinier, *Amy Robsart the wife of Lord Robert Dudley the favourite of Queen Elizabeth I. Her life and ancestry, and the true cause of her tragic death,* Norfolk Record Office, MC5/29, p. 166.
2. *Cal. S.P. Span.*, I, pp. 174–5.
3. See G. Adlard, *Amye Robsart and the Earl of Leycester* (1870), p. 32.
4. *Cal. S.P. Span.*, I, 175.
5. Ibid.
6. Ibid.
7. Ibid., 36–7.
8. *Hardwicke Papers* (1775), I, p. 123.
9. P. Yorke, ed., *Miscellaneous State Papers* (1778), I, p. 167.
10. *The Itinerary of John Leland*, ed. L. Toulmin Smith (1964), II, p. 109.
11. R. Laneham, 'A Letter Wherein Part of the Entertainment unto the Queen's Majesty at Killingworth Castle . . . is signified . . .' (1575), reprinted in G. Adlard, (op. cit.), p. 124.
12. Longleat, Dudley papers., IV, f.13.
13. J. E. Neale, *Elizabeth I and Her Parliaments, 1559–1581* (1953), p. 109.
14. Ibid., p. 127.

Chapter 15 – **Politics, Puritanism and Patronage**

1. *Cal. S.P. Span.*, I, 591–2.
2. See Conyers Read, *Mr Secretary Cecil and Queen Elizabeth* (1955), p. 362.
3. *Cal. S.P. Span.*, I, 415.
4. See P. Collinson, *The Elizabeth Puritan Movement* (1967), p. 53 and note.
5. L. S. Marcus, J. Mueller and M. B. Rose, eds., *Elizabeth I, Collected Works* (Chicago, 2000), pp. 178–9.
6. P. Collinson, ed., *Letters of Thomas Wood, Puritan, 1566–1577* (1960), p. 15.
7. *Cal. S.P. Span.*, I, 415.
8. Conyers Read, 'A letter from Robert, Earl of Leicester to a lady', *Huntingdon Library Quarterly* (April 1936), p. 25.

9. P. Collinson, ed., op. cit., p. 12.
10. *Cal. S.P. Dom. Addenda*, XIII, 73.

Chapter 16 – Love's Labours Lost

1. The National Archives, State Papers, 63/26/14.
2. British Library, Harleian MS, 6991, fol. 27.
3. *Cal. S.P. Dom.*, CXXV, 73; British Library, Lansdowne MS, 45, 34.
4. E. Lodge, *Illustrations of British History, Biography and Manners* . . . (1838), II, p. 17.
5. Conyers Read, 'A letter from Robert, Earl of Leicester to a lady', *Huntingdon Library Quarterly* (April 1936), p. 24.
6. A. Collins, ed., *Letters and Memorials of State* (1746), I, p. 48.
7. R. Laneham, *A Letter, wherein is signified* . . . (1821), p. 138.
8. *Cal. S.P. Span.*, I, 131.
9. Longleat, Dudley papers, II, f.190.
10. See I. Mahoney, *Madame Catherine* (1975), p. 172.
11. The National Archives, *State Papers*, XII/125/73.
12. *Cal. S.P. Span.*, I, 486.
13. D. Wilson, *The World Encompassed* (1977), p. 88.
14. See J. E. Neale, *Queen Elizabeth* (1934), p. 238.
15. J. B. M. C. K. de Lettenhove, *Relations Politiques des Pays Bas et de l'Angleterre* (1882–1900), X, p. 678.
16. A. Labanoff, *Lettres . . . de Marie Stuart* (1844), V, p. 94.
17. *Cal. S.P. Span.*, I, 592.
18. See Mahoney, op. cit., p. 262.
19. Ibid., p. 264.
20. *Cal. S.P. Span.*, II, 465.
21. de Lettenhove, op. cit., IX, p. 486.
22. R. C. Strong and J. A. Van Dorsten, *Leicester's Triumph* (1964), p. 13.
23. *Cal. S.P. Dom.*, XXXIX, 41.
24. G. M. Baker and R. W. Kenny, *The Papers of Nathaniel Bacon* (Norwich, 1979–83), II, p. 296.

Chapter 17 – Fair Means and Foul

1. F. J. Burgoyne, ed., *History of Queen Elizabeth, Amy Robsart and the Earl of Leicester* (1904), p. 49.
2. Letter under the royal sign manual to the Lord Mayor of London, see G. Adlard, *Amye Robsart*, pp. 56–7.

3. See A. G. Lee, *The Son of Leicester* (1964), p. 34.
4. H. Nicolas, *Memoirs of . . . Christopher Hatton* (1847), pp. 382–3.
5. *Cal. S.P. Dom.*, CLXXII, 37.
6. *DNB*.
7. See Conyers Read, *Lord Burghley and Queen Elizabeth* (1960), p. 295.
8. H. Nicolas, op. cit., pp. 348–9.
9. J. Bruce, ed., *Correspondence of Robert Dudley Earl of Leycester . . .*, Camden Society, series I, no. 27 (1844), p. 4.
10. Ibid., pp. 7–8.
11. Ibid., pp. 23–4.
12. Ibid., p. 112.
13. Ibid., p. 110.
14. Ibid., p. 151.
15. Ibid., pp. 367, 312, 426, 378, 394, 312.
16. Ibid., pp. 478–80.
17. Ibid., p. 446.
18. Ibid., p. 453.
19. *Leland's Itinerary*, I, p. 5.
20. J. Bruce, ed., op. cit., pp. 431–2.
21. See Conyers Read, op. cit., p. 391.
22. See G. Mattingley, *Defeat of the Spanish Armada* (1959), p. 60.
23. British Library, Cotton MSS, Galba D, I, 230.
24. Ibid., CCXIII, 38.
25. L. S. Marcus, J. Mueller and M. B. Rose, eds., *Elizabeth I Collected Works* (Chicago, 2000), p. 326.
26. Ibid., II, f.249.
27. Ibid., II, f.257.
28. The National Archives, SPD 12/215/65.

Chapter 18 – **Tudors and Dudleys**

1. British Library Cotton MSS, Caligula, D.I., f.333.
2. L. S. Marcus, J. Mueller, and M. B. Rose, eds., *Elizabeth I Collected Works* (Chicago, 2000), p. 329.
3. R. Hakluyt, *The Principal Navigations, Voyages and Discoveries of the English Nation . . .* (1899 ed.), III, p. 580f.
4. Ibid., III, p. 593.
5. J. Guy, *Tudor England*, p. 351.
6. G. Temple Leader, *Roberto Dudley, Duca di Nortumbria* (Florence

1896), pp. 202–3.

7. G. Temple Leader, op. cit., p. 220.

8. D. Starkey, *Elizabeth* (2000), p. 92.

9. Conyers Read, *Lord Burghley and Queen Elizabeth* (1960), p. 436.

10. C. Wilson, *Queen Elizabeth and the Revolt of the Netherlands* (1970), p. 102.

Bibliography

The place of publication is London unless otherwise specified

Manuscript and Printed Sources

Acts of the Privy Council of England, ed. J. R. Dasent (1890–1907)

Allen, P. S. and H. M. (eds.), *The Letters of Richard Fox, 1486–1527* (Oxford, 1928)

Ascham, R., *The Schoolmaster*, ed. J. E. B. Mayer (1863)

Aylmer, J., *A Harbour for Faithful and True Subjects* (1559)

Bacon, Sir Francis, *History of the Reign of Henry VII* in R. Lockyer (ed.) *Works* (1971)

Bain, J. (ed.), *Hamilton Papers: Letters and Papers Illustrating the Political Relations of England and Scotland in the Sixteenth Century* (Edinburgh, 1890)

Barthlet, J., *The Pedigree of Heretics . . .* (1566)

Ben, J. T. (ed.), *Early Voyages and Travels in the Levant*, Hakluyt Society, 1st series LXXXVII, (1838)

Bergenroth, G. A. and de Gayangos, P. (eds.), *Calendar of State Papers, Spanish* (1862–6)

Brodie, D. M., ed., Edmund Dudley, *The Tree of Commonwealth* (Cambridge, 1948)

Brooke, R., *Catalougue of Nobility* (1619)

Brown, R., Bentinck, C. and Brown, H. (eds.), *Calendar of State Papers, Venetian* (1864–98)

Bruce, J., (ed.), *Correspondence of Robert Dudley, Earl of Leicester, during his Government of the Low Countries . . . 1585–6*, Camden Society (1844)

Burgman, H., *Correspondentie van Robert Dudley, Graaf van Leycester*, 3 vols (1931)

Burgoyne, F. J., (ed.), *History of Queen Elizabeth, Amy Robsart and the Earl of Leicester* (1904)

Byrne, M. St. C. (ed.), *The Lisle Letters* (Chicago, 1980)

Calendar of Patent Rolls Elizabeth I, V, 1569–1572 (1966)

Calendar of State Papers, Domestic, Edward VI, Mary, Elizabeth I and James I (ed. R. Lemon and E. Green, 1856–1872)

Calendar of State Papers, Domestic, Edward VI, 1547–1553 (ed. C. S. Knighton, 1992)

Calendar of State Papers, Foreign, Elizabeth I (various editors, 1863–1950)

Calendar of State Papers relating to Scotland, 1509–1589, I (ed. M. J. Thorpe, 1858)

Camden, W., *The History of the Most Renowned . . . Princess Elizabeth* (ed. W. T. MacCaffrey, 1970)

Campion, E., *History of Ireland* (1571)

Caraman, P., *An Autobiogaphy from the Jesuit Underground* (1955)

Carr, C. T., (ed), *Select Charters of Trading Companies 1530–1707*, Seldon Society, XXVIII, (1913)

Cavendish, G., *The Life and Death of Cardinal Wolsey* in R. S. Sylvester and D. P. Harding (eds.), *Two Early Tudor Lives* (New Haven, 1962)

Clowes, W., *A Proved Practice for all Young Chirurgians* (1565)

Collins, A., (ed.), *Letters and Memorials of State*, 2 vols (1746)

Collins, A., (ed.), *Memorials of the Actions of the Sidneys* (1746)

Collinson, P., (ed.), *Letters of Thomas Wood, Puritan, 1566–1577* (1962)

Corrie, G. E. (ed.), *Sermons and Remains of Hugh Latimer . . .* Parker Society (Cambridge, 1844, 1845)

Corte, C., *Il Cavalerizzo*, trs. T. Bedingfield (1584)

Crowley, R., *Select Works*, Early English Text Society edition (1872)

Cunningham, W., *The Cosmographical Glass Containing the Pleasant Principles of Cosmography, Geography, Hydrography and Navigation* (1559)

De Lisle and Dudley Papers, Kent County Archive Office, Maidstone

Dee, L., *General and Rare Memorials Pertaining to the Perfect Art of Navigation* (1577)

Digges, T., *A Brief Report of the Proceedings of the Earl of Leicester for the Relief of Sluys . . .* (1590)

Digges, T., *An Arithmetical Military Treatise Named Stratioticos* (1579)

Diggs, T., *Humble Motives for Association to Maintain Religion Established* (1601)

Digges, D., ed., *The Complete Ambassador* (1655)

Dowling, M. (ed.), 'William Latymer's chronickille of Anne Bulleyne', *Camden Miscellany 30*, Camden Society, 4th series, XXXIX (1990), 23–66

Dudley Papers, Longleat, Wiltshire

Ellis, H. (ed.), *Original Letters, illustrative of English history* (1824–46)

Elton, G. R. (ed.), *The Tudor Constitution, Documents and Commentary* (Cambridge, 1960)

Fills, R., *Laws and Statues of Geneva* (1561)

Fish, S., *A Supplication for the Beggars*, eds. F. J. Furnivall and J. M. Cowper, Early English Text Society, extra. Ser. XIII (1871)

Florio, J., *Second Fruits* (1591)

Forbes, P. (ed.), *A Full View of the Public Transactions in the Reign of Queen Elizabeth* (1740–41)

Forster, R., *Ephemerides Meteorographicae* (1575)

Fortescue, J., *The Governance of England*, ed. C. Plummer (Oxford, 1885)

Foxe, J., *Acts and Monuments*, eds. G. Towsend and S. R. Cattley, (1939)

Frere, W. H. and Kennedy, W. M., *Visitation Articles and Injunction* (1910)

Fuller, T., *History of the Worthies of England* (1811 ed.)

Fulman, W., (ed.), *The Crowland Chronicle* (1684)

Gairder, J. (ed.), *Past Letters, AD 1422–1509* (1904)

Gale, T., *Certain Works of Chirurgery* (1563)

Gascoigne, G., *A Hundred Sundry Flowers Bound up in One Small Posy* (1572)

Gascoigne, G., *The Princely Pleasures at the Court of Kenilworth* (1575)

Gascoigne, G., *A Discourse of a New Passage to Cathay* (1576)

Gascoigne, G., *The Spoil of Antwerp* (1576)

Gentili, A., (ed.) *The Whole Works of Roger Ascham* (1864)

Golding, A., *A Confutation of the Pope's Bull . . . Against Elizabeth . . .* (1572)

Grafton, R., *Abridgement of the Chronicles of England* (1563)

Haddon, W., *Cantabrigiensis: sive Exhortatis ad Literas* (1552)

Hakluyt, R., *The Principal Navigations, Voyages and Discoveries of the English Nation . . .* (1904 ed.)

Hall, E., *The union of the two noble and illustre famelies of Lancastre and Yorke*, ed. H. Ellis (1809)

Hardyng, J. and Grafton, R., *Chronicle of John Hardyng . . .*, ed. H. Ellis (1812)

Harington, J., *A Brief View of the State of the Church of England* (1653)

Harington, J., *A New Discourse on a State Subject called the Metamorphosis of Ajax* (1596)

Harison, G. B., *Letters of Queen Elizabeth* (1968)

Hatcher, T., *G. Haddoni Legum Doctoris, S. Reginae Elizabethae a Supplicum Libellis Lucubrationes Passim Collectae* (1567)

Hay, D., ed., 'The Anglica Historia of Polydore Vergil' in Camden Society, 3rd series, LXXIV (1950)

Haynes, S. and Murdin, W. (eds.), *Collections of State Papers . . . Left by William Cecil, Lord Burghley* (1740–1759)

Herbert, E., Lord Cherbury, *The Life and Rayne of Henry VIII* (1872)

Historical Manuscripts Commission:
   Calendar of de Lisle and Dudley MSS
   Calendar of Hatfield MSS
   Calendar of Pepys MSS in Magdalene College Cambridge

Holinshed, R., *Chronicles of England, Scotland and Ireland*, ed. H. Ellis, 6 vols. (1807–8)

Hughes, P. L. and Larkin, J. F. eds., *Tudor Royal Proclamations* (New Haven, 1964, 1969)

Hunnis, W., *A Hive of Honey* (1578)

Inderwick, F. A. (ed.), *Calendar of the Inner Temple Records* (1896–1901)

Jordan, W. K. (ed.), *The Chronicle and Political Papers of Edward VI* (1966)

Knox, J., Works, ed., D. Laing (1846–64)

Labanoff, A., *Letters: Instructions et Memoires de Marie Stuart* (1844)

Laneham, R., *A Letter, wherein part of the entertainment unto the Queen's Majesty at Kenilworth Castle in Warwickshire in this summer's progress – 1575 – is signified*

Le Report de un Judgement done en Banke du Roi (1571)

Legh, G., *Accedens of Armoury* (1562)

Letters and Papers, Foreign and Domestic, of the Reign of Henry VIII, ed. J. Gairdner (1861–3)

Letters and Papers, Foreign and Domestic, of the Reign of Henry VIII Preserved in the Public Record Office, The British Museum and Elsewhere, eds. J. S. Brewer, J. Gairdner and R. H. Brodie (1862–1910)

Letters and State Papers relating to English Affairs, preserved principally in the Archives of Simancas, ed. M. A. S. Hume (1892–1899)

MacCulloch, D., ed., 'The *Vita Mariae Angliae Reginae* of Robert Wingfield of Brantham', in Camden Miscellany, XXVIII, 4th series, 1984, p. 181ff

Machiavelli, N., *The Prince*, trs. W. K. Marriott (1992)

Mancini, D., *The Usurpation of Richard III*, ed. C. A. J. Armstrong (1969)

Marcus, L. S., Mueller, J. and Rose, M. B., *Elizabeth I, Collected Works* (Chicago, 2000)

Merriman, R. B., *The Life and Letters of Thomas Cromwell* (Oxford, 1902)

Montgomery, J., *On the Maintenance of the Navy* (1570)

Neville, A., *De Furoribus Norfolciensium Ketto Duce*, trs. R. Wood (1615)

Nicholas, H., ed., *Memoirs of the Life and Times of Sir Christopher Hatton* (1847)

Nichols, J. G., (ed.), *Chronicle of Queen Jane and of Two Years of Queen Mary*, Camden Society, Old series XLVIII (1850)

Nichols, J. G., (ed.), *The Diary of Henry Machyn 1550–1563*, Camden Society, Old series XLVIII (1848)

Nichols, J. G., (ed.), *Greyfriars' Chronicle*, Camden Society, Old series XLXIV (1852)

Nichols, J. G., (ed.), *Literary Remains of Edward VI*, 1857

Nichols, J. G., (ed.), *Narratives of the Reformation*, Camden Society, Old series LXXVII (1859)

Osma P. d', *Report on the Royal Studs* (1576)

Parker, D. H., ed., Jerome Barlowe and William Roye, *Rede Me and Be Nott Wrothe* (Toronto, 1992)

Parsons, R., *A Conference About the Next Succession to the Crown of England* (1594)

Perlin, E., *Description d'Angleterre et d'Ecosse* (1558)

Read, C., 'A Letter from Robert, Earl of Leicester, to a Lady', *Huntington Library Quarterly* (April, 1936)

Robinson, H., (ed.), *Original Letters Relative to the English Reformation* (Parker Society, 1846–7)

Robinson, H., (ed.), *Zurich Letters*, 2nd series (Parker Society, 1845)

Rodriguez-Salgado, M. J., and Adam S., 'The Count of Feria's Dispatch to Philip II of 14 November, 1558', in *Camden Miscellany*, XXVIII, 4th series (1984), p. 302ff

Rosso, G. V., *Historia delle cose occorse nel regno d'Inghilterra . . .* (1558)

'R.S.', *The Phoenix Nest* (1593)

Starkey, Thomas, *A Dialogue Between Pole and Lupset*, ed. T. F. Mayer, Camden Society, 4th series, XXXVII (1989)

State Papers and Manuscripts Existing in the Archives and Collections of Milan, I, 1385–1618, ed. A. B. Hinds (1913)

State Papers and Manuscripts relating to English Affairs, existing in the Archives and Collections of Venice . . ., VII, VIII, 1558–1591 (1890–95) (referred to in the Notes as Cal.S.P.Ven.)

State Papers published under the authority of His Majesty's Commission, King Henry VIII (11 vols., 1830–52)

Stow, J., *Annales, or, a general chronicle of England*, ed. E. Howes (1631)

Stow, J., *A Survey of London*, ed. C. L. Kingsford (Oxford, 1908)

Stow, J., *The Chronicles of England, from Brute unto this present year of Christ* (1580)

Strype, J., *Annals of the Reformation* (1824)

Strype, J., *Memorials . . . of Thomas Cranmer* (1853)

'T.D.', *A Brief Report of the Military Services done in the Low Counries by the Earl of Leicester, Written by one that served in a Good Place there* (1587)

The Complete Works of St Thomas More (New Haven, 1963–)

Tomkyns, J., *A Sermon Preached the 26th Day of May 1584*

Tottel, R., *The Passage of Our Most Dread Sovereign Lady Queen Elizabeth Through the City of London to Westminster . . .* (1960 ed.)

Tyndale, W., *The Obedience of a Christian Man*, ed. R. Lovett (1888)

Veron, J., *Treatise on Free Will* (1562)

Vives, J. L., *On Education*, trs. F. Watson (1913)

Warner, G. F. (ed.), *The Voyage of Robert Dudley . . . to the West Indies, 1594–5*, Hakluyt, Society, 2nd series, III (1899)

Whibley, C., *The Triumphant Reign of Henry VIII* (an edition of Edmund Hall's *Chronicle*), (1904)

Wiburn, P., *A Check or Reproof of Mr Howlet's Untimely Screeching* (1581)

Wilson, T., *A Discourse Upon Usury* (1572)

Wilson, T., *Arte of Rhetorike* (1553)

Wriothesley, C., *A Chronicle of England During the Reigns of the Tudors*, ed. W. D. Hamilton, Camden Society, new series, XI, XX (1875–7)

Yorke, P. (ed.), *Miscellaneous State Papers* (1778)

Secondary Works

Adams, S. L., 'The Gentry of North Wales and the Earl of Leicester's Expedition to the Netherlands', *Welsh Historical Review*, VII (1974–5)

'The Accession of Queen Elizabeth', *History Today* (May, 1953)

Adams, S., 'The Dudley clientele, 1553–1563' in G. W. Bernard (ed.), *The Tudor Nobility* (Manchester, 1992)

Adlard, G., *Amye Robsart and the Earl of Leycester . . .* (1870)

Adlard, G., *The Sutton Dudleys of England and the Dudleys of Massachusetts in New England* (1862)

Aird, I., 'The Death of Amy Robsart', *English Historical Review*, LXXI

Alford, S., *The Early Elzabethan Polity: William Cecil and the British Succession Crisis, 1558–1569* (Cambridge, 1998)

Alford, S., *Kingship and Politics in the Reign of Edward VI* (Cambridge, 2002)

Allen, J. W., *A History of Political Thought in the Sixteenth Century* (1960 ed.)

Alvarez, M. F., *Charles V – Elected Emperor and Hereditary Ruler*, trs. J. A. Lalaguna (1975)

Anglos, S., *Spectacle, Pageantry and Early Tudor Policy* (Oxford, 1969)

Anglo, S., *The Great Tournament Roll of Westminster* (1968)

Anglo, S., 'Ill of the dead: The posthumous reputation of Henry VII', *Renaissance Studies*, I (1987)

Aston, M., *The King's Bedpost, Reformation and Iconogaphy in a Tudor Group Portrait* (Cambridge, 1993)

Aston, M., *England's Iconoclasts: Laws Against Images* (Oxford, 1988)

Aston, M., *The Queen's Two Bodies: Drama and the Elizabethan Succession* (1977)

Bacon, F., *History of the Reign of Henry VII*, ed. J. R. Lumley (1876)

Beatson, R. and Hayden, J., *Book of Dignities* (1851)

Beckingsale, B. W., *Thomas Cromwell: Tudor Minister* (1978)

Beer, B. L., *Northumberland: The Political Career of John Dudley, Earl of Warwick and Duke of Northumberland* (Kent State University Press, 1973)

Beer, B. L., *Rebellion and Riot: Popular Disorder in England During the Reign of Edward VI* (Kent State, 1982)

Beer, B. L., 'Northumberland: the myth of the wicked duke and the historical John Dudley', *Albion*, 11, 1979, pp. 1ff

Bellamy, J., *The Tudor Law of Treason: An Introduction* (1979)

Bennett, H. S., *The Pastons and Their England* (Cambridge, 1922)

Bernard, G. W., 'The fall of Anne Boleyn', *English Historical Review*, CVI (1990)

Bernard, G. W., 'Anne Boleyn's religion', *Historical Journal*, XXXVI (1993)

Bindoff, S. T., 'A Kingdom at Stake', *History Today*, III (1953)

Bindoff, S. T., (ed.), *The House of Commons 1509–1558* (1982)

Block, J., 'Factional Politics in the English Reformation', *RHS Studies in History*, LXVI (1993)

Blomefield, F. and Parkin, C., *An Essay Towards a Topographical History of the County of Norfolk* (1805–1810)

Brakspear, H., 'Dudley Castle', *Archaeological Journal*, LXXXI

Brenan, G. and Statham, E. P., *The House of Howard* (1907)

Brigden, S., *New Worlds, Lost Worlds, The Rule of the Tudors, 1485–1603* (2000)

Brigden, S., *London and the Reformation* (Oxford, 1989)

Brodie, D. M., 'Edmund Dudley, Minister of Henry VII', *Transactions of the Royal Historical Socety*, 4th Series, XV (1932)

Burnet, Gilbert, *History of the Reformation of the Church of England* (Oxford, 1865)

Bush, M. L., 'The Lisle-Seymour Land Dispute: A Study of Power and Influence in the 1530s', *Historical Journal*, IX (1966)

Bush, M. L., *The Goverment Policy of Protector Somerset* (1975)

Butler, L., 'Leicester's Church in Denbigh: An Experiment in Puritan Worship', *Journal of the British Archaeological Association*, 3rd Series, XXXVII

Cameron, E., *The European Reformation* (Oxford, 1991)

Chamberlin, F., *Elizabeth and Leicester* (1939)

Chambers, E. K., *The Elizabethan Stage* (2 vols., 1923)

Chambers, R. W., *Thomas More* (1976 ed.)

Charlton, K., *Education in Renaissance England* (1965)

Chrimes, S. B., *Henry VII* (1972)

Christy, M., 'Queen Elizabeth's Visit to Tilbury in 1588', *English Historical Review*, XXXIV (1919)

Clarke, P., *English Provincial Society from the Reformation to the Revolution* (1977)

Coleman, C. and Starkey, D., *Revolution Reassessed* (1986)

Collins, A. J., 'The Progress of Queen Elizabeth to Tilbury, 1588', *British Museum Quarterly*, X (1936)

Collinson, P., *Archbishop Grindal, 1519–1583; the struggle of a Reformed Church* (1980)

Collinson, P., *The Elizabethan Puritan Movement* (1967)

Collinson, P., *Elizabethans* (2003)

Condon, M., 'Ruling elites in the reign of Henry VII' in C. Ross (ed.), *Patronage, Pedigree and Power in Late Medieval England* (Gloucester, 1979)

Connell-Smith, G., *The Forerunners of Drake* (1954)

Cooper, J. P., 'Henry VII's last years reconsidered', *Historical Journal*, II (1959)

Cornwall, J., *The Revolt of the Peasantry, 1549* (1977)

Coulton, G. G., *Social Life in Britain from the Conquest to the Reformation* (Cambridge, 1926)

Cross, C., *Church and People 1450–1660: The Triumph of the Laity in the English Church* (1976)

Cross, C., *The Puritan Earl: Henry Hastings, Third Earl of Huntingdon* (1966)

Cross, C., Loades, D., Scarisbrick, J. J., (eds.), *Law and Goverment Under the Tudors* (Cambridge, 1988)

Cruickshank, C. G., *Elizabeth's Army* (1966)

Cunliffe, J. W. (ed.), *Early English Classical Tragedies* (1912)

Davies, C. S. L., 'The administration of the Royal Navy under Henry VIII', *English Historical Review*, LXXX (1965)

de Beer, E. S., 'The Lord High Admiral', *Mariner's Mirror*, XIII (1927)

Dickens, A. G., *Thomas Cromwell and the English Reformation* (1959)

Dickens, A. G., *Lollards and Protstants in the Diocese of York 1509–1558* (1982, revised edn)

Dickens, A. G., *The English Reformation* (1989)

Dickens, A. G., *Later Monasticism and the Reformation* (1994)

Dickens, A. G. and Tonkin, J. M., with Powell, K., *The Reformation in Historical Thought* (Oxford, 1985)

Dodds, M. H., and R., *The Pilgrimage of Grace and the Exeter Conspiracy* (Cambridge, 1971 edn)

Dollason, A. A., *History of the Owners of Dudley Castle* (Dudley, n.d.)

Dorsten, J. A. van, and Strong, R. C., *Leciester's Triumph* (1964)

Dowling, M., 'Anne Boleyn and reform', *The Journal of Ecclesiastical History*, XXV, I (January, 1984), 30–46

Duffy, E., *The Stripping of the Altars: Traditional Religion in England 1400–1580* (New Haven, 1992)

Elton, G. R., *England Under the Tudors* (1955)

Elton, G. R., *Reform and Reformation, England 1509–1558* (1977)

Elton, G. R., *The Parliament of England, 1559–1581* (Cambridge, 1986)

Elton, G. R., *The Tudor Revolution in Government: Administration Changes in the Reign of Henry VIII* (Cambridge, 1953)

Elton, G. R., 'King or minister? The man behind the English Reformation', *History*, new series, XXXIX (1954), 216–32

Elton, G. R., *Policy and Police: The Enforcement of the Reformation in the Age of Thomas Cromwell* (Cambridge, 1972)

Elton, G. R., *Reform and Renewal: Thomas Cromwell and the Common Weal* (Cambridge, 1973)

Elton, G. R., 'Sir Thomas More and the opposition to Henry VIII', *Studies in Tudor Politics and Government*, I (1974)

Elton, G. R., 'Thomas More, councillor', *Studies in Tudor and Stuart Politics and Government* (1974)

Elton, G. R., *Studies in Tudor and Stuart Politics* (1974–84)

Elton, G. R., 'Tudor government: the points of contact', *Royal Historical Society* trs. (1976), 211f

Elton, G. R., 'Henry VII, a restatement', *Historical Journal*, IV (1961)

Elton, G. R., *Thomas Cromwell*, ed. J. Loades, *Headstart History Papers* (1991)

Emmison, F. G., *Tudor Secretary: Sir William Petre at Court and Home* (1961)

Erickson, C., *Bloody Mary* (1978)

Fortescue, J. W., *History of the British Army* (1899)

Fox, A., *Thomas More: History and Providence* (Oxford, 1982)

Fox, A. and Guy, J., (eds.), *Reassessing the Henrician Age: Humanism, Politics and Reform, 1500–1550* (Oxford, 1986)

French, K. L., Gibbs, G. G. and Kümin, B. A., *The Parish in English Life, 1400–1600* (Manchester, 1997)

Gammon, S. R., *Statesman and Schemer: William, First Lord Paget – Tudor Minister* (Newton Abbot, 1973)

Garrett, C. H., *The Marian Exiles: A Study in the Origins of Elizabethan Puritanism* (Cambridge, 1938)

Geyl, P., *The Revolt of the Netherlands, 1555–1609* (1932)

Gibbons, G., *The Political Career of Thomas Wriothesley, First Earl of Southampton, 1505–1550* (Lampeter, 2001)

Gilkes, R. K., *The Tudor Parliament* (1969)

Gunn, S. G. and Lindley, P. G. (eds.), *Cardinal Wolsey: Church State and Art* (Cambridge, 1991)

Gunn, S. G., 'The accession of Henry VIII', *Historical Research*, LXIV (1991)

Gunn, S. G., 'The courtiers of Henry VII', *English Historical Review*, CVIII (1993)

Guttery, D. R., 'The Two Johns: Patron and Parson', *County Borough of Dudley Library, Museum and Arts Dept.*, Transcript No. 13 (1969)

Guy, J. A., *The Public Career of Sir Thomas More* (Brighton, 1980)

Guy, J., *Tudor England* (Oxford, 1988)

Guy, J., (ed.), *The Tudor Monarchy* (1997)

Guy, J., *My Heart is My Own: The Life of Mary Queen of Scots* (2004)

Haigh, C. (ed.), *The English Reformation Revisited* (Cambridge, 1987)

Haigh, C. (ed.), *English Reformations: Religion, Politics and Society Under the Tudors* (Oxford, 1993)

Hanham, A., *Richard III and His Early Historians, 1483–1535* (1975)

Harrison, C. J., 'The Petition of Edmund Dudley', *English Historical Review*, LXXXVII (1972)

Harrison, S. M., *The Pilgrimage of Grace in the Lake Counties* (1981)

Hassell Smith, A., *Country and Court, Government and Politics in Norfolk 1558–1603* (1974)

Haugaard, W. J., 'Katherine Parr: the religious convictions of a Renaissance queen', *Renaissance Quarterly*, XXII (1969), 346–59

Head, D. M., *The Ebbs and Flows of Fortune: The Life and Times of Thomas Howard, Third Duke of Norfolk* (Athens, Georgia, 1995)

Heal, F. and O'Day, R., (eds), *Church and Society of England: Henry VIII to James I* (1977)

Heller, A., *Renaissance Man* (1978)

Hoak, D. E., *The King's Council in the Reign of Edward VI* (1976)

Hoak, D., (ed.), *Tudor Political Culture* (Cambridge 1995)

Horowitz, M. R., 'Richard Empson, Minister of Henry VII', *Bulletin of the Institute of Historical Research*, LV (1982)

Hoskins, W. G., *The Age of Plunder: King Henry's England, 1500–1547* (1976)

Howarth, D., *Images of Rule, Art and Politics in the English Renaissance 1485–1649* (1997)

Hoyle, R. W., *The Pilgrimage of Grace and the Politics of the 1530s* (Oxford, 2001)

Hudson, W. S., *The Cambridge Connection and the Elizabethan Settlement of 1559* (Durham, North Carolina, 1980)

Israel, J. I., *The Dutch Republic, Its Rise, Greatness and Fall, 1477–1806* (Oxford, 1995)

Ives, E. W., *Faction in Tudor England, Historical Association Appreciations*, VI (1979)

Ives, E. W., 'Faction at the court of Henry VIII', *History*, LVII(FIF972), 69f

Ives, E. W., *The Common Lawyers of Pre-Reformation England: Thomas Kebell: A Case Study* (Cambridge, 1983)

Ives, E. W., 'Anne Boleyn and the early Reformation in England: the contemporary evidence', *Historical Journal*, XXXVII (1994), 389–400

Ives, E. W., 'The queen and the painters: Anne Boleyn, Holbein and Tudor royal portraits', *Apollo* (July, 1994), 36–45

Ives, E. W., 'Henry VIII: the political perspective' in D. MacCulloch (ed.), *The Reign of Henry VIII: Politics, Policy and Piety* (1995)

Ives, E. W., *Anne Boleyn* (Oxford, 1986)

Jackson, J. E., 'Amy Robsart', *Wilts Archaeological Magazine*, XVII (1898)

James, M. (ed.), *Society, Politics and Culture, Studies in Early Modern England* (Cambridge, 1986)

James, M. 'Obedience and dissent in Henrician England: the Lincolnshire rebellion, 1536', *Past and Present*, XLVIII (1970), 1–72

Jebb, S., *Life of Robert Earl of Leicester* (1727)

Johnson, P., *Elizabeth, A Study in Power and Intellect* (1974)

Jordan, W. K., *Edward VI, The Young King* (1968)

Jodan, W. K., *Edward VI, The Threshold of Power* (1970)

Knappen, M. M., *Tudor Puritanism* (1939)

Knowles, D. E., *The Religious Orders in England* (Cambridge, 1948–59)

la Ferrière, C. f. H. de, *Les Projects de Marriage de la Reine Elizabeth* (1882)

la Ferrière, C. f. H. de, *Le XVI Siècle et la Valois* (1877)

Lake, P. and Dowling M. (eds), *Protestantism and the National Church in Sixteenth-Century England* (1987)

Land S. K., *Kett's Rebellion* (Ipswich, 1977)

Lee, A. G., *The Son of Leicester* (1964)

Lehmberg, S. E., *The Later Parliaments of Henry VIII, 1536–1547* (Cambridge, 1977)

Lehmberg, S. E., *The Reformation Parliament, 1529–1536* (Cambridge, 1970)

Leti, G., *La Vie d'Elizabeth, reine d'Angleterre traduite de l'Italian* (1696)

Lettenhove, J. B. M. C. K. de, *Relations Politiques des Pays-Bas et d'Angleterre* (1882–1900)

Levine, M., *The Early Elizabethan Succession Question 1558–1568* (1966)

Lewis, C. S., *English Literature in the Sixteenth Century, Excluding Drama* (1954)

Loach, J. & Tittler, R., *The Mid-Tudor Policy, c.1540–1560* (1980)

Loach, J., *Edward VI* (New Haven, 1999)

Loades, D. M., *Two Tudor Conspiracies* (1965)

Loades, D., *The Tudor Navy: An Administrative, Political and Military History* (Aldershot, 1992)

Loades, D., *John Dudley, Duke of Northumberland, 1504–1553* (Oxford, 1996)

Loades, D., *England's Maritime Empire, Seapower, Commerce and Policy, 1490–1690* (2000)

Loades, D. M., *The Reign of Mary Tudor, Government and Religion in England, 1553–1558* (1979)

Loades, D. M., *The Tudor Court* (1986)

Loades, D. M., *Two Tudor Conspiracies* (Cambridge, 1965)

Lodge, E., *Illustrations of British History . . . in the Reigns of Henry VIII, Edward VI, Mary, Elizabeth and James I* (1838)

MacCaffrey, W. T., 'Elizabethan Politics: the First Decade, 1558–1568', in *Past and Present* (April, 1963)

MacCaffrey, W. T., *The Shaping of the Elizabeth Regime* (1969)

MacCulloch, D., *Thomas Cranmer* (Yale, 1996)

MacCulloch, D., *Tudor Church Militant* (1999)

Malkiewicz, A. J. A., 'An Eye-witness's Account of the Coup d'Etat of October 1549', *English Historical Review*, LXX (1955)

Historical Review, LXX (1955)

Marius, R., *Thomas More* (1984)

Marshall, P. and Ryrie, A., (eds), *The Beginnings of English Protestantism* (Cambridge, 2002)

Martienssen, A., *Queen Katherine Parr* (1973)

Mattingly, G., *Catherine of Aragon* (1942)

Mattingly, G., *Renaissance Diplomacy* (1955)

Mattingly, G., *The Defeat of the Spanish Armada* (1959)

McConica, J. K., *English Humanists and Reformation Politics Under Henry VIII and Edward VI* (Oxford, 1965)

McCoy, R. C., 'From the Tower to the Tiltyard: Robert Dudley's return to glory', *Historical Journal*, XXVII (1984)

Miller, H., *Henry VIII and the English Nobility* (Oxford, 1986)

Moat, D., (ed.), *Tudor Political Culture* (Cambridge, 1995)

Morley, B. M., *Henry VIII and the Development of Coastal Defence* (1977)

Motley, J. L., *The Rise of the Dutch Republic* (1956)

Muller, J. A., *Stephen Gardiner and the Tudor Reaction* (New York, 1926)

Neale, J. E., *Elizabeth I and Her Parliaments, 1559–1581* (1953)

Neale, J. E., *Queen Elizabeth* (1934)

Oberman, H. A., *Masters of the Reformation: The Emergence of a New Intellectual Climate in Europe* (Cambridge, 1981)

Oppenheimer, M., *History of the Administration of the Navy* (1896, 1988)

Outhwaite, R. B., *Inflation in Tudor and Early Stuart England* (1969)

Parker, G., 'The Dutch Revolt', *Tijdschrift voor Geschiednis*, LXXX 4 (1976)

Peck, D. C., 'Government Suppression of English Catholic Books: The Case of "Leicester's Commonwealth"', *Library Quarterly*, XLII 2 (1997)

Pennant, T., *A Tour in Wales* (1778–81)

Pickthorn, K., *Early Tudor Government: Henry VII* (Cambridge, 1934)

Pollard, A. F., *England Under Protector Somerset* (1909)

Pollard, A. F., *Thomas Cranmer and the English Reformation, 1489–1556* (1905)

Prescott, H. F. M. *Mary Tudor* (1952)

Prior, C. M., *The Royal Studs of the Sixteenth and Seventeenth Centuries* (1935)

Pulman, M. B., *The Elizabethan Privy Council in the Fifteen Seventies* (Berkeley, 1971)

Raid, R. R., *The King's Council in the North* (1975 edn)

Read, C., *Lord Burghley and Queen Elizabeth* (1960)

Read, C., *Mr Secretary Cecil and Queen Elizabeth* (1955)

Redworth, G., *In Defence of the Church Catholic: the Life of Stephen Gardiner* (Oxford, 1990)

Reese, M. M., *The Royal Office of Master of the Horse* (1976)

Richardson, A., *The Lover of Queen Elizabeth* (1907)

Ridley, J. G., *Thomas Cranmer* (Oxford, 1962)

Ridley, J. G., *The Statesman and the Fanatic: Thomas Wolsey and Thomas More* (1982)

Ridley, J. G., *Henry VIII* (1984)

Roderick, A. J., (ed.), *Wales Through the Ages* (2 vols, 1959–60)

Rosenberg, E., *Leicester, Patron of Letters* (1962)

Russell, J. G., *The Field of Cloth of Gold: Men and Manners in 1520* (1969)

Scarisbrick, J. J., *The Reformation and the English People* (Oxford, 1984)

Scarisbrick, J. J., *Henry VIII* (New Haven, 2nd edn, 1997)

Scott Pearson, A. F., *Thomas Cartwright and Elizabethan Puritanism* (1925)

Simon, J., *Education and Society in Tudor England* (Cambridge, 1966)

Simpson, A., *The Wealth of the Gentry 1540–1660* (1961)

Simpson, M. A., *Defender of the Faith, Etcetera* (1978)

Simpson, R., *Edmund Campion* (1867)

Simpson, R., *The Crisis of the Aristocracy (1558–1641)* (1965)

Slavin, A. J., 'The fall of Lord Chancellor Wriothesley: a study in the politics of conspiracy', *Albion*, VII (1975)

Slavin, A. J., 'Cromwell, Cranmer and Lord Lisle, a study in the politics of reform', *Albion*, IX (1977)

Smith, A. G. R., *The Government of Elizabethan England* (1967)

Somerset, A., *Elizabeth I* (1991)

Starkey, D., 'Court, council and the nobility in Tudor England' in R. G. Asch and A. M. Birkie (eds), *Princes, Patronage and the Nobility. The Court at the Beginnings of the Modern Age, c.1450–1650* (Oxford, 1991)

Starkey, D., (ed.), *Henry VIII: A European Court in England* (1991)

Starkey, D. R., *Elizabeth* (2000)

Starkey, D. R., *Six Wives, the Queens of Henry VIII* (2003)

Starkey, D. R., 'From Feud to Faction: English Politics c.1450–1550', *History Today*, 32 (November 1982)

Starkey, D. R., (ed.), *The English Court: From the Wars of the Roses to the Civil War* (1987)

Starkey, D. R., *The Reign of Henry VIII: Personalities and Politics* (1985)

Stewart, A., *Philip Sidney, a double life* (2000)

Stone, L., 'Anatomy of the Elizabethan Aristocracy', *Economic History Review*, XVIII (1948)

Stone, L., *The Crisis of the Aristocracy, 1558–1641* (Oxford, 1967)

Storey, R. L., *The Reign of Henry VII* (1968)

Strong, R. C. and Van Dorsten, J. A., *Leicester's Triumph* (1964)

Thompson, B., (ed.), *The Reign of Henry VII* (Stamford, 1995)

Tittler, R., *The Reign of Mary I* (1983)

Tjernagel, N. S., *Henry VIII and the Lutherans: A Study in Anglo-Lutheran Relations from 1521 to 1547* (St Louis, 1965)

Tucker, M. J., *The Life of Thomas Howard, Earl of Surrey and Second Duke of Norfolk, 1443–1524* (The Hague, 1964)

Tytler, P. F., *England Under the Reigns of Edward VI and Mary* (1939)

Waldman, M., *Elizabeth and Leicester* (1944)

Walker, G., *John Skelton and the Politics of the 1520s* (Cambridge, 1988)

Warner, J. C., *Henry VIII's Divorce: Literature and the Politics of the Printing Press* (Woodbridge, 1998)

Warnicke, R. M., *The Rise and Fall of Anne Boleyn* (Cambridge, 1989)

Warnicke, R. M., *The Marrying of Anne of Cleves, Royal Protocol in Tudor England* (Cambridge, 2000)

Wernham, R. B., *Before the Armada, The Growth of English Foreign Policy, 1485–1588* (1966)

Williams, D., *A History of Modern Wales* (1950)

Williams, E. C., *Bess of Hardwick* (1959)

Williams, N., *All the Queen's Men* (1972)

Williams, N., *Thomas Howard, Fourth Duke of Norfolk* (New York, 1964)

Williams, N., *Henry VII and His Court* (1971)

Wilson, C., *Queen Elizabeth and the Revolt of the Netherlands* (1970)

Wilson, D., *England in the Age of Thomas More* (1978)

Wilson, D., *Hans Holbein: Portrait of an Uknown Man* (1996)

Wilson, D., *In the Lion's Court: Power, Ambition and Sudden Death in the Reign of Henry VIII* (2001)

Wilson, D., *Sweet Robin, A Biography of Robert Dudley, Earl of Leicester* (1981)

Wilson, D., *A Tudor Tapestry: Men, Women and Society in Reformation England* (1973)

Wilson, D., *The World Encompassed. Drake's Great Voyage 1577–1580* (1977)

Woude van der, A. M., *Der Staten, 'Leicester en Elizabeth in Financiele Verwikkelingen', Tijdschrift voor Geschidnis*, LXXIV (1961)

Wright, T., *Queen Elizabeth and Her Times* (1938)

Yates, F. A. S., *The Occult Philosophy in the Elizabethan Age* (1979)

Yates, F. A. S., *Astraea: The Imperial Theme in the Sixteenth Century* (1975)

Unpublished Works

Adams, C. J., *Tudor Minister: Sir Thomas Wriothesley*, Manchester M.A. Thesis, 1970

Bush, M. L., *The Rise to Power of Edward Seymour, Protector Somerset, 1500–1547*, Cambridge Ph.D. Thesis, 1965

Fourdrinier, N., *Amy Robsart, the Wife of Lord Robert Dudley the Favourite of Queen Elizabeth I. Her Life, Ancestry and the True Cause of Her Tragic Death*, M.S. MC5/29, Norfolk Record Office.

Hodgkinson, L. A., *The Administration of the Earl of Leicester in the United Provinces*, Liverpool M.A. Thesis, 1925

Jong de, G., *The Earl of Leicester's Administration of the Netherlands 1586–86*, Wisconsin Ph.D. Thesis, 1956

Oosterhoff, F. G., *The Earl of Leicester's Governorship of the Netherlands 1586–87*, London Ph.D. Thesis, 1967

Starkey, D. R., *The King's Privy Chamber, 1485–1547*, Cambridge Ph.D. Thesis, 1973

Sturge, C., *Life and Times of John Dudley, Earl of Warwick and Duke of Northumberland, 1504(?)–1553*, London Ph.D. Thesis, 1927

Tighe, W. J., *Gentlemen Pensioners in Elizabethan Politics and Government*, Cambridge Ph.D. Thesis, 1983

Index